Making Indian Law

CHRISTIAN W. MCMILLEN

Making Indian Law

THE HUALAPAI LAND CASE
AND THE BIRTH OF
ETHNOHISTORY

Yale University Press
New Haven &
London

Published with assistance from the Kingsley Trust Association Publication Fund
established by the Scroll and Key Society of Yale College.

Set in Sabon by Keystone Typesetting, Inc.
Printed in the United States of America.

Library of Congress Cataloging-in-Publication Data
McMillen, Christian W., 1969–
Making Indian law : the Hualapai land case and the birth of ethnohistory /
Christian W. McMillen.
p. cm.
Includes bibliographical references and index.
ISBN: 978-0-300-11460-7 (cloth : alk. paper)
1. Hualapai Indian Tribe of the Hualapai Indian Reservation, Arizona — Trials,
litigation, etc. 2. Santa Fe Pacific Railroad Company — Trials, litigation etc.
3. Hualapai Indian Reservation (Ariz.) — Trials, litigation, etc. 4. Indian title —
United States — History — 20th century. 5. Hualapai Indians — Legal status, laws,
etc. — United States — History — 20th century. 6. Hualapai Indian Reservation
(Ariz.) — Trials, litigation, etc. I. Title.
KF228.H83.M38 2007
346.7304'32089975724 — dc22

2006029347

A catalogue record for this book is available from the British Library.

The paper in this book meets the guidelines for permanence and durability of the
Committee on Production Guidelines for Book Longevity of the Council on
Library Resources.

10 9 8 7 6 5 4 3 2 1

For my mother and in memory of my father

Contents

Acknowledgments

Many people and institutions helped me write this book. Yale University was very generous. During the research phase of the project, the Beinecke Library at Yale supplied a MacKinnon Family Fellowship in Western Americana, the Howard Lamar Center for the Study of Frontiers and Borders facilitated a full semester of research away from New Haven, and the Program in Agrarian Studies helped pay for a trip to the Hualapai reservation for much-needed interviews. A Robert M. Leylan Dissertation Fellowship provided a year's support while I wrote. New York University Law School's Samuel I. Golieb Fellowship gave me another year of freedom to write. All who have been Golieb Fellows know about Bill Nelson's tireless support of young legal historians; I'm pleased to have been among them. Many other institutions also gave me financial assistance: the Phillips Fund for Native American Research at the American Philosophical Society, the Charles Redd Center for Western Studies at Brigham Young University, which awarded me a summer grant, the Friends of the Princeton Library, who offered a research fellowship, and the American Historical Association, which awarded a Littleton-Griswold Research Grant in American Legal History. A summer grant from the University of Virginia allowed me to complete the book. Without such generous financial support this work never would have been completed.

Archivists at various branches of the National Archives have been helpful, especially Paul Worsmer in Laguna Niguel and Mary Frances Morrow in Washington, D.C. The law firm of Fennemore, Craig graciously allowed me to spend a week combing through its files on the Hualapai case. Dennis Casebier allowed me to spend several days in his private archive in Goffs, California, where I turned up a set of critical documents.

Many friends and colleagues at Yale University and elsewhere were unflagging in their support and criticism. John Mack Faragher directed the dissertation. Johnny allows his graduate students total freedom to pursue what they want; it was a luxury to have such a trusting advisor. Howard Lamar and Robert Gordon, at Yale Law School, served on my dissertation committee and offered helpful comments. Steve Pitti was never a teacher but always a good friend. Robert Johnston and Glenda Gilmore also deserve special mention. John Demos knows no peer. George Miles's unparalleled knowledge of the collections at Yale, as well as his devotion to students, aided me immensely. Florence Thomas made six years at Yale smooth sailing.

Graduate students make up the core of the intellectual community at Yale. Aaron Sachs, with whom I started and finished my studies there, had the greatest influence. If I could pay Aaron for all he has done, he would be a rich man. Those who shaped me in ways known and unknown also include Adriane Smith, Bob Morrissey, Rob Campbell, Dodie McDow, Daniel Lanpher, Kip Kosek, Kat Charron, Brian Herrera, Roxanne Willis, and Geoff Pynn.

Dan Flores got me started down this path ten years ago at the University of Montana — thanks, Dan. Mark Carey has been a critic and close friend since we started studying at Montana together in 1996. Mark is a model of dedication to teaching, scholarship, and friendship. Duke Richey, another Montana alumnus, took time away from writing his own dissertation to read and comment extensively on the manuscript. Jared Farmer helped, too. Jeff Shepard also wrote a dissertation about the Hualapais. He and I have shared resources, talked ad infinitum about Hualapai history, and become close friends along the way. A small group of experts in the law of land claims and native political history has helped over the years. Sidney Harring knows this book better than anyone; all young scholars should be so lucky as to have someone like Sid in their corner. Not only has the work of Bain Attwood in Australia been a critical source, but Bain has also been a sounding board for my interest in the connections between the United States and Australia. Hamar Foster, in Canada, has read the entire manuscript — some parts of it twice — and saved me from making many errors in Canadian history; his work on aboriginal title in Canada, and his comments on mine, have been essential. Arthur Ray shared his work on comparative land claims and the history of ethnohistory — work that proved critical for completing the final chapter. I am also grateful to Stuart Banner and Dalia Tsuk, both of whom offered comments on the project.

The University of Virginia, where I turned the dissertation into a book, has become home. All of my colleagues deserve thanks for so warmly welcoming me into the department. Chuck McCurdy, chair of the History Department, has been nothing but supportive, as has Steve Cushman, chair of American Studies. Chris Loomis did excellent work as a research assistant. At the Alderman Library, Barbie Selby and Lew Purifoy (and his staff) endured, with grace, countless requests for material. Risa Goluboff and Rich Schragger are simply great friends.

On the Hualapai reservation, Ronald Mann Susanyatame and Loretta Jackson arranged interviews and made me feel welcome. Mann's generosity and interest in the project, his understanding of Hualapai history, and his intimate knowledge of Hualapai country all helped me immeasurably. Sadly, Mann passed away just as I was finishing the book. Thanks also to Mabelene Mahone and Ardith Benn (now deceased) for sharing their memories of their father with me. And thanks to everyone who agreed to be interviewed formally and those with whom I talked informally.

Thanks to Lara Heimert and Molly Egland and Yale University Press. Lara and Molly, both of whom have now moved on, were early supporters of the project. Chris Rogers and Ellie Goldberg took over and saw it through to completion. Thanks also to the three reviewers for apt and insightful comments.

I reserve the greatest thanks for my family. Stephanie Tatel, the love of my life, has touched every page. Our children, Maya and Olin, are a pure joy. My mother, Mary Ellen McMillen, deserves the greatest thanks for, simply, everything. The support of my sister Frances and my brother Matt, too, has been unwavering. David and Edie Tatel have welcomed me into their family and taken a keen interest in my work. Writing this book has been a joy. My only wish is that my father, to whom it is dedicated and who died as I finished my first year of graduate school, were here to read it.

A portion of this book is reprinted from the *American Indian Culture and Research Journal,* volume 27, number 3, by permission of the American Indian Studies Center, UCLA © Regents of the University of California.

Introduction

Proving property rights for indigenous people has been tough. It still is: indigenous people worldwide, especially hunting and gathering peoples, who to Western eyes simply wandered like animals, have tremendous difficulty winning land claims cases. The idea that wandering people, so-called nomads, had no valid claims to a specific area of land has a long pedigree. But in 1941, with *United States v. Santa Fe Pacific Railroad Company* — the case in which the Hualapai people asserted their rights to their homeland — that situation started to change. Slowly, Indian land claims — what Felix Cohen, the founder of modern federal Indian law, called the "backwash of a great national experiment in dictatorship and racial extermination" — began to be taken seriously. The Hualapai case was the start of a new way of thinking about native people, their property, and their past. The complicated case took a long time to get to court. Lawyers and legal scholars, bureaucrats, courts, historians and anthropologists, Hualapais and other Indians, attorneys general, and secretaries of the interior went at it for almost thirty years. In 1946, exhausted after working on the claim for six years, Cohen wrote to a colleague, "This is really the most complicated case I have ever handled."[1]

The notion that Indians had discernable, legitimate claims to the land they had occupied since time immemorial was a hard pill to swallow at the beginning of the twentieth century. In theory, treaties, land cessions, and several

Supreme Court decisions granted that Indians had some rights to their land. But these were, in large measure, expediencies crafted to gain access to Indian land. To be sure, buried within these contrivances were essential principles that could (and would) be used to rethink Indian property rights, but it would take time to excavate them. Beyond the legal principles was the Indians' belief that the land was theirs on the basis of longtime occupancy and a set of mytho-historical stories that tied Indian people to a place. Yet until well into the twentieth century Indians' own ideas about their past and their property mattered very little to anthropologists and historians and much less to courts.[2]

That the legitimacy of Indian land claims was beyond the ken of most of those involved in Indian affairs at the beginning of the twentieth century should come as no surprise. The Indian population was at its nadir in North America. Laments (and cheers) about the vanishing Indian were common. Political and legal rights were fragile. The Bureau of Indian Affairs (BIA) worked in earnest to stamp out Indian culture through its nationwide system of boarding schools, use of field matrons, and other assimilation campaigns. And, most devastating of all, the Indian estate was quickly disappearing as a result of allotment, that ill-fated scheme to turn Indians into private property owners leasing to non-Indian ranchers, farmers, and oil companies, and of land cessions. The BIA, often in league with covetous non-Indians, provided the means, overseeing the transfer of tens of millions of acres.[3]

And the Supreme Court of the United States sanctioned it all. *Lone Wolf v. Hitchcock* is the most notorious case in the cannon of federal Indian law and one of the Court's most anti-Indian decisions. *Lone Wolf,* decided in 1903, declared that Congress had plenary, or total, power over Indian peoples. Treaty rights and Indian title made no difference; Congress could do with Indian land what it wanted. The Court decided that, despite their protests to the contrary and their treaty, the Kiowas' consent was not needed to open up their land to non-Indians. Thus, despite having voted against opening their nearly three-million acre reservation to leasing, the Kiowas' land base shrank to three thousand acres over the course of the succeeding generation. As the case made its way through the courts in the first few years of the century, the prominent investigative journalist George Kennan described the state of anxiety among Indians and their friends: "If this decision will be sustained . . . , it will mark the beginning of a new departure in our Indian policy. There will then be no legal bar to the removal of all American Indians from their reservations and the banishment of every man, women, and child of them to Alaska and Porto Rico [*sic*]." *Lone Wolf* was a mighty blow to all Indians. During the ensuing thirty years, tribal land holdings shrank on an order of magnitude that still leaves one breathless: 138 million acres whittled away to 52 million.[4]

It was in this climate that the Hualapais began the fight to retain their reservation, a fight that would eventually lead to a landmark Supreme Court decision. But the case also represented a formative moment in the development of native activism, reconceptualized the writing of Indian history, and ushered in the international land claims era in which we now live.

As the case made its way through the legal system in the period between the world wars, Indians and lawyers developed a way of talking about Indian land and history that was intelligible to the courts, shaping the writing of Indian history for the rest of the century. In the 1920s and 1930s, when historians wrote very little about Indians and anthropologists were concerned with ritual and religion, not time and the past, history was left to Indians and their lawyers. Because so little light had been shined on their past as the Hualapais began to fight for their land, a history of the tribe had to be written for the first time.

The Hualapai case is unique in many ways, but it also serves as a stand-in for the many other instances of litigation of land claims by Indians in the interwar years. And yet it is more. Not only did the Hualapais' long fight to retain control of their land mirror other tribes' legal struggles over lost land, squandered resources, and general chicanery, but the results of the Supreme Court's decision had a direct effect on the writing of Indian history. If it is true that the great outpouring of Indian history that resulted from the formation of the Indian Claims Commission (ICC) marks the more or less formal birth of ethnohistory, then the discipline was conceived during the Hualapai case. The seemingly simple provision in the Court's opinion that proving occupancy from time immemorial was the evidentiary bar the Hualapais had to leap in order to have a valid claim to their land had far-reaching effects. When the Court said that Indian occupancy of land was a "fact to be determined as any other question of fact," and the ICC adopted this standard as its basis for determining Indian title to land, ethnohistory began.[5]

As much of this story started to become clear to me, as I began to see that what began with the Hualapai case had its culmination in the 1990s in *Mabo v. Queensland* and *Delgamuukw v. the Queen,* the leading cases in Australia and Canada, respectively, I began to wonder: How did a case that looked from the beginning like a sure loser become one of the most important cases in federal Indian law? How did the Hualapai case give hope to other Indian people? How did the evidentiary standards of the case become the basis for decisions by the ICC? How did it come to pass that the Canadian Supreme Court in 1973 called this case — which originated from the protests of a small tribe in northwestern Arizona in the 1920s — the major decision of the twentieth century concerning native rights? And finally, why did the Australian

Supreme Court, in 1992, turn to the Hualapai case to answer key questions in deciding the contours of its own native title jurisprudence?

D'Arcy McNickle, the Salish novelist, founder of the National Congress of American Indians, and a former colleague of Felix Cohen at the Bureau of Indian Affairs, remembered when Cohen took the Hualapai case to the Supreme Court and attempted something that "had never been attempted before."[6] He rewrote history and won. It was hard work and it had taken a long time. Thinking back on the case in 1950, when the torrent of native land claims in the United States and abroad was just about to spill over the top of the dam, Cohen remembered that sorting out just how the Hualapais lost so much land, while figuring out how to keep some of it, was the "biggest Chinese puzzle" he had ever encountered.[7]

But he had not done it alone. In fact, Cohen became involved rather late. Twenty years before he took the Hualapais' case to the Court in 1941, Fred Mahone had been fighting for their land—documenting tribal land use, writing petitions, and badgering politicians. His cause consumed his life. Mahone was a Hualapai, a veteran of the Great War, and a pioneer Indian civil rights activist. Like many of the delegates present at the first meeting of the National Congress of American Indians in 1944, Mahone was one of the thousands of unknown Indians who between the world wars built the foundations for the post–World War II American Indian renaissance. No one knows who Fred Mahone was—at least, not historians; he is a well-known and complicated figure on the Hualapai reservation. Like the stories of most Indians in the twentieth century, the story of Mahone's singular pursuit of justice for his people is totally unknown. Like the lawyers involved in the case, and indeed Mahone himself, who dug Hualapai history out of the archives and the memories of the Hualapais, I have pieced together Mahone's life from the records left behind in archives and in memory.

Not until I got into the archives did I realize how unsettled certain questions in Indian law were and how great an effect the activism of one tribe could have on what was—and still largely is—a relic of a colonial mentality. The principles of Indian title, set down by the Marshall Court in the early nineteenth century, might have appeared to be embedded in judicial doctrine, but in everyday practice they were largely ignored by lawyers who knew very little about Indian law and even less about Indians. When it came to the day-to-day business of Indian land rights, principles drawn from precedent were hard to find. In addition, as we shall see, foundations laid in the nineteenth century regarding property rights were based on observable occupancy; in the twentieth century cases such as the Hualapais' were based on history.

Although many of the strictures of assimilation were firmly in place and quite active in the 1920s, so, too, were dozens of tribes working hard to hold on to their land and culture. But a study based on the experiences of many tribes would have lacked texture, characters, and the level of detail I wanted to explore and discuss. Writing with any degree of intimacy or certainty about just how Indian people in the early twentieth adjusted to and effected change would have been impossible. Then I found Fred Mahone. His story and the Hualapais' became the medium through which this story of Indian activism and the residue of colonial law in the 1920s and beyond would come alive. The questions that Mahone and the Hualapais raised about their land rights cut to the core of Indian history: land dispossession and all that entails — loss of subsistence and the adjustment to new forms of work and economy, loss of place, erosion of family and band ties, upsetting of gender norms, powerlessness in the face of a strong state. The Hualapais wondered why centuries of living in the same place meant nothing when compared to the rights of a railroad. Why was a reservation created for them in 1883 if they really had no claim to their land? Beginning in earnest in the 1920s and 1930s, many other tribes besides the Hualapai raised similar questions.

For most of the 1920s the government brushed aside the Hualapais' concerns; government attorneys generally worked hard to preserve the rights of the railroad and snuff out those of the Hualapais. But in the early 1930s, with the advent of the Indian New Deal, that situation started to change. Lawyers and others working for the Department of the Interior and the Bureau of Indian Affairs began to take the Hualapais' claims seriously. They took the land case to the Supreme Court. Along the way significant change occurred. For example, fundamental questions about the nature of the Indian past and what it meant to the law were first asked and answered, and Indian activism began to have a profound effect on policy. A return to older ways of thinking about Indian people became impossible. History works, at times, like a ratchet and pawl. Although there is slippage backward, certain pushes forward cannot be reversed.[8] This was one of those times.

The angles from which I tell this story are several. It is not a tribal history. At some times we are on the Hualapai reservation, at others, in Washington, D.C. The story that follows is as much about Indians and their encounter with colonial law as it is about non-Indian lawyers and their defense and partial destruction of that same colonial law. In asking the question, which came first, Indian activists or concerned lawyers? I come down decidedly in favor of the Hualapais. Very simply put, Fred Mahone and the Hualapais would not let their land go, and they held on until someone with more power came along and cared. Without this activism the case never would have gone to court.

Likewise, the case never would have been tried were it not for a group of lawyers gathered together by John Collier.

The Hualapai case has traveled the globe. To date, many of its principles have been adopted in Canada, Australia, New Zealand, South Africa, and Malaysia. Wherever and whenever indigenous land claims are litigated the shadow of the Hualapai case falls over the proceedings. Although what follows is largely a narrative history of the case, its legacy is important, too. That story is even more complicated. And it could fill another book. Were the Hualapai case not to have had an impact beyond its own set of facts it would still be a story worth telling. But because the facts of the case are *not* unique, it is a universal story.

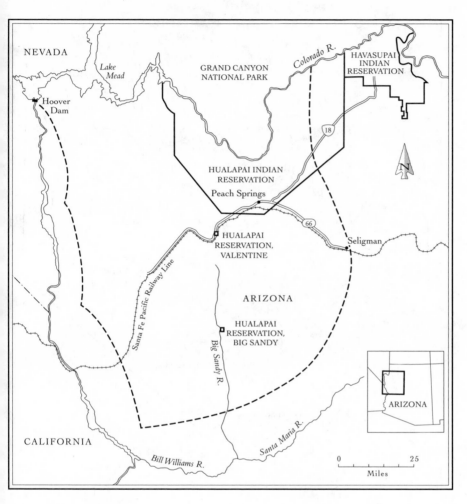

Original Hualapai Territory

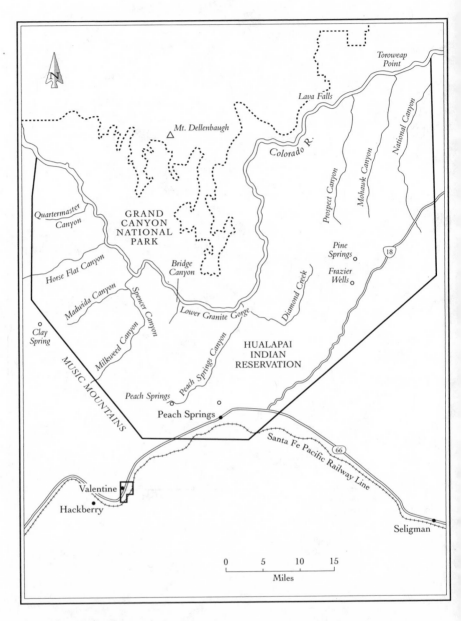

The Hualapai Indian Reservation

PART I

Keeping the Country Whole

I

The Hualapais

No one knows just how long the Hualapais have lived in the north-western corner of the Colorado Plateau. Science tells us one thing, and Hualapai origin stories another. Anthropologists and archaeologists disagree about just where the Hualapais came from: some scholars say they came from the west and the south when Yuman speakers of the Colorado river delta began to spread out around A.D. 1; others argue that the Cerbat people who preceded the Hualapais, after oscillating between nomadism and sedentism as the climate shifted from wet to dry periods between A.D. 850 and 1250, eventually settled, started to farm, and became the Hualapais; still others suggest that they were formed in situ, an amalgamation of several cultures. Making matters more confusing, a gap in the archaeological record between 1150 and 1300 suggests that what is now Hualapai country was abandoned along with many other areas in the uplands of the Colorado Plateau. Although archaeologists may never know where the Hualapais came from, most agree that by roughly 1300 they had arrived and were firmly in place.[1]

The Hualapais tell a different story — and offer an interesting example of the possible overlaps between scientific theory and Indian origin stories. According to the Hualapais, they come from Wikame, a mountain to the west of the reservation in present-day Nevada. Shortly after Kathat Kanave made all Indian people — Mojaves, Yavapais, Hopis, Paiutes, Navajos, Havasupais, Chemehuevis, and Maricopas—they began to quarrel. They went their separate ways, splitting into tribes. First the Mojaves and then the Paiutes left the fold. The remaining peoples moved east to Madwida, the sacred canyon in the northwestern area of today's reservation. Slowly, the people dispersed, some in peace, some not. The Hopis went east, and as they went a small group stayed behind in Cataract Canyon and became the Havasupais. When Madwida became crowded, more quarreling erupted. From within the ranks of people left in the canyon the Yavapais and the Hualapais became enemies. The Hualapais chased out the Yavapais, banishing them to the southeast. From then on, only the Hualapais lived in Madwida. The canyon is where they were born. But they, too, did not all stay in the canyon. They split into bands but remained one people—on this they and most scholars agree.[2]

Before contact the Hualapai world was enormous in geographical scale and in human diversity. Trade was so well developed that up to one-quarter of Hualapai pottery goods were imported from elsewhere. And the Hualapais, like just about all native peoples in the Southwest, were involved in the horse trade and to a lesser extent the slave trade and had been since at least the late eighteenth century. Horses came from Navajos and Hopis to the east, Mojaves to the west, and Paiutes and Utes to the north. This extensive trade network encompassed more than horses. The Hualapais acquired European goods from the Hopis as early as the late eighteenth century. Trade likely began much earlier between the Hopi mesas and people to the west. According to Spanish sources, the Hopis referred to the Coninas—the Hopis' generic term for the Hualapais and the Havasupais—as early as 1665. Via the Mojaves came shells from the Chumash on the Pacific coast. Shells were prized among the Hualapais and perhaps were akin to wampum in the East. To the more immediate west, just across the Colorado River, they exchanged corn for meat with the Mojaves. On occasion they acquired horses from and married the Mojaves. To the north, the Colorado River and the Grand Canyon made trade difficult but not impossible. Shivwit Paiutes and Hualapais built rafts to cross the Colorado, meeting regularly in the Grand Canyon to trade—the Shivwits provided guns and horses and the Hualapais brought hides and sometimes Mojave horses. Relations were friendly enough that for a time in the 1850s a group of Paiutes fleeing the Mormons lived with Ha'Kasa Pa'a (Pine Springs band) Hualapais, and on occasion Shivwit men and Hualapai women married. To the south, the Hualapais acquired goods from the Yavapais through raiding, not trading; marriage was off-limits.[3]

Trade tied the Hualapai to a large network of native peoples. They acquired vital and necessary goods through their far-flung contacts. But the Hualapais made their living largely by hunting, gathering, and farming. Their calendar revolved around agriculture and the harvesting of wild plants. Hundreds of years of accumulated knowledge allowed them to take advantage of a vast array of plants that might have appeared to others as useless. Contained within their territory was a virtual pharmacy, a wild vegetable garden, and a hardware store. The leaves of the globe mallow, for example, could be cut and dried and then brewed as a tea for a sore throat. Like the inner bark of the cliff rose, which worked well for making sandals and for lining sweat lodges, globe mallow was collected as needed. The Hualapais gathered other wild plants on a fairly strict seasonal schedule. The fall was a major harvest season for agricultural products and wild plants. Black walnuts were roasted and eaten and were also used to make dye. *I'ko'*, or pinyon trees, yielded one of the staples of the Hualapai diet, *ko'*, or pinyon nuts. The collecting of ko' was the cause for major movement to higher elevations in the fall. Women, for the most part, collected, roasted, dried, and stored the cones, and the nuts were used to make soup or ground into a paste. Families worked hard to gather enough ko' to last the winter. By the first decade of the twentieth century, ko' was not only a staple of the Hualapai diet but was also part of the cash economy. Hualapai women collected bushels of pine nuts and sold them to local Anglos and travelers. *Selé,* a staple of the aboriginal diet and high in carbohydrates and fat, was collected in late May and June.[4]

Water for farming, though not abundant, was plentiful. Every major canyon south of the Colorado that fed into the Grand Canyon contained springs. Madwida, Quartermaster, Spencer, Milkweed, Peach Springs, and Diamond Creek Canyons all were scenes of productive agriculture, as was the plateau region around Pine Springs in the eastern portion of Hualapai country. Wherever water was found so, too, was agriculture. Corn, pumpkins, watermelons, and beans were planted in the canyons in the late spring and harvested in the fall. Agriculture was important to all Hualapais but likely was a greater source of food for those who lived on the upland plateau than for those who lived in western Hualapai territory. The plateau country provided more ready access to the well-watered canyons, whereas the desert basins had a more abundant supply of harvestable wild plants.[5]

Although Hualapai pre-contact history is by no means completely clear, post-contact history is well documented — at least as far as the history of Indian-white relations is concerned. On June 10, 1776, the Hualapais had their first known contact with the non-Indian world. Leaving Tucson's Mission San Xavier del Bac sometime in January or February, Fray Francisco Garcés spent the winter and summer alone, exploring the greater Colorado River region. In June, heading east and north from Mojave country in what is now southeastern California, he crossed the Colorado and began a roughly six-week tour of Hualapai, Havasupai, and Hopi land. It is from Garcés's sparse diary entries, which yield just enough information to leave a reader begging for more, that we first learn about the Hualapais. We don't learn much: he says that they already knew about the Spanish from their friends and neighbors the Hopis (two of whom were visiting the Hualapais when Garcés turned up); they don't farm (not true); and they're spread out in small bands across a large territory. Garcés and the Hualapais drew maps for each other in the sand. The Hualapais showed Garcés the "nations of the vicinity"; he sketched a map of his route. And though Garcés gained a "clear understanding of the situation of all the nations," we know nothing. One can only imagine what the Hualapai map contained.[6]

Later explorers revealed only a little more. Although their sometimes ugly utterances about the Hualapais might call into question their reliability, they are the only sources available — Hualapais would create no written documentation about themselves until the twentieth century. Some speculate that the mountain man and trapper Bill Williams spent time with them in the early 1830s, but it was not until the 1850s that Anglos began heading into Hualapai country on a regular basis. In a flurry of visits that must have signaled to the Hualapais the advent of great change, four government-sponsored expeditions, all charged with exploring what remained a virtual terra incognita until the late nineteenth century, journeyed across Hualapai territory in rapid succession in the 1850s. Lorenzo Sitgreaves (1852), Alexander Weeks Whipple (1853), Edward Beale (1857), and Joseph Christmas Ives (1858) all caught glimpses of the Hualapais while they variously sought out the best train route to the Pacific or explored the meanderings of the Colorado River. Ives relied on Hualapais to help him navigate the intricacies of the "Big Cañon," but the others had little or no significant contact with them. Catching little more than occasional glimpses of them, the explorers gave them little thought, and the impact of these visits appears to have been fleeting. To Ives, for example, the Grand Canyon region was a wasteland best left alone. The grizzly bears of the region made "a capital soup," but there was little else of value. Convinced that his expedition had "been the first, and will doubtless be the last, to visit this profitless locality," Ives wrote the region off.[7]

Ives was, of course, wrong. In the 1860s, when army officers such as J. W. Mason and William Redwood Price were fighting Indians in earnest, the Hualapai began to have significant contact with the Anglo world. After gold was found, a stream of miners set their sights on Hualapai country. The founding of Prescott, the reinvigoration of Fort Mojave, across the Colorado, the construction of Fort Whipple, and the near constant wagon road traffic all brought rapid change. The murder of Hualapai leader Wauba Yuma in 1866 set off the

Hualapai War, a guerrilla war that alternately simmered and boiled for the next three years. It was a ruthless campaign fought in the arid valley of western Hualapai country and the tight canyons in the center of their territory in the extreme heat of July and the snow of January. Gun battles did less damage to the Hualapai than the destruction of resources—any later suggestion that they were not farmers could easily be dismissed by the reports of army officers who destroyed cornfields. War not only pitted Indians against the United States. It also stressed relationships among Indians: the Mojaves and the Hualapais, longtime friends, briefly became enemies as the army enlisted Mojaves in its fight with the Hualapais; Yavapai-Hualapai enmity reached new heights; and Paiutes to the north, heretofore shielded from the army by the Colorado River, were drawn into the regional war. For Indians in the greater Colorado River region, it must have seemed as if the world was at war.[8]

After heavy losses, the Hualapais signed a peace agreement in 1868. By this time, too, many of them had taken a new view of the army. Under the command of Captain Thomas Byrnes, the army founded Camp Beale's Springs on the outskirts of Kingman in 1871 as a buffer between Hualapais and Anglos. With their subsistence so badly disrupted by Anglo ranching—their hunting and farming grounds had all but been taken away—the Hualapais became dependent on army rations. Soon thereafter many Hualapai men became scouts in the war against the Apaches. Fighting, perhaps, for a paycheck or because of lost honor, boredom, coercion, hatred of the enemies to the south —we are likely never to know their motivations—at least 140 Hualapai men joined the army. Then, in 1874, the same army, following the wishes of the BIA, removed them from their homes against their will and sent them south to bake in the desert of the Colorado River lowlands, a place the officer in charge called the "Sahara of the Colorado." Many went, but some stayed, hiding out in the Grand Canyon. When those who left could no longer stand it, they returned home. The tribe's stay lasted less than a year, but it suffered heavy losses from disease, exposure, and malnutrition. This was the Hualapais' long walk.[9]

When they returned to their home, the Hualapais found much of the land occupied by miners and ranchers. Indeed, according to Mason, "every stream, water-hole, and square foot of arable land [is] taken up by white men, and the Indian has no place to call his own." And, again, many men scouted. Anglo ranchers and a new threat, the Atlantic and Pacific Railroad, generated a sense of urgency among the Hualapais. They needed a reservation. It remains impossible to say whether they knew exactly what "reservation" meant. It is certain that they wanted a specific piece of land to be protected. Able to see the damage done by the arrival of Anglo-owned cattle—the usurpation of springs, a drastic reduction in game due to overgrazing, and the destruction of selé, which rapidly declined as Hualapais stopped setting the seasonal fires that encouraged its growth and cows moved in — the tribe wanted to stem further losses. And now the railroad, fast moving across Arizona and headed straight for Hualapai country, soaked up whatever water it could find. Major General O. B. Willcox, as he sat watching the tracks of the Atlantic and Pacific Railroad — the Santa Fe's predecessor — make their way west of Albuquerque in 1881, observed that the "railroad now progressing through the country [the Hualapais] inhabit . . . is giving rise to new complications."[10]

The tribe knew that its land needed protection. In July 1881 a "majority of the tribe," including Cherum and other important headmen, met with Price and asked for a reservation. Aided by one Charles Spencer, the Hualapais marked out a territory that included key places in their aboriginal homeland. A shadowy figure who spent the late 1860s fighting the tribe, Spencer was first a foe and then a friend. After the army defeated the Hualapais, he joined them, marrying a Hualapai woman named Snyje. Calling himself a guide, Spencer acted as an interpreter and spokesman for the Hualapai.

Though little is known about him, Spencer was, without question, of singular importance — contemporary opinion suggested that he was instrumental in creating the reservation and possibly unifying the tribe. By the summer of 1882, the largest Hualapai band, numbering 215, lived in Madwida Canyon, some congregating around Spencer's Ranch. That fall, as he watched ranchers and the railroad approaching, he lamented that "our Country is filled up with thieves and desparadoes." Knowing that Peach Springs, the largest and most important spring in Hualapai country, would soon be coveted by the railroad, Spencer built a stone monument at the spring. A pile of rocks and a sign could not stem the tide, but it could at least stake the Hualapais' claim. Many contemporaries recalled that Spencer played a critical role in making clear the tribe's claim to Peach Springs. When Jim Fielding, a prominent Hualapai headman until his death in 1936, was a teenager, he said that when the Hualapais returned to their homes from their internment at La Paz to find that their water sources had been "taken by the new comers," he and Spencer traveled throughout Hualapai country to mark "a piece of land as an Indian Claim against the new comers." Mike Sue, Nora Schrum, and Jim Smith — Smith claimed to be an eyewitness — all remembered that Spencer put up the sign claiming Peach Springs for the tribe. His wife Snyje went further, claiming that he worked hard to shield Peach, Milkweed, and Pine Springs from white encroachment. And W. F. Grounds, one of the earliest white ranchers, claimed that Spencer negotiated with the army and was, in part, responsible for setting aside the reservation.[11]

Spencer helped the Hualapais get the army's attention, but it remains uncertain exactly how much he worked with them to map out the boundaries of the reservation. Included in the Hualapais' request for a reservation were important springs, as well as the core areas of most of the tribal bands. Beginning at Tinnakah (later Clay) Springs, the boundary would run north to the Colorado River, south and east two miles south of Peach Springs, and far enough into the eastern portion of Hualapai country to include Pine Springs. The half of the reservation that was west of Peach Springs is drier and lower in elevation than the well-watered and heavily timbered eastern half. Although the eastern half would eventually become more important economically—and thus desired by both the railroad and the Hualapais—both halves of the reservation preserved parts of the Hualapais' ancestral land.[12]

On July 8, 1881, Willcox issued General Order 16, setting aside a reservation for the Hualapais, subject to the approval of the president. Commissioner of Indian Affairs Hiram Price agreed with recommendations of W. R. Price and Willcox and suggested to the Secretary of War that he make it clear to the railroad that the Hualapai had a prior right to the water on their land, "that it must not be diverted to the injury of the Indians."[13] A year and half later, on January 4, 1883, President Chester Arthur signed an executive order creating the Hualapai reservation—the same reservation mutually agreed on by the tribe and the army in the summer of 1881. This seemingly simple series of events, played out over less than two years, would take more than twenty to untangle in the courts.

The creation of a reservation marked the birth of the Hualapai tribe. Dispersed across their vast territory in camps comprised of kinship networks and led by a headman, the Hualapais had never before been a unified political entity. Camps coalesced into bands based on regional affiliations, and these in turn made up the tribe. Although they were unified by a common language and culture, their day-to-day activities were carried out in the local camps, and regional bands had little contact with one another. It was only after contact began in earnest in the 1860s that the need for a more cohesive political entity emerged. In 1865, for example, three Hualapai "chiefs"—Wauba Yuma, Hitch-Hitchie, and Cherum—allied and negotiated an agreement with the Mohave and Prescott Toll Road Company granting Anglos safe passage across their territory in exchange for gifts. Hualapai leadership was loosely hereditary, and it remained so through the 1930s. It was also based on strong oratorical skills, one's war record—or descent from one with a strong war record—and, increasingly, on an ability to negotiate effectively with Anglos.[14]

Although the reservation indeed contained a portion of the Hualapais' aboriginal territory and was not simply a random swath of dusty desert, as was later argued, it nonetheless created a new Hualapai home—and a new relationship with the government. By taking the land out of the public domain, the government agreed to hold the land in trust for the tribe and protect it against non-Indian intrusion. The Hualapai also became a new legal identity: a U.S. government–administered tribe. For many years thereafter, because of white encroachment and limited economic opportunity, the reservation was the not the scene of much activity. And though the Hualapai bands made up a tribe, they operated autonomously well into the late nineteenth century. Band identity was more important than tribal identity.[15] The creation of the reservation is the single most important event in the Hualapais' modern history, but the change came gradually. The boundaries now hemming the tribe in, the ability of the government to monitor Hualapai behavior, however feeble at times, the Hualapais' new and uncertain property rights—all these things and more would, at different time and in varying degrees, have a profound impact on Hualapai life.

If the creation of the reservation initially had little direct impact on the Hualapais, the opposite was true of the coming of the railroad, the increase of Anglo cattle ranching, and the on-again, off-again mining in the area. Once the Anglo world rushed in, aboriginal land use and Hualapai life changed rapidly. Beginning in the 1870 and 1880s, wage work, for ranchers and for the railroad, began to attract Hualapai men; some women became domestics. Even the most isolated Hualapais, for example, the Pine Springs band, were affected by the changes. Owing to their remote location and proximity to the Grand Canyon, most members of the Pine Springs band, like their neighbors the Havasupais, were able to avoid the internment at La Paz. But in the 1880s their population diminished quickly—cattle pushed them out and railroad work drew them to Peach Springs, the fast-growing town in the middle of the reservation. Hackberry, a small mining town just west of the reservation boundary, where Hualapais lived among miners from Prussia, Saxony, Ireland, and all regions of the United States, also drew Hualapais toward wage work. By the mid-1870s they provided a key labor source for the mines. According to one observer, both men and women were able to "make considerable money." Men worked in the mines, and women did laundry and gathered hay. But the vicissitudes of wage work—Hackberry boomed and busted with alarming regularity—meant that Hualapais could not rely on a paycheck from the mines, and those who did, while forgoing hunting, gathering, and farming, risked becoming dependent on government rations. The railroad pumped new life into Hackberry, making it a major regional shipping point for cattle. During the 1880s the Hualapai population in Hackberry quintupled from 28 to 137. But it was also marked by disease and death. The cramped and poor living conditions and exposure to unknown diseases tore through the population. In one month—March 1887—pneumonia and measles killed thirty Hualapais.[16]

At the turn of the twentieth century the reservation was home to about five hundred to seven hundred Hualapais. Most were just barely scraping by, eking out a living in an unforgiving landscape. At the end of the 1880s and the beginning of the 1890s, briefly but with great intensity, some Hualapais also embraced the Ghost Dance. Seeing it as a way to revitalize Indian strength in the face of white power, Indians across the West adopted the Ghost Dance to varying degrees. Dancing in circles, sometimes for days on end, Ghost Dancers hoped for visions regarding the return of the buffalo, for example, or the destruction of whites. As with other Indian peoples, when the Hualapais welcomed the Ghost Dance they hoped it would lead to a tribal renaissance and rid their country of non-Indians. It didn't. As surely as it had begun in a great fury, it petered out with barely a sound.[17]

The Hualapais felt with far greater impact the opening of the Indian school at Valentine. Just to the west of Peach Springs, the school, started in 1894 by the Massachusetts Indian Association, took in many Hualapai children. In 1900, one of them was a young boy of about ten named Fred Mahone.[18]

2

The Conflict

On its long ramble across New Mexico and Arizona into California the Atchison, Topeka, and Santa Fe Railroad cut across millions of acres of Navajo, Pueblo, Hopi, Havasupai, Yavapai, Hualapai, Chemehuevi, and Mojave land. The land grant awarded to the railroad perforated Hualapai country just a few miles south of Peach Springs—the tracks can be found these days by looking on a map for old Route 66, where it arcs north off I-40 toward the Colorado River. Continuing west after leaving Flagstaff, the railroad heads out into Arizona's lonely backcountry, reaching the boundary of the Hualapai reservation at the intersection of Yavapai, Coconino, and Mohave Counties. The Aubrey Cliffs rise in the northwest, breaking the otherwise flat landscape. Just on the other side of the cliffs, still further to the northwest, lies Prospect Valley, which is cut by small canyons, each one making its way to the Grand Canyon and the Colorado River. Five miles further the tracks reach the reservation's only town, Peach Springs. The springs themselves are north of town a few miles, in the south central portion of the reservation; they once served as a crucial water break along the route and the only stop on the reservation. These days the train just blows its horn and stops traffic a couple of dozen times a day as it barrels by the Hualapai Lodge. The tracks then skirt the southern boundary of the reservation, and after about twenty miles the train leaves Hualapai land at Hackberry, heading westward to Kingman and California.

The railroad's voracious thirst for the water at Peach Springs, combined with the Hualapais' needs, set the two on a collision course. Water drew the railroad to Peach Springs; the railroad and the water drew the Hualapais. Although both considered the springs their own, neither party had clear ownership. But what seemed like a simple question — who owned the water at Peach Springs? — did not have a simple answer. Did the Atchison, Topeka, and Santa Fe (ATSF), a large corporation responsible for opening much of the American Southwest, own it, or did the Hualapai tribe possess inherent rights to land they had utilized since time immemorial? For many years no one had asked, and had the issue been raised, it is likely to have posed little debate. The railroad had been using the water since it first laid tracks through Peach Springs in the early winter of 1883. The uncertainty of the date is important: the railroad would claim that it had built the tracks before the reservation was created by executive order on 4 January 1883. It also would claim that it had bought the spring fair and square from two settlers. Both claims would later be disputed. The Hualapais, on the other hand, had no proof of ownership — or so everyone thought. They had no written language, which meant they had no documentation. Plus, they built no towns or permanent dwellings around the spring; it seemed that at best they occasionally wandered past it, stopping for a few days or more and then moving on. How could a people with such ephemeral ties to a place assert that they owned the rights to the waters there?[1]

In the years just before World War I, in fits and starts, the Hualapais and their reservation agents started to wonder why the tribe paid the railroad for water they considered theirs. At first the dispute revolved around ownership and use of Peach Springs, with little or no discussion of Hualapai rights to land. What rights did the railroad possess on the basis of its 1866 grant from Congress? This was crux of the matter. Was the spring contained in an odd-numbered section — all odd-numbered sections being granted to the railroad — or in an even-numbered section? In the early, stillborn discussions, only rarely were the Hualapais' rights mentioned. Yet despite the seeming narrowness of the question — and it was narrow originally, for no one had it in mind to interrogate Indian title — a Pandora's box had been opened.

Indian Inspector John Charles raised the first alarm in 1909 when he visited the Hualapai reservation and noted the strange state of affairs: the railroad charged the tribe for the use of Peach Springs — a spring well within the boundaries of the reservation. Charles thought it wise to determine title. Having heard that the railroad had purchased the rights from a couple of old settlers, he wondered how they had acquired title. But he only wondered. He filed his report and moved on. And the railroad continued to charge the Hualapais for water.[2]

Five years later the matter surfaced again. It might have been the onset of the intense summer heat that arrived in June, when the water from the spring became ever more precious, that set reservation superintendent Charles Shell to thinking. Water was scarce. And as the new government-sponsored cattle operation drew Hualapais toward Peach Springs from off-reservation towns such as Hackberry, the Hualapais and their animals needed all the water they could get. Why was the railroad taking all the water it needed and charging the tribe for the leftovers? Shell was indignant. He wrote to the Commissioner of Indian Affairs, "There is no record in this office that I can find showing what right the railroad Company has to this water. Please inform me as to what right, if any, the Railroad Company has to maintain this plant on the reservation."[3]

Inquiries went a little further this time. Shell did a little digging into the settlers' sale of land to the railroad. As he pursued the matter with alacrity for about two years, key pieces of the puzzle began to fall into place. Shell got the attention of the Bureau of Indian Affairs. Chief Clerk C. F. Hauke confessed that determining ownership would be tricky. The reservation had never been surveyed, and the lack of a survey meant that there was no way to demonstrate whether the land was in an odd or an even section—the key to learning who owned the springs. Only ten years earlier, because the reservation had become a "refuge for train robbers, horse thieves, and desperadoes," a survey had been planned, but nothing had come of it. No one could say what was Indian land and what was railroad land. But there might be evidence that the Hualapais used the spring before the railroad arrived. Hauke found a report written in 1882 by Major J. W. Mason discussing the establishment of a reservation for the tribe that included Peach Springs. Mason noted that Peach Springs was unique among springs in Hualapai territory in that no one else claimed it—it had not been settled and developed by whites. Mason observed with scorn that one fellow was making a sorry attempt at farming but showed little prospect of success and could easily be persuaded to relinquish his tenuous claim.[4]

The ATSF told a different story. The railroad claimed to have bought the rights to the spring in 1882, developing it the same year. The Mason report said otherwise: in 1882 no one except the lone settler, who was doomed to failure anyway, was using the spring. The railroad believed that if it could prove that it owned Peach Springs before it was set aside by executive order on January 4, 1883, as part of the Hualapai reservation, the matter would rest. Surely, its grant and its purchase of Peach Springs, both of which, it claimed, came before the creation of the reservation, gave it rights that trumped any the Hualapais might have had. And what was more, it had been using the spring, uncontested, for thirty years. Why the current concern?[5] After all, Indians, like railroads, had no rights in land other than those granted to them by Congress.

The answer to the problem appeared to be in the chronology: Did the railroad establish its rights first, or did the Hualapais? Shell didn't know what to think. On one hand, he sounded convinced — the railroad was there first and thus its claim to the water was solid. On the other, he still thought it wise to determine whether there was a cloud over their title, and if so, to see about getting the water for free.[6]

In the fall of 1914, at the urging of the Commissioner of Indian Affairs (CIA), the General Land Office (GLO) became involved and determined that, indeed, the land had not been surveyed. Was Peach Springs in an even or an odd section? Only two answers could be imagined: if the former, the railroad had no valid claim to the land as far as the GLO was concerned; if the latter, the Hualapais would get no free water. Peach Springs was either granted to the railroad or made part of the Hualapai reservation. It did not exist as property until conferred on one owner or another. But was a survey really necessary? What use were the Hualapais making of the water? The commissioner was concerned about costs — the survey would not be cheap. Would the benefits of finding title in the Hualapais justify the expense? And if it were found to be so, would the water be put to beneficial use?[7]

While the BIA was pondering the wisdom of a survey, Shell had begun to contact some of the old settlers to see if he could sort out the sale of Peach Springs. He made some initially promising discoveries after trying to contact three old-timers. All three agreed that the same man, Sam Crozier, had sold Peach Springs to the railroad. First, W. P. Grounds told a confusing tale of squatters and settlers buying and selling the rights to the spring; W. B. Ridenour, barely literate in his response, was more reticent; and T. G. Walter's widow had no sure idea of whether the sale had taken place in 1882 or 1883. As best Grounds could remember it, Crozier sold the land to the railroad sometime in 1884 or 1885 — information that helped neither side and was almost assuredly incorrect because the railroad, whether or not its title was good, had developed the spring by 1883. He also averred that "no white man lived on it or laid claim to it until 1874." This was likely correct, but of little use at that time.[8] All three — and many more in the years to come — would have another chance to tell their stories.

Having satisfied himself, Shell gave up the chase. "The rights of water in this country are vague," he concluded.[9] The chain of title might never be untangled. Yet he never bothered — as far as the documentary record reveals — to ask the Hualapais. This would be the last time the tribe got no say in determining whether it had a history.

With matters in such a muddle Shell thought it might be best to let things lie. If a survey were conducted it might be discovered that the railroad owned choice grazing land — something he was loath to give up. He also came to think that the cost was too great; the benefits would not justify the expense. But paying for the water continued to get under his skin; he was unwilling to let the matter go. Shell considered the price of fifty cents per thousand gallons "exorbitant" and still believed that the railroad was utilizing Indian land unlawfully.[10]

Just what did Shell want? If he pressed further a survey would be the result — too costly and too risky. If he let the matter go, then the Hualapais would surely lose their right to the water. His ambivalence — the first sign of a pattern — precluded real action. He threatened to close the road to the spring that the railroad operated but then was afraid to have the reservation surveyed for fear that doing so might benefit the railroad. His intuition told him that the railroad was trespassing on Hualapai land, but the notion that perhaps it wasn't still lingered. In the end, he didn't want to find out. And in the end, nothing was done. Shell opened the new year of 1916 by declaring that the "matter is now satisfactorily settled."[11] As far as he was concerned, the ownership of the title to the land remained a mystery.

But to the Hualapais, of course, there was no mystery. The land was theirs. They had recognized the threat posed by the railroad and the settlers in the late nineteenth century and done what they needed to do to protect their land: they had requested a reservation. They asked that the government, in creating the reservation, mark off an important portion of their ancestral land, including, specifically, Peach Springs. The government agreed. But when confronted by the claims of the railroad, the government appeared willing to forgo its commitment to protect Hualapai land. The Hualapais would not give up their land easily; the desire for its protection became a unifying force.

3

The Hualapai Awakening

Fred Mahone, shortly after leaving Chilocco Indian School and before
shipping out for France, took time in the summer of 1918 to reflect on the past
and think about the future. Whiling away the time at Michigan's Selfridge
Field, Mahone put pencil to paper in the language he had only recently learned
to write and announced to the world, "I am a full blooded born from . . . Ancient
descendent who has gained three fourth of an education." From that moment,
far from his home in Arizona, Fred Mahone became the voice of the Hualapais.
He urged: "Let us forget to-day the sole object of the mere early savagery of the
passed period. Wearing apparel of peculiar specimens, long hair, feathers,
blankets, moccasins are curiosity for to-day . . . the redmen of the western
hemisphere must make up our mind to be . . . in the modern History of to-day."
After all, he said, the "ancestors of the redmen remains the same. But their
present generations are aiming themselves toward the modern life." And to
help them aim straight Mahone drafted an eighteen-page manifesto. Divided
into nine parts and thirty-seven sections, his letter from Michigan was a thoroughly modern and quite detailed blueprint for self-government and education, as well as a clear demand for citizenship and all its privileges and burdens
— the right to vote and the responsibility of paying taxes, for example. When he
came home to the Hualapai reservation after the war, a new tribal organization,
"The Redmen Self Depentendent [sic] of America," would carry out his plan.[1]

Eventually embracing the views of the radical, southern California–based Mission Indian Federation (MIF), Mahone became politicized, and once he became an activist the tribe was able to articulate, for the first time, a set of collective political goals. The Hualapai, to be sure, had been coalescing into a coherent tribe since its first contact with whites in the 1860s. But Mahone's influence was unique. When Mahone returned home, he inaugurated a twenty-year program to rid the reservation of ranchers and the railroad. Although these had long been Hualapai concerns, Mahone gave them new urgency. But he never became a sanctioned Hualapai leader.[2] And in time many Hualapais came to think of him as an upstart. He was an agitator, an activist, and his often troubled and always complex relations with the Hualapais earned him their scorn as well as their admiration.

The Hualapai elder Ben Beecher says that Mahone was both loved and hated. According to Beecher — whose family allied with Mahone in the 1930s in the Hualapais' fight against the railroad — something dawned on Mahone when he was in the service that caused him to ask a lot of questions. He came home a different man. Beecher says that Mahone advocated big changes that scared some Hualapais. Indeed, after a time Mahone's activism so raised the ire of some that he came to fear for his safety. After the Hualapais formalized the reservation government under the Indian Reorganization Act in 1939, forming a tribal council, Mahone served but one term, and only as secretary.[3] Impatient, impetuous, and frustrated — that was Fred Mahone. But once he became politicized, he was also dedicated to securing Hualapai land rights.

Mahone's politicization and his modernity, his intense desire to "forget today the sole object of the mere early savagery of the passed period," stand in counterpoint to the better-known story of more prominent Progressive Era Indian leaders and activists such as Arthur Parker and Charles Eastman. The image of Indian America crafted by Parker, Eastman, and the Society of American Indians (SAI) had little to offer men such as Mahone. For him, the past — or at least popular images of the Indian past — crippled the Hualapais. The exterior symbols of primitiveness that Parker and Eastman at times donned as authentically Indian — symbols used to gain favor with white America — Mahone found to be barriers to progress. Mahone had no need to drape himself in Indian costume; playing Indian had no appeal for him. He set his sights on the future in order to aim toward "maximum equal rights. The maximum Equal Opportunity. The good homes, the good roads. The common wealth and the well fare for [today] and the days to come."[4]

Fred Mahone was born in 1888 and spent his childhood on the reservation. By the age of ten he could read, write, and speak English. He was among what reservation superintendent Henry Ewing characterized as the "noisy, howling horde of dirty untrained savages, who had never before felt what it was to [be] restrained or corrected, [who] were soon transformed into orderly, quiet, attentive children, eager to learn, each striving to conform his savage nature" by attending the agency school at Valentine. He remained there until he was sixteen. In 1914, just as the troubles over Peach Springs began, he left the reservation, a place where tuberculosis infected almost 15 percent of the tribe, a tribe that the U.S. Public Health Service had declared "a menace to the public health." There were few opportunities for a young man like Mahone. He headed off to Chilocco Indian School in Oklahoma, where he stayed until 1917.[5]

Fred Mahone, pan-Indianism, and assimilation all matured together in the years before and after World War I. Among the multiple reasons for the origins of pan-Indian activism, the influence of the boarding school experience ranks near the top. When the SAI, the nation's first pan-Indian organization, was formed in 1911, most of its founding members had attended such schools; at its first annual conference at least one-third of the delegates were graduates of either Carlisle or Hampton, two other boarding schools. The influence of this experience on the SAI was unmistakable: assimilation and education, tinged with a healthy dose of nineteenth-century evolutionism, were markers of the society's ethos. To be sure, the formation of the SAI signaled a change in Indian politics: for the first time Indians organized on a national scale, and, unlike other reform organs such as the Indian Rights Association, the SAI was run by Indians. But its assimilationist tendencies, along with its failure to make strong connections to Indian reservations, led to its ultimate downfall by the mid-1920s.[6]

The society's largely nonreservation leaders celebrated Indianness in a generic, at times romantic way. But at a time when most American Indians lived on reservations in countless diverse settings, the SAI's appeal was minimal. "Bridge figures" such as Parker, the Seneca pan-Indian activist and eventual president of the SAI, tried to join the primitive past to the present and the future. Such leaders aimed to reconfigure Indians as essentially American by diminishing the presence of reservation Indians — or more accurately, by masking what they represented: unreconstructed primitivism. If this meant mixing and matching Indian cultures, so be it. For example, when the Iroquois donned Sioux regalia at their celebration of the five-hundredth anniversary of the founding of the Iroquois League, Parker admitted that "Indians to be recognized as such must 'play' Indian." Indians were loyal and close to nature; they were thrifty and honest — "the American Race," according to Parker. By rendering the past more palatable, by reframing it as romantic, Parker, Eastman, and the SAI worked hard to disarm those who saw Indians as savages. They vigorously asserted their Americanness. Doing so, however, relegated Fred Mahone to embracing an image of the past that he wanted to transcend.[7]

Confronting the challenges of this new world was not possible for everyone; inevitably, evolution left some behind. From the beginning, the SAI wanted to cultivate "race leaders" — Parker's term — from among the "small company of Indians of broad vision" — those with just the right mix of Indian and non-Indian traits. Yet because most Indians lived on reservations, the SAI's program fell largely on deaf ears. In truth, very few were listening. One who was, Cahuilla leader Francisco Patencio, bristled at what he heard. At the SAI's 1919 meeting, Patencio said, "My friends, you are different from my people. . . . I hear that you want citizenship. I and my people, we do not want citizenship, because we have already been citizens in this country always."[8]

Fred Mahone was a Hualapai first and an Indian second. The SAI would have had difficulty understanding his ties to a place and to history. Or, perhaps, it understood the link all too well — and feared it. It knew that the strong ties that connected reservation Indians to their homes could not be severed. On the positive side of the ledger, they had a link to the past, a loyalty to place, and a closeness to nature, but, on the negative side, they were trapped by that same past, living in the rude conditions of the reservation. They inhabited a place of *permanent* primitiveness, rather than being able to travel at will between the reservation and the modern world. Indians such as Eastman and Parker tapped into that primitiveness when it suited them, when it jibed with the few positive notions that Americans had of Indians. But in their celebration of antimodernism they risked keeping real Indians from gaining modern rights. Relegating native peoples to the past, of course, is not a uniquely American practice; it has an been effective tool elsewhere in world, explicitly or implicitly, in denying native people modern rights.[9] Mahone recognized the danger in seeing the Indian past this way; he did not want to be considered a primitive, "[w]earing apparel of peculiar specimens."

Ultimately, Indians might become like whites: progressive and not wedded to the past. Parker rejoiced in the knowledge that some Indians had "attained great distinction as leaders in the white world[, which] proves the virility of the race and demonstrates its capacity." Although Indian virility could lead to achievements valued by whites, redemption must come first, so Parker cryptically counseled his readers to "make good where we have sinned." Parker's "we" was both Indian and white. He played both, and at times he could mask his Indian identity entirely. In 1916, contrasting Indians' and immigrants' efforts to assimilate, Parker posed as if he were not native at all: "The Indian . . . comes out of his own peculiar form of civilization, an undeveloped form, *to*

our way of thinking, and into the full glare of twentieth century enlightenment. Little wonder that he is for the moment dazed and stumbles as he
walks."[10] The allusions to evolution, so obvious that they hardly rank as
metaphor, are nonetheless instructive: the Indian was a work in progress.
Parker, of course, held himself out as an example of an Indian who was no
longer dazed and stumbling; he had emerged from the depths and become an
American, clear-eyed and walking tall.

The SAI's was a model Indian — stripped of tribal affiliation, cast off the
reservation, and educated — ready to take on the future. The pan-Indian activists of the Progressive Era, like Parker and Charles Eastman, crafted a generic
Indian with a primitive yet idyllic past. Coupled with Parker's virile American
Indian, this new man (for "virile" was nothing if not a masculine signifier) was
ready for the challenges of modernity.[11]

Fred Mahone's politicization began in the pan-Indian atmosphere of the Chilocco Indian School. In his long letter to Cato Sells the influence of the boarding school experience is clear. For example, his new tribal organization, the
Redmen Self Depentendent of America, would ensure that Hualapai boys and
girls received a Chilocco education; in fact, uneducated Hualapais would not
be allowed to serve in the new tribal government that Mahone envisioned. At
Chilocco, Mahone began to get a sense of the scope of the forces lined up
against the Hualapais. Surrounded by young people from more than forty
tribes who were trading stories from their homes, it is easy to imagine, given
his later tendency toward outspokenness — one could never call Fred Mahone
a wallflower — that on meeting other Indians he began to air some of his
complaints. Whether he did or did not, like many other young men at Chilocco and other boarding schools, Mahone went to war to fight for the United
States. And like 75 to 90 percent of his fellow Indian soldiers, he went as a
volunteer. In a photograph from 1918 he stands erect in his new uniform,
looking stern and a bit stiff but ready for action. While stationed in Michigan,
he kept up with the news from Chilocco, trained for war, and began to wonder
about the past and the Hualapais' place in the future. When the war had
begun, Chilocco's newspaper, the *Indian School Journal,* steeped as it was in
patriotism and proud of its men in uniform, had urged its Indian men to
"follow the flag" and avoid the shame of being labeled "slackers in this critical
period." Mahone joined the American Expeditionary Force and shipped off to
France in 1918.[12]

Service in World War I exposed Indian men to the wider world and forever
altered their perspective on America. A new generation of leaders emerged
from the war demanding citizenship for all Indians and settlement of land

claims in exchange for service — their country owed them something. Time spent in boarding schools and loyalty to the United States during the war made these men more Americanized than any previous generation of Indians — and more demanding.[13] Men such as Mahone came back from Europe hoping to regain lost ground in a new world. He returned to Hualapai country an American, to be sure, but his newfound faith in American democracy and equality did not simply cause him to cast off his Indian clothes and step in line with white America. On the contrary, Mahone returned with a deep sense of purpose: to get back the land taken from the Hualapai by the Atchison, Topeka, and Santa Fe Railway.

Although journalists, Indian Service officials, and other commentators could not contain their excitement at finally seeing Indians — Indian warriors at that! — embracing such American values as discipline, loyalty, and service, men such as Mahone were preparing to pick away at the past. If Mahone became a true American as a result of his wartime service, if he came home "with a new light on his face and a clearer conception of the democracy in which he may participate and prosper," as Cato Sells hoped, he also returned from the war with a keen sense that something was amiss in Indian country.[14]

Mahone stood poised to be the kind of Indian that Arthur C. Parker envisioned: one who embraced aspects of the white world and retained a vestige of what was good about being Indian. Mahone achieved what Parker, at his most optimistic, hoped all Indians could achieve: as firm a place as possible in two worlds, with equal reverence, and not a little disdain, for both. Yet Parker's vision could also be bleak. He might have been imagining Mahone when he wrote: "The solitary educated Indian sent back to his own tribe could do little for it. Moreover, he could do little for himself, for he has lost all his skill as an Indian, and his knowledge of most things was of little use to his tribesmen."[15] Parker could not have been more wrong, at least about Mahone. He returned to the reservation alone after the war, mobilized the Hualapai, and used his education to secure Indian rights. He did what he was supposed to do: he used his education as a tool to help his people become Americans.

After the war, Mahone briefly attended college. Two-quarters of a full course load at Valparaiso University in Indiana was enough, and in the spring of 1920 he was off to Riverside, California, where he reenrolled in the military, joining the U.S. Air Service at March Field.[16] In California, his life went in a new direction. A version of his vision, the Redmen Self Depentendent of America, had come to life. He discovered the Mission Indian Federation (MIF).

The MIF, a radical group founded in Riverside in 1919, demanded Indian self-government, pressed for land claims legislation, called for the abolition of the BIA, and generally lobbied for sovereignty. The MIF quickly gained influence in southern California, and by the summer of 1921 the BIA feared that most Mission Indians were solid supporters. If the organization was not stopped, wrote two BIA inspectors, unrest would "spread to other reservations with very harmful results." Also popular, but less radical, was the state-wide Indian Board of Cooperation, based in San Francisco, which worked hard on a California claims bill and lobbied southern California tribes for their support. The board even garnered some positive reviews from the BIA.[17]

The MIF, in contrast, heard nothing but criticism. It was too antagonistic, too radical. If the Society of American Indians' hallmark was equal rights through assimilation, the MIF's was sovereignty and separation. Although founded and run in its early years by a non-Indian, Jonathan Tibbet, whom one inspector called "the enemy of the Government," as well as an "unscrupulous impostor and a flagrant criminal," the MIF was eventually led by reservation Indians for reservation Indians. Tibbet, a lifelong resident of the Riverside area, claimed that the MIF was "conceived in the minds of the Indians." But because it challenged BIA control of Indian land and people, BIA tolerance of it was short-lived. Unlike the SAI, the MIF presented a real threat. Whereas Indian reformers such as Carlos Montezuma, an on-again, off-again member of the SAI and at least a tepid supporter of the MIF, wanted to end BIA control and dismantle the reservation system as a method of assimilation, the MIF wanted the same as an assertion of sovereignty. Its appeal to a largely reservation-based constituency explains the group's rapid ascent; in 1921, only two years after its first stirrings, the BIA feared that the MIF controlled most Mission Indians in southern California. The SAI's support base was more diffuse. It had no center. The BIA never feared it. Although the MIF, to be sure, was a regional and not a national organization, its support was densely concentrated. It was also more effective. Mahone naturally gravitated toward the latter group.[18]

Mahone arrived in Riverside just as the MIF took off. Several large-scale gatherings held there garnered the support of Indians from across the region. First, Frederick G. Collett and George Wharton James of the Board of Indian Cooperation held a meeting about the status of a bill to settle California Indian claims in October 1920 — before Mahone arrived. Then Jonathan Tibbet held at least two large MIF meetings at his home in Riverside — one that ran for nearly a week in late January and early February 1920 and another in the spring of 1921. Hundreds of Indians attended both meetings, and several Hualapais — Kate Crozier, Richard Magee, and Fred Mahone — were present at the spring meeting. By then the MIF's influence was both wide and deep, reaching out across the region to all of the Mission tribes and to the Hualapai, Havasupai, and Mojave tribes — with whom Tibbet met in the fall of 1920 at Needles, California.[19]

The spring meeting worried the BIA. Until then Tibbet and the MIF had been carrying their message of Indian liberation without interference from the BIA. Initially, the MIF had been sanctioned, if not encouraged, by the government and given free rein to visit reservations in the region. But that spring, everything changed. Too many Indians were now involved; agents were being ignored; the MIF's radical politics were spreading. Fueled by fear, the BIA asked the Department of Justice to prosecute Tibbet and fifty-three Mission Indians for conspiracy for their attempts to alienate the Indians from the government. Although no crimes had been committed in its name, the BIA had come to consider the MIF's message seditious. Charles Burke, the Commissioner of Indian Affairs, thought it "absolutely necessary that the Government enter into the prosecution of these cases vigorously and with a determination to bring about the undoing and elimination of these men." If the Indians of California and the Southwest were to be "amalgamated into the citizenship of the community," then the message of the MIF needed to be stamped out and Tibbet and his followers stopped lest it lead to a "very unfortunate uprising." Unwilling to believe that the Indians of the various Mission reservations were capable of having a political consciousness separate from a white man's, the BIA and the Justice Department resolved to prosecute Tibbet. If Tibbet were removed, the Indians would straighten out. The government resolved to "strike down and destroy the organization." But Tibbet tapped into grievances that were already present — distrust of the government foremost among them. One of Tibbet's co-conspirators, Joe Pete, a Torres-Martinez Mission Indian living on the Malki reservation, had led a troublesome draft resistance movement during the war. Assistant Attorney General Raymond Benjamin feared that "unless stopped," Pete and Tibbet's activities posed a "great danger."[20]

Hundreds of radicalized Indians demanding their rights, the government clamping down, tension mounting: this was the climate in which Mahone found himself. Riverside was where Mahone first saw Indian activism, and the MIF had what he wanted. Already primed for action, Mahone was finally set in motion during his time in Riverside. Prior to the war Mahone had imagined forming his own group; now he saw that it could be done. After soaking up all that the MIF and Tibbet had to offer, he made plans to go home.

But back on the reservation he lamented, "We are all depressed." Poverty and disease were rampant. And because of "all these laws rules and regulations by the united states . . . we are ruled like slaves." But things were not all bad. As a result of Hualapai service during the war, there were signs that relations between local whites and the tribe were thawing. Mahone was recognized in the local community as "a splendid fellow" and was respected for his military service. And while the MIF stirred his anger, the memorial services held for two other Hualapai soldiers — Sam Swaskegame and Clarence W. Watson — in May and September, 1921, respectively, likely filled him with a sense of hope. First the Hualapais held a large-scale funeral attended by people from tribes all across the region. And then, in a cross-cultural affair, Swaskegame's body, which lay in state for several days at the American Legion post, was given a hero's welcome. Residents of Kingman helped plan the homecoming, and Hualapais and Anglos joined together to hold a funeral at the Methodist church. Mahone, along with three other Hualapais and three non-Indians, served as pallbearers in a service that combined Christian and Hualapai funeral rites. To honor Swaskegame, who died in combat in 1918, the American Legion post in Kingman was named after him. The funeral came at an auspicious time and is remembered as a turning point in the tribe's history, a moment when the Hualapais were considered citizens. Mahone's involvement with the MIF was at its height, and his new group was still young. Excited by the prospect of organizing the Hualapais and homing in on the tribe's single most important struggle — regaining their land from the railroad — he felt that the joint Anglo-Hualapai funeral signaled a changed climate. After all, the funeral honored a Hualapai veteran like himself. In death, Sam Swaskegame was honored by whites and Hualapais for his service; in life, Fred Mahone wanted the same recognition. In some respects, Mahone came back to a new world: Indians were honored by whites, and they were organized.[21]

Mahone hoped to capitalize on the changed climate and to change the lives of Hualapais by bringing his own brand of the MIF to Hualapai country in early 1921. Operating at first below the BIA's radar, Mahone embraced the MIF's message — what he called "Human Rights and Home Rule" — and, using its constitution and by-laws, Mahone and other members of the tribe formed the American Wallapai and Supai Indian Association on January 1, 1921. With Tibbet on hand as counselor, Mahone declared that the group's "work is principally based upon restoration means on Indian land and rights."[22] The Hualapais "authorized and empowered" him to lead the tribe because, he said, "[I] know with clear under standing the Ways my Wallapai Indian lives at present. They are suffered to great extent and many lives lost yearly." He wrote, "We are now seeking for [an] immediate time to elect by our own selves a highly recomended a college graduate and must deal and justify any of our rights with all our delgates of American Wallapai Indian Association. . . . We want some right to [make] immediate changes at Valentine, Arizona. What ever changes shall be It shall be known to or be for the delgtes and member of American Wallapai Indian Association." Rendered in elegant penmanship, Mahone's English, though fractured, nevertheless made his message clear: Hualapais knew their needs best and should be in control of the reservation.[23]

Charles Burke, the commissioner of Indian affairs, disagreed. Mahone's role as head of the newly formed group, Burke told him, was "without lawful authority." The commissioner cautioned Mahone to watch out or he might be subject "to punishment for possible violation of the Federal Laws."[24] Burke's threat contained no mention of particular laws that Mahone might be breaking. But the warning was more than toothless bluster. It was an effort to scare Mahone, to silence his protests and stop his organizing.

The American Wallapai and Supai Indian Association was not only a threat to the BIA, however. It would have been at least a foreign idea, if not a threat, to many of the Hualapais. Decision making had not been done in such a fashion in the past, nor could someone like Mahone simply declare himself a spokesman and leader. A single supreme tribal leader was unknown; a young man who had been gone for almost seven years with only weak hereditary links to power had no legitimacy. Jim Fielding, an older leader, had ascended to power because of lineage and because he was a *pa-kawha't* ("a good talker"). None of this deterred Mahone. He was not willing—then or later—to follow a traditional path to leadership. When he came home, band affiliations and family ties remained important. But since contact, and especially since the coming of the railroad in 1883, more and more people had moved to Peach Springs or outlying towns for work.[25] As a result, older social structures had become fragile or were not able to meet new challenges. A space opened up for a man like Mahone. The timing could not have been better for a young, eager activist: Mahone returned to the reservation at a time when increased threats to their land from ranchers and the railroad had many Hualapais worried, and their new agent had made few friends. Because Mahone could write he had a unique ability to reshape the tribe's fears and concerns into articulate protests. He gave the Hualapais a political voice in a new world—one where skills that older leaders such as Jim Fielding, who remained a respected leader until he died in 1936, did not have.

But Mahone did not bypass Hualapai leaders; he allied himself with them. Prominent elders such as Kate Crozier and, at first, Jim Fielding lent legitimacy to Mahone's cause. Indeed, many years later, Jacob Honga remembered that Mahone wisely enlisted the aid of recognized leaders. If he had not done so, no one would have listened to him. Having already made an alliance with Kate Crozier by 1921—the two men were together at Riverside MIF meetings—Mahone needed to reach out to others. Fred's uncle, Jim Mahone, was one of them. In 1922 the elder Mahone applied for a pension. Reported to be 120 years old when he died in 1949, Jim Mahone was a revered elder who had served under Generals George Crook and Nelson Miles in the army's hunt for

Geronimo in the 1880s. Mahone's service in the fight against the Apache was a mark of pride, as it was for all of the Hualapai scouts and eventually the tribe. One of Jim Mahone's most prized possessions was a letter of introduction of sorts written by an army major on his behalf vouching for his good character. Crook apparently had said that "no braver man ever trod shoe leather." Jim Mahone carried it with him everywhere. His pride may have run deep, but his memory of specifics was shallow — he no longer remembered precisely who he served under or who was in his unit. Nor could his name be found on the muster rolls. In order to receive a pension one must prove that one had served, and much of the evidence pointed in that direction, such as the corroborating testimony of fellow scouts. But the pension bureau denied Mahone's request; despite his testimony and that of others no definite record of his service could be found. Fred Mahone surely knew of the denial. Although he never specifically alluded to the incident, it is plausible that it angered him. The ex-scouts' army service was an exceptionally important part of their identity as Hualapai men and leaders; some, such as Huya, remembered that by helping to fight the Apache the Hualapai secured peace for themselves.[26] To be denied a pension for that service was unjust.

Jim Mahone was not the only Hualapai elder who might have influenced young Fred Mahone. Jim Fielding, who had made his own bid for power in 1910 when the revered Cherum was on his deathbed, also lent Mahone his support. Another former scout and de facto leader of the tribe, Fielding had a memory that stretched back before the coming of whites, when "we were all Indians." He knew that times had changed, however. Young Indians now went to school, "to make them capable of competing with the whites." Despite Fielding's disapproval, sending children away to school was not entirely a bad thing. Some, indeed, came home having learned a valuable lesson: "Some of the boys [who] have been sent away to school, they have discovered many things are wrong." Whether he was referring to Fred Mahone is unknown, but Mahone's activism resonated with Fielding, and they were soon allies.[27]

A third elder, Steve Leve-Leve, the official leader of the Hualapais, also lent Mahone's cause critical support. Already a supporter of the Mission Indian Federation — he had affixed his name to an MIF petition demanding that all reservations in the lower Colorado River region be solely reserved for and governed by Indians and that they all have water and education for children and not be subject to allotment — Leve-Leve was an obvious ally. Aligning himself with a hereditary leader (Steve Leve-Leve was the son of the important nineteenth-century band leader Leve-Leve) was a shrewd move.[28] If Mahone's activism was to have an impact on the Hualapais, it would need the sanction of a recognized leader; Mahone could not simply thrust himself into that role, despite his eagerness to do so. Now that at least some elders approved of his work, and with their sanction, Mahone's political career was firmly under way.

Mahone spent the winter and spring traveling back and forth between Arizona and California, keeping the formation of his new group a secret. But when news of a "plot" making its way from southern California to Arizona reached the Havasupai reservation in April, the superintendent grew concerned. Gaining information, however, proved difficult. The superintendent was wary, but any Havasupais who were involved would reveal little; they were "guard[ing] all their plans with the utmost cant . . . to find or understand the exact scheme is quite difficult." In August, when the military reduced its forces, Mahone received a discharge and headed back to Hualapai country for good. Organized and energized, he had identified what became his lifelong pursuit: "the protection of our sacred lands." Threatened by the railroad and by Anglo ranchers, he declared, "We claim the Indians' right of prior occupancy of the lands and the water."[29]

When Fred Mahone moved back to the reservation in the summer of 1921, the reservation superintendent, William A. Light, hoped that he could find out about the plot developing in Riverside, perhaps because of Mahone's background. After all, Mahone fit the profile of a progressive Indian: he was an educated veteran and had escaped the reservation, if only temporarily. Light had struck out with others who had traveled to Riverside in the spring: Kate Crozier, although "quite a reliable man and one of the most industrious Indians among the Hualapai," remained tight-lipped. As for Richard Magee, Light let loose with a torrent of invective. Magee was a "parasite, an imposter," and likely the ringleader of any plan to defraud the Hualapais of their money. But Light had no luck with Mahone, either; he soon learned that Mahone was the leader of the possible insurgency, and within a couple of months the two were bitter enemies. Light might have had high hopes for the returned students, but he found instead that "one or two of them are full of self conceit and imaginary knowledge and think they are able to solve the problems of their fathers, and are denouncing the Government, and biting the hand that has fed them throughout their earlier lives, and attempting to sow the seeds of dissatisfaction and discontent. These fellows are never seen at work. They are beggars, parasites, ne'er-do-wells, and live upon the industry of better men and women. . . . I have also to say that a few of these educated Indians are the worst element in the tribe."[30]

Tempers began to flare on the reservation in June 1921. Light, on the reservation only since 1919, had made few friends among the Hualapais and soon would engender the enmity of most of the tribe. Prior to the summer of 1921 Mahone had had no direct dealings with Light, but on the basis of reports from other Hualapais he came to distrust him. Sparking the action that June was a plan to build a highway across the reservation — what would become an important section of the famous Route 66. Mahone was furious, claiming that the BIA had granted the state of Arizona a permit to build a road on Hualapai land after Light allegedly reported that the tribe was in favor of the plan. It did not want a road, Mahone averred, and if it did, that was for the tribe to decide democratically through the newly formed American Wallapai and Supai Indian Association. Organized by Mahone as the first formal tribal government, the association was to make all decisions. Mahone declared: "The organization of American Wallapai Indian Association has right to bring any matter before the state and Federal Court to justify any wrongful causes amongst the Wallapai Indians and others." He assured the governor and the state highway engineer that the Hualapais would meet to discuss the new road and "settle it out right in a political manner."[31] In the meantime, he urged them to postpone construction. Despite their profession of faith in American values such as democracy and representation — values that the BIA had been hoping Indians would embrace for generations — this new group threatened Light's already weak hold over the Hualapais. He would not tolerate any attempt to diminish the autocratic role the reservation superintendent played in Indian life.

Deeply affected by lessons learned in school and the war, Mahone and others sincerely believed, perhaps naively, in the power of what they saw as American democracy. Appealing to his "white friends the loyal hearted American citizens of the State of Arizona," Mahone hoped to achieve equal rights for the Hualapai. Having served his country, it was time "to carry out the suffrage Indian in a busines manner and civilize them thru my education." The first step was having a representative group of Hualapais who could speak for the tribe. Others echoed Mahone. Richard McGee, the secretary and treasurer of the association and the object of so much of Light's scorn, was also a returned student, and to him the biggest problem was the inability of the Indian Service to cede any power to educated Indians. What, then, he wondered, had been the point of their education? And Roger Havatone, another Mahone supporter, angry and fed up with the BIA, appealed to "our true hearted white friends of America." He said, "We are not free people. We are prisoners." The Hualapais' subordinate position made no sense to Havatone because "we were here first before any whites came to this country." Tongue in cheek, he wondered: "Who was that person discovered America first and meet Indians on that country[?] [H]e did not brought any Indians along with him to this Country from other Countries across the ocean." By Havatone's reckoning, the fact that Indians were here first gave them the "right to bring this matter [of others' claims on reservation land] up before some one . . . who are working to help to get back my rights or the Indians rights on the reservation." Havatone lamented that as a result of having had their land alienated, their attempts at improving the reservation thwarted, and their rights compromised, they were "all depressed." Continuing, he declared that "we Indians are greatly suffered by these undesirable matter of rights and we raised our hands and called our white brothers to help us, for we help the white people when the world wars is going on." They had offered their aid, and, in return, hoped for "great help" from whites.[32]

But the Hualapais' declarations of independence and demands for rights were shunted aside. William Light mocked them, calling their protests simply "complaints of creatures so small mentally" that they were hardly worthy of reply. Mahone fared the worst. Light dismissed him because he was "so unwise, so brainless, and so much of a fool." Allegiance to the MIF and his "miserable use of English" marked Mahone as an Indian on whom the government had wasted thousands of dollars — his education and training as a soldier were all for naught. But worse, his attitude toward the government — the same government, Light intoned, that had done everything in its power for Mahone and the Hualapai — was traitorous. Mahone, in fact, had sunk "his record as a soldier into the slimy ooze of treason."[33]

Like the Mission Indian Federation in California, the American Wallapai and Supai Indian Association was a threat to BIA control. It scared Light, and his fear fueled threats: "I will say further, if these Indians do not use their reservation, live upon it, and cease their indolence, gambling, and immorality, they deserve to lose it, and it should be opened for settlement by men who would use it, and make good homes thereon."[34]

When the tense summer of 1921 was over, Fred Mahone was known as a troublemaker and marked as a source of unrest among the Indians of the Colorado River region. The government began to monitor him. His letters and statements to the BIA about Indian rights, conditions on the Hualapai reservation, and the formation of the American Wallapai and Supai Association made their way from Commissioner of Indian Affairs Charles Burke to the assistant U.S. attorney in Los Angeles. His missives were being used as evidence in the conspiracy case pending against Jonathan Tibbet.[35]

Unhappy with Light and unable to get him to take them seriously, in December 1921 Steve Leve-Leve and Fred Mahone asked the CIA to send an inspector to the reservation to look into Light's management of cattle sales. Burke showed little interest; until the Hualapais fleshed out their vague petition with the particulars of Light's malfeasance, the BIA would not act. But they pushed on, renewed their demands and petitioned the government again in 1922. This time Leve-Leve and Mahone drafted a petition and had it signed or thumbmarked by one hundred others. They demanded to know just how the Santa Fe got possession of the Hualapais' land and water, asked that the tribe be given total control of the reservation, and ordered all non-Indian ranchers out of Hualapai country. Four years earlier, the latter two of these three demands had figured prominently in Mahone's letter from Michigan. Now, with the aid of Hualapai leaders such as Leve-Leve and Fielding and of the American Wallapai Indian Association, Mahone could begin to carry out his plans.[36]

The BIA disregarded their complaints, and matters on the reservation only became worse. Early in the new year, Light was assaulted. A group of Hualapais accused Light of cheating them out of the proceeds from cattle sales. In his office on the school grounds, Mary Tokespeta, believing herself the rightful recipient of any money earned from the sale of the cattle of her former husband, Dude Ross, made her case to Light. Rejecting her initial appeal, Light tried to convince her that an heirship hearing would have to be held. Jim Fielding intervened. Siding with Tokespeta, he urged Light to skip the hearing, pay her, and avoid tangling with the BIA. According to Hualapai rules of inheritance, if the cattle had been hers when she married Ross — cattle could be owned by both husband and wife in a Hualapai marriage — then they became hers again when the union ended in divorce or death. Light refused, and the confrontation turned violent. Having expected Fielding to side with him and enforce the law, Light was livid when Fielding questioned his authority. They argued at length. In the thick of their exchange Tokespeta struck Light in the back. Reading his account, one imagines Light crumpled on the floor, flattened by her blow, pleading in vain for Fielding to arrest her. Light threw her out of the office. Once outside, in rapid succession, first her husband attacked him and then she did, hitting him several more times. They wanted their money. Fielding only watched. When the brief melee was over, Light collected himself and suspended Fielding, declaring him useless as a policeman. Believing Light's story, Burke backed him and had Fielding fired.[37] The incident shook Light: he lost confidence in a once-trusted ally and was subjected to a violent reprisal.

But what had caused Fielding to abandon Light? Mahone's influence had. Fielding had been, according to Light, "well coached" by Mahone. The two were now the "self styled and self constituted leaders" of the Hualapais. Light was losing control. Needing proof that Mahone was "guilty of violating the law against interfering with the duties of a Superintendent of an Indian reservation," he pleaded with the BIA to send a "Secret Service representative, or some other Officer" to spy on him. The unrest on the reservation caused Light to characterize Mahone's gang as "the most insolent and ugly spirited Indians, I have ever met in the Service." The Indians, Light averred, "have been trained by transient miners, who were I.W.W.'s, socialists, and communists, and by this man Mahone, whom your office has cautioned as to his conduct." As a result of their actions "they should be severely punished for their attitude toward the Government, the local officers, and the Indian Office."[38]

Despite Burke's dismissal of the Hualapais' initial complaints, the fight got his attention, and he dispatched an inspector to the reservation. Traveling auditor L. E. Murphy, charged with looking into the cattle sales but not the more general unrest, arrived on the reservation in mid-February 1922. He reached a conclusion quickly: Light had not intentionally done anything wrong but had merely mishandled the proceeds from the fall 1921 cattle sale.[39]

Although he found that Light had scrupulously accounted for all the sales and had come up with a plan to distribute the funds, Murphy nonetheless chided him for the way he handled the sale. But that was it. He largely dismissed the Hualapais' concerns. Learning that Mahone and Fielding had caused much of the trouble, he sought them out. But when asked, neither Mahone nor Fielding would offer any specific information as to Light's wrongdoing, and they both refused to sign anything attesting to Light's alleged malfeasance. The investigation ended there: Murphy left, and Light was exonerated.[40]

Conditions deteriorated. And in the fall, the BIA dispatched another inspector to Hualapai country, this time to investigate the unrest unleashed by the MIF. When John Atwater came to the reservation in October 1922, Hualapai political unity was beginning to gel. Early in his three-week stay he discovered that the fight with the railroad, control of the reservation, the ejection of Anglo ranchers, and the dismissal of Light were on the Hualapais' agenda. Led by Fred Mahone, a good man, Atwater surmised, but "obsessed with Utopian dreams for his people," the Hualapais were at a turning point, rallying around a set of issues for the first time. Their political awakening was just beginning, but Indian Beecher already knew what they wanted: "We want no white people to use this land anymore."[41]

Jim Fielding was angry. Speaking to a group of Hualapais gathered together for Atwater's benefit in the fall of 1922 and reminding them that "with the increase in cattle we will soon need all of the range very much," Fielding advocated ridding the reservation of Anglo ranchers. Money earned from their leases mysteriously made its way to Washington, never to be seen again, non-Indian cattle crowded the reservation herd, and at times stray Hualapai livestock was not returned, spirited away, he suggested, by Anglo ranchers. Fielding's idea was simple: Allow the Hualapais to run their own cattle operation on a reservation that was entirely theirs. Fielding had used his influence with the BIA just before World War I to get cattle operation running; now he wanted the tribe to control it.[42]

Hualapai political activity began to coalesce around what Fred Mahone called their "foremost urgent need," the need to foment "action to prevent the Santa Fe from acquiring title to the land in the Walapai reservation." Because it was possible that they would find refuge in the courts, they did what any property owner would whose land was threatened: they got a lawyer, Washington attorney Everett Du Four—who, poetically enough, lived on John Marshall Place. Mahone, Fielding, and Leve-Leve, supported by ninety-seven male members of the tribe who either signed or made their thumbmark on the contract with Du Four, laid out for the first time, and in explicit detail, their demands and grievances. Mahone drafted the documents and decided to bypass the BIA, electing instead to try to enlist the support of Arizona's congressional delegation. He hoped that he could count on their aid in exposing "the ill treatment accorded [the] Walapai Indians and in helping to secure for them their rights which have been withheld."[43]

Along with a secure title to the land and control of the water at Peach Springs, they also wanted the proceeds from grazing and mining leases turned directly over to them. Documenting the various non-Indian uses of the reservation, Mahone made clear that non-Hualapais profited from the use of their land; he thought the tribe should share in the bounty. He, Fielding, and others believed that Light routinely ignored them, squandering any money earned from leases. By getting rid of Light and securing title, the Hualapai hoped to gain total independence. They wanted to manage their own affairs on the land that "Chester A. Arthur set aside and reserved for the use and occupancy of the Hualapai Indians. . . . It is our desire to make this tract our everlasting home for ourselves and our future generations."[44]

Their greatest wish was to be free to do with their land as they saw fit. For forty years every agent had denied them their rights. According to the tribe's petition, a three-pronged assault had been waged on the Hualapais: the agents did not take care of them, the railroad claimed land that did not belong to it, and the money from leasing went to the government, not to the Hualapais, where it belonged. Mahone declared: "We want to be as AMERICANS are, free to develop our resources, as a community, and to hold as community property, our reservation."[45]

Mahone invoked the government's promise of land to the tribe and, for the first time, played on the historical relationship between the government and the tribe. According to Mahone, when the army "sent out a call or official order for all Wallapai Indians to meet," they did so willingly, and made peace, amicably ending hostilities. And when they were asked to scout for the government in its fight against the Apaches, they agreed to do so with no protest. Mahone condensed many years of Hualapai-government relations into a page and a half but in the process left out what has come to be called the Huapalai War. Mahone wanted to relinquish what he thought of as the savage past, but in truth the Hualapais had been formidable enemies of the army. Hostilities had lasted several years. In 1869, the army had defeated the Hualapais, who then made peace with the government. Mahone called their truce "a treaty of brotherhood with the Whites," although the tribe never signed a formal treaty with the government. Bound to abide by American law, the Hualapais had made "friends with the white people." Shortly afterward their new friends had needed them for, according to Mahone, "Conditions were bad. Apache Indians were on the war path killing government mail carriers and committing many depredations." The army's solution was to call out the Hualapais to "clean up the country and rid it of hostile Indians." That done, the government decided that the "Wallapai Indians were to have the privilege of education which meant the Americanization of the Wallapai Indians of to-day."[46]

From this deal came a new world, or at least Mahone saw it that way. As a result of their "treaty of brotherhood," and in return for their service as scouts, they were given a reservation. He looked back in time and saw this as the moment in which the modern Hualapais emerged. They were now the American Wallapai Indian Tribe, in possession of rights the U.S. government was bound to respect. But they were hindered from "advancing with equal rights, such as the new civilization includes for others." In Mahone's vision, commencing with the treaty of brotherhood, the Hualapai were bound to become Americans, but the government was also committed to honor the Hualapais' most basic right: the right to their property. If allowed to have their entire reservation, the Hualapai would "advance in the new civilization in sociallity [*sic*], politically or as a citizen not a ward."[47]

Fred Mahone created a new historical consciousness for the Hualapais. Past events took on a new meaning, or, rather, they were *given* meaning and put to use in the present. Grasping that the past — which was marked by peace and cooperation — could be used as a tool in the present, Mahone had great power. To be sure, he alone did not craft the tribe's past. But it was he more than anyone who, as one of the few educated Hualapais, articulated that past to the outside world. His reverence for his elders — at least as far as can be documented — likely went a long way in determining what was important in Hualapai history. Scouting, for example, clearly meant a great deal to the older men of the tribe. But Mahone knew its political value as well. He also knew that the Hualapais would have to be seen as good Indians; thus, they needed a counterpart, the Apaches. The Hualapais' petition was passionate and clear: Give us control of the reservation. They also extended the terms of the debate when they included the entire reservation, not only Peach Springs, in their demands. Up to that point the discussion had turned on title to the spring. The Hualapais were now talking about much more than Peach Springs. The implications of this shift would be vast.

4

The Government Versus the Hualapais

Fred Mahone and the Hualapais had good reason to be worried. In 1919 the government hashed out plans for a survey of their reservation — the last piece of the last unsurveyed railroad grant in the country. When first contemplated by the General Land Office the survey appeared routine — simply a matter of allocating the even-numbered sections to the tribe and the odd-numbered sections to the railroad. Any worries about title were brushed aside. As far as the GLO was concerned, the matter had been settled: the railroad had filed its map of definite location — which simply meant that it had identified where the tracks *would* lie, not where they did lie — eleven years before the creation of the reservation, and thus the "grant was superior to the reservation." It was now time to make it official.[1] Once the GLO figured out where the springs lay, determining who owned the water at Peach Springs would be simple.

Commissioner of Indian Affairs Cato Sells had a different idea: instead of a survey he suggested a lawsuit challenging the railroad and the GLO to prove the validity of the railroad's claim, not the validity of the Hualapais'. By pointing out that the Hualapais had never voluntarily ceded their land to the railroad and that the land that the railroad claimed was not Indian land, Sells argued, long before anyone else in the BIA or elsewhere did so, that the 1883 executive order simply recognized what was already known by the tribe and the military as Hualapai land. After repeated attempts to make his case Sells lost. Holding fast to the belief that "no such Indian claim as prevents the railroad grant from attaching to these lands" existed, Assistant Secretary of the Interior Alexander Vogelsang quickly quashed the possibility of a suit. Railroad land could not be beholden to the claims of Indians. Vogelsang made Interior's position clear: "Our unanimous conclusion is that the railroad company has full, complete, and incontestable title to the odd numbered sections in this reservation and embraced in grant limits."[2]

For the Hualapais, the consequences of Interior's position were potentially devastating. In June 1920, after a winter's wrangling, Interior decided to cleave the reservation in two. Two parcels, one for the railroad and one for the tribe, would be carved out of the whole.[3] In order to avoid turning the reservation into a checkerboard made up of Indian and railroad parcels, and wanting to avoid going to court to determine who really owned the land, Interior thought it best simply to split it in two. After talks with the railroad about a possible land trade broke down and after disagreement with the BIA about the wisdom of legal action, in 1923 Secretary of the Interior Hubert Work decided in favor of splitting the reservation in half. By mid-fall a draft bill was complete. In order to justify it, Work made a case for the "considerable trouble and embarrassment" the dual ownership caused the Indian Service. As proof of the difficulties the railroad claimed that the Hualapais were riding roughshod over their land, cutting valuable timber and grazing cattle, and showing no regard for the railroad's rights. Despite admitting that it "would reduce by about one-half the area the Indians have heretofore used," Work welcomed consolidation.[4] After all, ease of administration and the forestalling of future lawsuits from the ATSF would mitigate this unfortunate outcome.

Then, at the height of the summer of 1924, when it learned that the springs fell in an even section and that the Hualapais had clear title, the BIA conceded that the railroad had no rights to the spring. Charles Burke quickly advocated a suit to quiet title in favor of the Hualapais, noting that they had occupied the land "long before the coming of the white man and the building of the railroad."[5] Records in the Indian Office made this clear. But why should this be of any consequence when the survey determined that the spring was in an even section? Didn't that settle the matter? It didn't. The ATSF averred that it had bought rights to the spring from an early settler and thus contended that, wherever located, the spring belonged to the railroad. The case entered a new realm; history now mattered, and Burke's allusions to Hualapai occupancy needed to be taken seriously. Preliminary moves to initiate a suit for the spring were under way.[6]

But the government moved in two directions at once, pulled one way by legal obligation and the other way by expediency. On February 12, 1925, the Department of Justice instructed the U.S. attorney for Arizona to initiate a suit for Peach Springs on behalf of the Hualapais. And then, a little more than a week later, on the twentieth, the bill to consolidate the reservation into two parcels became law. The railroad, recently so interested in an exchange, now waited to see what the government's next move might be. Would it enforce the consolidation or sue? For most of the year, the parties watched each other. Shortly after the consolidation bill passed, reservation superintendent William Light voiced concern about the fate of the Hualapai cattle operation should the reservation be split in two. Few other concerns surfaced, and it would be late fall before the U.S. attorney in Phoenix, George Hill, began the Justice Department's investigation of Hualapai land rights. He started with a trip to the reservation.[7]

When Hill arrived in Peach Springs in late November there was no doubt about what was at the top of the Hualapais' agenda: saving their land. Coincident with Hill's visit, a group of eleven headmen — among them Steve Leve-Leve, Jim Fielding, and Kate Crozier — made this clear in an appeal to the CIA. The Hualapais were represented for the time being by Homer O. Davidson, chair of the Welfare Committee of the Mojave tribe and an active member of the Mission Indian Federation, and their letter and petition were part thank-you, part history lesson, and part demand:

> We now understand what the federal [Government] (done for us) . . . when we are in the stage, incompantant to the living ways and laws of the white people. our protection from the newcomers [is] by Executive Orders in setting aside a reservation. . . . We are law abiding people according to the reports made by military reports and we will continue to be so as to nature we are contented people no matter what the conditions looked to us and aiming to make some improvements and for this certain matter [the right to water and land], with good reason we are taking this stand and writing to you. . . . We herewith ask you a special favor to give us a complete map of our reservation. . . . Our land grants by the government is sufficient for our protection, the water rights must be acknowledge by the state, therefore we need a map and we are glad to do this part and cannot depend on the government that is if we can help ourselves, we will try and go as far as the law of our country permitts us.

The reservation, in the past and the present, afforded the Hualapais protection, and the headmen were pleased that it had worked as a bulwark against white encroachment. Without it, all their land might be gone; what was left was enough to get by on. Now that their land was newly threatened by the railroad, the protection afforded by the reservation was even more greatly appreciated. By writing a history that included their scouting, their peaceful relationship with the military, and their grateful acceptance of the reservation, the Hualapais, Homer Davidson claimed, were "preparing . . . a history and a benefit to the future generation."[8] They were consciously constructing a past that served present needs.

They passed on some of that history to Hill, who discovered that they had been using the spring since long before the coming of the railroad. Taking Hill to the spring, the Hualapais showed him the remnants of the stone monument that Charles Spencer had built there around 1881. In the face of a steady stream of ranchers, they explained, the cairn claimed the spring for the tribe.[9]

At Hill's urging, the DOI searched for any correspondence by Spencer and two other Anglos that the Hualapais had mentioned. They looked in vain. But in its search the DOI unexpectedly found copies of other critical documents: the report on the Hualapais by William Redwood Price from July 1881 recommending a reservation and Major General O. B. Willcox's General Order 16. Documentation had been found that agreed with what the Hualapais said: they had occupied and used the land before the coming of the whites and the railroad. The Price report and Wilcox's order were just what the Secretary of the Interior needed: written proof of Hualapai occupancy.[10] With new evidence in hand, a case appeared to be building.

In early 1926, a little less than a year after Congress passed the consolidation bill, Assistant Attorney General B. M. Parmenter began to wonder about the railroad's two claims — to ownership of the odd-numbered sections within the reservation stemming from their grant and the ownership of Peach Springs based on purchase from the settlers Decker and Crozier. Not only did Parmenter consider the railroad's claims suspect, but he thought the tribe might have a strong case: "If . . . as some things in the correspondence appear strongly to indicate, the present reservation was a part of the original home of these Indians so that they had therein the usual right of Indian occupancy and use from a time prior to the railroad grant of 1866, then their rights did not originate with the executive orders creating the reservation but those orders were merely a recognition of their pre-existing right of occupancy. . . . If in fact these lands were a part of their ancient possessions then the railroad company has not at this time and never has had any right to the possession and use of either the odd or any even sections, nor could there be any squatters' right to an even section which could be of an validity when conveyed to the company." Parmenter dug deeper than anyone and struck the core of the case: Did Hualapai occupancy pre-date the creation of the reservation? Enough evidence had accumulated to make an investigation necessary. Certain that the Hualapais had never voluntarily ceded their land to the railroad, Parmenter reasoned that if they had title to the reservation then the railroad didn't. But Parmenter was concerned: Did the Hualapais occupy an identifiable homeland, or had they "merely wandered from place to place over a wide range so that it could be said that they had no definite home to which there was attached the Indian right of occupancy and use?" He needed to know what type of Indians they were and how they lived before the railroad — or any whites — came. Having "[no] doubt oral evidence could be obtained upon this subject from the old Indians themselves," he sent George Hill back to the Hualapai reservation in early 1926.[11]

The first news from Arizona was encouraging for the tribe. Hualapai witnesses could attest to long prior use of the spring. Babies had been born there. Entire lives had been lived at Peach Springs — the proof was in what the Hualapais said and the ample physical evidence that Hill said he saw scattered about. But their ties to the place, though strong, had been forged in the past; no Hualapais had lived near the spring for decades. And this might be a problem, for the railroad, according to Hill, "drove off the Indians" and had been using the spring for many years. With Hill in the field collecting more and more evidence in favor of the tribe, and fed up with "conferences and delays," Parmenter pushed for a suit.[12]

As 1926 wore on the mood at Interior and the BIA shifted with the seasons — one moment favoring a suit, at another preferring a settlement. The railroad, for its part, still wanted consolidation, taking comfort in Senator Carl Hayden's continued support. The Department of Justice, confused and caught in the middle, called off its search for evidence of Hualapai occupancy pending a settlement. And the Hualapais were puzzled. As Peach Springs band leader Bob Schrum said in 1927, because "the Great Creator has give us this county," tribal elders were determined that "we must act at all times to hold our country from the white race." The railroad's claim to half the reservation was a challenge to this commitment, a legacy handed down to the tribe from one of its most famous and revered leaders, Cherum. Now Schrum, his oldest son, wanted to develop their reservation, make homes there, and bring back tribe members who had been forced to leave in search of work. Ridding the reservation of Anglo cattlemen by asking time and again that their leases not be renewed was one of Schrum's preoccupations. But the government, he now learned, was intent on putting a stop to those plans by giving "about half our country . . . to the Railroad Company." How could this happen, Schrum wondered, to land set aside for the Hualapais by the president?[13]

Yet by the summer of 1927 Interior and the BIA, working at a dizzying pace, had decided to sue. After extensive research in government archives and interviews with some Hualapais, Interior thought that a case based on a combination of law and fact could be waged against the railroad.[14] The ATSF's confidence began to wane. Because of its close ties to the BIA, the railroad's Washington attorneys were given access to the bureau's confidential file. Once they were able to take a close look at the government's case they began to wonder: Could it be that the Hualapais actually used water from Peach Springs before the arrival of the railroad or Anglo settlers? With no firm idea of exactly when Anglos began taking water from the spring but certain now that the Hualapais and settlers used the water in common, the railroad worried that the tribe might have a claim.

The railroad did not worry for long. By the time it learned of the government's intention to sue in mid-autumn it had little to worry about.[15] The government's hardened position in favor of the Hualapais soon dissolved.

Ethelbert Ward, a Justice Department lawyer, had been practicing law and litigating Indian water rights cases for more than fifteen years. Because he was based in Denver, Ward knew the West, which meant he knew about water rights. Asked to weigh in on the Hualapai case, he was blunt: "The proposed suit against the railroad will fail."[16] Ward relied on two cases. First, he took a look at *Winters v. United States* (1908) — a case that he had helped litigate and that had changed Indian water rights — and reasoned that because the ATSF appropriated Peach Springs before the reservation was set aside, it belonged to the ATSF. According to the decision in *Winters,* Indians had a prior appropriation right only *after* a reservation had been set aside. If the ATSF was already using the water it retained that right. At best, Ward thought, the Hualapais might have a right to some of the water for domestic use or for watering livestock — if they lived at the spring. But Ward knew they didn't, which meant that the Hualapais did not meet the test laid out in the Court's most recent ruling on Indian occupancy, *Cramer v. United States* (1921): definite, settled, agricultural use of a specific area. Comparing the circumstances of the Hualapai case with the particulars of *Cramer* and *Winters,* Ward pronounced the Hualapai case dead on arrival. The tribe possessed no inherent right to the land based on occupancy. The government either granted the rights to the tribe or it did not. The law would not help.[17]

But history might, and so Ward began to wonder: Who was there first — the railroad, the settlers, or the Hualapais? Playing historian proved tough. He was not very good at it. Making several questionable claims, Ward came to the conclusion that even if the railroad had arrived after the creation of the reservation the Hualapais' rights had already been extinguished. He decided that the forced removal of the Hualapais to the Colorado River reservation rendered their home vacant public land. In a series of memos to the attorney general

Ward argued that between 1869, when the Hualapais were ordered to leave their territory, until 1883, when the reservation was created, the land had fallen into the hands of white squatters. As a result, the Hualapais had lost any aboriginal rights to the land that they may have had. He pulled no punches: "The Act of Congress establishing the Colorado River Indian Reservation and forcibly removing the Hualpais [sic] *destroyed the Indians' original right of occupancy and possession.*" If the Hualapais did not lose their rights to the railroad, they lost them to squatters. When Ward used forced removal as the basis for his decision, however, he ignored a key provision in the language of the grant and a principle embedded — at least theoretically — in U.S. and international law: consent.[18]

But had the Hualapais vacated the land? In Ward's version of events — and this is critical because it would become common wisdom — the army "herded" the Hualapais onto the Colorado River reservation in 1869, thus leaving their land empty in 1872, the year the railroad filed its map of definite location. With no evidence for his claim, Ward merely stated what he thought was a fact. Were Hualapais still there? Yes, according to white settlers interviewed the previous spring. When W. F. Grounds arrived in 1871 Indians were everywhere, he said. And John Bozarth, who had lived in Arizona since 1875, testified that "[m]yself and everybody else regarded [Peach Springs] as Indian land. It was occupied entirely by Indians . . . and [there was] no evidence that there had been any whites there." Of course Grounds and Bozarth saw Indians everywhere: the Hualapais did not leave for the Colorado River reservation until 1874 — two years *after* the railroad filed its map of definite location. Even then, not all Hualapais went south. Another witness, Harvey Hubbs, came to Hualapai country as a miner in 1878, living in the settlement of Cerbat. He worked for the railroad hauling water from Peach Springs in the spring of 1882 and was at the spring every day for months. He said that he saw no whites and a lot of Hualapais: the "Indians were always there." Hubbs also recalled seeing white ranchers negotiating with Hualapais for the privilege of running cattle on Hualapai land.

The railroad's witnesses, too, saw Hualapais everywhere; they testified to their presence at Peach Springs, as well as the arrival of the railroad after the reservation was set aside on January 4, 1883. John Hewlett, the first Anglo to attempt settlement at Peach Springs and thus one of the railroad's most highly prized witnesses, said he settled with his cattle at the spring in 1874 or 1875. Shortly after he had set up camp a band of Hualapais came and "made great speeches to me about that country and all that. They said that was their grass, and their water, and they wanted all of that." This had been Hualapai country, Hewlett confessed; the signs were everywhere. Finally, O. W. Decker, who with Crozier had sold the deed that was believed to be so critical to the railroad's claim, said he never actually lived at Peach Springs. In fact, he grazed cattle there only with the *express permission* of the tribe. In the summer of 1926, Decker said, "All the testimony I could give would be in favor of the Indians, as they was all that had any rights when I was there [from 1876 to 1882]." Decker's statement was corroborated by Sam Crozier's wife, Mrs. Tony Walters, and by W. F. Grounds.[19] Obviously, Hualapai country had not been abandoned and rendered vacant between 1869 and 1883. The few Anglos who had been there before 1875 attested to the tribe's presence. And, after the Hualapai left the Colorado River reservation in 1875 they returned home and reoccupied the land to such an extent that whites who settled there after 1875 recognized it as Indian land.

Like Fred Mahone, Homer Davidson was an agitator. A Mojave who was active in the Mission Indian Federation, a good friend of Jim Fielding, and able to speak Hualapai, Davidson was the official paid spokesman for the tribe. Because he was at the hub of Indian political activity in the lower Colorado River region, Davidson had earned the suspicion of the new superintendent at Truxton Canyon, F. T. Mann, who thought of Davidson as a shyster who was only interested — "like so many of his type" — in cheating Indians out of their money and raising their expectations. Holding large meetings at Pop's laundry or at agency headquarters in Valentine, Davidson did stir up the Hualapais. Having lived among white people in Needles, California, he was, one elder recalled, well versed in the ways of the outside world and helped the isolated Hualapais. The tribe's investment paid off. Not only did Davidson arrange visits with the governor of Arizona, but in the spring of 1927 he persuaded Lynn Frazier, chair of the Senate Subcommittee on Indian Affairs, to take an interest in the tribe's case. After a visit to the West and a meeting with Davidson, Frazier agreed to look into it.[20]

Davidson was pleased; he didn't trust the Indian Service. Neither did the Hualapais. They were not satisfied with the investigation made by Ethelbert Ward, and after a visit to Hualapai country in 1927 from Assistant Commissioner of Indian Affairs E. B. Merritt, their distrust of the BIA was only heightened. When talking about land and history, they communicated best in their own language, but when Merritt met with the Hualapais he demanded that Jim Fielding — whom Merritt designated as their leader — discuss their claim in English. Fielding's limited command of English ensured confusion and anger. Not allowing Fielding and others to speak Hualapai, Davidson told Frazier, meant that "the real language and meaning of the Indians are lacking." Well-meaning men such as William Light had already tried the best they could in their own language to flesh out the tribe's history. But much was still missing. And language was not the only concern. The identity of the speaker was equally important. Because of their knowledge of their people and their lands Davidson and the Hualapai wanted the headmen—Jim Fielding, Philip Quasula, and Bob Schrum—to represent the tribe. Davidson warned that when "the thinking party of the Wallapai Indians [were] left out" and "the incompetent Indians [were] used" the Hualapais' true concerns could not be voiced. Now Davidson and the Hualapais were fed up. Not able to trust the BIA, they addressed their concerns to the president via Congress, in the hopes that Congress would act.[21]

For all the foregoing reasons—lack of trust, annoyance at not being allowed to speak in their own language or use interpreters of their own choosing, and the choosing of improper leaders—the Hualapais, Davidson told Frazier, had been working on their own history. Beginning in the late fall of 1927, William Light and Fred Mahone—once enemies but now committed to documenting the tribe's history—interviewed tribal elders. When asked, they had a lot to say about their former lives at Peach Springs. People had lived there for generations, as far back as memory stretched. It was a scene of great activity, not ephemeral use. It was home: the Hualapai built houses and sweat lodges. It was a transportation hub: a network of trails radiated into and out of the canyon to the mesas above and to the Colorado river below. And it was a place of production: they processed corn and mescal and made arrows. Mike Sue remembered that the Hualapais grew the peach trees in the canyon from seeds acquired from the Hopis, their long-time trading partners. Mahone's and Light's informants could name individuals as far back as their grandparents' generation who had lived at Peach Springs. But after the railroad came and began to take the water, Jim Smith said, Hualapais' use of the spring diminished. Everyone claimed that the Peach Springs band had never given the railroad their permission to use the water. Late in December 1927 a group of Hualapais, including Fielding, Quasula, and Schrum, met with Light, discussed the evidence he and Mahone had collected, and, believing they had a good case, asked that the government supply them with attorneys. A newly formed organization, the Executive Committee of the Walapai Tribe, led by Fielding, Quasula, and Schrum, presented their demands.[22]

Light's report, written later the following spring and based on the evidence that he and Mahone had collected, constituted some of the first detailed ethnohistorical work concerning the Hualapais—research that would soon convince Assistant Attorney General Seth Richardson that the Hualapai had a claim. Light was sure that the tribe's history stretched back beyond memory, lodged firmly in the stories passed from generation to generation. He documented Hualapai occupation in eleven single-spaced pages and sounded not unlike a modern ethnohistorian when he wrote: "Evidence of their undisputed occupancy and ownership of this territory is contained in their family and tribal records, traditions and legends; unwritten, but faithfully transmitted from parent and leader, to offspring and follower, from a stock that lived in the dim and distant past, to the present generation."[23] By cross-referencing the Hualapais' history with the histories of their neighbors — the Havasupais, the Yavapais, and the Mojaves — Light hoped to verify Hualapai accounts of their past. All three tribes, who were at various times either friends or foes, according to Light, acknowledged the same territorial boundaries for the Hualapais.

Mixing polemic and analysis in equal measure, Light did three remarkable things. First, he went to Indians for their history; second, he believed them; and third, by seeing that the Hualapais and their neighbors vacillated between being friends and enemies he tacitly recognized that they had a history. Light was concerned most with one date: January 4, 1883. The railroad contended, as did Ethelbert Ward, that any rights the Hualapais might have to their land were conceived on this day. In Light's view this was entirely wrong. All Hualapai rights came from their history of land use and occupancy leading up to January 4, 1883. Because Light — doubtlessly echoing the Hualapais — took the radical stance that no one else had ever had rights to the land, the history of the tribe was of paramount importance. "I hold that the rights of the Indians have existed for all time, and that their claim to occupancy, possession and use of the reservation and the water thereon, antedates not only the claim of the Curetons [some of the early settlers] or the Railroad but that of the Government also; that the land in question has never been Government land, and therefore has never been subject to grant by the Government."[24]

A new batch of affidavits, collected in 1928, buttressed the tribe's case. Again white settlers said that the area was Hualapai country. In the spring of 1883, as a boy of twelve, William Nelson had moved to Peach Springs with his father, a railroad worker. Hualapais were everywhere; they lived at Peach and Pine Springs, according to Nelson. "It was Indian Country, and was occupied by the Indians of the Wallapai Tribe." Warren Day, a doctor employed by the government, began visiting the Hualapais in late 1879. He ministered to the tribe's ills at Pine and Peach Springs, at Milkweed and Madwida Canyons, and recognized it all as Hualapai country. Even James Cureton, despite his belief that the Hualapais drifted, admitted that they did have definite territory and always returned to the same spots. And, of course, Hualapais such as Snyje, Charles Spencer's wife, claimed Peach Springs as their own.[25] Evidence of the tribe's occupancy was strong.

Not only were the Hualapais gathering evidence to prove their case, but the

Indian Rights Association (IRA) began applying pressure, too. Herbert Welsh, past president and founder of the IRA, sent out a circular letter to various friends of the Indian, and Samuel M. Brosius wrote a passionate plea to the president. Both urged that the government take the Hualapai case to court. The Interior Department disingenuously responded that it had always been interested in a suit; it hoped that Justice would see things its way. And Brosius, soon to become embroiled in the case, was prescient enough to realize that the case "may be groundwork for future compensatory legislation." Ethelbert Ward continued to be pessimistic about the case's success, but by the spring of 1928, after dogged criticism from Parmenter, his firm belief that the Hualapais' use of the spring was merely part of a life of aimless wandering was beginning to loosen. Interior, for a time, remained committed to bringing suit.[26]

But none of this mattered to Justice Department lawyer G. A. Iverson. He had just spent the summer of 1928 amassing evidence which convinced him that the Hualapais did not have a claim based on their right of occupancy. The settlers did. Many of his conclusions mirrored Ward's: no precedents applied, there was little or no evidence of Hualapai occupation, and the railroad had rightfully appropriated water on public land. To Iverson, the Hualapais' land use did not amount to much. They were "wild, shiftless, and hard to control"; they "preyed upon white settlers." Anything they had to say was disregarded out of hand. Iverson's lengthy opinion misrepresented all testimony — Hualapai and Anglo — that was contrary to his belief that the tribe did not make sustained, permanent use of Peach Springs. Iverson was so committed to upholding the rights of the railroad that he ignored key parts of two critical settler statements, those by Decker and Crozier. To be sure, Iverson noted that Decker had said that the Hualapais lived at Peach Springs and used the water. But Decker had gone further, claiming that the Hualapais "was all that had any rights when I was there [from 1878 to 1882]." The railroad claimed that it had purchased the rights to Peach Springs from Decker. Yet here was Decker, clearly stating that he never had any rights to the spring in the first place. If one factored Crozier's statement into the equation, the sum was the same: Ida Crozier, wife of Sam Crozier, testified in 1928 that they only used the water at Peach Springs after the Hualapais had taken what they needed. After all, according to Crozier, the tribe "had lived there from time immemorial." Testimony from Hualapais did no good, either. Mike Sue said that he had lived at Peach Springs "until the railroad took possession" and for a number of years thereafter, and Nora Schrum said that her grandparents and their grandparents had lived at Peach Springs all of their lives. Nothing the Hualapais or the settlers said could convince Iverson that the tribe had a valid claim. Nor did a trip to Peach Springs in July do any good; in fact, the visit convinced him of the need for some sort of settlement.[27]

That others besides the Hualapais used the water is not in question. But the squatters' use was ephemeral. It was not the length of time that they stayed but the way they used the land that gave the settlers a claim. Their fleeting attempts were efforts at permanence; the Hualapais' centuries were mere shadows. But Iverson, Ward, and the railroad were so committed to the idea that Hualapai land use gave them no legal rights that they ignored and misrepresented all evidence to the contrary. Decker, according to his own testimony, had come and gone in four years. A cow would wander to the spring at times; a settler might plant a vegetable patch. No one ever stayed for long. James Cureton, in whose opinion regarding Hualapai occupancy the railroad placed great stock, remained only two years at Peach Springs; by 1927, when the railroad first interviewed him, he had lived outside Arizona for fifty years. And in at least one instance, the railroad's attorneys either misrepresented the testimony of a witness or simply heard what they wanted to hear about Anglo versus Indian occupancy. The Arizona attorneys alleged that Ida Crozier supported their claim, backing up the stories of Cureton and Grounds. But Crozier became one of the government's strongest witnesses, testifying on three separate occasions that the land around Peach Springs — and beyond — was Hualapai country.[28]

After digesting the rest of the affidavits and depositions collected for the case, including six from Hualapais testifying that they had always lived at the spring and four white settlers saying the same, Iverson still was not convinced. His intransigence is, at times, bewildering. "Considering the question of Indian occupancy in its most favorable light, and assuming it can be shown that bands of Hualpi Indians at times camped at the springs and in the vicinity, and used water for themselves and their ponies, still this falls short, in my opinion, of constituting this territory Indian country in the sense of establishing title by Indian occupancy."[29] Iverson did what he could to convince the government that a suit would fail.

Wanting to stay out of court, Attorney General John Sargent agreed with Iverson. But the pressure was on from the Department of the Interior. Because the case was so important to the tribe and because a compromise in their favor looked unlikely, litigation appeared to be the only solution. What's more, if litigation were put on hold again, Interior worried, the government would "come under much criticism" from the friends of the Indian. Interior finally realized that the Hualapais deserved their day in court.[30]

The Hualapais were, of course, adamant in their belief that the entire reservation should remain theirs. "I believe," said Fielding, "our friend Commissioner Chas. H. Burke do not realize that we know our country." That they had not gone to school did not mean that the Hualapais did not know how much they owned before the white man came. Fielding and Bob Schrum, for example, wanted no more permits "for white people" to be issued for the eastern half of the reservation. Specifically, they wanted rancher Abe Cauffman to leave. Not only did Cauffman's cattle operation conflict with theirs — which had been ever more successful since first begun in 1914 — but his permit kept the Hualapais from building homes in the east. After three years of careful investigation they had determined that the title and the water were theirs; after all, the "Executive Order reads in plain English that these lands are set aside for the sole purpose of the Indians alone." Because they knew the land was theirs, Fielding, Quasula, and Schrum told the governor of Arizona that Ethelbert Ward may have been "a good water attorney etc., . . . but there is no case since the water belongs to the Hualapai Tribe."[31]

Despite Ward's and Iverson's opinions, Justice believed for a short time that it had a strong case. When he could no longer ignore the similarities between *Wismer* and the Hualapai case, in the spring of 1929 Ward, so long a foe of the Hualapais, finally relented. After being challenged by Assistant Attorney General Seth Richardson, Ward said simply, "I am now of the opinion that the date of this reservation is July 8, 1881." The Justice Department's change of heart was brought about by a close reading by Richardson of the evidence in the Price, Willcox, and Mason reports (the last of which was newly discovered). He established a chain of correspondence similar to Ward's but determined that the Secretary of the Interior had signed off on Willcox's Order 16. Richardson and Ward, to say nothing of Iverson, looked at the same documents but read them differently. At many points the Hualapais' case turned on new readings of the evidence.[32]

In addition to his own reading of the facts, Richardson also took seriously the work Light and Mahone had done documenting Hualapai land use and history. Richardson now believed that

> these Indians lived at and around Peach Springs since time immemorial, being removed against their wishes and by armed forces and for a short time only to another reservation. . . . With the exception of the few years spent in this new reservation, the Indians made their homes at or near Peach Springs before the formal reservation was established. Their ancestors participated in the establishment of the reservation so that Peach Springs might be included herein. None of those Indians have ever relinquished their claims to the springs or the lands adjacent thereto. They have used the water of the springs from a time so far distant in the past that it has been forgotten. It appears that upon the

approach of the railway, Charles Spencer, who was either an Agent . . . or just an Indian friend who had married an Indian woman, posted notices in all of these springs claiming the water for the use of the Indians.

Richardson went on to say that although the Hualapais were supposedly removed, he now knew that many of them had stayed in and around the Peach Springs area. Richardson based his opinion on Light's research and on the Hualapais' and early settlers' memories, saying that the "evidence of the Indians and some whites will show that Decker and Crozier had never claimed the land or the water and in fact had *rented the same place from the Indians.*" Richardson's opinion refuted virtually every point of the Ward and Iverson opinions: whereas they put no stock in Hualapai testimony, Richardson believed it; whereas Ward and Iverson considered the Crozier and Decker deed definitive in proving that the Hualapais lost their water rights, Richardson contended they used the water only at the sufferance of the tribe. Most important in supporting the Hualapais' claim was proving long-term occupancy of their homeland. And in order to prove this Justice would need to find testimony "among the ancient Indians" that the Hualapai reservation had been a "de facto reservation which the Indians had occupied since time immemorial." The removal to the Colorado River reservation, so important to Ward and Iverson, Richardson considered moot; the tribe had never consented to it. The most substantial claim to the reservation, however, was not the Hualapais' long-term occupancy, Justice reasoned; it was the creation of the reservation via Willcox's order. Richardson hoped to win the case under the guidelines set out by *Wismer,* which meant arguing that it was only official state sanction that guaranteed the Hualapai land rights. With Ward and Iverson out of the picture, Justice authorized litigation once again. This time, however, it meant it: Justice filed a formal complaint on 1 November 1929, reported that same day by the *Arizona Republican* as the "famous 'Peach Springs' case."[33]

5

Taking Hualapai Land

The Justice Department's resolve was more apparent than real. What looked like commitment from Washington turned out to be collusion with the railroad. In March 1930 Herbert Hagerman, who during the consolidation discussions of the mid-1920s had mediated between the ATSF and the BIA and successfully brokered an agreement that avoided a suit, was hired by the BIA to finish working out a deal with the railroad and finding a solution to the Hualapai land problem. Hagerman came primed for the job. Before his official appointment in March as Special Commissioner of Indian Affairs, he had already met with the railroad's attorneys in Chicago, where he was briefed on its and the government's respective cases. Worried about various pieces of evidence suggesting that the Hualapais might have been at Peach Springs first, as well as such precedents as *Cramer* and *Wismer,* lawyers and others at the railroad's headquarters were eager for Hagerman to dispose of their problem. So when he arrived in Washington in March, he hit the ground running, likely already armed with a plan. The railroad was confident that he would do a good job for it. And why not? Railroad officials knew he had the trust of the Santa Fe and of the BIA.[1]

Hagerman was one of a quartet including Commissioner of Indian Affairs Charles Rhoads, his assistant Henry Scattergood, and Secretary of the Interior Roy Lyman Wilbur, who propped up the aging twins of past Indian policy:

allotment and assimilation. The governor of New Mexico in 1906–7, Hagerman was long thereafter a fixture in southwestern politics. In 1923, in order to facilitate oil and gas leasing on the Navajo reservation, Secretary of the Interior Albert Fall appointed him special commissioner to the Navajos. Also serving as a member of the Pueblo Lands Board, Hagerman was ever-present in southwestern Indian affairs. Like Fall, he favored opening reservations such as the Hualapais', which had been created by executive order, to mining and mineral prospecting. Hagerman and Fall were among many who considered the executive order reservation a lesser type of reservation. Unlike reservations created by treaty, they were created solely at the sufferance of the president; Hagerman and Fall viewed them as essentially public domain, regarded as Indian land until a better use was found for them. Having worked on a similar consolidation effected between the railroad and the Navajos, Hagerman had a great deal of experience with the Santa Fe and possibly close financial and political ties as well — the railroad funded Hagerman's organization, the New Mexico State Taxpayer's Association.[2]

Hagerman didn't let the Santa Fe down. After a hasty trip to Washington, he quickly returned to Chicago, where again he met with railroad officials. They came up with a new compromise — just what the railroad wanted. It offered to exchange Clay Springs, in the far west of Hualapai country but just off the reservation, for clear title to Peach Springs. (It wanted to settle only the Peach Springs controversy at the time; talk of consolidation could wait.) Hoping to exploit the inevitable delays by the Justice Department in getting the case off the ground, Hagerman thought he might have enough time to craft a compromise. The railroad would play along, too, dragging its feet as much as it could, allowing Hagerman to work on a deal with the BIA.[3]

That Hagerman and the ATSF had sympathetic interests, and that they conferred about them, is not altogether surprising. What is surprising is that the local U.S. attorney in Arizona was involved as well. John Gung'l, unbeknownst to Seth Richardson in Washington, conspired secretly with the railroad to abandon litigation. Gung'l agreed to bring work on the case to a standstill, giving the railroad enough time to work out a deal with Hagerman and the BIA. After an April visit to the reservation, Gung'l proposed that the Santa Fe deed Clay Springs to the government, that it run a pipeline from Peach Springs to a holding tank so that the Hualapais could have water year-round, and finally that the railroad provide this water to the tribe for free. The catch was that the Hualapais would have to cede title to Peach Springs *and* give up half of their reservation to the railroad — exactly what Hagerman and the railroad had agreed on. Gung'l told Justice in Washington that this compromise was not only in the Hualapais' best interests, but a measure of what they wanted. It was not, of course, what they wanted at all. Gung'l did not really care what they wanted. As far as he was concerned, they were disappearing, and in a few years the Hualapais would be gone and the reservation abandoned. He worked out his plan with this outcome in mind.[4]

In order to convince his boss, Seth Richardson, to accept the plan, Gung'l claimed that Clay Springs was a verdant paradise that offered the best hope for gardening and grazing. The way Gung'l saw it, Peach Springs and the rest of the eastern half of the reservation, which offered few grazing opportunities and where only a handful of Indians lived anymore, couldn't compare with Clay Springs. He was both silent about the Anglo and Hualapai ranching long under way in the east and unrealistic about reclaiming the western half of the reservation. And, of course, he ignored the Hualapais' obvious desire to hold on to the entire reservation. His plan was ill-conceived. It was also cynical: when he urged a compromise and not a suit he hoped that the attorney general would "abide by the wishes of the Indians."[5]

After his visit to Peach Springs, in spite of the Justice Department's commitment to litigation, Gung'l satisfied the railroad's desire for delay and brought work on the case to a virtual standstill.[6]

In late April Hagerman and representatives from the railroad made plans to head west to Hualapai country. The railroad's Arizona counsel armed the Hagerman convoy with the Gung'l plan *before* Gung'l told the attorney general about it. Thus, with the help of the Hualapais' own lawyer, Hagerman might be able to effect a settlement — one the railroad had had a hand in crafting. In Chicago, railroad officials were pleased but nonetheless wondered whether Gung'l had the authority to work out a settlement.[7] He did not, but Hagerman did, and he was on his way to Peach Springs.

The Hualapais were without counsel. John Gung'l, the tribe's government-appointed attorney, had done a better job representing the railroad than he had the Hualapai. No one in Washington knew this, and Justice still insisted on litigation. The attorney general, unaware that Hagerman, Gung'l, and the ATSF's counsel had conferred, told Gung'l in early May that a "vigorous prosecution of this suit" was the best way to solve the Peach Springs problem. Richardson was tired of delays and hoped that Gung'l would get his reply back before July 1 and get to work on depositions. But save colluding with the railroad, Gung'l had yet to do any work on the case. The depth of his neglect is startling: he was so unfamiliar with the progress made that though he knew that the railroad had taken depositions — none of which he had read — he had to ask it to suggest witnesses for the government! And when Gung'l told the railroad of Justice's continued commitment to a suit, he confessed that his boss's eagerness to push ahead meant that he would now have to start working on a reply—taking depositions, reading the ones already completed, and doing research. In short, Gung'l would have to do his job.[8] His foot-dragging worked as planned. Herbert Hagerman and the ATSF had all the time they needed to strike a deal. And two months after their March meeting they did so.

Agreement in hand, Hagerman and representatives from the railroad and the BIA convened on the Hualapai reservation in May 1930, met for a day, and, without the input of anyone from the tribe, confirmed their commitment to a compromise. The deal was simple—and familiar. First, instead of a straight acre-for-acre trade—as proposed in the 1925 consolidation plan—each party would get land of equal value, with the railroad still taking land in the east and the Hualapai receiving land in the west. (The Hualapais were also to receive a little less than two hundred thousand acres of unsurveyed land along the Colorado River, land that was of little use for grazing and had no timber.) Second, the railroad agreed to grant the government thirty-six sections of land on the western edge of the reservation as a bonus in exchange for clear title to Peach Springs and enough adjacent land for maintenance. Exactly which thirty-six sections were granted would be determined later, but from the third point of the agreement it was evident that they did not include the valuable Clay Springs. Instead of trading Clay Springs for Peach Springs the railroad agreed to lease Clay Springs—something it was already doing on a year-to-year basis—for ten years. And finally, the railroad would continue to sell water to the government from Peach Springs as it always had. This arrangement, of course, looked a lot like the consolidation plan that had been passed in 1925. It varied in certain details—specifying a contract for Clay Springs and setting aside the unsurveyed land, for example—but the sentiment was the same: give the railroad title to Peach Springs and split the reservation in two. After the meeting, the negotiations were over. Both sides were satisfied. But Hagerman anticipated "dissension and unpleasantness." On the day of the hearings, he warned Commissioner Rhoads that "in all probability the Indians and perhaps some of their over-zealous friends will, if consulted, object to this or any other proposed settlement."[9]

With a consensus reached, it was time to meet with the Hualapais. At 9 A.M. the following day, Hagerman, district supervisor Chester Faris, and the new superintendent of the reservation, D. H. Wattson, gathered with about thirty-five Hualapais at the Truxton Canyon School. Within minutes the mood had been set, the battle lines drawn. After hearing about the plan, and obviously angry, Hualapai leader Bob Schrum spoke. "Once we had this whole country to ourselves but were put on a small reservation by the Government, and the Railroad is now after this reservation. We lived here long before the white men came into this country; therefore it is ours." Schrum wanted the railroad to leave Peach Springs. It made no difference to him, he thundered, that the Santa Fe pumped water out of the canyon; easier access to water could not ease the pain of losing half of the tribe's land. He would prefer to pack water out on his back than allow the railroad to stay. Sounding weary, Hagerman expressed the wish that the Hualapais would not protest at every turn. After all, he was trying "to reach an agreement whereby the Indians are going to have much more than half of the land." But the tribe wanted all of the land.[10] Hagerman knew it.

That morning the Hualapai barely had a chance to open their mouths. Bob Schrum and Kate Crozier were allowed only enough time to reiterate their familiar refrain—the entire reservation was theirs. Faris and Hagerman took up the rest of the meeting with patronizing patter, chastising the Hualapai for their dissent. "Everything the Government can do for you, it is trying to do," Faris reminded them. "But the Great Father in Washington is just a little sick at heart because you can't do a little for yourselves."[11] After sermonizing for a few more minutes, Faris stepped aside. Wattson then ended the meeting.

But the Hualapais were not finished. On the same day Bob Schrum, Kate Crozier, Young Beecher, and his wife headed west on Route 66 into the heat of the desert. They followed Hagerman to California. It was after dark when they arrived at Fort Mohave. The following day, after securing their Mojave interpreter—likely Homer Davidson—the Beechers, Schrum and Crozier were ready to confront Hagerman. He refused to meet them.[12]

That summer, the Hualapais mulled over the May meeting. In August, Fred Mahone, who had not been present at the meeting, talked with Bob Schrum, Kate Crozier, and Roy Winfred and heard their versions of the event. Because they did not trust the transcript made by the BIA and because Hagerman and Faris had given the Hualapais little time to voice their sentiments about the Hagerman plan, thus erasing the depth of their views and their anger, Mahone wrote his own description of the meeting. Once approved by the tribe, Mahone sent it to the Indian Rights Association (IRA) and hoped that the "association's power [would] save the lives of the Walapai, Restore their intrinsic value of their land and water, and too, restore a new birth of Walapai Tribe." Instead of adding significant new details to the official version, Mahone's made it clear the Hualapais not only were unhappy with Hagerman's plan but also found the man threatening. For instance, in response to Crozier's claim that they disliked buying back their stolen water, Hagerman lashed out at Crozier, saying, "If you Walapai dont [sic] quit talking over Peach Springs Water the railroad will get mad and they will hold the water much longer time.

Not only that but they will get ½ of Reservation land and $40,000 of the Treasur[y] money." Mahone's version also belied the image of the docile Hualapais conveyed by the official version. They did not sit patiently as Hagerman told them that they would lose half of their land; rather, their anger was evident. Kate Crozier and Bob Schrum argued with Hagerman. Words flew every which way. The meeting moved at such a pace, and so many voices were being heard, that Ray Winfred, the interpreter, could not keep up. His efforts to translate the "rapid speeches" failed, and he was "unable to catch all meaning and explain it to [the] Tribe."[13]

The Hualapais' frustration was at its peak. Kate Crozier and Bob Schrum declared that the meeting had been a waste of time, or, as they put it, "A BLUNT." Committed to having a say in the fate of their reservation, they chased Hagerman to California, where he ignored them. Mahone wished he had been there. Perhaps he could have helped by better articulating the Hualapais' position. His disappointment was deeply felt: "This party made a trip more than one hundred miles just to finish their business properly, on their land and water within their reservation boundary. They have failed."[14]

While Hagerman, the railroad, and Gung'l hashed out their respective compromises and the Hualapais rallied support in the fight against them, the case threatened to overwhelm John Gung'l, and by June he needed help. Panicked and in need of direction from Justice, he was stymied. The deadline for the government to file its reply to the railroad's answer to its complaint was fast approaching, and a hearing on the motions from both sides was scheduled for 28 July. Gung'l still had not done any work. And by that time the welter of facts in the case made less and less sense to him. Organizing history proved difficult.[15]

In July, frustrated with Justice's insistence on a suit, convinced that the attorney general would not listen to his objections, and with less than ten days until the hearing, Gung'l turned to the railroad. Racing from Tucson to Phoenix, he made his plea in person to the railroad's Arizona attorneys. He wanted the case put on hold, but he needed the railroad's help. Using its influence with Rhoads — and playing on his preference for a compromise — the ATSF asked him to put a hold on the suit. Rhoads obliged.[16]

The railroad's attorneys, of course, were willing to accommodate Gung'l's desire to stall, but they were still not entirely pleased with his compromise. And with the Hagerman plan beginning to look as though it would fail, the railroad was unsure that it would get what it wanted. For one thing, the railroad was loath to provide free household water to the tribe. If required to give water to the tribe the railroad at least wanted it made clear that it had priority over the

Hualapais in the event of a shortage. During his July visit Gung'l assured the ATSF that it had nothing to worry about, confessing that he had made free water a feature of his compromise in order to appease the BIA and facilitate the deal. The BIA would continue to buy water for any Hualapai cattle that were being watered at Peach Springs. And, what's more, the railroad already had a good plan worked out for household water: it charged local traders for the water, who then gave it to the Hualapais for free as an incentive to do business with them. Gung'l admitted that he merely wanted to give the appearance of conciliating the Hualapais; dangling the illusion of free water in front of the bureaucrats at the BIA was the best way to do it, he said.[17]

But Gung'l made an even more startling admission at his conference with the railroad's attorneys: if the case went to trial the government would beat the ATSF! All the evidence was in the tribe's favor; the railroad had no legitimate claim to the water. But Gung'l feared reprisals from the railroad were it to prevail. He claimed to be afraid of extortion: if the government won the railroad might then turn around and charge the Hualapai exorbitant fees to use Clay Springs. Perhaps he was right. The railroad did nothing to allay his fears.[18]

With the 28 July deadline only days away, the BIA asked that the Department of Justice back off the suit. Again, the case was on hold. At a meeting held at Hagerman's Santa Fe office in late July, Rhoads, Hagerman, and E. E. McInnis of the ATSF worked out a deal suitable to all but the Hualapais. Half of the tribe's land would vanish. The secretary of the interior agreed to the suspension of the suit.[19]

In Santa Fe, at the end of that long summer of negotiating, while the Hualapais were still reeling from the May meeting and pondering what to do, Herbert Hagerman, Carl Hayden, and W. B. Collinson, land commissioner for the ATSF, met and talked about problems the railroad was having with the Navajos and the Hualapais. They all agreed: consolidation was best. Hagerman remained in Santa Fe that fall and waited while his plan was considered. And once Hayden's interest in the matter grew, he realized that the Hualapais' relation to their land and the government since contact needed a thorough examination.[20]

By the close of the summer of 1930, things were not going well for the Hualapais: the meeting with Herbert Hagerman had not gone in their favor; the failed attempt at catching Hagerman in California angered the tribe; the U.S. attorney in charge of their case was acting in the interests of their adversary; and they were now stuck with a land deal that was at odds with what they wanted. Yet despite the setbacks, the Hualapai leadership, according to Mahone, looked for "other way[s] to convince our reason to our U.S. Government why we want to hold our entire reservation land and water." Their frustration and anger energized them. So later that fall, a group of Hualapais including Jim Mahone, Kate Crozier, Bob Schrum, and Little Jim sought out the U.S. attorney for Arizona. Unable to speak at the May meeting, when a "very bitter objection" to the agreement was lodged by Crozier and Schrum, they now wanted to make formal statements regarding the reservation's boundaries and to discuss the Hagerman plan.[21]

Having been active in Hualapai politics for nearly a decade, Fred Mahone was by that time considered a "well known Wallapai Indian," recognized in Kingman as the tribe's spokesman. He was also the wealthiest; he owned his home and ran cattle on the open range. Mahone made the fifty-mile trip to town in August, hoping to drum up support for the Hualapais and get help preparing a petition to be sent to their congressional representatives. Also around this time — possibly as a result of Mahone's trip to Kingman — almost two hundred Mohave County residents sent a petition of their own to their congressional representatives, urging them to allow the Hualapai to "retain all of the lands original intended to be apart to them."[22]

Mahone's petition contained three clear and simple provisions. It was his fullest statement yet of the Hualapais' wishes. The forty-three Hualapais who gathered at Peach Springs in the August heat to sign or thumbmark the petition did not regard "their treatment by the United States Government in this instance as just." Their demands: repeal the 1925 consolidation act; allow the ATSF to select land of equal value outside the reservation; and "create, set apart and confirm" the original Hualapai reservation as envisioned by the 1883 executive order. For too long the tribe had been kept from its reservation by the railroad, the ranchers, or both. The petition was more than a statement of their demands, however. It was also a detailed description of the reservation, stressing the aridity of the western half while emphasizing the excellent grazing in the east — leased now to white ranchers and coveted by the railroad. Their cattle operation suffered as a result.[23]

Seeing themselves as loyal Americans, they were incensed by this unjust treatment, and they played their trump card. Although on several occasions Fred Mahone had cashed in some of the Hualapais' historical capital by invoking their loyal service as scouts and soldiers, the tribe had yet to articulate as clearly that "they felt [the reservation] was guaranteed to them, in recognition of their friendly services to the military forces of the United States during the period of Indian Hostilities." Kate Crozier and Jim Mahone both remembered that "after quieting the rebellions of hostile Indians," an army general had called them and their fellow Hualapais to a conference at Fort Whipple. Their commander urged them to return to their portion of Arizona, where a reservation would be set aside in gratitude for their service. The two former scouts further recalled that they had been promised that any white miners or ranchers would be arrested if caught trespassing; the land was to be solely theirs. The Hualapais were not suggesting that the only legitimate ties they had to the land originated with government's guarantee. Rather, they were adding the power of that promise to what they already saw as unassailable: their longtime ownership and occupancy of the reservation. Rhetorically speaking, this was a good move. By reminding the government that they had aided the army in ridding the country of hostile Indians, the Hualapais hoped to stake a moral as well as a historical claim to the reservation. Perhaps most pragmatically, they wanted to date the pledge of a reservation before the coming of the railroad.[24]

Thanks in large part to Fred Mahone, word of the disastrous May meeting had spread, and the Hualapais were now joined by others. An editorial in the *Native American,* the newspaper of the Phoenix Indian School, criticized the deal and argued that the Hualapai were right not to accept it. Samuel Brosius of the Indian Rights Association, in a diatribe replete with underlined passages and capitalized words emphasizing his outrage, attacked the Hagerman plan. At such a time, when "the public is aroused as it has never been aroused before to the wrongs suffered by our Indian wards," he implored Charles Rhoads, "Let us not add another chapter by compounding the injury to the Walapai through lack of care in protecting their rights in the past." Brosius's anger appealed to the Hualapais—they had an advocate at last. Eighteen Hualapai men petitioned Brosius and the IRA for their help.[25]

The public might have been aroused, the Hualapais might have been angry, and the IRA might have been putting its considerable weight behind the Hualapais' claim, but none of this would matter if a powerful set of ideas about Indians and their property held sway over those in government—and those outside it.

6

Writing Indians out of Their Land

When government attorneys declared the railroad's claim superior to the Hualapais', and when Hubert Work, Charles Burke, and Herbert Hagerman so readily favored consolidation, they did so reflexively, giving their decisions little thought. It had been easy for them — as it would be for others later — to write the Hualapais out of their land.

The lawyers, courts, and bureaucrats did not write in a vacuum, and such keywords as "roam," "wild," "wander" were part of a larger discourse about Indians. Native peoples had a difficult, if not impossible, time mounting effective land claims in an intellectual climate in which, as a matter of habit, anthropologists, historians, writers, and jurists wrote off their land use as ephemeral. And writers drawn to the native people of the Southwest ignored, did not see, or openly disparaged wandering peoples such as the Hualapais. Popular and governmental conceptions of them were mutually reinforcing. The result was that the Hualapais had no legitimate claim to their land.

They flitted about where game and their fancy took them; the land now encompassed by their reservation meant no more to them than any other dusty piece of desert. When the Massachusetts Indian Association purchased land near Valentine for a school in 1894, it thought that the reservation had been "assigned to them . . . because of its barren and useless quality."[1] For those who gave the matter any thought, it would have been far easier to imagine cutting the reservation in half than it would have been to imagine keeping it whole. By the time the Hualapais began to think about how to preserve their reservation, judges and legal thinkers (considered in chapter 8), anthropologists, and popular writers had already put a lot of thought into the reasons why Indians should not maintain control of their land.

And some had given a great deal of thought to why Indians' own versions of the past mattered very little. For example, although he considered himself a proponent of historical anthropology and strongly supported the notion that some native people possessed individual property, the influential Berkeley anthropologist Robert Lowie determined in 1917 that "Indian tradition is historically worthless." Indians could not be trusted as historians "because the occurrences, possibly real, which [Indian tradition] retains, are of no historical significance; and because it fails to record, or to record accurately, the most momentous happenings." To Lowie's mind an Indian rendering of history would be akin to a "picture of the European war as it is mirrored in the mind of an illiterate peasant." Of course, illiterate peasants would become the social historian's bread and butter, but to Lowie and others, the lack of documents meant that there was no history. Lowie was not uninterested in reconstructing the past; to the contrary. But it could only be done via science—archaeology or linguistics, for example. He was emphatic: "I cannot attach to oral traditions any historical value whatsoever under any conditions whatsoever."[2]

The Hualapais' case, which rested on competing versions of their history, would be especially difficult. Could they prove that they had occupied the land since before the coming of the railroad? In the 1920s and 1930s, little was known about the Indians' past; virtually nothing was known about the Hualapais. In 1921 Superintendent William Light had written that along the rim of the Grand Canyon "there are evidences of old ruins. Exploration may develop abandoned cliff dwellings, but at present they exist only in rumor, and legend." By 1930, not much had changed. Although rumor and legend had become fact—Superintendent D. H. Wattson had actually seen ruins, saying that "there are in various places in the eastern portion of the reservation ruins of the homes of an ancient people"—he nonetheless acknowledged that "as far as I can ascertain, little has been done on this reservation in the way of archeological research." Wattson was right. Southwestern archaeology was in its infancy and only recently had concerned itself with chronology. The time-depth of pre-contact history in the Southwest remained guesswork until A. E. Douglass perfected dendrochronology (better known as tree-ring dating) in the 1920s and 1930s.

The first archaeological fieldwork—financed by the ATSF and used as evidence in the case against the Hualapais—would not be conducted in Hualapai country until the late 1930s. Only basic research had been done into the documentary and ethnographic record. Indeed, so little was known about the Indian past that the anthropologist Leslie Spier cautioned his fellow scholars to move with caution when writing the Indian history of the Southwest. Historical work, he wrote in 1929, "had hardly even begun." Spier's work among the Havasupais was, in part, the cause of his conservatism. After extensive fieldwork and exhaustive research in the literature Spier would only hazard a guess as to a basic outline of Havasupai history — his effort was more a demonstration of the difficulties of doing Indian history than a profitable venture. The Hualapais remained such a mystery that William Duncan Strong, in the comprehensive survey of southwestern societies that he published in 1927, was forced to use Spier's field data about the Havasupais to make a guess about Hualapai social organization.[3] The government's attorneys in the Hualapai case showed no such reluctance.

Although historians and anthropologists spent little time on Indian history, Indians were becoming preoccupied with the past. Scholars such as John Swanton and Roland Dixon, who looked to Indians as bearers of their own history and wrote in 1914 that along with manuscript sources the "Indians themselves" supplied key documentation of the past, were exceptions. Most historians gave Indians little thought or considered them obstacles to the evolution of American society. One went so far as to say that "fortunately" a plague had wiped many coastal Algonquian peoples just before English settlement began in 1620. As the Hualapai case gained momentum, the government increasingly came under attack from other tribes that were suing for treaty violations and land theft. The Sioux case, launched in 1923, is only the most famous; there were many more. Seeing the past in new ways and actively documenting their history, tribes from coast to coast, from the Duwamish in western Washington to the tribes of the Iroquois confederacy in the East, began to pursue their land claims during the 1920s.[4] They enlisted history as their most trusted ally.

The Crows in Montana rallied around a claim against the government based on violations of treaty rights. So did the Western and Northwestern Shoshones, two tribes that allied in the 1920s in pursuit of claims against the government. But others, just like the Hualapais, based claims on the principles of Indian title laid down by the U.S. Supreme Court under Chief Justice Marshall in the nineteenth century and immemorial occupation. Tribes such as the Lower Spokanes, the Lower Pend D'Oreilles, and the Kalispells, as well as the Colvilles and the Okanogans, had never ceded title to the United States, and now they wanted compensation for its taking. To shore up their claims, Spokanes such as Charlie Thompson, about ninety years old in 1926, put their history into writing and documented their longtime use and occupancy of a vast portion of Montana, Washington, and Idaho. And because of agitation related to claims, the violent and sordid but largely unknown, forgotten, or repressed history of Indian-white contact in California was finally coming to light. Indians such as Alfred C. Gillis, a Wintun from far northern California, had a chance to recount their versions of the past. Indians might not write it down as whites do, but they knew their history. As Gillis said, there "are historians among the Indians that make it a practice in the wintertime to gather in the great council house and these stories [of the past] are sifted over, just like a great historian would gather facts and place them in good order to hand them down to their children." Using those stories, a group of California Indians, representing the native membership of the Indian Board of Coopera- tion, said in a joint statement regarding their claims that their "right of occu- pancy is clear." Though Indians, they continued, do not "depend on written records[,] the rights and history and legends of our people are handed down from generation to generation by word of mouth." Further north, the treaty and nontreaty tribes in the Puget Sound region organized the Northwestern Federation of American Indians in 1914 to address land claims; by the mid- 1920s they had an attorney and sophisticated spokespeople carrying their cause to Congress. By taking the statements of older Indians—such as Chief Charles Satiacum, a roughly ninety-year-old Duwamish man present at the signing of the Point Elliott treaty in 1855—and presenting them to Congress, the federation hoped to demonstrate the depth of its historical claims. Finally —although many other examples are available—in the Midwest, the Wichita Nation Association of Oklahoma prepared what it called a "splendid history in brief form" of their claims based on aboriginal occupancy, and the Omaha mapped their aboriginal territory in numerous depositions taken during the litigation of their claims case.[5]

The government found the suits not only alarming—between 1914 and 1923, eight tribes filed claims against the government, and between 1924 and 1927 the number rose to thirty-seven—but also daunting in their historical complexity. The chair of the House Committee on Indian Affairs worried in 1924 that if all the Indians wanting to sue the government won all their cases it would be more costly than World War I. By the early 1930s, in more than one hundred cases, Indians were suing the government for almost $1.5 billion. And that was principal alone; if one factored in the interest the amount more than doubled. For this reason the attorney general considered claims cases to be the most important pending litigation the Department of Justice handled. In this adversarial climate the government was loath to grant that Hualapai history and land use conferred property rights. What all the claims shared, of course, was a reliance on history. Gathering documents, taking testimony — the day-to-day grind of collecting evidence to prove occupancy or show that a treaty had not been upheld — was hard work. Harder still was convincing courts that all this evidence *meant* something.[6]

Before mid-century, American anthropologists generally considered wandering people to be without a sense of property ownership that was legible by Western eyes. Forever simply engaged in the chase, people such as the Hualapais, wrongly thought to be completely ignorant of agriculture, followed game from place to place with no more attachment to the land than the animals they stalked. Cultivated fields were like anchors, and aboriginal peoples without them simply drifted. That property rights flowed from property ownership, which in turn could only be had in conjunction with agriculture, was, of course, a prominent feature of the law. But it also characterized most anthropological thinking. Largely an idea developed from the legal circumstances surrounding colonization and from Enlightenment ideas about the growth of civilization, the notion was that the adoption of agriculture represented a critical stop on the evolutionary path. Without agriculture, cultural evolution would stop. Cultures, according to a dominant strain within anthropology, moved through a series of stages from savagery to barbarism to civilization, and critical to evaluating the development of a culture was whether it had adopted agriculture. If it had not, the culture in question was still in a state of savagery. And because these stages were universal, all cultures either did or did not move through them. The ones that failed to keep up were destined to die. Having failed to achieve a key marker of civilization, cultures that were without agriculture were in no position to claim property rights based on aimless wandering. Hunting and gathering peoples — or at least those perceived to be hunters and gatherers — were seen as lesser peoples. Viewed with suspicion and distrust, hunters and gatherers have been at the mercy of the ever-moving, always restless farmer for millennia.[7]

Some did dissent. Using oral sources alongside evidence drawn from ethnographies and other writings about a variety of American Indians, Frank Speck developed an elaborate defense of individually owned property among hunters. Contradicting anthropologists who were under the sway of Lewis Henry Morgan, such as George Bird Grinnell, who believed that "there is nothing in the Indian's traditions or experience that enables him to even imagine the ownership of land by persons," Speck worked hard to convince the anthropological community that individually owned hunting territories existed among Indians and that their claims to land were legally enforceable property rights. Focusing his attentions on the Algonquians of the far Northeast and hoping to counter a "number of fallacies current among historical writers which do injustice to the Indians by putting them on a lower cultural scale than they deserve," Speck wrote in a style that combined advocacy with anthropology. He made two radical moves. First, he used Indians as sources for their own past, and, second, he attempted to overturn the commonly accepted idea that Western concepts of property did not exist among Indians. Speck specifically hoped to counter ideas about hunters, arguing that they did not merely wander, forever aimlessly chasing game. Rather, they had legally recognizable — and enforceable — property rights. Regardless of his good intentions, Speck inadvertently reified Western ideas about property. In insisting that Algonquian notions of property were identical to Western ones, Speck left out of the equation Indians who *did not* possess such a sense of property, such as the Hualapais and most other hunting and gathering peoples. Speck's idea of what constituted viable property was no different from the law's in that it recognized only a narrow range of possibilities — property was individually owned, transferable, and inheritable. Like Grinnell, some anthropologists recognized the existence of tribally owned land — land owned by one people to the exclusion of others with definite boundaries and passed on over time. But they were as yet unable to imagine a relationship to land that was both different from the Western conception of ownership *and* could be called property. Thus, they did not find one.[8]

In the discourse of dispossession, population was a major theme — that is, even if Indians had proper respect for private property, there were not enough of them to warrant such large landholdings. Low figures, based on scanty research, allowed for the easy dismissal of the Indian presence and were used for political ends, repeated time and again to suggest that the land was virtually vacant. Whether the population was high or low, Indians could not win. If the pre-contact population was high, then their demographic decline was evidence of the weakness of their race; if it was low, that was evidence that few had ever existed and thus their claims to the continent were weak.[9] These ideas left the realm of theory when Indian agents and others, as we shall see, applied them directly to the Hualapai. As justification for cutting the reservation in half, they had great appeal, for if the Hualapais were never there or were a dying race, what would be the point of keeping their land intact?

Some, such as Flora Warren Seymour, an attorney, a prominent writer about Indian affairs, and a member of the Board of Indian Commissioners (a quasi-governmental group of philanthropists and reformers charged with checking up on the BIA), held that natives' numbers barely reached three hundred thousand when Columbus first set foot in the Americas — a figure suspiciously close to the reported population of Indians at the turn of the twentieth century, suggesting that some thought there had been no decline in the Indian population.[10] And low numbers begged the question: What had the Indians done with all that land? The answer, generally, was nothing.

A small number of Indians was, as Seymour put it, no match for the "irresistible movement of world population." She reasoned that Indians could have little claim to so much land. After all, "a hundred and ten millions have overspread the land where four hundred years ago three hundred thousand natives scratched a scanty living from the soil, tramped about in search of wild berries and nuts, or tracked wild game. There must have been vast solitudes across our great country; for the moccasin leaves no wide track. . . . In a word, America was in the Stone Age when the Spaniard's flag was planted on the beach at San Salvador."[11]

Where had Seymour obtained such a low number? Population estimates had been batted about since Indians and Europeans met. If by Seymour's time a precise number could not be agreed on, one thing was certain: the Indian population had never amounted to much. In 1894 the U.S. Census Bureau claimed that the aboriginal population of the United States "could not have exceeded 500,000."

Five years later, Cyrus Thomas, in the introduction to Charles Royce's authoritative and oft-cited *Indian Land Cessions in the United States,* averaged Indian population figures and came up with 315,000. Thomas's methodology, however, was questionable — laughable, really — by any standard. For example, Thomas began his survey more than two centuries after contact, in 1820, when the population was given rather precisely as 471,036. Remarkably, only five years later the number had plummeted to 129,366. By 1829, a miraculous recovery had occurred: the Indian population shot up more than 100 percent. The wild fluctuations that plagued Thomas's fifty-six-year survey never caused him to pause and wonder about the veracity of his average. And what was the purpose of his foray into Indian demographics? He hoped to show "the absurdity of admitting the Indians' claim to the absolute right of the soil of the whole country." He compared population figures with the land claimed by Indians in an effort to demonstrate that "it is apparent . . . that the requirements of the human race and the march of civilization could not permit such an apportionment [to the Indians] of the soil of the American continent, . . . even were the estimates trebled." Indians were selfish. They claimed too much land and kept it out of the hands of needy farmers. Indians, in fact, needed very little land — about what was included in the state of Illinois. Allowing them "the exclusive use of the whole territory of the United States" simply by virtue of their being here first was "inconsistent with any true theory of natural rights. Moreover, it is not required by humanity, religion, nor any principle of human rights." If the absurdity of Indian claims to land was not enough to justify the righteousness of dispossession, then, Thomas and others averred, social evolution would take care of the Indian problem. "It is an inevitable consequence of the increase of population and of human progress that civilization and savagery must come in contact; and as the higher culture is the stronger in the process of evolution, its customs and activities must survive as the fittest."[12]

The Hualapais were the targets of much vitriol. In 1930, for example, the *Native American* — "a fortnightly journal devoted to Indian education" — published an article titled "Wild People" by former Hualapai reservation superintendent Frank Mann. According to Mann the Hualapais lived lives that hovered between savagery and civilization. "From the white man's viewpoint it is a sordid, even a revolting life, filthy, immoral, and without any of the things that to us make existence worthwhile." Belying the impression that Mann got from "their squat figures, low brows, and . . . forbidding aspect," he reported that the Hualapais were as intelligent as, and spoke English as well as, the average rural white person. Their apelike features, however, were suited to the way they lived, "in their rude domiciles, often no more than a framework of poles covered with juniper boughs and furnished with an old stove and a pile of rags." This all added up to the conclusion that "they are indeed wild — wild as the mysterious region of awful depths and terrific heights that lie silent in its shadows and glories behind them." Indeed, in 1894, Mary Dewy of the Massachusetts Indian Association simply said: "They live very much as mere animals do."[13]

Other writers fostered equally ugly images of the Hualapais. In 1929 Mary Roberts Coolidge published *The Rain-Makers: Indians of Arizona and New Mexico* to high praise. At more than three hundred pages it was a comprehensive survey of the Southwest, written largely for a lay audience. Coolidge's book was a mixture of admiration, pity, and disgust. "Physically," she wrote, "the race is well formed and symmetrical, with extraordinary power and endurance." The "Desert Indian" is much like his environment: tough. Coolidge's environmental determinism — the notion that the place makes the race — coupled with her commitment to cultural evolution led her to believe that, like the animals, southwestern Indians had evolved into perfect desert-dwelling creatures, limited only by their surroundings. She reserved most of her praise for the Navajos and the Pueblos and had little but disgust for the Hualapais. They were nomads, and "on account of their nomadic habits and the barrenness of their reservation, they scarcely stay upon it even now, but wander to the Navajo and

Hopi reservations." She wrote them off as "an all but homeless and degenerating tribe."[14] Coolidge reinforced the ideas that many government officials had of the Hualapais and their reservation. If any of this were true it would be difficult to justify a trial. It would be tough work for the tribe to counter images constructed by friends of the Indian such as the Massachusetts Indian Association and writers such as Coolidge.

Alongside such images sat misinformation. Under the auspices of the Committee on Social and Religious Surveys — an umbrella group representing Protestant interests on reservations around the country — G. E. E. Lindquist and a team of researchers traveled the United States in the early 1920s taking the pulse of Indian America. They did not like what they found on the Hualapai reservation. Littered with mistakes, not the least of which was the claim that the reservation consisted of only 73,940 acres, the survey contained in Lindquist's *Red Man in America* was woefully inadequate. They trotted out the usual tropes: the Hualapais wandered; they were a "primitive" people whose "superstitions and customs" were only slowly fading. In addition, the book made what would become a common claim in the case to come: most Hualapais did not even live on the reservation. They had abandoned their home and now they trespassed on Hopi and Navajo land.[15]

Only one person wrote against the grain. George Wharton James — desert wanderer, photographer, and writer — spent time among the Hualapais in the early twentieth century. Taking seriously their origin story, lamenting the generally unpleasant contact they had had with whites, and promoting their uplift, James wrote more about the Hualapais than had any other writer to date. He filled two chapters of his 1903 book *The Indians of the Painted Desert Region* with observations about the land and life of the tribe. With Jim Fielding as his guide, James got to know the Hualapais and more or less liked what he saw. Although some of his observations now ring a little off-key, such as his surmise that the Hualapais' large nostrils denoted "good lung power and capacity," mostly he accorded them a level of respect found nowhere else. Not until 1935, when *Walapai Ethnography* appeared, did anyone write in any greater detail about the tribe.[16]

Images of the Hualapais were, of course, part of larger discourse about Indians. Historians have argued that between the turn of the century and the New Deal Anglos came to like Indians. But the sanitized image of Indians that emerged before World War II looks more like what Patrick Wolfe has called "repressive authenticity" than a true measure of Indian life. The Hualapai case is a perfect opportunity to examine how Anglos came to see nomadic Indians — and, to a lesser extent, Indians in general. Were people willing to change the way they thought about all Indians? In most cases they were not. Nomadic peoples were the hardest to understand, and though changing views of the Pueblos might suggest that non-Indians were shedding time-worn conceptions of native people, what they thought about groups like the Hualapais—their land rights, their "racial capacities," their history, and their future—suggests the distance whites would have to travel if they were truly going to reimagine Indians.[17]

There is no doubt that Anglos came to have great sympathy for the Pueblos and that they imagined their culture as an antidote to modernity. John Collier, future commissioner of Indian affairs and leader of the non-Indian reform movement of the late 1920s and 1930s, is, of course, the most famous example. But groups of effete urbanites, eager to recharge their souls in the desert sun, rarely went to Hualapai country—or to the homeland of the Apaches, Pimas, Tohono O'odhams (formerly the Papagos), Mojaves, Chemehuevis, Paiutes, or Western Shoshones. They went to Santa Fe and Taos. By celebrating the village life of the Pueblos and to a lesser extent the warrior culture of the Plains, the so-called antimodern primitivists constructed ideal Indians that looked nothing like the Hualapais and others. If the ideal Indian lived in an adobe village or hunted the high plains, what, then, would be made of Indians who did neither?[18]

None were more explicit about the answer than Charles Fletcher Lummis. Traveling across the West at the end of the nineteenth century, Lummis, one of the first popularizers of the Pueblos and the Southwest, found himself near Peach Springs. There, he encountered "the nastiest human beings [he] ever saw." They were a "race of filthy and unpleasant Indians, who were in world-wide contrast with the admirable Pueblos of New Mexico. These unattractive aborigines, ragged, unwashed, vile, and repulsive faced, were the Hualapais." Having been "thrashed into submission by the noblest and greatest of Indian fighters," Lummis found the Hualapai harmless and "worthless as a pair of last year's linen pants." Unlike the Pueblo, who were industrious, artistic, and pious, the Hualapai "don't make blankets, pottery or anything else." Prostitution appeared to be their only industry. As with the Navajo, whom he also disdained, the absence of farming and a sedentary life sent Lummis off into paroxysms of verbal abuse—such as suggesting that a pregnant cow, terrified after looking a Hualapai in the face, would have a "miscarriage forthwith."[19]

Others, though not focusing on the Hualapai and using less extreme language, were similarly disdainful of some Indians. Mary Austin, for instance, often hailed as a progressive thinker—forward-thinking with regard to feminism and the environment, sympathetic to Indians—held less-than-palatable ideas about Indian people. Below the surface of Austin's sympathy lurked a quotidian racist. Her belief in social evolution was not simply a quaint though misguided marker of her milieu. It was indicative of a deeper commitment to the racial superiority of whites. Austin was an advocate of elevating Indians' place in the national psyche. Yet she meant this in terms of national monuments akin to the "big trees of California and the geysers and buffaloes of Yellowstone," and not as people.[20] They were symbolic of what was natural and unique about America; they stood mute, like the giant redwoods and sequoias, as Austin and others spoke to America about what they meant.

Late in her career as a writer and advocate, once she had removed to the Southwest permanently, Austin's racial views had hardened. In a 1929 article titled "Why Americanize the Indian?" a good deal of her romanticism was replaced by a grim vision of Indians' racial capacities. Their abilities were so limited, in fact, that "to spend time and money trying to force Indians beyond their natural capacity is just a stupid waste." What did this mean in practice? For one thing, education was futile. Austin pontificated: "There is no good reason why ninety-eight per cent of the Indians should be forced to continue their schooling beyond the age of fifteen or sixteen. The small number who exhibit capacity beyond that age should be admitted to the white schools." If Austin's forty years in the desert—her forty years of experience with the Indians of the Southwest—had taught her anything, she said, it was that Indians did not have it in them to learn by reading. And the ability to understand the printed word was for her a mark of a civilized, modern mind. Indians could learn, of course, but by means of "oral teaching and ocular demonstration." Their inability to learn by reading was "just one instance of the natural limitations of the primitive mind." These ideas were born of what Austin thought it meant to be a primitive. Romantic, indeed, but far from liberating. Ideas such as Austin's trapped Indians. Did she want to preserve Indian culture? Was this primitive being something that could be saved? Yes, but only because "we have come to realize that our Indians mean more to us [as Indians] than as imitation whites." But Indians, too, could meld into white society. Amalgamation—the mixing of races—could work to the Indians' advantage—provided, of course, that the right races mixed. According to Austin, "among the world's rapidly shrinking group of aboriginals—such as the African, the Australian, the Polynesian—the Amerind ranks high. Ethnically his stock is superior, and . . . he could pass into the American strain to our advantage, especially if he were mixed with Nordic stocks rather than Latin."[21]

Writers such as Austin offered a nonthreatening Indian to a small reading public; they had no effect whatsoever on the people with power: lawyers and bureaucrats. When they celebrated primitiveness by heightening people's awareness of it in order to ameliorate the effects of the modern world, such writers offered more of an anodyne for than an antidote to modernity. For Indians such as Fred Mahone, a celebration of primitivism would have been offensive. He wanted Indians to be seen as citizens of the modern world, not as relics of a reimagined past.[22]

7

The Hualapais and History

As far as Ray Tokespeta Winifred was concerned, the Hualapais' historic presence was not in doubt: "We can see the different signs or marks on numerous walls of rocks. This shows we live here long before the white people came to this country, or long before Columbus discovered American in the year 1492."[1] But the Hualapais were burdened with proving their historic ties to Peach Springs and saddled, too, with the notion that their current presence on the reservation did not amount to much. They had to challenge the government's narrative of invisibility. As they mounted their challenge, the government's resolve against them hardened and two stories emerged: one from the Hualapais, claiming that they had always occupied the present reservation, and another from the government, claiming that they did not, that they were mere wanderers. As earnestly as the government tried to erase them from the landscape, the Hualapai worked to write themselves back into it. They created a landscape with history.

The Pine Springs country—country in the eastern half of the reservation long leased out to ranchers and long off-limits to the Hualapais—was especially important. Beginning in the late 1920s many Hualapais decided that they wanted to move back. Proving their ties to Peach Springs was now combined with efforts to retake Pine Springs. But to at least one BIA inspector who toured the reservation in the summer of 1927, the Hualapais' desire to return to Pine Springs after their long exile was not a deep-seated desire. It was nothing more than a recent impulse "at least in part fomented and accentuated by the activities of one of the younger Indians, Fred Mahone, who is clearly of a very Bolshevistic turn of mind." Mahone was "doing all he [could] to stir up anger and agitate these Indians." Mahone might have been simply stirring up trouble in 1927, but by 1930 he had focused his energies. In order to shore up Hualapai claims to the Pine Springs country, Mahone embarked on his biggest project yet: documenting the tribe's history and land use in the eastern half of the reservation in September and October of that year. Mahone gathered testimony from important Ha'Kasa Pa'a (Pine Springs band) such as Dr. Tommy—whom some Hualapais now call the last of the traditional medicine men—to give credence to his claims. He documented their historic ties to the place "before white men and cattle were seen, But when only horses were seen to the Walapais," as well as their persistent efforts to homestead in the east, alongside the government's equally dogged attempts to run them off. No written records existed; Mahone knew that memories were all they had. As Indian Honga said, the Hualapais "do not read and write to keep such records of the past in books. . . . They keep all things in their brains." Were Mahone and the Hualapai to lose, landscapes sacred to them such the Qua'da graveyard, where Dr. Tommy and others are buried, or Diamond Creek canyon would be lost.[2]

The urgency of his task was, of course, brought on by the threat of losing half of the reservation, but it might also have been inspired by the sense among those in the BIA and elsewhere that not only did the Hualapais have no valid claim but also that they were disappearing. The common refrain "Too much land for too few people," so often used to justify removing Indians from their land, was being applied to the Hualapais. Indeed, as early as 1911 their agent had made predictions about their imminent extinction. Because the Pine Springs country was already devoid of Hualapais, Hagerman declared, by 1940 or, at the latest, 1950 the tribe would be gone entirely. Carl Hayden called them a "dying race." Hagerman and Hayden liked to tell the timeworn tale of the vanishing Indian. So did assistant U.S. attorney John Gung'l. While working out the settlement with the railroad, in fact, Gung'l reasoned that because the Hualapais were disappearing so fast—they would all be gone in a few years, he averred—he saw no reason to exchange the respective holdings of the Hualapais and the ATSF. Superintendent Wattson parroted Gung'l and Hagerman. No Hualapais lived on the eastern portion of the reservation and had not done so for twenty or thirty years, he claimed. Why? Because it was being leased to white cattlemen.[3] Thus, ceding that half of the reservation to the railroad would be of no consequence to the Hualapai; they weren't there anyway. They were being written out of the past and the present.

But Mahone called this convenient narrative into question. By interviewing several families and individuals who had historic band ties to the Pine Springs country, as well as Hualapais who had been purposefully kept out of the east, Mahone documented the Hualapai presence. They remembered their time there well. After all, only fifty years earlier — well within the memories of his informants — one of the largest bands had occupied the Pine Springs country. But after the coming of the railroad and cattle ranching the Pine Springs population diminished quickly — cattle pushed them out, and railroad work drew them to Peach Springs.[4]

One of Mahone's best informants was Dr. Tommy (or Wa'thee'ima, as Mahone transliterated his name), a Hualapai elder and a powerful medicine man still revered by Hualapai elders. He ranged across the east, traveling frequently between the area around Mohawk and National Canyons and into Supai, ministering to the spiritual and physical needs of the Hualapais and the Havasupais. Mahone, in his imperfect English, said that Dr. Tommy "was told time after time as, *long, long ages* have passed our fore ancestors, ancestors were borned and raised in the Pine Springs regions classed as the Pine Springs Indian[.] Their ruins of homes and other relics are numerously found in this Pine Springs country." The medicine man himself intoned: "I want to say that us Walapai Indian does not come in this country recently from other sections of the country. Therefore we sign our signatures in good faith to prove that we wish no one from out side of Reserve to crowd us out from our original home and garden ground."[5]

All the individuals and families he interviewed agreed that the Pine Springs country had been good for gardening and that Hualapais had been farming and living there for generations. The family of Mrs. Philip Sullivan (Headama), for example, "raised corn and pumpkins on a place about two or three miles south of Pint [sic] Springs before the white men came." Continuing to raise crops after the arrival of whites, Mrs. Sullivan dated her family's removal from the region to the coming of cattle. She wanted to return. Others told similar stories. Frank Beecher wanted a home in the Pine Springs country because, he said, "I know no other place." In 1930 his garden, partly shaded by two Ponderosa pines and watered by a simple well-fed irrigation system, produced abundant corn. Having recognized it as a nice spot, Beecher had wanted to settle there for some time, and in about 1923 he had pointed out the place to William Light, the BIA agent at the time. Light warned him off the spot, telling him that he'd disturb the cattle. But Beecher had a secret that he did not dare share with Light: he had discovered water and had been developing a well. He worried that if he told Light about it, his water would be usurped and he would be asked to leave. Years later, being a cattleman himself, as well as a farmer, Beecher sold his stock and used the money to buy timber for a house. Unable to get permission to build his house, and with his savings spent on a pile of stacked timber, Frank Beecher lived the life of a clandestine farmer, watering his garden with his secret well—of whose existence everyone but William Light knew. Speaking for a group of Hualapais who wanted to return, Beecher said, "We want to make ranches or homes and gardens in the Pine Springs Country."[6]

Indian Honga and his son Jacob had been having trouble becoming gardeners at Pine Springs even longer than Beecher had. Since 1914 Indian Honga had been told time and again that he could not settle there because the land was leased to white ranchers. But, he protested, "this Place Pine Springs country has been a home for my parents before the whiteman. Therefore, I want to build a home." Fencing off a plot of land sometime in the 1920s, Indian and Jacob Honga started gardens about a mile east of Pine Springs, planting corn, beans, and squash—the great triumvirate of native North American gardening. They built a cabin, too, not far from Frank Beecher's garden. When their crops were nearly mature and ready for harvest, the Hongas said, Light asked them to leave: they scared cattle away from the springs. "So we left this garden stand and let it abandoned." Indian Honga wanted a permanent home for his family, including his eight children, all of whom, he felt compelled to point out, had attended the government school. He wanted them to "live decently and be a prosperous Indian in the future." But before he could see his children prosper they had to await "the land question to settle in favor of the Walapai Tribe so that we may go back to this place to rebuilt home, garden, etc." Almost forty years later, Jacob's wife Jane remembered what would happen to Hualapais when they tried to live on what was considered ATSF land: "They'd shoot us."[7]

The list continues: Kate Crozier had been trying since 1912. Shortly after he built a house near Pine Springs the land was leased, and the agent told him to leave. Each year he waited, hoping that the leases would run out and that he could move back to the house, which still stood in 1930. The new agent, D. H. Wattson, followed the familiar pattern, and Crozier continued to wait.[8] And, finally, Fred Mahone himself had tried to farm the Pine Springs country before being warned off. Taking over Crozier's homestead in January 1923, Mahone spent seven months laying in a garden, fixing up the cabin, and developing his well. But come summer, Light told him to leave; until the leases expired he could not come back.

Light corroborated all of this testimony, admitting in 1923 that he had not let the Hualapais build houses near the springs lest they use them for "their own selfish interests." He claimed that both Jim Fielding and Mahone had been running an extortion scam and that their interest in farming was merely a ruse. Light imagined that they and others whom they coaxed into joining them would set themselves up on ranch land, refuse to leave, and then extort exorbitant payments from ranchers whom they bullied into submission. Ridiculous as it sounds, Light's fear of this plot kept the Hualapais from homesteading on their own reservation.[9]

The government had ruled much of the Pine Springs country off-limits. Frank Beecher, the Hongas, Kate Crozier, Dr. Tommy, Mrs. Philip Sullivan, Fred Mahone, and Charles McGee made it clear that it was the superintendents, and not an imagined rate of natural attrition, that led to the demise of the Hualapai population in the eastern half of their reservation. But with consolidation being considered, the government claimed that the absence of Hualapais was a consequence solely of a weak people's inevitable decline.

It was a busy autumn for Fred Mahone. Not satisfied with demonstrating only the desirability of the eastern portion of the reservation, he decided he would also make clear the worthlessness of the west. In order to do this, Mahone compiled a history of all the attempts he could find to drill wells in the country between Peach Springs and Clay Springs. He knew it was dry country, and he proved it: Indians, ranchers, and agents all failed to find water. Clay Springs notwithstanding, the eastern portion of the reservation was the better half. Mahone knew it, and so did the nearly two hundred citizens of Mohave County who signed a petition supporting the Hualapais' efforts to secure the entire reservation. Mary J. Musser of Kingman summed up the west country in five words: "A goat would starve there."[10]

Petitions and editorials in Indian school newspapers, however, were not enough to save the land. They needed help, and luckily the Indian Rights Association had one good fight left. Long an assimilationist organization, the IRA was now past its prime and within a generation would fade from view, eclipsed by a new brand of pro-Indian activism. The IRA might have thought the Hualapais were a "backward people," but it still had connections and some pull. Matthew K. Sniffen and Samuel M. Brosius, in particular, fought hard for the Hualapais' land. Brosius, a long-time champion of assimilation in his eighties, had been with the IRA since the 1890s and had battled with the courts before over Indian land—he and the IRA were instrumental in bringing *Lone Wolf v. Hitchcock* to the Supreme Court in 1903. Brosius now mounted one last campaign for Indian land rights.[11]

The Hualapais needed more help, and Brosius knew where to find it. Taking Brosius's advice, Mahone asked William Light, the retired superintendent, if he would agree to work on the Hualapais' behalf. Among other things, the Hualapais wanted Light's assistance in getting the Act of 1925 repealed, ridding the eastern half of the reservation of Anglo cattlemen, and guaranteeing that they had title to the whole reservation. Mahone, once so at odds with Light, now needed him. Worried that if the Hagerman deal went through it would "debar the Tribe from meeting their general resources which would be derived from the Walapai reservation land, water, etc., and they [would] never become worthy citizens to our community, State and Nation," Mahone turned to one of the few non-Hualapais who knew anything about their history.[12]

In addition to making what had become their standard set of demands, the Hualapais also took the first steps down a new path. Fred Mahone argued, perhaps at the urging of Brosius, that the tribe had a claim under the 1848 Treaty of Guadalupe Hidalgo. The land they now inhabited was, Mahone said, a "part of their ancient habitation," and the "rights of possession and occupancy recognized by Mexico was guaranteed to the Indian by the foregoing treaty and has never been voluntarily abandoned by the Indian."[13] The Hualapais had earlier argued that the military had set aside their reservation as a reward for their service as scouts against Geronimo's band. They were now contending that they had a claim to their land that was recognized by Mexico and thus predated the establishment of the United States. The dispute over Peach Springs had grown into a fight over title to the entire reservation—a dispute that looked as if it would be resolved in favor of the Santa Fe.

After a long but inevitably temporary separation, the question of title to both the reservation as a whole and to Peach Springs in particular began to run together in late December 1930. The funnel was Herbert Hagerman, who by that time was not only directing the consolidation negotiations but was instrumental in reaching an agreement concerning Peach Springs. Hagerman, his allies at the ATSF, and his sympathizers in the BIA spent the fall working out an agreement. Convening in Washington in December 1930, Hagerman, representatives of the railroad, the secretary of the interior, and the commissioner of Indian affairs reached an agreement. The railroad, remarkably, ceded title to the water. The Hualapais could have it. But there was a catch—in fact, there were several. Under the agreement, the railroad would be granted a permanent easement to the water; because of the improvements it had made, it would continue charging the tribe; and the tribe would only receive water *after* all the railroad's needs were met. The railroad now hoped that it could finally put the Peach Springs controversy behind it and have the case dismissed.[14]

Worried about the bad press that the new compromise might receive and the inevitable protests from the various friends of the Indian, the BIA hoped to keep it confidential until a decision was made. The IRA, because of its close ties to Commissioner Rhoads, got wind of the deal but was sworn to secrecy. Not knowing what to do, but thinking that this latest deal was the worst yet,

Samuel Brosius mentioned it to no one — least of all the Hualapais. Though he lacked hard proof, Brosius suspected that Hagerman was behind the new deal. Hoping he could help the Hualapais but not wanting to betray Rhoads, Brosius was conflicted. Which was more important, the confidence of the commissioner, or his obligation to the Hualapais? His worries paralyzed him.[15]

With Brosius stymied, the Hualapais' interests were now in the hands of a government that was against them. With informal talks out of the way, the negotiation of the legally binding stipulation between the railroad and the government began in early 1931. Piecing together the negotiations is impossible because John Gung'l wanted it that way. Under scrutiny from his superiors in Washington owing to his close relationship with the railroad — the Justice Department had finally begun to catch on — Gung'l was nervous because any draft stipulation he might write would have to be vetted by the attorney general. But his worries were not enough to stop him from closely collaborating with the railroad on the stipulation — a stipulation that only made its way to Justice once the railroad gave it a stamp of approval.[16]

Unaware of the meeting in Washington and blind to Gung'l's relationship with the railroad, Mahone waited patiently. Early in 1931 he was hoping for the "joyful news" that a "fair decision" would be made in their case. "The tribe pray that you preserve for us our land and water titles," he wrote to President Hoover. Eager to generate interest in the case, Mahone also wrote to Samuel Brosius and the CIA, mailing them affidavits of longtime Hualapai occupancy. He had already sent the same materials to Gung'l, having heard that he was their lawyer.[17] And then Mahone waited out the winter.

Word came in March. It was bad news for the Hualapais: Rhoads voiced his support for the Hagerman consolidation agreement and told Mahone about the new deal regarding Peach Springs. And because Rhoads admitted that a final agreement still eluded the BIA, Mahone, ever optimistic, said he thought that Rhoads's "very kind letter" was a sign of hope — all was not lost.[18] But his optimism was likely feigned. Mahone was just being politic. He was deeply worried.

The ruptures that had begun to appear among the Hualapai by the end of the summer burst open over the winter. Because their land was in limbo many Hualapais were losing patience and getting angry. They began to blame Mahone for their problems, thinking that he had gotten them into this mess in the first place or, at a minimum, was not doing enough to get them out of it. He feared he was in danger. And he had lost the confidence of Jim Fielding. Initially, Mahone and Fielding had been allies against Light, but lately they had been drifting apart — Fielding's name turns up less and less often on Mahone's various petitions, and he is never a witness in one of Mahone's several affidavits. Fielding and Homer Davidson were in league with one another against Mahone; for the better part of a year, likely longer, Mahone had been sparring with both.[19] Mahone — educated, articulate, fluent in English and Hualapai — had the ear of the IRA and carried some weight with people in Kingman. Fielding did not. Mahone was a political force and thus a threat to Fielding. The rift between them would eventually widen and would never be bridged.

Clear signs of the fissure opening up between Mahone and some members of the tribe were evident after a general meeting held in early March. Not having heard from Samuel Brosius in months, Mahone worried about his safety and wondered where his friends had gone. "The Indians will endanger me or trouble me when I lose in this fight to gain their land and water title. The tribe are still criticizing the work that I and other Indians are working together on to the finish where we can reach a fair settlement to satisfy the Walapai tribe. . . . The meeting was an embarrassment for several hours to the tribe. I am much sorry to say this meeting proves that the Walapais will turn quickly against me and endanger me and also others who are working together to settle their land and water problem for them."[20]

Alone, possibly feeling abandoned, and certainly angry about the recent approval of the Hagerman plan, Mahone took no comfort from Brosius when he finally received a mysterious letter from him late in March. The heat was on in Washington. Brosius, anticipating a possible visit by the Senate Committee on Indian Affairs but not wanting to confirm anything, and still conflicted by dual loyalties — to Indians and to his needed allies at the BIA — implored Mahone to keep all correspondence between them strictly confidential. Brosius warned Mahone that "parties" in Washington were "intent on making trouble."[21]

Two months later, in May 1931, hope arrived. The Senate Subcommittee on Indian Affairs was coming to the reservation. The timing could not have been better. The Interior Department had recently come out in favor of a consent decree between the railroad and the government that backed the Hagerman plan and would legally bind the agreement.[22] Whereas the government wanted to settle the case quietly, and fast, Fred Mahone looked forward to a public airing of the Hualapais' claim, even sending out an invitation to the *Albuquerque Journal*. When the Hagerman deal had first appeared the previous spring the Hualapais had not been able to voice their views. Now, almost exactly a year later, he hoped they would have the chance.[23] Others were hopeful, too, that the hearings would help the Hualapais: dozens of members of the Kingman business and civic community, including Mahone's American Legion post, supported the tribe.[24]

The tone at the day-long hearings held at Valentine was tense. For a year the Hualapais had not only been shaking off the memory of their last meeting with government but living under the very real threat of having half of their reservation taken from them. And for their part, after listening to unending descriptions of government malfeasance and Indian poverty, the team members were travel-weary, too. They had just come from days of exhausting hearings on the Navajo reservation, where Hagerman had also been a topic of discussion. Three years into their work when they reached Truxton Canyon, the survey team was fatigued. At times, it seemed as if the committee disdained the Hualapais' concerns, impatiently suffering speeches about justice or long-term occupancy and only letting a few among many speak. At others, the railroad appeared to be on trial. The investigators — Senators Burton K. Wheeler, considered a heckler of witnesses, and Lynn J. Frazier — bristled at the ATSF's arrogance. The obvious goal of the hearings — it was almost all anyone wanted to talk about — was to investigate the Peach Springs case.[25]

Assembled like judges above the crowd gathered in the school auditorium, seven non-Indians presided. As Fred Mahone hurried fellow Hualapais into the room, shuffling his papers, Senator Carl Hayden began to speak — and speak and speak without interruption. Nervous and excited, and missing most of what Hayden said, Mahone took his time settling down. This picture fits the memory that some elders have of Mahone: hurrying from place to place in Peach Springs, always burdened by a stack of books and a mass of papers, always busy, always on the move. If Mahone had been listening to Hayden's opening remarks, he would have heard him say that the Hualapais' claim to the entire reservation was weak. First, he harked back to the early discussions of the case at the Department of the Interior in 1919 and reminded the audience that the government conceded that the railroad had title. And, second, the Hualapais were disappearing. Demographic work proved it. Hayden suggested that the only way to secure the entire reservation for the Hualapai — he knew that was what they wanted but was convinced that they had no legal claim to the land — was to purchase the railroad's sections. But, based on their population, that would be too costly. Citing the prohibitive cost, Hayden considered consolidation to be the best solution.[26]

Jim Mahone, almost one hundred years old, it was said, testified next. Fred Mahone interpreted his story of scouting for the army against Geronimo with other Hualapai men. In return for their service they received army protection and a permanent home free from white encroachment. Likening settlers to "a bunch of worms" who would crowd out Indians, General Willcox had set aside the Hualapai reservation, the elder Mahone said. Unable to recite dates, Jim Mahone had a hard time being specific. But specificity did not matter. Not much did, in fact. All Burton Wheeler cared about was whether the railroad lived up to the provisions of its grant. As soon as the elder Mahone tapped into the past — his scouting and his meeting with Willcox and the Havasupais and Mojaves to hash out a deal for a reservation — Carl Hayden stopped him: "We are not interested in all that history." Wheeler lectured him: the Hualapais did not possess any inherent rights to their land based on occupancy; they might have rights to their land only if the railroad had somehow abused the privileges of its grant. But if the railroad satisfied the requirements of the grant, Wheeler did not "think the Indians would have very much of a chance to recover all of such lands."[27]

Bob Schrum, hereditary leader of the Hualapais, took a different view of the reservation's creation. Also speaking through Fred Mahone, Schrum agreed that the military had set aside a reservation for the tribe, but he challenged the reason. Jim Mahone was wrong. It had been set aside not in gratitude for military service but in recognition of what was already theirs. They owned the land and the army simply recognized that and made it official. Schrum, too young to have been a scout, would have no part of any explanation that suggested the reservation was an artificial creation based on service to the government. He wanted it made clear: This was the ancestral home of the Hualapais, not a gift from the government.[28] Wheeler had now heard enough. His patience worn thin, he stopped Schrum right there. Wheeler did not want to hear what he considered irrelevant testimony about the past. This was a legal question, and he insisted that the hearing move on.

Fred Mahone was next. His message: In the reservation's return would be their salvation; the Hualapais could then work their land, raise cattle, and return to their homes. Wheeler listened as Mahone angrily recounted the Hualapais' removal from the Pine Springs country. Then, as Mahone later put it, there was a "clash between Wheeler and I." Like Hayden before him, Wheeler invoked the image of the vanishing Hualapai. From his testimony, it is almost possible to hear Mahone's voice rise as his temper flared. It had been a long and trying year for Mahone. He did not need to be reminded on this day, when his hopes for a reckoning were so high, that few Hualapais lived on the eastern half of the reservation. He knew that. The dangers posed by the white cattlemen made it unsafe to the point at which they "could never live there at this time." And the tribe's various agents had been no help. They sided with the ranchers, offering the Hualapai a litany of unsatisfying excuses for why they could not live in the Pine Springs country. Wheeler kept challenging him, asking what use he would make of the land, since he was doing nothing with it now. "We are not allowed to make anything from any part of the reservation," Mahone shouted back. His anger rising, three times he shot back at Wheeler: "We can prove to you why we do not live there. We can prove to you right now why we do not live there. We can prove by these statements why we do not live there." But he was ushered away before he had a chance to air all the evidence he had collected the previous fall detailing longtime Hualapai use and occupancy of the Pine Springs country. Given no opportunity to prove that the Hualapais had always been there, much less to demonstrate that it was the government that had kept them from returning, Mahone must have been bitterly disappointed.[29]

The hearings ended after one day, and from the transcript it would be difficult to see what effect — good or bad — they would have on the tribe's case. Fred Mahone was frustrated. The committee had not spent enough time on the reservation and had not cared enough about "vital matters involving the welfare of members of [the] tribe." Without a visit to the Pine Springs country, how could the committee have hoped to understand the "true conditions as they actually exist"? He was not only frustrated; he was worried, too, because the "Santa Fe railroad has talented men looking out after the interests of their company, while we must fight this battle alone with but little talented help outside of our own ranks."[30]

And if they lost, valuable land would disappear. More than material needs had to be met. Mahone, in a sentence that is tantalizing in its brevity, alluded to the importance of the *place*. The water was important, the cattle operation was important, arable land was important. But so, too, was the land itself to the tribe's identity as a people: "A great many parts of the Reservation are dear in history to our Tribe and to the whole Nation and you are aware of how our Tribe perishes [cherishes?] and keeps scared [sacred] its historical places and traditions."[31] The reservation was not only a source of potential income but also the wellspring of Hualapai history. Mahone gave the lie to past and future statements to the effect that the reservation had simply been carved out of one among many parcels of barren desert. But, of course, none of this would matter if no one intervened and stopped the Hagerman plan.

By the end of the summer the Hualapais — forever kept in the dark — wondered where the case stood. Responding to Mahone's request, in July the IRA sent Matthew K. Sniffen to Hualapai country, where "the Indians were suspicious of everything and almost everyone." A year earlier Sniffen had favored consolidation, but after the Hualapais — especially Fred Mahone — convinced him that the land was theirs, he confessed that he "had seen the light." What had looked to him like good pasture the previous year — after abundant rain — had become parched grassland. He now knew that the best water was indeed on the eastern half of the reservation, around Pine Springs. And he, too, soon realized that the Hualapais "had been discouraged . . . if not actually prevented" from settling there.[32]

For a time the hearings appeared to have no impact, for the stipulation worked out among the BIA, Hagerman, the ATSF, and Gung'l made its way to court on 7 July 1931 and became legally binding on that day. The tribe now had title, and the railroad got the water. The Peach Springs controversy was over. John Gung'l likely sighed with relief on that same day when he wrote, "As this now completes this matter I have closed my files." But Fred Mahone had not closed his. He immediately wrote to Lynn Frazier, chair of the Senate Subcommittee on Indian Affairs, rushing off a raft of documents — a petition from the American Legion, a citizens' petition, and five more affidavits.[33]

Sharing Gung'l's relief, Carl Hayden, too, was glad that it had worked out so well. In fact, the resolution of the Peach Springs case so pleased Hayden that he hoped Hagerman could do the same for a similar dispute between the Navajos and the ATSF. Most of all, he wanted a deal just as "well done [as] on the Walapai reservation, so that neither the Senate Committee on Indian Affairs or any of the uplifting brethren can pick any material flaws in it."[34] He could hope.

The Hualapais' version of their past, Fred Mahone's documentation of their longtime occupancy, and the support of the IRA would not matter if they had no *legal* claim to their land. After visiting the Hualapai reservation in the spring of 1931, the Senate Subcommittee on Indian Affairs asked for an opinion on Hualapai land rights from the attorney general. Consolidation was a serious matter. And because the Hualapai made a potentially strong case, the members of the committee wanted to know, Is this legal? Lynn Frazier asked that until that question was answered any steps toward consolidation be halted until he and his colleagues had a chance to "further investigate the rights of the Indians."[35]

They asked for one opinion, but they got three — one from the Justice Department and two courtesy of the Interior Department. All three opinions worked hard to write the Hualapais out of their land; they were willfully ignorant of the tribe's past — and shameless about it. Although evidence of Hualapai occupancy — Fred Mahone's interviews and photographs, Light's report, depositions and affidavits, and the testimony taken at Valentine, for example — was mounting, it could not overcome deeply embedded ideas about Indian property rights and history. All three opinions rewrote the past and provide remarkable testimony to the power of history.

The solicitor of the Department of the Interior issued his opinion in September 1931. The solicitor's opinion was the first official, published stance taken by the government concerning the question, and it demonstrates in clear, unbridled prose exactly what it thought of the Hualapais' claim — and by extension Indian property claims in general. Solicitor E. C. Finney laid out the case history. Beginning with the original discussion between the Indian Office and Interior in 1919 and ending with the 1931 Peach Springs agreement, Finney mapped out what appeared to be a seamless, consistent course from start to finish, free of controversy. By highlighting Interior's 1919–20 position that the railroad's title was valid, the 1925 consolidation act, and the 1931 Peach Springs agreement Finney attempted to show that the government had consistently ruled against the Hualapais.[36]

These were the facts according to Finney: the Hualapais had no treaty with the United States, nor did any congressional action or administrative order set aside these lands prior to the executive order, save Willcox's General Order 16; at the time of the granting act it appeared that the Hualapais "roamed" the mountainous county of northwestern Arizona; they "vigorously" resisted army and settler efforts to control them; they fought a war; they were then "forcibly removed" to the Colorado River reservation, a place "unsuited to their wants [where] many of them died of disease"; after a brief, unhappy time they fled the reservation and became "wanderers and fugitives in the desolate mountain regions where they previously roamed, part[s] of which were later embraced in the Walapai Reservation"; the Hualapais pleaded with the army to create a reservation for them in 1881; the army complied and Willcox issued General Order 16.[37]

The railroad's rights to the land attached, according to Finney, on the date they filed their map of definite location in 1872, but he cited no authority for this claim. At the time, he wrote, no Hualapais were living on the land, nor had a reservation been created for them by treaty, by act of Congress, or by other administrative action covering the areas they roamed. In fact, they were living nowhere nearby. In 1872, he claimed incorrectly, they lived on the Colorado River reservation, created for them and others in 1865. Thus, their land was public land when the railroad filed. When the Hualapais made their "unauthorized" return, a reservation was created for them. But it was too late. They had lost their rights to the land when they left for the Colorado River reservation, though their journey south was forced upon them:

> There is nothing to show that, prior to the time of the removal of the Indians from northwestern Arizona to the reservation created for them on the lower Colorado, there was such use and occupancy of the lands subsequently embraced in the reservation, separate and apart from the vast area of the public domain, to impress upon them the status of Indian lands. In any event, the fee was in the United States, and it was within the power of Congress to transfer such lands without restriction, to terminate any right which they might have to further use and occupy the lands and to provide other lands for their use

and occupancy. In my view, their removal to the reservation provided for their use by act of Congress under the circumstances disclosed by the reports, extinguished any right which they might have acquired to use and occupy any of these lands, and they became subject to disposition under public land laws, unburdened with any title based on aboriginal occupancy.[38]

Finney made two key points. First, there was no evidence that the Hualapais had done anything more than roam across the land now set aside as their reservation prior to the coming of the railroad, and even if they had a stronger claim — the second point — Congress had the power to extinguish any rights flowing from that use. Forced removal and their wandering ways extinguished the Hualapais' rights. After reading the solicitor's opinion and considering the political opposition to the tribe's claim, Samuel Brosius wrote to Fred Mahone in despair, saying, "It is apparently a hopeless case."[39]

Matters worsened when the Justice Department weighed in. Seth Richardson, who had recently favored litigation and been interested in exploring the Hualapais' historic ties to their land, now shared Finney's view of their past. Richardson began his opinion by noting that the Hualapais did not have fixed homes but rather "were a wandering, warlike, hunting people that followed the herds of game." Their "present reservation was merely a part of their hunting ground, differing not at all from the rest of their range." They had no claim to the land because "it is clear that the Walapais did not occupy the territory of the present reservation in any other manner than they did the mountainous regions generally in Arizona." Based on the facts he had, such as his erroneous belief that the Hualapais were confined to the Colorado River reservation in 1872, he was "very strongly of the opinion that a suit attacking the title of the railway to odd numbered sections . . . would fail."[40]

The third appraisal of Hualapai history completed the government's hat trick and offers a final example of the ways in which the Hualapais were not seen. The BIA's A. C. Monahan crafted a version that was similar to Finney's and Richardson's. After combing through a variety of documents he could find little or no positive evidence of Hualapai occupancy of the land within the present reservation prior to the arrival of the railroad. Monahan's survey of the few extant explorers' reports convinced him that the Hualapai had lived west and south of the present reservation. They may have occasionally wandered east and north, but they never stayed for long. His interrogation of the evidence was strange. Citing reports that did not mention the Hualapai as confirmation of their absence, while discounting material that attested to the Hualapais' presence as incorrect, Monahan appeared to be trying *not* to find the Hualapais. Reports from the commissioner of Indian affairs that listed the Hualapai population at six hundred one year and at fifteen hundred a mere three years later did not cause him to wonder about the reliability of his sources. In addition, when quoting the Ives report on Hualapai occupation of Diamond Canyon and the Pine Springs country — which he discounted as a likely mistake — Monahan extracted Ives's ugliest utterances, inserted, no doubt, to suggest that whatever occupancy the Hualapai might have claimed was illegitimate.[41] Not only was all evidence used, in one way or another, to prove the Hualapais' absence, but Monahan's source base was also extremely limited; he neglected the Mason and Willcox reports, as well as all of the affidavits collected by Light and Mahone.

History was used in strange ways to justify a legal conclusion. And the Hualapais were written out of their land. Legal reasoning regarding occupancy and the property rights of native people trumped history — or, history in this case was made to serve the law. And those who dealt with the law — courts, judges, lawyers — were already well versed in keeping Indians from their land.

8

Land and Law

Why did the attorneys in the case routinely work against the Hualapais? Was it because, as the legal historian and counsel for the British Crown in *In Re. Southern Rhodesia* (1918), the Right Honourable Earl of Birkenhead, put in 1926, "As a rule, the settlement by white people of a country already occupied by natives raises problems of extreme complexity"? The short answer is yes, and the attorneys in the Hualapai case gave easy answers. By the early 1920s those extremely complex problems had been heard in courts and been debated by public officials in Australia, Canada, New Zealand, Rhodesia, Nigeria, and the United States for more than a century. But their thinking had been inconsistent; settled law on the property rights of native people did not exist.[1] Armed with only a dim understanding of Indian law, the lawyers eventually involved in the Hualapai case had to discover and remake Indian law. Cases such as *Johnson v. M'Intosh* (1923), which we now view as canonical, had largely been forgotten.

What came to be variously known as native title, Indian title, or aboriginal title was an American invention. Based on the notion that indigenous people could not possess free and clear title to land, Indian title was a contrivance developed from the colonial encounter, a way to grant native peoples some property rights while allowing the European sovereign — the ultimate power — to maintain control over land, especially its sale and distribution. Indian title was also an American export. By the time the Hualapai case began, Indian title had, in one form or another, became part of the law of Canada, Australia, and New Zealand. And although it is unlikely that the lawyers who worked on the Hualapai case were aware of this, they were nonetheless part of an international conversation about the rights of native people to property, a conversation to which native people generally were not invited. The Hualapai case developed on multiple fronts: on the reservation, at the U.S. attorney's office in Phoenix, at the Departments of Justice and the Interior in Washington, D.C., and at the BIA. But many of the legal contours of the case had been developing far afield for decades before the Hualapais ever wondered why so many did not think that they owned their land.

The precedents may have been many, but the attorneys who knew anything about them were few. Indian law was barely a field of inquiry among legal scholars in the early decades of the twentieth century. Defenders of the Hualapais' rights to their land might have been able to wring some support from past precedent, but fashioning a well-buttressed argument in their favor would not be easy: Indian law can be, and has been, manipulated to serve many interests. It is notoriously slippery. What's more, federal Indian law was developing so rapidly — and so inconsistently — that no one could be expected to keep up with the changes. Between 1900 and 1940 the Supreme Court heard more than twice as many Indian cases as it had heard during the entire nineteenth century. And even if a solid strategy could be devised, theory and practice rarely coincided. In addition, legal scholarship concerning Indians was pitifully undeveloped. Because most attorneys knew as little about Indian law as the average citizen knew about Indians, as one lawyer reckoned in 1922, few attorneys possessed the expertise needed to navigate Indian law. After all, according to another lawyer, who comically understated the matter in 1917, "The laws relating to the rights of Indians on the public lands are somewhat complicated." The period in which the Hualapai case was batted about — Do we take it to court? do we cut the reservation in half? — was a time of flux and uncertainty. The case raised questions thought, by some, to have been answered; others, as we shall see, thought the case novel. Although it is important to keep in mind the unique features of the case, it is also wise to note that the contours of Hualapai case could be found throughout the British Empire. The case marks a tipping point between one way of seeing Indian land rights and another. But these ways of seeing had been changing for centuries; oscillating between recognition and denial, colonial land policy was anything but definite.[2]

By the time the Hualapais were beginning to wonder about their property rights and the railroad and the government were working hard to cut the reservation in half, legal opinion—in the United States and abroad—stood firmly against them. If the Hualapai were to win their case a new way of thinking about native peoples and their property rights would have to emerge. Unlike Australia, where aboriginal peoples' existence was legally erased, New Zealand, Canada, and the United States did not question the fact of native occupancy in the nineteenth century. When the foundational Indian property rights cases were decided, recognition of occupancy was an entirely different matter—the Indians' presence was obvious. For example, *Worcester v. Georgia* (1831), revolved around current rights derived from current occupancy, not rights based on historic occupancy as in the Hualapai case.[3]

But after World War I the Hualapais no longer practiced their aboriginal lifestyle, and as the years went by, they moved still further away from precontact ways; long-term occupancy was *not* a readily obvious fact. In deciding that the railroad had title, government attorneys and other officials relied, in part, on a novel argument: the Hualapai simply were not there. In the twentieth century, when jurists and judges could no longer see Indians as they had in the nineteenth century, when historic occupancy was not always so obvious, aboriginal occupancy had to be proved. Many tribes either no longer lived on their historic homelands or practiced an entirely different way of life. And so the courts, lawyers, and Indians turned to history.

The Supreme Court and Indians first met in 1810. *Fletcher v. Peck,* which did not actually involve any Indians directly, was concerned with sorting out title to western lands that were bought and sold by speculators. The suit arose when the state of Georgia attempted to repeal legislation that had granted land to John Peck's New England–Mississippi Land Company. This land had formerly been Indian land and had never been lawfully ceded to Georgia via treaty. Robert Fletcher, who bought land from the company, sued John Peck when he got wind of the pending repeal. The Court was asked to decide whether the land was state-owned or federally owned. In the midst of deciding this question—which was answered in favor of Georgia—the Court noted that all land was at base subject to what Justice John Marshall, in his opinion, called "Indian title"—at the time, a neologism. The Court found that Indian title must be extinguished before another party's rights can attach to the land. In *Fletcher,* Marshall tried to have it both ways by allowing Georgia to have property rights that were subject to the Indians' right of occupancy, creating two owners of the same land. But he declined to sufficiently define Indian title. Marshall's associate, Justice William Johnson, had no such trouble. In his dissenting opinion he argued that Indian title was no different than fee simple, or absolute, title. While Marshall vaguely sketched out a new form of property rights, Johnson contended that the only applicable type of title was fee simple title. If Indians had fee simple title to their land, grants from the government would be void. But Johnson lost.[4]

Thirteen years later Marshall got his chance to elaborate on Indian title. *Johnson v. M'Intosh* is the most important Indian property rights opinion handed down by the Supreme Court. Decided in 1823, *Johnson*, like *Fletcher*, involved no Indians directly. Two parties in Illinois had bought the same land — Johnson from a private company, and M'Intosh from the federal government. Both sellers claimed to have acquired their right to the land from the Illinois and the Piankeshaws, who sold the same land twice. The question — Can Indian tribes sell land to private parties, or can they only cede or sell such land to the government? — appeared simple; the answer was not. In one of the Court's most thoroughly analyzed opinions, Marshall ruled that tribes only had what he called the right of occupancy. They can do what they want with the land while they occupy it, but they cannot sell their land to anyone but the sovereign. The sovereign alone retains the right to extinguish Indian title. Whence does such a powerful right flow? Discovery. According to Marshall, discovery of a given territory granted the discoverer the right, against other nations, to purchase Indian land and then grant that land to non-Indians. Colonial and federal law and policy prevented tribes from selling land to anyone but the sovereign or those authorized by the sovereign, but it was not until the early nineteenth century that lawmakers and jurists began to conceive of Indian property rights as something less than fee simple ownership. And for Marshall, it was this long-term practice of preventing private purchasers from acquiring Indian land directly from tribes or requiring potential purchasers to obtain permission first that convinced him that Indians did not possess fee simple title. Rather, they only had occupancy rights. In other words, because colonial governments prevented private purchasers from contracting directly with Indians, Marshall took it to be a matter of settled law that that this was a restriction on Indian property rights.[5]

The decision was both a blow and boon to Indian rights. The Court created a new property right for Indians, one that all parties, including the sovereign, were bound to respect. At the same time, the Court took away absolute control of Indian land by Indians. The Court said that Indians possessed an occupancy right that only the discovering sovereign could extinguish with the tribe's consent. Thus, discovery did not vest title in the discoverer; it gave the discovering nation the right to extinguish a tribe's title via purchase or conquest. The rights of the discover were against those of other nations staking a claim to Indian land; they were not necessarily rights over Indians. The Court now said that tribes could convey their land to the discovering sovereign and to no one else. If Marshall ruled that the sovereign's rights derived from discovery, from where did the Indian's rights come from? Occupancy was the bedrock of Indian title. Residence in a given area conferred Indian title upon a tribe.[6]

The decision was a compromise. As Justice Johnson had noted in his dissent in *Fletcher,* Anglo-American common law included no notion of Indian title; the only type of right he would recognize was fee simple. In *Johnson v. M'Intosh,* Marshall was faced with a choice: either Indians possessed the fee or the United States did. But Marshall would neither strip Indians of all property rights nor vest them with the fee. So he invented Indian title, which awkwardly sat somewhere below fee simple title but above the rights of a renter. More than a century later, Felix Cohen noted that "Chief Justice Marshall's doctrine [held] that the Federal Government and the Indians both had exclusive title to the same land at the same time."[7]

Called both a "brilliant compromise" and "judicial mythology," Marshall's opinion in *Johnson v. M'Intosh* left Indians with a property right that was unique in American law. Although the United States had the ultimate fee and the right to extinguish Indian title, it could only do so with the permission of the tribes. Marshall's decision was really a limitation on European powers, not on Indian tribes. Marshall realized the oddity of his decision. In fact, he confessed that his version of the doctrine of discovery was unjust, calling it "pretentious." But he saw no other way out. It was the custom of the country. And though Indian title was not to be taken lightly — it was as close to fee simple title as possible — *Johnson* was still an unbridled assertion of power. Marshall could find no other justification for his theory of discovery than his belief in the power of colonialism and the concomitant notion that the question of colonial power was solely a political, not a justiciable, question.[8] But *Johnson* was not the last word.

Both *Worcester v. Georgia* (1832) and *Mitchel v. United States* (1835) modified Marshall's stance. In *Worcester,* the Court ruled that the laws of Georgia did not apply to the sovereign Cherokee and that thus Samuel Worcester broke no law when preaching to the tribe without a permit from the state. In order to establish sovereignty Marshall reworked the conquest aspect of his decision in *Johnson.* He admitted that the conceit that discovery gives the discoverer title was a fiction. He made it clear that a European nation could claim title to land only if the Indians consented to sell. He repudiated his earlier belief that discovery and conquest were, in essential respects, synonymous. By ruling that Indian tribes possessed all their aboriginal rights at discovery and could only relinquish those rights to the sovereign power with their consent, he demolished *Johnson's* conflation of discovery with conquest. And if discovery and conquest were not the same thing then discovery did not automatically confer title on the discoverer. Marshall now circled back to Johnson's dissent in *Fletcher*: Indians were masters of the soil until they relinquished those rights to the new sovereign. But, for all its strong words in defense of Indian sovereignty, *Worcester* still endorsed colonialism and left its legacy largely outside the arm of the law. The historical processes of colonialism — alienation of land, for one — were not justiciable, but the "ongoing process of colonialism," such as Samuel Worcester's trouble with the state of Georgia and Cherokee sovereignty, might be handled in court. *Worcester* was a pivot point. The questionable practices of colonialism up to that point were beyond repair, but, after *Worcester* was decided, colonialism had to answer to a limited Indian sovereignty. *Worcester* had little practical effect. States continued to routinely trample Indian sovereignty by trying native people in state courts.[9]

Finally, *Mitchel v. United States*, while not giving or taking away rights, further refined the definition of Indian title. *Mitchel* was Marshall's last case, but Justice Henry Baldwin wrote for the Court. In this case, the Seminoles of Florida had sold land, with the permission of the sovereign, Spain, to a private purchaser. The Court found that because Spain had granted the Seminoles permission to sell, Colin Mitchel, and not the United States, had the greater claim to the land. Baldwin's opinion was the clearest expression of Indian property rights up to that time: "Indian possession or occupation was considered with reference to their habits and modes of life; their hunting grounds were as much in their actual possession as the cleared fields of the whites; and their rights to exclusive enjoyment in their own way, and for their own purposes, were as much respected, until they abandoned them, made a cession to the government, or an authorized sale to individuals. . . . The merits of this case do not make it necessary to inquire whether the Indians within the United States had any other rights of soil or jurisdiction; it is enough to consider it as a settled principle, that their right of occupancy is considered as sacred as the fee simple of the whites".[10] *Mitchel* was an unequivocal endorsement of Indian property rights, but it remained to be seen whether any of its principles would be applied to the Hualapai case — if it ever got to a court.

Although the question of native title did not regularly come before courts outside the United States until the final third of the twentieth century, concerns about native land rights — or, just as often, concerns about settlers' rights in the face of native demands — were regular features of colonial policy discussions. A look at the few cases that did arise, alongside a glance at policy, not only demonstrates the shaky ground on which native peoples' property rights rested. A brief tour of the British colonial world also makes clear that the

Hualapai were embedded in something far larger than themselves. The barriers to their success were formidable: for more than a century policy makers and courts had been working hard to ensure that people such as they enjoyed few rights to land. Canada, Australia, New Zealand, Southern Rhodesia, and Nigeria all offer important examples of the status of native property rights under colonial regimes. These cases differ in details from the U.S. cases but have some features in common. Taken together, they indicate the status of native property rights before common law courts as the Hualapai case developed. They all answered, in one fashion or another, the question of exactly what rights native peoples had to land, and they all relied, explicitly or implicitly, on precedents set down by the Marshall Court. The importance of the Marshall decisions cannot be overstated. As early as 1836, the English legal scholar William Burge was called upon to decide whether John Batman's purchase of land directly from Australian Aborigines was valid. Citing *Johnson v. M'Intosh* as his primary authority, Burge concluded that Batman and his associates had not made a legal purchase. The land was the Crown's. Five years later the Superior Court of New South Wales noted the influence of American law when discussing aboriginal affairs in Australia.[11]

The Marshall Court had its greatest influence in New Zealand, where indigenous land rights were the subject of extensive litigation and legislation well before similar issues came to the fore in Canada and Australia. The nature of Maori land rights, the applicability of *Johnson v. M'Intosh* and U.S. law generally, and the question of whether Maoris could rule their own affairs were major concerns of the British. In 1840, writing in *The New Zealand Herald*, Henry Chapman, who would go on to prominence as a member of the New Zealand Supreme Court, wrote of the U.S. Supreme Court's Indian decisions: "Among the reported decisions of that court, is to be found a body of international law, which does not exist in any other country." In the same year, a vicious debate took place between the governor of New Zealand, George Gipps, and the prominent colonial attorney William Wentworth, over the applicability of the Marshall Court's jurisprudence. Gipps justified following American law when writing the New Zealand Land Claims bill by saying that the U.S. Supreme Court was the most important court "in the whole of the Christian world. . . . It is an international court, and one of its objects is to construe the law of nations; and it is the only court in the civilised world which has that object." Wentworth, as a prominent private citizen and member of the New Zealand Company who stood to profit greatly by purchasing land from Maoris to sell to settlers, predictably disagreed. At base, the debate about who controlled land in New Zealand was not a debate about what rights the Maori had; rather, as in *Johnson,* the question swirled around who stood to profit from the sale of land once native title had been extinguished. Would the government or private persons profit? Subsequent events would assure that state power ruled over private purchasers.[12]

In 1840 settlers and Maoris entered into the Treaty of Waitangi. The treaty was a cession of sovereignty from the Maoris to the British, but it was also a protection of rights to land, fisheries, forests, and other resources; the treaty made Maoris British subjects and gave the Crown the exclusive right to purchase Maori land. The provisions of the treaty have been contested ever since: What exactly was ceded? Did the Maori chiefs and the British negotiators have a similar understanding of sovereignty? Did the Maoris retain the ability to govern their internal affairs? Seven years later *R. v. Symonds*, citing *Johnson v. M'Intosh* in likely the first export of a U.S. Indian case into another country's case law, ruled that something akin to aboriginal title applied to Maori land. Like *Johnson*, *Symonds* involved no native people. It was a test case brought in order to settle the question of what rights settlers had to land purchased from natives, to determine, as in *Johnson*, who had the ultimate title to that land and all remaining land. The *Symonds* court, like the U.S. Supreme Court, ruled that the Crown had both the ultimate title and the power to extinguish native title, and, too, that land could not be purchased by settlers directly from the Maoris. An inquiry into the common law — especially the Marshall Court's decisions — legislation, and custom found no other answer.[13]

By 1850 it looked as if New Zealand would have a land rights regime similar to the one laid out by John Marshall — the system of dual ownership outlined above, that allowed only the Crown, and not settlers, the right to acquire native land. But Maoris continued to lease land to white settlers after the treaty was in force and after *Symonds* had been decided. This practice was a holdover from pre-treaty days, and Maoris and settlers saw no reason to discontinue the mutually beneficial practice. The Colonial Office and the government in New Zealand, desiring total control over land transactions, would not tolerate trade in land between natives and newcomers. More important, the government worried that if Maoris could alienate land to settlers there might not be any left for the government. As in the United States, if courts and treaties were going to uphold native land rights, then a legislative solution was necessary. Before *Symonds* two attempts had been made to outlaw the practice: the Land Claims Ordinance of 1841 and the Native Lands Purchase Act of 1846. In 1852, the Constitution Act further buttressed the Crown's prohibitions on buying or leasing land from Maoris. Then, in 1856, virtually all control over land was taken away from Maoris with the passage of the Native Reserves Act. In 1865, it became easier still to take land away from Maoris. A new Native Lands Act and a Native Lands Court designed to convert customary title to individual freeholds facilitated the process. Communally held land was converted to fee simple, individually held land that was able to be alienated — and it was alienated at an alarming rate. By the end of the 1860s, after a decade of fighting, the dispossession of Maori land was entering its final stages. A new Native Land Act passed in 1873 sped up the pace of dispossession, which by the late twentieth century resulted in Maoris' owning about 4.5 percent of New Zealand. As a final blow to Maori title, which was at least in part a response to a favorable Judicial Committee of the Privy Council decision concerning native title in 1901, the legislature passed yet another Native Lands Act in 1909. It became illegal to bring claims against the Crown based on native title, and by the time World War I broke out, *Symonds* and its protection of title had fallen into obscurity.[14]

The Marshall Court's jurisprudence was a matter of theoretical debate in New Zealand, and land rights in general were a feature of the country's political landscape right from the beginning, but Australia was a different story. There the Marshall Court scarcely affected the law of the land, and dispossession occurred through physical violence and not the structural violence of the law. Australia was considered *terra nullius* — vacant, occupied by no one, and generally free for the taking — by early historians, anthropologists, and settlers who crafted a narrative of invisibility that hardened into law by the end of the nineteenth century. For more than a century after *Cooper v. Stuart* (1889) — the Judicial Committee of the Privy Council case that determined that Australia was "practically uninhabited" — Australian law did not recognize any property rights for Aborigines. As defined in Australia, land did not have to be *actually* vacant in order to be considered terra nullius; it only had to be *legally* vacant. Forty thousand years of aboriginal occupancy notwithstanding, until the High Court decided the *Mabo* case in 1992, Australia was legally empty when white settlers first arrived.[15]

How did this come to be? Why did Australia, ruled by Britain, differ so from the United States in ignoring aboriginal occupancy? Terra nullius did not arrive in Australia with James Cook, the explorer who claimed the continent for Britain. Although Cook might have landed in Australia fully intending to secure native consent, on arrival he found that much of Australia was inhabited by hunters and gatherers, people like the Hualapais who appeared to know no property lines, tend no gardens, have no law, and live in a dispersed manner all about the countryside. Such people had no valid claims to land. Like Cyrus Thomas in the early twentieth-century United States, discoverers and settlers in late eighteenth- and early nineteenth-century Australia echoed a long line of European thinkers who considered it absurd that a small, dispersed population could claim a continent. In short, what Cook and others thought they found in Australia was a small number of technologically primitive people who did not farm, a people who by the early decades of the nineteenth century were considered to be the lowest form of humanity living in a "state of nature." And, of course, living in a state of nature meant they had not yet appropriated land as private property.

By 1822 James Stephen—who was then only a law clerk in the Colonial Office but would later become undersecretary of the colonies—could reasonably argue that the governor's power to make law in the territory was based on Australia's legal status: it "was neither acquired by conquest or cession, but by the mere occupation of a desert or uninhabited land." Two decades later Stephen could simply say: "The whole country is vacant." Despite occasional and vigorous protests to the contrary by such groups as the Aborigines Protection Society, as well as colonial policy that at times appeared to favor aboriginal land and legal rights, the notion that Australia's land was unclouded by aboriginal title—that it was terra nullius—was firmly lodged in the law by the middle of the nineteenth century. By then, all landowners in Australia had a vested interest in protecting terra nullius and thus their property rights. As one settler put it in the *South Australian Register* in 1840, "If the land is indeed [the aborigines'], the Colonists of South Australia have no title to their land, for a 'voluntary surrender' of it has never been made."[16] It would be more than a century before the law of the land would change.

In Canada, the specifics were different but the outcome was similar: the law there was just as hostile to Indian property rights as it was in Australia. The recognition of Indian title to land in British Columbia in the mid-to-late nineteenth century—as evidenced by the signing of treaties on Vancouver Island and the not infrequent references to its existence by Canadian officials, including the Ministers of the Interior and Justice—meant little when the question of aboriginal title came up in court or when making policy. Indian title meant nothing. As in Australia, a case that made its way out of Canada to the Judicial Committee of the Privy Council would define native property rights for more than a century. Like *Johnson* and *Symonds* before it, *St. Catherine's Milling v. The Queen*, decided in 1888, did not directly involve any native people. Deeming aboriginal title in Canada to be a "personal and usufructuary right" granted by the sovereign (much to the consternation and confusion of future courts), *St. Catherine's* provided a definition as similar to and as bedeviling as the one laid out in *Johnson v. M'Intosh* (except that Marshall did not suggest that Indian title was *given* to Indians; they possessed it by virtue of occupancy). Lord Watson, writing for the Judicial Committee, did not define the content of aboriginal title. But he knew that the Ojibways didn't have it and largely agreed with an Ontario lawyer who had written that "amongst the Indians of North America there was usually no more conception of private property in land than in the atmosphere or the sea."[17]

The case arose from a dispute concerning land that once had been occupied by the Ojibways. Though they continued to hunt and fish on the land, they had ceded title to their land under Treaty 3 in 1873 to the Dominion government; the government then granted St. Catherine's Milling and Lumber Company a lease to some of the land for logging. The Province of Ontario sued, saying that it was the owner of the lease. The Dominion, in defense of St. Catherine's, based its claim to the land on the proposition that the Ojibways had possessed full title to the land at the time of cession and that their title was recognized by the Royal Proclamation of 1763. The province countered that the Ojibways had a mere usufructuary right. The Supreme Court of Canada agreed with Ontario, and so did the Judicial Committee. And both, in part, relied on a misinterpretation of *Johnson v. M'Intosh,* one which suggested that Indian title was given to aboriginal people and not something they already possessed. At all levels of appeal, the trial court judge's views were upheld: the Ojibways had no legally enforceable property rights. And thus, because they never had full title, they could not grant title to the Dominion. Despite talk of taking a native title claim to court in British Columbia as a test case, nothing was done, and so, as in Australia, a case decided in the late nineteenth century remained the law of the land in Canada until the late twentieth. The former special commissioner for Indian affairs, J. A. J. Mckenna, writing in 1920 in the *Canadian Magazine,* went so far as to say, "Aboriginal title is not a claim enforcible at law."[18]

But it did not mean that native peoples in Canada were silenced. On the contrary, although the courts remained mute until the 1970s, native peoples in British Columbia, where very little land had been ceded by treaty, became increasingly vocal. Like the Hualapai and others in the United States, native peoples in British Columbia formed committees, wrote petitions, and hired attorneys. The Nisga'a, firm in their belief that they possessed title, served notice to settlers in 1910, forbidding them to come onto their land "until such time as a satisfactory settlement be made between the representatives of the crown and ourselves." That the recognition of native title was at the top of the native political agenda was not lost on provincial authorities—in 1919, the recently formed Allied Tribes of British Columbia made it abundantly clear in a sixteen-page petition to the provincial government. In 1927 the head of the Canadian Department of Indian Affairs, Duncan Scott, affirmed the half-century's agitation on the part of native peoples in British Columbia for recognition of their title. "From the year 1875 until the present time there has been a definite claim, growing in clearness as the years went by, gradually developing into an organized plan, to compel the Provincial and Dominion Governments . . . to acknowledge an Aboriginal title and to give compensation for it."[19] As the result of hearings before a special joint committee of Parliament—itself the result of political pressure brought on by the ever more powerful, organized, and growing Allied Tribes—claims based on aboriginal title were, in effect, banned across Canada between 1927 and 1951. Because of fear of land claims of native peoples in British Columbia, it became illegal for natives and lawyers to raise money for the purpose of pursuing claims against the government. With its modus vivendi taken away, the alliance disbanded; it no longer had any reason to exist.

Two major though somewhat contradictory cases—*Re Southern Rhodesia* (1919) and *Amodu Tijani v. Secretary, Southern Nigeria* (1921)—came before the Judicial Committee of the Privy Council from Britain's colonial possessions in Africa. Called the "greatest land case in British history" by the Anti-Slavery and Aborigines Protection Society and followed daily in the *Times* of London, the decision in *Re. Southern Rhodesia* was a stinging blow to native land rights. Despite years of lobbying and political pressure to secure land rights for the Matabele and the Mashona of Southern Rhodesia by such groups as the society, the Judicial Committee preferred to dodge an investigation into the nature of aboriginal title—claiming, for one thing, that World War I prevented significant research into records in South Africa. In a decision that upheld the supremacy of Crown title, the Judicial Committee of the Privy Council ruled that the Matabele and the Mashona had not lost land rights to the Crown or to the British South Africa Company. They never had any in the first place. The Judicial Committee put it succinctly: "The estimation of the rights of aboriginal tribes is always inherently difficult. Some tribes are so low in the scale of social organization that their usages and conceptions of rights and duties are not to be reconciled with the institutions or the legal ideas of civilized society." Because the Matabele and the Mashona "clearly approximate . . . to the lower rather than the higher limit" of the earth's peoples it would be a folly to accord them property rights akin to those of civilized nations.[20]

Amodu Tijani v. Secretary, Southern Nigeria was not a cause celebre in England, but it was front-page news in Nigeria. The *Tijani* case was, in its respect for native land rights, at odds with *Re Southern Rhodesia*. This time the Judicial Committee found that aboriginal land rights pre-dating the colonization of Nigeria survived the change in sovereign powers. When the Crown assumed title to land in Nigeria on annexation, it did so without disturbing the existing rights to land — an important principle that would affect future claims cases. Electing to soften some of the ethnocentrism of *Re Southern Rhodesia* and also to take native title seriously, the Judicial Committee wrote that there was "a tendency, at times unconsciously, to render . . . [native] title conceptually in terms which are appropriate only to systems which have grown up under English law. But this tendency has to be held in check closely." It cautioned future courts not to apply "abstract principles fashioned a priori," for they were of little use and potentially misleading, but, rather, to take into account each peculiar mode of native land holding.[21] The committee took its own advice, inquiring into the history and patterns of land holding in Lagos, and it found a system of communal property rights different from the English system but in the main no less valid. Amodu Tijani won his case; his land rights survived the British annexation of Lagos, and he was entitled to compensation for the land he lost.

Despite taking different paths, New Zealand, the United States, Canada, and Australia all arrived at more or less the same place by the end of the nineteenth century: property rights had become fragile or had disappeared, and dispossession had occurred on a massive scale. This was the climate in which the Hualapais found themselves in the mid-1920s. By the time their case began to gain momentum, the law had sided against them. Anyone making predictions about the Hualapai case at the time would not be faulted for predicting a loss. Indeed, in 1921 the United States Supreme Court, in *Cramer v. United States,* one of the last major Indian title cases before the Hualapai case twenty years later, appeared to confirm that wandering peoples had no property rights. *Cramer* involved a disputed grant to a railroad, and the Court said that the Indians were there first and were using the land. In contrast to the Hualapai case, *Cramer* was about three individual Indians in California and their rights to small plots of land that were settled and cultivated by Indians whose valiant attempt to adopt white ways by "abandoning their nomadic habits and attaching themselves to a definite locality, reclaiming, cultivating and improving the soil and establishing fixed homes thereon[,] was in harmony with the well understood desire of the Government." *Cramer* made it clear that if Indians could prove that they had occupied a tract of land in accordance with the settled government policy of turning Indians away from nomadism and toward farming, then they had a claim. In fact, to do otherwise, "to hold that by so doing they acquired no possessory rights to which the Government would accord protection, would be contrary to the whole spirit of the traditional American policy toward these dependent wards of the nation."[22]

The Court clearly was not talking about the Hualapais; if the *Cramer* standard became a test for occupancy rights, the Hualapais would fail. The Court said further that possessions must be "definite and substantial in character and open to observation."[23] This made Hualapai land use uncertain. It was surely "definite," but was it "substantial" or "open to observation"?

Jurists and theorists had been thinking about Indians and their property rights since first contact. But by the twentieth century, with a few notable exceptions, legal scholarship concerning Indians was virtually nonexistent. The thinking about Indian property rights had hardened, more or less, into several different variations on the same theme: Indians had few land rights. In 1909 Isaac Franklin Russell, writing in the *Yale Law Journal,* opined on occupancy rights, Indian title, cultural evolution, and treaties and wrote that "the feudal law of property, when applied to the holdings and bargains of the natives, showed the Indian to be without title to real estate. No deed of record or written testament showed ownership in the actual occupant; and a convenient rule was developed that no instrument of conveyance from an individual Indian could give a valid title to a purchaser. What knew this simple son of the forest of fee simple? . . . As a rule, tribal Indians in reservations occupy the land at the will of the government."[24]

Like others, Russell latched onto the notion of population. Thinking that the number of natives in the area occupied by the United States "in historic times" had likely been only three hundred thousand, Russell gave little credence to Indian property rights. And now, he wrote, Indians were "soured on the civilization of the white man." Tired of seeing their "happy hunting grounds" taken over by whites, and "quickly contract[ing] the vices of civilization," Indians were "undergoing a process of self-extermination." There had never been many to begin with, and now, in the face of white encroachment, Indians had given up, deciding it was best to pass from this world. If one viewed property rights from Russell's perspective it was indeed "convenient" — as he put it — that a system of relieving Indians of their land had been put in place. The system was working well: the most recent report of the commissioner of Indians affairs showed that "progress is still being made in disposing of the clouds that hang over many of the titles to Indian lands."[25]

Some commentators believed that benevolence was at the heart of Indian policy and likely would have agreed with Grant Foreman when he professed in 1913 that "the attitude of our Supreme Court toward the Indian should bring a glow of pride to the cheek of every lover of justice and fair play." But benevolence had many measures. Clinton R. Flynn, another in the small group of legal writers who took up the subject, cautioned those who might argue that U.S. law and policy could have handled the Indian problem more justly by saying that at least we had not killed them all.[26]

Based in part on her belief that the Indian population never amounted to more than a few hundred thousand, Flora Warren Seymour held the common view that Indians had occupancy rights to their land solely at the sufferance of the sovereign, the United States. As the Hualapai case picked up momentum in the 1920s, Seymour, like many, believed in cultural and social evolution. She lamented that the "attitude toward land ownership which long centuries had bred into our race was still lacking in the Indian." With time this was likely to change, she thought. But in the 1920s the idea of letting Indians have title to their land went against almost one hundred years of Supreme Court opinion and Indian policy — or, so Seymour said.[27]

As the Hualapais' troubles began, legal scholars began to investigate anew questions concerning native peoples and the law. Two major treatises concerning this subject appeared. Alpheus Snow's *The Question of Aborigines in the Law and Practice of Nations,* first published in 1919, would have provided little encouragement for the Hualapais. Snow painted a grim picture, for he believed that colonial law had been developed for the twin purposes of "fitting the aborigines for civilization, and opening the resources of the land to the use of the civilized world." Contact, especially in South Africa and Australia, was reduced to a pitched battle for land, in which "economic competition tends to lead to war between colonists and aborigines, which invariably results in the more or less complete extinction of the aborigines." For the few left alive, reserves were set aside that were as large or small as the "embittered feelings of the colonists will allow." The native population, reduced to a fraction of its original strength, was herded onto vacant tracts of land and thus the problem was solved. Generally speaking, hunting and gathering peoples such as the Hualapais and many aborigines in Australia and native people in South Africa, had it worst of all. They were exterminated.[28]

More nuanced and better versed in the vicissitudes of American law was M. F. Lindley's *The Acquisition and Government of Backward Territory in International Law.*[29] Backward territory was, of course, occupied generally by backward people, and Lindley's massive book was written as a guide for those who needed to know how to legally acquire title to and govern the land they claimed. But it was also a history. Lindley's global survey of the literature about occupation, conquest, and discovery, as well as his examination of case law, encompassed the entire history of European expansion from uninhabited lands to those occupied by nomads, pastoralists, or farmers.

Lindley began by discussing the work of jurists, theologians, and philosophers who had taken up the question of aboriginal property rights. Whereas Seymour and Russell, as well as BIA officials and attorneys, suggested a longstanding consensus on Indian property rights, Lindley demonstrated controversy. He classified commentators who ranged across a historical spectrum from the fifteenth century to the twentieth. Commentators in Class I, which included the famed Spanish missionary Bartolome de las Casas and the less well known Spanish philosopher and theologian Francisco de Vitoria, generally thought that aborigines had a right to the land they inhabited, a right, according to Lindley, "which is good against more highly civilized peoples." Class II offered a more restrictive view of native rights to land: Indians had title, but it was conditional. Included in this class was Emeric de Vattel, the influential mid-eighteenth-century jurist who believed that land not being cultivated or put to efficient use by aborigines was fair game for settlers. Vattel's opinion had held sway in the United States. Indian landholdings, extensive but underutilized, were reduced in the face of greater potential need by settlers, who would farm, not roam as the Indians did. Reservations, set aside for Indians' exclusive use, were carved out of the leftovers.[30] Commentators in Class III accorded no property rights to aborigines when opposed to civilized nations. People without a recognized form of governance — nomads, hunters, pastoralists — were seen as having no rights to the land they occupied.

What is more, peoples who had not attained civilization were not recognized by international law. John Westlake perhaps summed up this group's position best when he wrote in 1894 that the "inflow of the white race cannot be stopped where there is land to cultivate, ore to be mined, commerce to be developed, sport to enjoy, curiosity to be satisfied." Characterized by commentators such as Westlake, David Dudley Field, and T. J. Lawrence — all writing between 1876 and 1923 — the opinions of the so-called legal positivists were closest to those of E. C. Finney, Seth Richardson, and G. A. Iverson, who were lawyers in the Hualapai case. The positivists held that all authority in international law stemmed from the state; nonstate entities — tribes, indigenous confederacies, and the like — could not be sources of law and were bound to adhere to the dictates of the state. In general, Lindley argued that the views expressed by the positivists, though of a more recent origin, were at once gaining influence and being contested; as more restrictive legal regimes ascended, so, too, did protest increase. Lindley believed in the protection of native rights to land because indigenous people possessed property rights that colonizers were bound to respect. He did not share the positivists' creed that any rights that indigenous people might have came only from the sovereign. Lindley took from international law the two key principles that land sufficient for subsistence must be reserved and that compensation must be paid when land is taken.[31]

One of the most difficult problems, as Lindley noted, was the chasm between theory and reality: the courts may recognize the theoretical rights of Indians, but real people needed to enforce them. Chauncey Goodrich, a California attorney and member of the Indian Defense Association of Central and Northern California, who shared Lindley's frustration with the administration of the rule of law, observed in the *California Law Review* in 1926 that "as noble declarations of a standard of conduct, these decisions [in favor of Indian rights] are convincing. . . . But any attempt to clarify the status of the Indian must be abortive that does not frankly recognize that the status thus described by the courts is largely ideal and fictitious, no more, indeed, than a counsel of perfection, seldom in fact approached."[32] Goodrich's sobering analysis — that decision by the courts were well and good, but without a base of support on the ground they could be rendered largely meaningless — was especially apt at a time when Indians had so little political power.

Goodrich and Lindley offered rare examples of serious scholarship concerning Indian law. And though their company was small, they were not alone. Joining them from amid the struggle over Indian claims in California was the Washington, D.C., attorney and chief counsel for the California-based Indian Board of Cooperation Jennings C. Wise. Before he wrote his 1931 classic *The Red Man in the New World Drama: A Politico-Legal History with a Pageantry of American Indian History,* Wise crafted one of the most thorough defenses of Indian title offered up to that time. Beginning with a series of articles in the *California Indian Herald* published in the spring and summer of 1924, Wise mounted an assault on the notion that Indians were without property rights. Recognizing that the "courts have been greatly puzzled by the problem of Indian title and estates since these questions were first presented," he hoped to clear things up.[33]

Like some before him and many after, Wise found that Indian rights were both trampled and upheld with baffling inconsistency. Lamenting that one branch of government often had no idea what another was doing and that most in power "know nothing of Indian litigation," Wise recognized that the government's master was expediency. At the same moment when the Justice Department might be fighting Indians, the Interior Department could be found defending them. His description fit the Hualapai case like a glove: "The Indians are left to the mercy of subordinates who are naturally more bent on winning their cases than they are in seeing that justice is done by the United States to the Indians." As a result, Indians "have learned by a century and a half of sorrowful experience that their rights are deemed by the Government to be more or less on a parity with those of the buffalo — to be ignored when they stood in the way of the Government notwithstanding the declarations of Congress and the courts." As if predicting the Hualapais' inability to get good legal representation, Wise indicted the government for its dismal record of defending Indians, a "people who require the best possible legal advice and representation in a contest with the Government that is inherently unequal." Indians, he continued, "are denied that aid. Instead of deterring their exploitation, the prevailing system tends to promote it."[34]

In the 1920s the pro-Indian bar consisted of lawyers such as Wise, Lindley, Goodrich, and the odd attorney here and there who represented tribal claims. If asked whether the Hualapai had any chance of winning control of their land, most would likely have said no. Although the Hualapais' title might be protected in theory — protection based on occupancy embedded in Marshall court decisions of the early nineteenth century that had not yet been excavated — they would be hard pressed to find a good lawyer to argue their case. Few knew the law, and most had no interest in Indians. And the lawyers who were involved in their case, John Gung'l, Ethelbert Ward and G.A. Iverson and still others to come, worked against the tribe's interests. If the tribe's land was to be protected, a radical rethinking of the law was necessary.

9

Saving Hualapai Land

In the fall of 1931 tensions were high on the reservation. Any optimism generated by the spring hearings had vanished. The unsettled land dispute wreaked havoc, and the Hualapais' distrust of the government grew. Not only was there bad news from Washington, but Fred Mahone worried that violence might break out at home. The Hualapais and Superintendent D. H. Wattson were engaged in a war of words over Hualapai livestock on the eastern portion of the reservation, and Mahone warned that it threatened to turn ugly. In what he claimed was simply a range restoration effort, Wattson attempted to move the Hualapai herd from the few sections it occupied in the east to the reservation's center. He was quickly thwarted by Mahone and "several of the ignorant old men [who were] on his side." Accusing Wattson of trying to rid the east of the Hualapais and their cattle, Mahone thought the plan was actually a ploy to buttress the government's position that no Indians lived on or used that portion of the reservation. His fears might have been well-founded: Wattson was one of many who believed that the Hualapais' absence from the east was justification enough for ceding the land to the railroad. And Wattson did not like Mahone. He called his complaints and concerns those of an "inveterate troublemaker" and warned that the Indian Office could expect constant trouble from Mahone as long as he and the IRA were in league. He had had it with Mahone: "If we are ever to be free from dissension and from the petty annoyances of such men as Mahone we must do one of two things; give them entire control of their cattle or assume absolute control ourselves, allowing the Indians no voice in their affairs."[1]

In blaming the unrest on Mahone and claiming that he did not speak for the rest of the Hualapai cattlemen, Wattson had misread the situation. True enough, Mahone did not speak for everyone. But other Hualapais were unhappy with Wattson, too. Kate Crozier did not think there was a conspiracy; he simply thought he was being robbed. He accused Wattson and the cattle agent of selling the tribe's cattle at a price far below market value. The rival cattlemen's association, the Wallapai Livestock Protective Association, did not like Wattson or his cattle manager, either, and were suspicious of their actions. The feeling was mutual: Wattson had complained about the association. He was unhappy with the influence that a Mojave—who could it be but Homer Davidson?—had over the group and claimed that the Mojave man "work[ed] with the chief and headmen and is constantly agitating resistance to the plans of the office." It was not one individual Indian troublemaker that objected to Wattson; it was the entire cattle interest on the reservation. Blaming Mahone, however, allowed Wattson to downplay the sense of dissatisfaction and threat of possible unrest on the reservation. The simmering anger among the Hualapais and Mahone's constant agitation were getting to him. The Hualapais whom Herbert Hagerman had characterized as "old men, idlers, and agitators" a year earlier simply would not brook any more intrusion into matters concerning their land.[2]

If the spring and summer had been marked by optimism and eager anticipation, then the fall of 1931 was a season of diminished hopes for the Hualapais. Brosius had been realistic and had warned Mahone not to have much faith in the Interior Department's interest in protecting their reservation. And now the "legal officials" were doing their part to write the Hualapais out of their land. But despite two legal opinions recommending that thoughts of a suit be forgotten, the Senate subcommittee remained interested, and word was now afoot in Washington that Lynn Frazier might take up the tribe's case. In confidence, and with some trepidation, Brosius let Mahone know there might still be hope. After all the bad news, he must have been elated. But, too, Mahone had to be weary after more than a decade of watching the BIA, and the Interior Department, and the Justice Department—at their whim, it must have seemed—change their minds again and again and again. Weary or not, he pushed on, collecting more signatures. Choosing to bypass his state senators, likely agreeing with Brosius's sentiment that Hayden was a "great stumbling block in the Walapai case," he passed on to the subcommittee another petition, this one from the citizens of Yavapai County.[3]

Tensions on the reservation brought into relief the frustration and anger the unsettled land dispute injected into daily life, but there was still hope. It seemed as though Mahone's years of letter and petition writing, badgering, and history collecting might finally pay off.

It might have seemed that the hearings at Valentine the previous year had been forgotten. In the intervening time the opinions of the Interior and Justice Departments, the intransigence of Hagerman and Hayden, and the impotence of the Indian Service surely made any progress made at Valentine seem fleeting. But early in the new year, Lynn Frazier requested a review of all the material gathered up to that time in the Hualapai matter. And then, in the summer of 1932, the Senate Subcommittee on Indian Affairs, after reviewing the evidence, put a temporary stop to the consolidation lest the "rights of the Walapai Indians . . . be forever foreclosed." Frazier requested that the consolidation be stopped while the subcommittee pursued two lines of investigation. First, it needed "all the facts pertaining to the Walapai Indian title and occupancy as it existed prior to" the railroad grant and the map of definite location, and, second, it wanted to know whether there was any voluntary cession by the Hualapais of any of their Indian title. Once Interior had concluded its investigation it was to submit its findings to the subcommittee.[4] Maybe something had come from the hearings after all.

John Collier, the future commissioner of Indian affairs, was by the early 1930s the single most important and prominent "friend of the Indian." He whirred into high gear in the summer of 1932. As he crisscrossed the country in his capacity as director of the American Indian Defense Association (AIDA), Collier agitated on behalf of the Hualapais. Not even a serious car accident in June diminished his interest; he simply wrote from his hospital bed. The AIDA, largely Collier's one-man operation, had for the past decade been in the vanguard of Indian policy reform. At the forefront of the battle for Indian land and legal rights since the mid-1920s, Collier now turned his considerable energy to the Hualapai case. He aimed straight for the Hagerman plan.[5]

"Shall the Hagerman Agreement Divesting the Walapai Tribe of Arizona Be Confirmed?" was classic Collier — intemperate, impolitic, shrill, and a withering critique of government policy. In this eleven-page analysis of the case Collier rightly noted that the courts had never had a chance to rule on the question of title. He put the matter bluntly: "Shall the courts be allowed to settle whether the Indians or the Santa Fe Railway own the contested properties, or shall the Interior Department, substituting itself for a court, settle the question adversely to the Indians?" He contended that the Hualapais' possessory, or occupancy, rights had never been extinguished. He was outraged by the Finney and Richardson opinions, which he carefully picked apart. After his own examination of the facts, which he gleaned from the report that William Light had written in 1928, Collier said that Finney's and Richardson's work "exhibit[s] historical misunderstanding *of a most peculiar kind.*" Based on his reading of the history, Collier thought that proceeding with the Hagerman deal would be a "sinister act."[6] And although history surely established the Hualapais' claim, Collier knew that this was largely a legal question and should be left to the courts. His faith in the courts—in particular, the Supreme Court—far overshadowed any hope he placed in the political process. Going to court was the only way to air the historical evidence that until that time had been manipulated to serve the railroad's, Hagerman's, and the government's purposes—if one could, in fact, tease them apart.

Because Collier and Hagerman operated within the very small world of Indian politics in the early 1930s it was only a matter of time before Hagerman learned of Collier's defense of the Hualapais—and Collier's critique gnawed at him. Mocking Collier, and mocking Indian claims, Hagerman sarcastically suggested that Collier wanted to rid Arizona of non-Indians. Hagerman thundered that the Hopis thought they owned Arizona as far west as the Colorado River. And, in light of that ridiculous claim, the Papagos (now the Tohono O'odhams) surely had a better claim to Arizona than did the Hualapais. In the world that Collier envisioned, when the whites were finally gone, the Indians would adjudicate their respective claims. "It may prove best perhaps, after having ousted the whites, to let the Indians fight it out amongst themselves," Hagerman wrote. "That will give them the opportunity which their friends have for so long been seeking for them, namely, to revert unrestrainedly to their grand, glad, aboriginal instincts, and, at the same time, perhaps, it may be a solution to this very vexing Indian problem."[7]

Hagerman's outburst was born of frustration. The Hualapai claim was not going away. The agreement that he and the railroad had reached more than two years earlier still languished. Resistance to it only mounted. Sharing his frustration but not necessarily endorsing Hagerman's extreme solution, Commissioner Rhoads drew a line between the two of them and more radical friends of the Indian such as John Collier.[8]

And Collier continued his attack in another dispatch from the AIDA. He now accused Finney and Richardson of "willful suppression of factual material of controlling importance." The two opinions, on which Interior and the BIA had based their decision to abandon the case, distorted the record in order to argue that the Hualapai had lost title to their land. Their "mythical recital of facts," according to Collier, was entirely wrong, and it led them to give up prosecution of the case. Finney and Richardson got swept up in the tide that was about to wash away the Hualapais' land rights, unable to resist. Hagerman had the Indian Office and Interior wrapped around his finger; Rhoads and Interior Secretary Work withered under his "hypnotic sway."[9]

Collier had crafted a trenchant critique. With considerable precision he exposed the structure of the anti-Hualapai position. A warped view of the tribe's past and a malleable jurisprudence added up to the Hualapais' loss of half of their land. "Within this framework of events already completed, of policies already adopted, and of the Indian Bureau's determination to fulfill the Hagerman compact with the Santa Fe Railway, the two attorneys may inevitably have found themselves practically driven to render the opinions which they did render and to become, as they did become, special pleaders against Indian rights and distorters of historical fact." Finney and Richardson operated within a bureaucracy that was pitted against Indians, lamented Collier. What's more, he claimed, because the Sante Fe was "an exceedingly powerful corporation," the Indian Service often buckled under its pressure where Indians were concerned.[10] Collier's involvement was good for the Hualapais but bad for Hagerman and the ATSF.

The spring of 1932 was a hopeful time. Perhaps buoyed by the news that consolidation had been put on hold, and definitely impressed by the Collier memos, Fred Mahone was happy to have so much support. Pleased that Collier had laid out a careful and clear summary of their case, the Hualapais extended their "highest appreciation and thanks to you the American Indian Defense Association, and our kind friends the Indian Rights Association." Because the Indian Office "is fighting us hard," Mahone lamented, the help the two organizations gave to the Hualapai was much needed. Collier and Samuel Brosius of the IRA assured them that, at least temporarily, the consolidation would not go through, and they worked hard to see that the Hualapais' interests were kept at the fore of Indian politics in Washington. And though Collier may have had his finger on the pulse of Indian politics, he was unaware of Hualapai activism; he called them a "peculiarly voiceless tribe." Mahone, for his part, kept superintendent Wattson wondering whether the Hualapais would ever accept consolidation. They retained a lawyer in the spring of 1932.[11]

But thinking in new ways about the Indian past would take time. In 1932 Commissioner Rhoads sat in the July heat and listened patiently as the Hualapais tried hard to convince him that because of their deep ties to the land, he should not cut their reservation in half. History, they made clear to Rhoads, was the tribe's only defense. "Our country," said elder Jim Smith, "is bounded by the countries of the other tribes." Those ancient boundary lines and proof of Hualapai occupancy rested in the memories of the Hualapais and all the other tribes of the greater Colorado River region. He and the other elders needed no map or reservation boundary line to tell them where their country began and ended. "Imaginary lines" marked their territory. The tribes in all four cardinal directions—the Mojaves to the west, the Yumas, the Yavapais, and the Apaches to the south, the Havasupais to the east, and the Utes to the north—had these mental maps. They all knew their own territories, and they all knew, as Jim Smith said, that the Hualapais "did not come from any other place." They had always been there.[12] But now they needed to prove it. They had to show that since the creation of the reservation, according to Butch Clark, Hualapai country had shrunk to only a third of its original size. And now it was slated to be diminished further still, this time by half.

The Pine Springs country was the sticking point. Hualapais, of course, challenged the government's belief that no one had ever lived there—Mahone's interviews and photographs provided evidence. Indian Honga, for one, said that his presence was proof enough. "A lot of people claim no Indians ever lived there. I stand here to give proof that there were Indians there," Honga declared. When the army came to round up the Hualapais and take them to the lower Colorado his parents hid; Honga's family had been in the Pine Springs area ever since. He claimed that the ruins of cliff dwelling proved it. Huya echoed Honga: "We never left this country." Annie Beecher said she had lived in the Pine Springs country all her life. The bands living at Peach Springs and Pine Springs retreated below the rim of the Grand Canyon when the soldiers came to take them in 1874, and a year later "they came out again," she said. She confirmed that there were ruins that showed Hualapai occupation, evidence in the form of utensils and cooking pots of lives lived in the Pine Springs country.[13]

It was not only the Pine Springs country to the east that was in dispute. Kate Crozier, an elderly Hualapai and former scout, claimed Clay Springs as part of the reservation. When the military first consulted the tribe about reservation boundaries Crozier said that Clay Springs, far to the west of Peach Springs but just outside the boundary line, was to be included. Charley Spencer and General Crook marked off the territory with cairns, some of which still kept a lonely watch over the western boundary. All the Hualapais' water sources were included in the reservation, Crozier averred, and Clay Springs was one of them.[14]

If Hualapai memories were not enough, one could turn again to the testimony of whites. Proof of Hualapai occupancy was also firmly lodged in the mind of Ida Crozier, the wife of the settler Sam Crozier. "We considered that they owned the country," she said. "The Wallapai Indians have always claimed the land which is now in the Wallapai Reservation, there was always a large number of Indians living around Pine Springs Country. No other tribe of Indians claimed the lands that are now in the Wallapai Reservation. . . . All the other tribes recognized this land in the present Wallapai Reservation as belonging to the Wallapais." She had heard that when the army came for the Hualapais in 1874, the year before she arrived, many had stayed, hiding out in the canyons that cut away toward the Colorado. She was right. John Smith, Mike Sue, and Jim Smith all remembered heading to Havasupai country when the army came, going down into the canyon with dozens of their fellow band members and staying with their neighbors for about a year.[15]

Rhoads sat and listened to the Hualapais; he knew about all the whites' testimony. And when the Hualapais were done Rhoads agreed with them, saying, "Our only chance is to prove what you have been telling me today — that you and your ancestors occupied this land for generations before the Railroad got that grant." History was the answer. Had the Hualapai finally found an advocate? Not yet, for Rhoads was forced to admit that it was "not a very strong case for us or for you." The shallow conceptions of Indian history that Rhoads and others possessed would not be cast off overnight. And listening to Indian versions of the past was something he would not do. Hualapai testimony, he told Brosius, had "no weight whatever." His meeting with the Hualapais made no impact. According to Brosius, Rhoads ridiculed the Hualapais' claim.[16]

Rhoads's view of Hualapai history, however, was not shared by all. He might not have been persuaded by Hualapais' stories of the past, but Matthew Sniffen of the Indian Rights Association was. Because of increased IRA interest and at the urging of Samuel Brosius, the IRA dispatched Sniffen to the Hualapai reservation for the third time in as many years. Brosius needed someone on the ground to get the facts by interviewing Indians and settlers. "There are now so many angles to the Walapai case," Brosius wrote, "that it is difficult to write them down definitely." Because the Finney and Richardson opinions had been written without the benefit of facts, Brosius urged Sniffen to arm himself with the tribe's history. It was the Hualapais' best chance for a strong defense — after all, wrote Brosius, a final decision in the case would "revolve around the ancient residence of the tribe." He urged Sniffen to remember that the tribe did not want money: "it is the land that the Walapais want." Encouraged by the hold that Frazier had put on the consolidation, Brosius now hoped that the tribe's land rights could be thoroughly investigated. But he added something that had the potential to spin the case off in a new direction: Sniffen must impress on the Hualapais the fact that they "should make no admission that they accepted the present reservation in [fulfillment] of any claim that they might have to all the country they might have claimed prior to March 12, 1872."[17] It was possible that their entire "ancient habitation," of which the reservation was but a part, could be claimed.

Brosius knew whom Sniffen had to contact: Fred Mahone. Writing Mahone in June, Brosius asked him to collect more stories from older Hualapais who could remember life before the coming of the railroad, for "no doubt your elder members have a well-defined history of your tribal claim in that matter." The eastern portion of the reservation, of course, was a big concern, and the Hualapais' claim needed to be shored up. In addition, Brosius wanted to make sure other tribes did not share the east with the Hualapais. This was critical. If the Hualapais did not use the land exclusively and if there were not recognizable boundaries — property lines, in effect — then they would have a problem. It needed to be clear that other tribes respected their claims. The Havasupais posed the biggest threat, but Brosius thought there was evidence of a distant connection between the two tribes.[18]

Mahone was happy to comply, fairly leaping at the chance. But it would take time. Because the reservation was so big and because so many Hualapais lived in towns that were off the reservation — Kingman, Seligman, Prescott, Valentine, Hackberry — Mahone could not gather them immediately. Moreover, it was also the height of summer, and as they did each summer in those days, most Hualapais had already left for the Navajo and Hopi country, as well as Flagstaff, for Fourth of July trading and celebration. Mahone lamented to Brosius, "It is bad to say that July holidays delayed us in the matter of action," but he was certain that when everyone returned he would "hear from us those exact stories from older men of the Wallapais of their ancients home countries."[19]

Mahone assured Brosius that they and they alone used the east. As soon as he could arrange it,

> the whole subjects of these Historical facts shall be formed in plain language and attach with a sketch map showing districts of which the individual group of wallapais had posseessed land and water by ancient posseessory right. I will also show the line, for instance a line between Mohave-Apaches and Wallapais. . . . My grand parent with others as a South eastern (group) Wallapai Indian constantly fought against the Mohave apache and the Apache Tontos, Each bands on either side of their possessory boundary line had fought against each others to hold possession of their own Tribal's possessory right of Territories. Our Wallapai's ancients land was about three times larger then the present granted reserve to the Wallapai Indians.

He further claimed that "once the Wallapais were noted warriors, was never been defeated by these tribe enimies which surrounded their ancients home country." Along with Hualapai stories, Mahone said, he had Apache (but he likely meant Yavapai) and Mojave testimony to prove it. They had not discussed this at the Valentine hearings because their white advisors had told them not to; the reservation case was big enough, and adding the "ancestral occupancy case to the present reservation case means two big things."[20]

Sniffen left Washington and headed to Hualapai country in July, his visit briefly overlapping with Rhoads's. Later in the month, Sniffen returned alone and talked at length with older Hualapais, hoping to strengthen their claims. He traveled the reservation and saw evidence of long-term use everywhere. In addition, interviews with Hualapai elders and white pioneers convinced him that the entire area claimed by the tribe had always been theirs. Anson Smith, publisher and editor of the *Mohave County Miner,* published continuously since 1882, was representative. He told Sniffen that Hualapais had always used the Pine Springs country, and because "water was everything," they must have also taken advantage of the springs. Others agreed. Sniffen also learned that Hualapais had been buried in the Pine Springs region for many years and that members of what he thought of as the Pine Springs band still wanted to be buried there. To him, these were sure signs of long-term occupancy in that section. What's more, if the Hualapais had not been using the eastern portion of the reservation at the time the army drew the original boundaries, why would it have been included? From the Hualapais he also heard about what he called Medda Wittica (Madwida) Canyon, the place where, the Hualapai say, all Indian people came from before dispersing across the continent.[21] To Sniffen there was no doubt that the tribe had been there since time immemorial. It only had to prove it to others.

Mahone was pleased with the visit. Proud that their command of their history was such that Sniffen was "naturally convinced that us Walapais must regain and hold our ancestral possessory Rights," the Hualapais now began to speak less about their service as scouts and more about their rights as the original occupants of their homeland. Though they had no written history, no proof on paper of their lives, Sniffen was astute enough to realize that, in Mahone's words, the "aged Walapais and the Pioneers official statements may be are the two important factors to support our present Walapais case." After his five-day visit, Sniffen, according to Mahone, "declared The Walapai Tribe should have the entire area of our Reservation by Rights of our ancient occupation." Especially important was his tour of Hualapai country, where,

Mahone reported, Sniffen was shown "pre-historic sites which sites were generated by those ancients Walapais."[22]

Their confidence buoyed by the IRA's interest in the case and the Senate's delay of the consolidation, the Hualapais now retained their own lawyers—the Kingman firm of Smith/Faulkner. In November 1932, Fred Mahone and Kate Crozier, acting as representatives of the tribe, drew up an agreement giving J. H. Smith power of attorney. One-hundred and seventy-nine Hualapais either signed or thumbmarked the agreement—a significant percentage of the adults in the tribe and a sure sign of the growing support on the reservation for their claim.[23] The Hongas and the Beechers from Pine Springs were there, as was Mahone's wife Nellie, his brother Dewey, and his uncle Jim; Mack Tokespeta, the Havatones, and the Schrums signed on; Dan and Maggie Mapatis pressed their thumbprints onto the agreement, as did Butch Clark and the Susanyatames, among dozens and dozens of others. Almost every family was represented. Mahone and Crozier got people from as far as Kingman and close as Peach Springs to sign their agreement. Only Jim Fielding's name was absent.

The land dispute was not over, but the tide was beginning to turn in their favor. The Indian Rights Association and John Collier's American Indian Defense Association were firmly on their side, the consolidation was on hold, and Herbert Hagerman and Charles Rhoads would soon be out of their jobs.

With the election of Franklin Delano Roosevelt and the subsequent appointments of John Collier and Harold Ickes, as, respectively, commissioner of Indian affairs and secretary of the interior, a sea change in Indian policy got under way. To be sure, a current of reform had pulsed through the 1920s, but it had been erratic. Although Collier had been the single most important force in the 1920s, he was not very effective. No one was. Pro-Indian activists were scattered about the country and for the most part worked in the private sector. Indians needed friends in the government, and until they got them little would change.

The hallmark of the "Indian New Deal" was the Indian Reorganization Act (IRA), which, after a lengthy gestation, became law on 18 June 1934. The legal scholar Ray Brown—the author of the law section of the *Problem of Indian Administration*—declared at the time that the law marked "a revolutionary change in the principle and method of treating the native Indian population by the federal government of the United States." As originally drafted in late 1933 and early 1934, the IRA was a large and rather unwieldy piece of legislation. The bill lost considerable weight after enduring a rigorous workout in the winter and spring of 1934. At several regional Indian congresses, and in the U.S. Congress, the bill came under attack from Indians and members of Congress who were suspicious of its aims. Taking a keen interest in the new administration, Mahone attended the two-day congress in Phoenix in March to see for himself what all the fuss was about. Some tribes had a direct impact on the final shape of the bill. When delegates at the Rapid City, South Dakota, congress, including the Oglala Tribal Council, made it clear that they would withdraw their support if the bill effected tribal claims, or if it compelled individual members to cede their allotments to the chartered community the drafters of the bill listened and changed the bill accordingly.[24] As a result of congressional concerns, the provision for a new federal court of Indian claims, for instance, did not make it into the final bill, and, as a result of Indians' worries, tribes were given greater latitude in deciding whether to accept the IRA.

Depending on one's perspective, the IRA was aimed at restoring or creating Indian self-government. Intended to improve the lot of Indians, the IRA — and the Indian New Deal generally — also symbolized the paternalistic attitude of most people in government when it came to Indians. In the broadest terms, perhaps one of Roosevelt's first public statements in favor of bill is most representative. Pitched to all the American people, not simply the legislators charged with passing or rejecting the bill, Roosevelt's statement suggests, at once, the guilt and the pride Americans feel with regard to Indians — guilt for all the wrongs done, pride in having the wisdom and kindness to make up for them. "This administration is working out a new deal for the original forgotten men of America — The Indians. We cannot undo all the wrongs that have been done to these original possessors of the continent, through generations of mismanagement, error, and repression. But we do propose to do all that can now be done to atone for those wrongs. It is an obligation of honor and duty of a powerful nation toward a simple people living among us and dependent on our wise protection."[25]

Platitudes from the president aside, real change was under way. But though the treatment of the Hualapais' land claim was emblematic of the new climate in Indian affairs, it demonstrates just as well the persistent residue of an earlier time. John Collier and his allies made up only part of the federal bureaucracy. The behavior of Justice Department lawyers, such politicians as Arizona's Carl Hayden, and the federal courts would make it very hard to notice any evidence of an Indian New Deal.

The sea change in Washington, especially Collier's vigorous attack on the hated Hagerman plan, pleased Mahone. Although Hagerman's deal was still the most likely option for the tribe, his most bitter enemy was now in power.

And to help matters, the new superintendent, Guy Hobgood, thought that consolidation was a bad idea. He agreed with the Hualapais: the best farm and grazing lands were those in the east, the very land the railroad claimed. With change under way it might be an auspicious time to act. Writing to the attorney general in early 1933 as president of the Walapai Tribal Association, Kate Crozier, an old man now, said, "We the Walapais are yet long, long wanting to give you a Faithful proofs direct from us Tribe in Verbals the cause which anciently made us tribe to possess this land and water." They did not have their history in writing, but if given the chance they could recite it. He continued, "I beg to request the Honorable Attorney General: Are you going to stand by us Walapai Indian Tribe to protect our reservation?" Knowing that they needed to act fast while the hold on the consolidation was still in effect and while the Senate subcommittee investigated their claims, Kate Crozier called a May meeting of the Walapai Tribal Association to discuss what to do next. The majority agreed to have Mahone promptly get in touch with the Commissioner of Indian Affairs John Collier.[26]

Mahone wrote to Collier later that day, making it clear, again, that the Hualapais felt that their rightful claim to the land was based on "Historical Possessory Rights which lies within the Heart of our Reservation area." From east to west and north to south, ruins scattered across the reservation proved their longtime occupancy: "These points of ruins or Historical Sites are the Walapais ancient homes." Included in these areas were Pine Springs and other places in the eastern portion of the reservation. This being the best land, the tribe wanted all cattle leases cancelled. Because many Hualapais wanted to build ranches in the Pine Springs country during the coming summer, Mahone urged Collier to formulate a plan immediately that would allow them to start ranching. Because of his "earnest experience, and earnest sincere effort," Collier could make this happen, but only if the Hagerman plan and consolidation, which, Mahone said, would "consume the last chunck of our original prehistorical lands," were abandoned.[27]

Collier radically altered the BIA's position with regard to the case. Under his care, any semblance of a conciliatory attitude toward the railroad vanished. After taking a look at the case, the new BIA shifted gears. Deciding that the Atchison, Topeka, and Santa Fe's occupation of the Hualapai reservation was illegal, Collier asked that the consent decree signed two summers earlier be set aside, and he wanted the railroad to hand over the deed to Clay Springs. Not sure of the legality of his plan, Collier requested that the new solicitor of the Department of the Interior, Nathan Margold, render an opinion. And when he did, a year later, everything would change. For the first time, forces within the Indian Service were lining up in the Hualapais' corner. Collier was so confident that the land was and would be theirs that he told Guy Hobgood that when making "plans for the development of the Hualapai Indians and their Reservation you may assume that the entire Reservation is Indian land."[28]

Since it appeared that the Hualapai might hold on to the reservation, Mahone decided it was time to tell the new commissioner about his development plans. He had been working on plans for a tourist operation for several years. Pressing his scheme on Collier in early 1934, Mahone asked for his blessing and assistance and again reminded the BIA that the Hualapais had faithfully served the government as scouts against the "Apache Indian Nation." Mahone had perfected his plea: "We are poor people, very poor, so all we can give to our country is our lives and this we have always done." In case loyalty was not enough he turned to economics, saying that because "our land question has never been settled favorable to the Indians, . . . we must look to other sources for livelihood." Mahone looked to Indian tourism. Telling Collier that the cattle business was failing and reminding him that the Hualapais were forced to pay for water from Peach Springs — water that was rightfully theirs — Mahone hoped that Collier would see that they needed the money.[29]

Beginning around 1930 Mahone struck up a four-year correspondence with A. P. Miller, a photographer and ATSF employee from Needles, California. Miller was an old friend of Jim Mahone and Jim Fielding and was allowed by the tribe to photograph a variety of events on the reservation, including, eventually, Fielding's funeral in 1936. Miller also had a keen interest in documenting the lives of the last of the Hualapai scouts. He wrote down the life stories of Fielding and of Jim Mahone, and the images he made in the early 1930s of the surviving scouts are now iconic — portraits painted after his photos hang prominently in the Peach Springs school. And because he worried that as old Hualapais passed away the tribe's history would go with them, he urged Fred Mahone to take down the oral accounts of Hualapai elders. He even offered to type up for the tribe's records anything Fred sent him.[30]

Miller did more than take pictures of the scouts. He used his skills as a photographer to help Mahone document Hualapai land use. He prepared a commentary on the 1931 Senate hearings at Valentine, highlighting what he saw as the malfeasance of the railroad. Assuming that the tribe had not seen the transcript, he mailed a copy to Fred Mahone. Miller wanted to help but cautioned Mahone not to spread the word or the railroad would fire him.[31] Because of his long friendship with the Hualapai and his intimate knowledge of their history, Miller believed they had a valid claim.

Miller and Mahone, with their sights set on the Grand Canyon, had big plans. Sightseers were already heading toward the South Rim in great numbers, and the time seemed ripe. The railroad Mahone had been fighting for so long had been cashing in on the tourist trade for a generation, not only running a lucrative tourist train and the luxury El Tovar hotel but also playing a key role in planning Grand Canyon National Park. Thousands of railroad passengers heading east and west every day passed right through Peach Springs. Motorists, too, traversed the reservation on Route 66. Why not lure some of that tourist traffic to Hualapai country by developing a variety of places on the reservation into tourist attractions, Mahone and Miller wondered? In 1923, park administrators had even considered Long Mesa — up along the northeastern boundary of the Hualapai reservation, where it meets Havasupai and park land — worthy of addition to its holdings.[32] Capitalizing on the obvious interest in canyon country was Miller and Mahone's goal.

Indian tourism was a proven success. The ATSF pioneered Indian gazing in the Southwest with its "Indian Detours" and via the promotion of such ceremonies as the Hopi Snake Dance, which the railroad called "perhaps the weirdest of all American aboriginal ceremonials." First as advertising symbols, then as makers of marketable pottery, and finally as attractions themselves in the 1920s, southwestern Indians made for good business. Through its longtime partnership with the Fred Harvey Company, the railroad tapped into the antimodern vision of uncorrupted Indians living a life of primitive virtue — and put it up for sale. The railroad's interest in Indians fit into its larger campaign to promote tourism in the Southwest.[33]

The Indian Detours, trips that embarked from Santa Fe and traveled to the pueblos and to Navajo country, promised to show tourists "real" Indians, allowing them a chance to "see archeology alive." With the men who drove outfitted as frontier guides and the women who led the tours dressed as Navajos, the tours went nearly everywhere — but not to Hualapai country. The Indian Detours did not merely stop short of the Hualapai reservation; they literally left it off the map. In their 1930 brochure, which ran to sixty-four pages and offered tours throughout Arizona and New Mexico, the centerfold map depicted what the company called "Roads to Yesterday" — a history lesson with Indians at its center. The map told a four-hundred-year story in pictures. The ATSF sold white tourists a nonthreatening version of Indian history that they could see in their own time. In its version of the past, battles were not fought, Indians were not killed; their populations experienced what the brochure called "shrinkage." Now, in the "modern" pueblos — the ironic quotes are the brochure's — one could see lifestyles which all "mirror an America unbelievably ancient." But the ATSF did not always play fast and loose with semantics: in another promotional piece it called the coming of the railroad and the displacement of Indians a conquest — and it was proud of it.[34]

Because the railroad had created a market for Indian tourism, the interest was already there. So were the means. Before Interstate 40 was built, Route 66 was the main east-west artery running through the Southwest. Although the half-dozen or so filling stations that used to cater to motorists are now all gone, it is still the main street on the Hualapai reservation. The hundred-mile stretch from Kingman eastward to Route 40 makes for a breathtaking drive. In 1930 Miller suggested to Mahone that a simple billboard on Route 66 would lure motorists onto a toll road off the highway that would lead to cabins on the rim of Diamond Creek Canyon. Because of its awe-inspiring view into the Grand Canyon, the site was an ideal vacation spot. Mahone liked the idea and agreed to talk with the original Hualapai owners of the land around Diamond Creek, hoping they would allow their land to be developed for tourism. It had been done before—the first tourist hotel in the Grand Canyon was built on the Hualapai reservation. But Mahone worried that the BIA would quash the plan. Many years earlier, Mahone told Miller, a man from California had interested the Hualapais in developing their "scenic wonders." But the superintendent ran him off the reservation, nearly arresting him, Mahone claimed, because he had tried to enliven the tribe's entrepreneurial spirit. Other interested "white fellers" had come to take photos only to be hustled off the reservation by the superintendent. Tongue-in-cheek, Mahone told Miller that he understood why: the "natural wards of the government" were not supposed to behave like that. Mahone and Miller would have to be careful not to raise the suspicions of D. H. Wattson. But they also needed to be wary of Hualapais, many of whom might be opposed to letting tourists come onto the reservation, disrupt their cattle operations, and generally be a nuisance. Mahone worried that others would not support his plans.[35]

Mahone and Miller picked a nice spot. For sheer beauty the canyon rivals many of the better-known side canyons along the South Rim. At the mouth of Diamond Creek, where it widens and joins Peach Springs canyon and flows in to the Colorado River, a large, sandy beach is hemmed in by canyon walls. Trails wind through the thick tamarisks. Another beach on the north side of the river and just upstream is a popular spot for river runners to spend the night. The south side beach is Hualapai country — part of the 108 river miles in the Grand Canyon that belong to them—and the put-in point for a thriving Hualapai-owned and -run river rafting business. The road built more than one hundred years ago is still there. The twenty-mile descent is the only place in the Grand Canyon where a car can make it from rim to river.[36] On the beach are some picnic tables, a few firepits, and a couple of ramadas for shade from the sun. The Diamond Creek rapids roar.

Mahone and Miller's plans for this spot coincided with the Bureau of Reclamation's bigger plans for the Colorado River. The bureau was about to plug up the river. Construction of Hoover Dam was under way. Mahone hoped that the lake created by the dam would back up all the way to the mouth of Peach Springs canyon. If it did, it would be a tourist bonanza, "a Desert playground for the sight seeing American people." In the finest booster tradition, Mahone boomed, "No doubt there will be power boats operated on this body of water taking tourists up into the Grand Canyon and the Indian country of the Walapai and probally [*sic*] the Havasupai people." Tourists would be taken into the canyon on horseback, with corrals at the rim and and on the river's edge. The tribe would build a road to the rim of Madwida Canyon and a trail to the "Ancient old deserted Indian village, so that those interested in Indian lore can visit." The surviving scouts could "relate the history of our country and its people as it was in the days gone before the coming of the white man." He went on: women could make baskets for the tourist trade, men would get work on the road building projects or cut firewood for the camps along the rim. Hualapai cowboys could act as guides and wranglers. Mahone wanted to turn the reservation into an Indian theme park, making it "a desert play ground in the Ancient Old Indian Country which has never been open to the whites as a whole." Like the Snake Dance at Hopi, some ceremonies would be open to white tourists. To what end would all of this be done? Mahone hoped that by opening the reservation to this type of large-scale tourism the Hualapais would "become self supporting which has been and is our life long aim."[37]

Created entirely by non-Indians, the Indian Detours aimed to give tourists a safe and memorable experience in Indian country. Mahone, along with Miller, envisioned a Hualapai-run program. Tourism on the reservation would fill the coffers of the Hualapai. To be sure, he wanted to present an ideal Indian past, one that, like the railroad's was free of strife and tragedy. After all, he wanted to make money. But he wanted to do it on Hualapai terms. And so, apparently, did others. "All the Indians and I were anxious to rush the matter right away," Mahone told Miller. It's doubtful that all Hualapais agreed. Besides Diamond Creek, he proposed developing Madwida Canyon — site of the Hualapais' origin story and so sacred that non-Hualapais are now forbidden from entering the canyon. Mahone had been in discussions with W. A. Farr of the Kingman Motor Company and hoped to present his plan to the Kingman Chamber of Commerce in the spring of 1932.[38]

It is hard to know exactly how the rest of the tribe received Mahone's plans. Mahone reported to Miller in January 1934 that after a meeting called to discuss the scheme most of the Hualapais agreed and wanted him to contact John Collier. But there were dissenters: Jim Fielding, Bob Schrum, and Jane Huya. Miller understood. Fielding, Schrum, and Huya had been there a long time and had seen a lot chicanery on the part of whites; their fear of losing control of more land was understandable.[39]

Mahone had a keen understanding of the cash value of the romantic Indian. If tourists were willing to spend money on Indian Detours, which took them into Pueblo and Navajo country, then why not direct some of that interest toward the Hualapais? He could give the public what it wanted: Indians playing Indian. But he also knew that if tourists celebrated Hualapai history the government could not deny the tribe's long-term occupancy — how could people pay to see that history if it did not exist? Mahone probably had made the connection when he had documented Hualapai land use in the Pine Springs country in the fall of 1930.[40] He could use history both as a way to save the tribe's land and as a tool for development. Mahone's plans for an Indian theme park may never have gotten off the ground, but his — and others' — documentation of the Hualapai past would be the key to keeping their land.

Most winters on the reservation were quiet, and the winter of 1934 was no different. But matters were different in the spring. Despite the recent change of heart at the BIA and the beginning of work relief programs on the reservation, the Hualapais' land was still in limbo; drought and lack of grass only exacerbated the problem. And some Hualapais began blaming Mahone. Anger erupted at a tense May meeting about the status of Clay Springs. Younger members of the tribe, represented by the Hualapai Livestock and Protective Association, had been urging Collier to purchase Clay Springs for their use, reasoning that for the amount they paid to lease it every year it made more sense to buy it outright from the railroad. But according to Mahone, older members from some of the bands in western Hualapai territory, whose "forefathers and their fore fathers' fathers original owned water and land," did not want the government to purchase the land. The elders believed that the original boundaries of the reservation extended well beyond Clay Springs, encompassing a far greater chunk of their aboriginal land than currently embraced in the reservation. The government's purchase of Clay Springs from the railroad would forestall any efforts to regain a greater swath of their original land. Moreover, why should they buy what they already considered theirs? The younger members of the livestock association were being shortsighted and impatient, Mahone implied. The elders from the Clay Springs band wanted to preserve a key piece of their ancestral land; the Indian cowboys wanted only grass and water for the cattle.[41]

These concerns came to the surface at the meeting when the elders found an unwilling audience in the younger Hualapais. Not willing to listen, the young cowboys simply wanted the land; the means were unimportant. Charles

McGee and Jim Fielding's son Swim urged Hobgood to write to Collier on their behalf. The discussion grew heated, and as the pace picked up arguments were carried on at such a clip that older Hualapais were left wondering what was happening. Their protests went unheard. According to Mahone, "There were many older Indians who were descendent, from the primitive race of the Tinnaka, Grass Springs, Clay Springs and the Milkweed Springs (west Side reserve area) made a protest against the signing of the letter thru such hurriedly acts made by these to young members of the Walapais."[42]

Not only did tension arise among segments of the older and younger generations, but a longstanding rivalry between Mahone and Fielding began to cleave the leadership. Mahone's bid for leadership, Fielding said, was unwelcome. Mahone might want to be a "big leader," but "the Indians don't want him." Two organizations — the Hualapai Livestock and Protective Association, led by Fielding, and the Walapai Tribal Association, with Kate Crozier at the helm — now vied to be the voice of the tribe. According to former superintendent D. H. Wattson there was "considerable jealousy and rivalry" between Fielding and Mahone. But Fielding was in charge, said Wattson. Mahone's attempts to use Kate Crozier's influence were in vain; he had no authority to speak for the tribe.[43]

Fred Mahone had a knack for getting into trouble. He was fighting with Fielding and fanning the flames of discord between the Clay Springs band and the young Hualapai ranchers. And he kept getting on the nerves of the reservation agent. "Mr. Mahone," Guy Hobgood wrote Collier, "has for several years been a tireless troublemaker." When Mahone got in the way of Hobgood's range management plans that summer — Mahone was convinced that his interest in culling the herd was one more plot to rid the eastern portion of the reservation of Hualapais — Hobgood could only shake his head in disbelief. "Poor blundering Fred Mahone, who has a mania for becoming the great leader of his people, and believes that the way to gain this leadership is to be different from all the rest of the crowd. This necessarily puts him on the 'wrong side of the fence' most of the time." But Mahone simply would not go away; he'd been working too long to save the Hualapais' land. His resolve was impressive, Hobgood thought: "He hangs on with the tenacity of a whole litter of bulldogs."[44]

Yet despite the new government's support of their claims and despite the tensions within the tribe, the Hualapais united to reject the Indian Reorganization Act in a tribal vote. It became law without their blessing. It is hard to say with precision why they did not vote for it in 1934 — they would do so only a few years later, in 1939. Initially, many Hualapais had supported the new law. Early in 1934 the Walapai Livestock and Protective Association, the tribe's decidedly anti-Mahone "official" organization, came out in favor of the proposed changes in Indian policy. But its support was qualified. Inserted within its resolution of support for the IRA was a demand for title to the entire reservation. Though the Hualapai reservation had never been broken up by the General Allotment Act, the Livestock Association was keenly aware of the damage done to other tribes and their land bases. It would not allow the same thing to happen to the Hualapais. As long as the railroad claimed half of the reservation, the effect was the same: the land was out of their control. And when it came time to vote, the Hualapais realized that the IRA would not keep their land intact. They withheld their support. Those on the other side of the Hualapai political divide, it seems, did not vote for the bill, either. Hobgood thought that some of the elders were reluctant to pass favorably on the bill because they did not understand its provisions. He blamed Mahone. But the image of a cabal of "old Indians," in league with Mahone, lobbying against the bill seems crudely rendered. Only a majority needed to approve the bill, but according to Hobgood the Mahone faction was tiny. How did it prevent the IRA from being accepted? It didn't. The fractured tribe formed a united front around one issue: keeping the reservation whole.[45]

And keep it whole they did, for amid the political turmoil and ill will on the reservation there was some good news, too. That spring, the leases of white ranchers on Hualapai land on the eastern half of the reservation ran out. They were not renewed. The land fell back into Hualapai hands. And in May, just after the rancorous meeting about Clay Springs, the tribe celebrated with a weekend's worth of events at Frazier Wells in the east. Organized by Mahone and his friend Frank Beecher of the Pine Springs band, it included a barbecue, chicken pulling, calf roping, shoeing of wild horses, a performance by the Hualapai band, a meeting of the returned students' club, a boxing match, and a Supai dance, among many other activities. The Hualapais invited everyone, Indians and whites alike. Havasupais, Navajos, Hopis, Paiutes, and friends from Kingman came. Everyone, it seems, was happy that the Hualapais now controlled the eastern part of their land.[46]

Though the Hualapais' land was back in their hands, actual ownership was still in dispute. But their case was about to get a complete legal makeover.

PART II

Making Indian Law

10

Building a Case

The attorneys who worked with John Collier and implemented the Indian New Deal saw federal Indian law so differently from their predecessors that it was as if they were a separate species. The difference in practice was simple: Ethelbert Ward, E. C. Finney, John C. Gung'l, Seth Richardson, and G. A. Iverson did their best to discourage litigation and weaken the Hualapais' position before the courts. Felix Cohen, Richard Hanna, and Nathan Margold worked hard to get cases to court and win. They revolutionized Indian law.

Nathan Margold was a brilliant lawyer. Though no stranger to civil rights when he became solicitor of the Department of the Interior in the spring of 1933, Margold was relatively new to Indian affairs. But he was a quick learner. Formerly a professor at Harvard University, and protégé of Harvard law professor — and future Supreme Court justice — Felix Frankfurter, Margold came to Washington with the flood of lawyers that rushed to the city during the first days of the New Deal. Frankfurter, for one, thought him supremely qualified for the tasks that lay ahead, writing in a recommendation, "I cannot imagine a man more alertly and effectively equipped to stand guard against all the enemies, often very fairseeming, who attempt to make inroads on Indian moral, material and cultural interests." Historians know him well as the architect of the NAACP's first comprehensive school desegregation strategy; he drafted the blueprint in 1931 when he wrote the "Margold Report."[1]

But he had a great impact on Indian law, too. It was Margold's work for the Institute for Government Research, begun in 1929, the year after *The Problem of Indian Administration* was released, that got him started in the field. Enlisted by the Institute to examine Indian claims against the government, Margold's bill was one among many in a series of proposals to finally settle the question of how to compensate Indians for land unlawfully taken. Although his bill never became law, it gave Margold invaluable and rare experience that led to his being named chair of the Indian Affairs Committee of the ACLU in 1931. While chair, Margold worked closely with Collier, helping him to draft pro-Indian legislation.[2]

In 1930, San Juan Pueblos in New Mexico and their long fight for land rights provided Margold with his first contact with Indian people — and a partnership with Richard Hanna, soon to become special attorney in the Hualapai case. Having spent most of the 1920s battling with Anglo and Hispanic settlers over land titles, the Pueblos were being afforded no relief from a government wedded to expediency. Margold was outraged by government attorneys' easy dismissal of Indian concerns, not to mention the ineffectiveness of the Pueblo Lands Board. A theme that sounded throughout his career as a solicitor was first stated: the government had routinely shirked its duty to represent Indians in court, preferring instead to dispense with their cases as quickly as possible.[3]

When Margold became solicitor for Interior in 1932 he came with a wealth of experience in protecting civil rights. And in the fall of 1934, when he finally found time to write his opinion on the Hualapai case — a memo that ran to more than 150 pages and turned the case around — he showed no mercy to the lawyers who had handled it to that point, nor to the government that had supported them. Near the end of his memo, after leaving previous arguments against the Hualapais smoldering in ashes, Margold turned his attention to the lawyers themselves. He showed little but contempt for Finney, Richardson, and the rest of the attorneys, who had "sadly neglected, if not entirely disregarded" the rights of the Hualapais. To begin with, Finney's and Richardson's opinions had been written *after* the 1931 consent decree had been entered; they had merely propped it up. And they were both wrong with regard to the history, which was, in Margold's words, "utterly inexcusable." Richardson, whose "performance was disgraceful," faired the worst. He "blithely" pronounced that title had been extinguished in 1869 without offering a shred of evidence — no citations and not a single relevant case. Margold thought Richardson's opinion egregiously wrong and shamefully misguided. Richardson's performance was so poor, fumed Margold, that he considered Richardson lucky that informal opinions did not make their way into the official reports of the opinions of attorneys general. Otherwise, his reputation would be worthless. But worse than the flimsy legal reasoning and fictitious history was that each step had been taken without the consent of the Hualapais. In fact, the consent decree, and the consolidation agreement before it, had been executed against their express wishes. All along, Margold argued, the government "assumed without reasonable cause the validity of the railroad's claims to the land and Peach Springs and acted accordingly." The government did nothing to protect the Hualapai and everything to accommodate the railroad. For all of these reasons, not to mention the facts in the case, Margold recommended litigation. He aimed to buck the pattern of compromise and stamp out the incessant kowtowing to more powerful interests, especially in cases such as this one, in which a powerful non-Indian party was at odds with Indians.[4]

Margold's opinion was not only the fullest statement of the case to date but also the first legal analysis to come from the new administration. It was a departure that cast off completely the reasoning of his predecessors. Margold broke new ground in several areas. First, he dismissed the notion that the Hualapais gave up title when they were forcibly removed to the Colorado River reservation, labeling absurd previous attorneys' arguments that this was the case. Second, considering the absence of written documentation, he asserted that Hualapai versions of the past mattered. Oral evidence "must be admissible proof even in a lawsuit [where it would normally be hearsay] if 'immemorial' possession is required, since it is absolutely the only evidence available." This was a remarkable concession.

Third, Margold turned to anthropology, something rarely used in Indian cases. Along with oral testimony, the work of anthropologists could illuminate the Indians' past. Margold placed great value on an unpublished paper by the cultural geographer Fred Kniffen. Kniffen, part of the team led by Alfred Kroeber that conducted the first and only ethnography of the Hualapai, mapped their occupancy in their aboriginal territory. Kniffen's work, though similar in nature to Mahone's, and done independent of the case, boosted the Hualapais' claims. Based on interviews with older Hualapais, his findings were sympathetic, but they also agreed with the available documentary record. Fourth, the laws of the United States, Mexico, and Spain all honored the rights of wandering tribes and not only settled, agricultural people. Established in the United States, by the decision in *Mitchel v. United States* (1835), this principle protected all Indians. What is more, Indians living in the territory ceded by Mexico were afforded the protection of U.S. law. And finally, Indians did not need formal recognition by Congress in order to have rights to land. They possessed rights based on occupancy. This well-settled feature of federal Indian law was often overlooked. But Margold went to great lengths to reiterate it by paying close attention to *Cramer v. United States* (1923) — the same case found to have no bearing by previous attorneys.[5] Margold effectively took all the arguments used against the Hualapais in the past, turned them on their head, and employed them in the tribe's favor. Margold's reading of the case was radical because it departed so thoroughly with the past, radical simply because it advocated actually *defending* the Hualapais, and radical because it took Hualapai history seriously. The opinion did not search for reasons why the Hualapais might lose their claim; rather, it took seriously the notion that government attorneys were charged with helping Indians win. That in itself was a reversal of past practice.

The biggest change in Indian law in the 1930s came when Felix Cohen joined the Department of the Interior. Hired by Margold in the fall of 1933 as an assistant solicitor, Cohen had never given the "Indian problem" a shred of thought, much less met an Indian, before he came to work for the government By the time he left, he had invented modern federal Indian law. At his death at forty-six in 1953 Cohen was the recognized leader in the field. He worked against the grain of assimilation, against the notion that in order to survive Indians must adopt white ways and jettison their land, language, and culture. To Cohen, Indian assimilation was cultural death and a mask for the government's real intention: to get out of the Indian business and abandon its fiduciary duty. Over the course of his thirteen years at Interior his resistance to assimilation only hardened. From the beginning of his career in 1933, Cohen saw the law as a way to protect Indian communities from disappearing.[6] He would eventually use his considerable skills to take the Hualapais' case to the Supreme Court.

While Margold worked on the Hualapai memo, Cohen simultaneously drafted — after he was finished co-writing the Indian Reorganization Act — what in many respects has become the guiding philosophy for Indian law ever since: an opinion titled "Powers of Indian Tribes." The Margold opinion and "Powers" appeared within weeks of each other in October 1934. Attributed to Margold but written by Cohen, this official solicitor's opinion was a powerful piece of work — it has rightly been called "revolutionary." Cohen wrote, in what one scholar has said is "without question the single most influential passage ever written by an Indian law scholar," that "the most basic principle of all Indian law, supported by a host of decisions . . . , is the principle that *those powers which are lawfully vested in an Indian tribe are not, in general, delegated powers granted by express acts of Congress, but rather inherent powers of a limited sovereignty which has never been extinguished. . . .* What is not expressly limited [by treaty or statute] remains within the domain of tribal sovereignty." Tribes, in other words, possessed a bundle of rights and powers that had their origin outside the Congress. Congress could only limit rights; it did not grant them. A series of rights, however, had never been curtailed. Tribes still possessed the right to adopt a form of government, regulate their internal affairs, set the conditions of membership, prescribe rules of inheritance, levy taxes on members and nonmembers doing business on the reservation, remove nonmembers from the reservation, "regulate the use and disposition" of tribal property, spend tribal money for the benefit of the tribe, administer a system of justice, and, to a limited extent, oversee the duties of federal employees working on the reservation.[7] When Cohen argued that tribes could control their internal affairs, he departed from more than a century of policy which dictated that tribes were not capable of providing themselves with the most basic services.

Designed to clarify the government's position regarding the powers of Indian tribes after the June passage of the Wheeler-Howard Act, Cohen's opinion recognized those powers as inherent and not delegated powers and thus signaled the beginning of the modern era of tribal sovereignty. By not including these powers within the Wheeler-Howard Act—which Cohen co-drafted—and thus keeping them from being powers that Congress could take away, Cohen made the powers of Indian tribes inalienable.[8] It was a brilliant move.

Felix Cohen was a legal realist committed to the idea that the law was not a set of abstract, natural principles waiting to be plucked out of the air by mortal lawyers but a fully human-constructed set of rules and expectations that changed as societies changed. The law was made, not found. Although legal realism was a descendent of the sociological jurisprudence and progressive legal thought of the previous decades and thus was not in itself a radical break with the past, its effect on Indian law was decisive—one era began and another ended. Until Cohen's brand of realism infiltrated Indian law in the 1930s, none of the earlier signs of progressive legal reform present in other areas of public law had made their way into the field. Indian law had been free of innovation and expertise and full of many of the tenets of classical legal thought—chief among them the belief in immutable laws about Indians and their rights. Cohen put politics into Indian law, or, more accurately, he realized that politics had always been there. Law was part of daily life for most Indians. Cohen would say many years later that "Indians have suffered for decades under complexities of law so involved that most . . . are inextricably entangled in red tape from birth to the grave."[9]

Cohen came to Indian law at a time when, according to Ray Brown, writing in the *Yale Law Journal*, "the federal government's power over the property of its Indian wards cannot fail to strike one with its arbitrary and almost unrestrained character." Cohen agreed. Not only did the federal government wield considerable power over Indians, but its attempts during the Indian New Deal to cede some of that power to Indians had up to that time been ineffective. In 1937 Cohen wrote, "We must . . . recognize that the administration of Indian affairs is not yet something of which we can be proud. The achievements of the present administration represent the beginning of a liberal Indian program, . . . a good beginning but only a beginning." A lot of work remained. Individual states' control over Indians, for example, galled Cohen. "Denial of Indian civil liberties through oppressive State legislation is a serious problem which the present administration has not met." The administration must mount a "vigorous attack upon statutes and local rulings that deny to Indians in several States such elementary rights as the right of franchise and the right to attend white schools." Cohen aimed to shift power back to Indians, with whom he thought it belonged and originated, and take it away from states and the federal government. Perhaps naively, he believed the way to do this was to establish democratically elected tribal councils—an institution that he hoped would be the bulwark for establishing sovereignty and self-government. When asked by Antoine Roubideaux, a member of the Rosebud Sioux tribal council, for his advice on setting up tribal courts and making membership based on blood quantum, Cohen was happy to oblige. But he quickly reminded Roubideaux, "As I have already suggested, this is a matter that the council itself should decide and you should pay as little attention as possible to my own views."

Despite Cohen's optimism he wondered whether the federal government would ever allow Indians to truly achieve self-government. "The vital question is: 'Will the promise of self-government embodied in the Wheeler-Howard Act and in the tribal constitutions and charters actually be fulfilled or will these promises be treated like so many earlier promises of the United States embodied in solemn treaties with the Indian tribes?' " In short, Cohen did not believe that the government was doing enough to change the real purpose of its ever-evolving Indian policy: the transfer by legal, illegal, and violent means of Indian lands to white hands.[10] But he would do his best to dismantle that policy as well as make up for past wrongs when he joined Nathan Margold in radically rethinking the Hualapai case.

Cohen not only worked hard to ensure that the government's rhetoric of sovereignty had some teeth, but he was also fully aware of the debates within anthropology and recognized the power of history. Cohen joined John Collier's short-lived efforts to infuse a little anthropology into the BIA, especially when it came to land rights. "The extent of our ignorance of the basic facts of

Indian land tenure is amazing," he wrote in his 1937 article "Anthropology and Indian Administration." It was so scanty, according to Cohen, that "one might read in an hour all that anthropologists have had to say on this subject." Exaggeration aside, he was generally right: the BIA made policy with little knowledge about Indian life and culture and then wondered why so many of its best-laid plans went awry. It is perhaps unsurprising that, given his later outrage at the courts' conception of the Indian past, Cohen was disheartened by this dearth of historical knowledge. On the other hand, he was also optimistic: some anthropologists were finally seeing that the Indian frozen in amber was a fiction and that "the dynamic aspects of culture in the process of change" — history, in other words — was itself worth studying.[11]

History did not know what to make of Indians. Although a few anthropologists were indeed thinking about how to reconstruct the Indian past, most historians paid but scant attention to it. When historians considered Indians they did so fleetingly, casting them as obstacles to settlement or as lesser creatures that evolution had passed by, to be dispensed with in a paragraph. They also generally ignored anthropologists, whose work had little effect on the writing of history. Beyond the well-known debate about objectivity in the 1930s was a separate struggle within anthropology about whether history had any value at all. Those who gave the matter any thought might have asked: What could a study of the past, after all, tell us that we don't already know about Indians? And who cares about the Indian past anyway? A structuralist might have answered: they lived in a timeless world, where nothing much changed; habits, customs, and so on developed in response to biological or environmental needs. When, in 1940, Alfred Kroeber charged anthropologists with too easily "disregarding the complications of the past, especially if it means wading through traveler's narratives or the *Jesuit Relations*," he could just as easily have been criticizing lawyers such as Finney and Richardson and judges who later ignored the Hualapais' past.[12] What would Finney and Richardson have gained by looking at the evidence collected by Mahone and Hanna over the years — the hundreds of pages of depositions, letters, memos, photographs, and archaeological data? Their answer: nothing.

To suggest that Finney, Richardson, and their predecessors were working under the influence of the British structural functionalists would be absurd. It is unlikely that either one had ever heard of, much less read, the works of Bronislaw Malinowski or A. R. Radcliffe-Brown. It is even more certain that Finney and Richardson never spent a moment wondering about the functional value of the *quipu* (a knotted rope used to keep track of time) or the taboo against eating fish in Hualapai culture. Yet there are similarities: they all ignored history or, at the very least, refused to look at evidence that might complicate their strongly held ideas about the "primitive" past. Structural functionalists put little or no faith in what is known as diachronic analysis (time perspective), preferring instead a synchronic approach (the study of cultures as they are found at a given moment in time). In the 1930s two distinct schools, each in opposition to the other, dominated anthropology: the historical particularists, largely American and led by Franz Boas and Alfred Kroeber, and the structural functionalists (sometimes called the scientific school), who were overwhelmingly British. It was, for practitioners, a starkly drawn dichotomy: the functionalists ridiculed the historicists as petty antiquarians hopelessly gathering facts with no chance of discerning the structure of human culture, and the historicists were baffled by the structuralists' total lack of interest in change over time. According to the anthropologist Robert Redfield, a colleague of Radcliffe-Brown at the University of Chicago during his brief American sojourn, "No one in America [had] offered a strictly non-historical scientific method" to the study of human culture. The structuralists held that looking into the past of primitive peoples was not possible—there were no documents, for one thing. But more than that, it was pointless. Structure was as it was found.[13] Structuralists would have said that there was nothing to be learned by looking into the Hualapais' past, and therefore they would not have bothered to do so.

A cursory glance at the structuralists serves simply to highlight problem of Indian history—the problem, that is, of taking it seriously. By the time the Hualapai case was making its way to court, the field was still in its infancy. Alfred Kroeber, the most well-known practitioner of the historical method within anthropology and the lead author of the only ethnographical work about the Hualapai, knew well the difficulties of getting anyone to think of Indian history as anything more than a fool's errand. Added to his frustration with the structuralists was his wish to be taken seriously by historians. Writing in 1935, just as *Walapai Ethnography* was published, Kroeber wondered sarcastically: "That historians pay little attention to us, their poor relations, is expectable enough: who are we to enter the houses of the substantial when we do not possess even one document written before our day?" More seriously, he lamented the fact that when anthropologists attempted the history of "the people without documents," their efforts were written off as a waste of time. He went so far as to characterize his own historical efforts, which he thought quite sound, thus: "It may gratify those who react differently to learn that these reconstructions have brought me some censure, no commendation whatever that I know of, and for the most part have been as completely ignored by my colleagues as I expected them to be by the larger world."[14] Self-deprecation aside, Kroeber had a larger point: by the mid-1930s there was open hostility to historical ethnology.

Cases that relied heavily on interpretations of treaties, land cession negotiations, historical occupancy, native testimony, and so forth came to court in a climate in which the value of the Indian past was up for grabs. New ways of seeing the Indian past were in dire need but in short supply. The Hualapais' historical consciousness, their unique way of narrating the past, of ordering and prioritizing events generated by the threat to their land, supplied a structure for other Indian histories. Likewise, the Hualapai case forced new ways of seeing the Indian past onto the intellectual stage and into courtrooms in the 1930s.[15] Professional historians, to say nothing of anthropologists, had little to do with this change. But lawyers did: using the work done by Mahone and others, government attorneys not only changed Indian law, they helped change the way the world viewed aboriginal history.

Richard Hanna was not a legal realist. One will never find his name in the pantheon of legal thinkers pedigreed by Harvard, Yale, Chicago, or Columbia Law School who changed the way we think about the law. Hanna was simply a lawyer — one who took the Hualapai case in a new direction. He had once been Chief Justice of the Supreme Court of New Mexico and a Democratic candidate for governor. And he was one of the few lawyers recruited by the government who had a wealth of experience in Indian affairs. A longtime associate of John Collier, Hanna had been active in securing Indian land rights since 1919, when Cato Sells appointed him attorney for the Pueblos. By the mid-1920s he was doing piecework for the American Indian Defense Association, defending, among other things, Taos Pueblo's right to its sacred Blue Lake. Collier called his office in Albuquerque "another headquarters of the Indian Defense Association." When Collier approached Hanna for advice on the Hualapai case in the fall of 1935, he and future Commissioner of Indian Affairs William Brophy shared a private practice in Albuquerque.[16]

By then, no one would disagree that the case was a difficult one, astonishing in its complexity and full of portent for land rights in the West. Few lawyers had been able to make sense of it, and after the Margold memo appeared it only looked more unwieldy. And Arizona senator Carl Hayden still, of course, pushed for consolidation.[17] Both the Interior Department and the BIA wanted to pursue the case, but neither had enough lawyers to go around. They came up with a singular solution: hire an attorney whose only job was overseeing the Hualapai litigation. After gathering advice from both agencies, Secretary of the Interior Harold Ickes made his pitch to the attorney general. "The matter is one of such magnitude and complexity," Ickes wrote, "that, were it referred in ordinary course to the appropriate United States Attorney, this official, no matter how marked his ability or how ardent his desire for action, could not by reason of his other duties have sufficient time to act effectively in the litigation." One overworked government attorney was no match for the "dogged and resourceful opposition which the defendant — the Santa Fe Railroad — is certain to muster." Thus, "the appointment of a Special Assistant to the Attorney General, who can devote his whole time to the intricacies of the case, seems indicated, and I earnestly request that you make such an appointment in order that the great injustice which has heretofore been done the Walapai Indians may be righted." Ickes made his recommendation at the end of October, Hanna received endorsements from New Mexico's two senators, and two weeks later Collier made an informal offer to Hanna. And by late December, the Justice Department hired Hanna solely to oversee the Hualapai case. Eager to get started, he reviewed the case and the Margold opinion on the train and was in Washington early in the new year. The case would be his life for the next several years; in fact, it outlived him. Five years after his appointment he mused, "I sometimes think that when Gabriel blows his 'Trumpet,' I will still be busy on the Walapai case."[18] And indeed he was; he died before its resolution.

Before Hanna did anything else he and his assistant Harlow Akers had to secure all the files in the case and begin preliminary research; by the time this was done, the spring of 1936 was almost gone. The research was tough, largely because of the nature of the evidence — or lack of it. Hanna was also in touch with former reservation superintendent William Light, whose earlier research in the documentary record was becoming increasingly valuable. Hanna found himself playing historian more and more. But he was stymied time and again because of the lack of complete records on the subject. Reconstructing Hualapai history was difficult enough, but Hanna made it more so when, before the season slipped away, he echoed a suggestion made in the Margold memo. It was something the Hualapais had pressed for in the past but that no other attorney had wanted to pursue. Along with setting aside the 1931 consent decree and quieting title to the reservation, Hanna suggested, it might be possible to file a claim on land lying outside the reservation's boundaries. "The long lapse in time in connection with these matters is going to make any and all efforts difficult," Hanna recognized, but it was worth a shot. He now wanted to expand the case beyond the immediate conflict with the railroad. He wanted to recover aboriginal land lost to the Hualapai, but the task was daunting. And the case was further complicated when new, confusing information regarding the location of Peach Springs turned up.[19] In his short time in the position Hanna had made a lot of work for himself.

The Hualapais were frustrated, too. "I am now an old man," Tomanata said, "ready to die, and I haven't seen any of these promises [to protect Hualapai land] fulfilled, and I hope that the younger generation will live to see these promises fulfilled." Like Tomanata, many of the elders were ready to die or, like Dr. Tommy, were already gone. Born before the coming of the whites in the 1840s, 1850s, and 1860s, Jim Mahone, Jim Fielding, Tomanata, Indian Huya, Kate Crozier, Annie and Young Beecher, Bob and Nora Schrum, and others had one last wish: to see the railroad gone and their land restored. Jim Fielding, soon to pass, summed up their sentiments: "We have a big battle with the railroad and we want to fight it now while us old fellows who were here before the railroad are still alive."[20] In statements collected in 1936 by the government and the railroad for use in the trial, these men and women again recalled the way their lives had been before the whites and the railroad came. Shifting from the high country to the low, from canyon rim to river, and from desert to pine forest, year by year these Hualapais took advantage of a vast territory.

Life before contact had not been idyllic. Shelters made from hides, sticks, and bark left them wet whenever it rained, according to Jim Smith. He wondered whether these simple shelters were the reason for what he thought was a once high mortality rate for the tribe. Narrating their lives in brief, at times reticent statements, Hualapai elders did not wish for the past to return. Rather, they merely tried to make clear that before the railroad and the white people arrived this country was theirs. Some, like Indian Huya, did not mind that the railroad crossed their land, but now railroad officials said it was theirs. The Hualapais, according to Huya, had relinquished war and embraced peace, but the railroad was testing their resolve. "Before the railroad came through here we lived here having our wars, and now we have been having peace with the exception of this claim of the railroad on our land. . . . [We] made war on Geronimo, then we decided to live in peace only to return to find that the railroad was coming through this country and now they have made this claim to part of the reservation." His frustration was obvious: "[We] would like to live in peace, but how can we when our lands are being taken away from us[?]" Old and tired of fighting, Huya, like others, left it to the younger generation to ensure that this country remained theirs.[21]

They, of course, knew where they had always lived and emphasized that the land remained theirs after contact. Even the earliest white settlers, who were also deposed again in 1936 and 1937, admitted that the Hualapais "roamed" across country they identified as their own. At their urging, Hanna traveled to the reservation late in the spring to hear their side of the story. After meeting for two days with leaders of the tribe Hanna returned to Albuquerque more convinced than ever that he could recover lost land. According to the Hualapai, the army's original 1881 survey of their land denoted the true boundaries of their reservation. But the *official* survey conducted in 1920–21 to settle the Peach Springs controversy had moved the reservation's boundary six miles to the east on the western and southwestern borders. As a result, five to six springs, including the valuable Clay Springs, were left outside the reservation. Hanna aimed to get all of this land back. Pete Grounds and Mike Matuthania, two Hualapais, said that during the 1920–21 survey the old boundary markers on the western edge of the reservation were moved eastward. They believed that when the official survey was done Clay Springs was intentionally left off the reservation, once and for all making it railroad land. Indian Sampson, whose family had lived at Clay Springs long before the railroad, had heard the same thing from Bud Grounds. Hanna's interest in the western boundary was growing.[22]

Hanna's May visit to the reservation was a turning point. "I spent five days on the reservation, had a conference with the older members of the tribe, and gained a picture of the situation which was of substantial importance and better than I had been able to gain from the study of extensive material which has been sent to me by the Department and by the Indian Office." After spending the winter and spring digging through the old files concerning the case and revisiting some of the same musty army reports the other lawyers had pored over, talking with the Hualapais was a welcome change. He now thought that the 1920–21 survey likely was a fraud perpetrated against the tribe. A search was on for army files with evidence of the original survey. But proving malfeasance was going to be tough; by mid-summer Hanna was losing faith. The evidence was simply not coming in. The army and the Hualapais may indeed have conferred about the boundaries for a reservation, but could this be thought of, in any official sense, as a survey? Although Hanna may have begun to have doubts of ever proving anything, he still wondered why important springs were left off the reservation in the official survey when they appeared to have been included in the army's and the Hualapais' original conception of the reservation; it did not make any sense. And what was worse, the army could find no records of any survey. A resurvey of the western boundaries of the reservation would raise many questions.[23]

The evidence of an incorrect survey was tantalizing enough to warrant a second look. Joseph Schaffhausen, working jointly for the Soil Conservation Service and the BIA, and Peter Grounds, a Hualapai, spent a few days in September hiking the boundary, looking for old cairns. Grounds, a lifelong resident of Clay Springs, had little trouble finding the markers. Starting due west of Clay Springs, they quickly came to the first marker, five and a half miles from the current boundary. Schaffhausen made a note on his map. Heading roughly south by southeast from Clay Springs toward the Music Mountains, they found another marker. After they found several more, an obvious pattern emerged. Then they hit a snag. The next monument on their list should have been near Iron Springs, about seven miles northwest of Clay Springs, located on a ranch run at the time by Mather Willis and his wife. Willis, a former superintendent of livestock on the reservation, granted the pair permission to look for the marker and told them to return the next day. They did, but Willis rebuffed them that day and the next. On the third day Willis took Schaffhausen and Grounds into the hills. Schaffhausen quickly found the marker. Oddly, Willis denied seeing it at first, but after a second look he admitted it was there. That evening, after returning to the ranch, Willis's wife took Grounds aside and warned him that he and Schaffhausen should not come back. At the office in Peach Springs Schaffhausen surprised everyone, including Superintendent Hobgood, when he drew a line through the four markers and found them running in a straight line about five and a half miles west of the 1921 boundary. Curious, he returned to the field a couple of days later to do some follow-up research — he had heard that old Land Office stakes could be found along the boundary. When hiking with John Metuck, chief of the reservation police, at Iron Springs he was shocked to find that the monument he had located only a couple of days earlier was gone. Fresh horse tracks led right to where it had stood. Shaking off the surprise and frustration, he headed further into the Hualapai valley. A lone man on horseback approached. For the sake of his health he had better not continue to prowl around, the man warned him. His work was done. When he returned to Peach Springs, Hobgood thought it best that he quit.[24]

It is hard to know what to make of this. No more evidence of threats exists, the horseman never returned, and Schaffhausen vanished from the scene. But the issue of the western boundary was obviously a touchy one — and it still is today. Hanna was confused: Schaffhausen's report was not enough to build a case, but it raised enough questions to convince him that "some fraud . . . has been perpetrated upon the tribe." Hanna would make the boundary question a feature of the legal battle to come. But because the ATSF had a friend at the General Land Office in Phoenix who was willing to help, the railroad remained confident that the boundary question would be settled in its favor.[25]

The western boundary, the problem of evidence, the resources of the railroad — the case flummoxed Hanna. After almost two decades practicing Indian law, he had to confess, "[The] more I go into the problem presented by the Walapai case the more troublesome I find it. The questions in the Walapai case seem to be so much out of line when compared with every other Indian land problem that I have had any contact with." When Hanna began digging into the "trunks and boxes in the basement of the War Department" he realized that the scope of research required to prove that the Hualapais had lived on land "undoubtedly occupied by the tribe . . . for centuries" was massive. The problem, of course, was evidence. Hanna was having a hard time gathering proof of the exact location where the Hualapais lived. As winter turned to spring and he got further behind in the complaint, Hanna found that he needed help scouring documents in the congressional library for further mention of Hualapai occupancy in Arizona. Encouraged by the recently published monograph *Walapai Ethnography*, authored jointly by a team lead by Alfred Kroeber, but disheartened by the vagueness of the Hualapais' memories, Hanna pushed on. By May he had enough to convince himself that he could prove Hualapai occupancy outside the present reservation — land claimed by the railroad.[26]

Calling the construction of the railroad tracks an "invasion of the reservation," Hanna was confident that he could prove that the Santa Fe's presence was illegal. Congress had made a mistake, he argued. The land granted to the Atlantic and Pacific in 1866 was not public land; it was Hualapai land. And the railroad had been occupying it unlawfully since 1883. Hanna also hoped to convince a court that the Hualapai never gave up rights to land outside the reservation; accepting a reservation did not mean that the Hualapais relinquished the rest of their territory. Estimated by Hanna to contain roughly seven million acres, the Hualapais' ancestral home extended as far west as the Colorado River on the present California border. The same evidence used to prove occupancy of the reservation — the Kniffen map, army reports, Hualapai testimony, and the government's own recently completed study of Hualapai occupancy — would be used to shore up this much larger claim.[27]

Dissent arrived quickly from Washington. The Justice Department warned Hanna that trying to apply the doctrine of Indian title to formerly Spanish and then Mexican — and not English — land was a fool's errand. Hanna risked it. Firm in his belief that occupancy from time immemorial applied to the whole tribe and all its territory, regardless of whether the Hualapai resided on formerly Mexican land, he now embarked on his mission to prove Hualapai occupancy outside of the reservation.[28]

The railroad and its longtime ally Carl Hayden were working on Hualapai history, too. Hanna was feeling the pressure. The railroad already had a researcher digging through the army's files at the Presidio in San Francisco and interviewing Hualapais. To match the railroad's efforts, Hanna wanted someone from the government in San Francisco, too. He aimed to show the extent of the tribe's territory, but he also hoped to demonstrate that the original reservation laid out by the army was different from the one surveyed by the General Land Office in the 1920s. Still convinced that the western boundary had been tampered with, Hanna hoped that research in the Presidio's archives would prove him right. But he had to hurry.[29]

The railroad's researcher, Sara Jones Tucker, a graduate student in anthropology at the University of Chicago, had been hard at work since the fall of 1936. She operated under the radar of the BIA, preferring to keep her affiliation with the Santa Fe to herself. The railroad's limitless resources worried Hanna. Totaling more than eight hundred pages when complete, Tucker's report to the Atchison, Topeka, and Santa Fe Railway was thorough. The product of coast-to-coast research in government archives and several trips to Hualapai country (under the auspices of the Museum of Northern Arizona), the scope of her research was daunting. The railroad also employed a couple of top scholars: Professor Herbert Bolton, a historian at the University of California at Berkeley, and Lyndon Hargrave, an archaeologist at the Museum of Northern Arizona. The railroad had struck out with Leslie Spier, author of a massive ethnography of the Havasupai published in 1928. Spier said his "sympathies all lay with the Walapai." But Bolton, long considered the founder of modern borderlands study, agreed to work for the railroad. And Hargrave and the Museum of Northern Arizona joined with the railroad in doing the first archaeological fieldwork on Hualapai country. An expert in Spanish exploration of the Southwest, Bolton knew about Garcés. Excited by the prospect of a trip to the Southwest, Bolton told Joyce Cox, lead attorney for the railroad, that he would be glad to make a trip with him to Hualapai country. Tucker and Bolton did their jobs well. Bolton joined Tucker, Cox, and others in May 1937 for a trip across Hualapai territory. Retracing the trail of Garcés, Bolton determined that there was no way the Spanish friar could have encountered the Hualapais in the summer of 1776. And Hargrave went further: there was no connection between the Hualapais and the people who prehistorically occupied what was now the reservation.[30]

And if the work of Bolton, Hargrave, and Tucker were not enough, the railroad could count on Hayden. Eager to aid the Santa Fe and ensure that the Hualapais lost their case, Hayden did his part to help write Hualapai history. In 1936 he and his staff compiled *The Walapai Papers: Historical Reports, Documents, and Extracts from Publications Relating to the Walapai Indians of Arizona.* Unique — and indispensable — the work is a collection of documents spanning the period from Garcés's 1776 trip across Arizona through the Senate hearings of 1931. Hayden intended the 350-page Senate document to serve as proof that the Hualapais had no claim to the land. For example, although it includes ample evidence of Hualapai degradation, there was a void in Hayden's chronicle of Hualapai history where one would expect to find abundant documentation of the government-sponsored, reservation-based cattle operation begun in 1914. Hayden compiled the *Walapai Papers* not only for his Senate colleagues but also for the railroad, welcoming its attorneys to peruse the documents as they were being compiled. Writing to a constituent once the case was wrapped up, Hayden confessed: "I had [the *Walapai Papers*] prepared for the purpose of endeavoring to establish before the Interior Department and the Federal courts that this group of Indians had no well-founded claim to the very large area of land the Interior Department has long sought to procure for their use." Government archives — soldiers' letters and reports, for the most part — were scoured to find data supporting Hayden's view that the Hualapais had never lived on the land now encompassed within the reservation. For this reason, Felix Cohen thought the *Walapai Papers* so biased and incomplete that he called it simply a bundle of "heterogeneous and often worthless documentary material." Although the compilation was a massive undertaking, Hayden did more. He passed on documents to the railroad's attorneys and kept in touch with Tucker, aiding her in her research. As the case made its way through the courts Hayden's support never flagged. Indeed, Hayden "offered to the Santa Fe attorneys all of the assistance of my office to fight the suit."[31]

While Hanna, Collier, and Margold — and, of course, the Hualapais — worked to document the tribe's long-time occupancy, Hayden and the railroad, with their team of experts, attempted to counter their efforts. Everyone now knew — if they had not known already — that the case turned on whose version history was more convincing.

Hanna filed his complaint with the District Court in late August 1937. After wrestling with his superiors at Justice, who, as ever, were dawdling, and threatening to resign if action was not taken against the railroad, he had given the ATSF the government's formal declaration of intent to sue. Throughout the fall the government and the railroad — still wanting to compromise but unwilling to give up title to the odd-numbered sections — wrangled over particulars, going so far as to head to court to hammer out the details of the government's position. Stalling further, the railroad announced early in 1938 that it would be filing a motion to dismiss the case entirely, which it did in April.[32]

The Hualapais, according to the motion to dismiss, were without rights. In blunt language that echoed conclusions reached by earlier government attorneys, and fully in line with the discourse concerning wandering peoples, the railroad argued that "the Walapai were . . . disunited bands of non-agricultural, nomadic savages who occupied exclusively no definable territory and no place or places for any great length of time. They were wanderers in a land of other

wanderers with whom, as between various Walapai bands, there was competition for food and water which accentuated, for the competitively unsuccessful
at least, the necessity, already imposed by a barren country, of continuous and
far-flung searches for the necessities of life. They were thus true to the shifting
pattern found generally in the Southwest."[33]

In its fifty-seven page memorandum in support of the motion to dismiss, the
railroad made four points, all designed to buttress the conclusion that the
Hualapai "have no rights in conflict with" the railroad's. Arguing point 1, that
the policy and laws of the United States had never accorded the Hualapai any
possessory right in the lands involved in the suit, took up more than half of the
memo. And half of point 1 was taken up with proving that the Hualapai were
wild, nomadic savages who by definition had no land rights; they had only such
rights as "Congress has seen fit to give" — which was to say, none. Filled with
quotations from myriad sources such as the records of the early explorers
Garcés, Sitgreaves, and Wheeler, army reports, and nineteenth-century anthropological theory from Adolph Bandelier, the memo showed that the Hualapais
were, indeed, a wandering people. And wandering people, the so-called "wild
tribes" acquired by the United States at the end of the Mexican-American War,
had no rights that the courts were bound to respect, though this idea had never
been tested in the Supreme Court. Further, the railroad argued, the Hualapais'
status as a wild tribe meant that the clause in the granting act mandating that
the voluntary cession of Indian land must occur before the land passed to the
railroad did not apply. The Hualapai had no land to cede. The railroad then
proceeded to argue that the government's "affirmative policy was not to recognize any possessory right in the Walapai." It quoted the secretary of the interior's 1872 annual report, which said, "We are assuming, and I think with
propriety, that our civilization ought to take the place of their barbarous habits.
We therefore claim the right to control the soil they occupy," among other
sources, to make its case for the government's disregard for the Hualapais' and
other Indians' land rights. From the evidence it mustered it would be hard to
argue that the U.S. government had ever made an effort to protect Indian
land.[34]

Yet it undermined the validity of its argument in point 2, when it argued that
"any Walapai right or title has been extinguished." First it contended that the
settled policy of the government had been to not recognize any title in the
Hualapai; then, just to be sure, it argued that in case the Hualapais had possessed any property rights, they no longer did. The railroad trotted out examples of past policy. Again, based on the railroad's examples it would be hard to
argue that the government did not possess a policy designed to transfer land
from Indians to whites. The railroad hoped to demonstrate that the Hualapais

lost any rights they may have had because various "acts of Congress which threw all the territory open to settlement by extending the land laws and protecting settlers by the military operated as a withdrawal of any recognition of Indian right." And if the argument that the Hualapai had no inherent rights failed, it also showed, in point 3, that its title had "been vested and confirmed by the political authorities in such manner that it is beyond challenge." Finally, point 4 asked that the court dispense with the hearing and take the foregoing facts concerning the Hualapais' lack of rights, savagery, and nomadism, as against the railroad's vested rights, as true and beyond dispute.[35]

The railroad wanted the Hualapais' claim thrown out of court. It hoped that the court would accept its version of the facts on what is called judicial notice. Judicial notice means simply that a judge can accept something as fact — "the sun rises in the east and sets in the west" or the "Civil War ended in 1865" — without needing it proved via evidence. Statements such as these, a judge can say, are known by all to be true; they thus can be taken on judicial notice. The railroad asked that Judge David Ling rule that it is well known and indisputable that a tribe such as the Hualapai has no vested property rights in the face of the ATSF, that it has been the policy of the United States to aid in the transfer of land from Indians to non-Indians, that the railroad, and the not tribe, was the rightful owner of the land in question.

The railroad had nothing to lose and everything to gain. After all, if it could convince a judge to dismiss the case it would avoid the expense of a trial and likely quash the government's newfound resolve. If it lost, at least it would have succeeded in delaying a trial. The motion was exhaustively researched and made some forceful arguments. It was so good, in fact, that Carl Hayden congratulated the railroad on it efforts, and said, "I shall have this splendid material bound for my library."[36]

But Arizona's attorney general, Joe Conway, was worried. He feared federal encroachment on what he considered state land. Hysterical, Conway hoped to inspire fear in the citizens of Arizona by saying, "If the contention of the United States in this case is upheld, there is not a livestock man, farmer or homeowner in Mohave county today who is safe from confiscation of his lands." Conway warned that the same fate awaited the rest of the state if the federal government was not stopped.[37]

Hanna had his work cut out for him in preparing the government's brief. Indeed, after several weeks' work it was "assuming substantial proportions."[38] But he appeared sanguine, and he hoped to dispose of the motion before his summer vacation.[39] By late July it was finished, and in August Hanna felt confident that the railroad's motion would be crushed. Anticipating ten days' worth of hearings on the motion — time enough for both sides to air all the evidence and call expert witnesses such as Fred Kniffen — Hanna set aside a couple of weeks that month to travel to the federal courthouse in Prescott.[40] The hot weather and the five days spent arguing the case wore Hanna out. Carl Hayden, of course, continued to take an active interest in the case and did what he could to ensure that the Hualapai lost — in the midst of the dismissal hearing and at the government's expense, Hayden helped the railroad secure critical evidence.[41] Hanna, meanwhile, left Prescott hopeful and eagerly anticipating the judge's ruling. It would be a long wait.

I I

The Case in Court

Judge David Ling dismissed the government's case on 1 March 1939. Carl Hayden was delighted — that same day he telegraphed the railroad's lead attorney, Joyce Cox, to offer his congratulations and a couple of days later wrote to say, "I am certainly pleased that your suit has had such a successful termination and I only hope that there now will be no further difficulty." John Collier was "shocked" and said that the "court bowled us over like tenpins."[1] And the Department of Justice began a campaign to ensure that an appeal by the Hualapais would fail.

At first, there was no opinion. Ling simply ordered the case dismissed. Not satisfied — and incredibly curious — Hanna asked for a written opinion. Six days later he got one. Ling found that the Hualapais — in his words, one of the "savage tribes" — had no rights to land under the laws of Spain and Mexico, and thus the Treaty of Guadalupe Hidalgo afforded them no protection. Ling also agreed with the railroad on virtually every point concerning past policy toward the land rights of the Hualapais: Congress had never explicitly granted them any rights, and so they had none. And like the railroad, Ling found that even if the Hualapais had possessed land rights, they no longer did; the government had snuffed them all out. Ling, accepting every point the ATSF made, wrote what amounted to an abstract of the railroad's motion to dismiss. But perhaps most important, Ling argued that no evidence could be found to

contradict the position that the Hualapai had no rights. His powers of ob-
fuscation could match anyone's, but the principle stated in his final paragraph
was clear:

> The controlling elements of this case, namely, the laws of Spain and Mexico,
> the Legislation of Congress, and the course of administration, are matters of
> judicial knowledge. It is perfectly clear that no evidence adducible would in
> any way affect the result of the case. The plaintiff [the government] has con-
> ceded that the only evidence it can offer cumulating what the Court judicially
> knows would go to the question of tribal organization of the Walapai, the
> issue whether the Walapai possessed any country at all (as distinguished from
> being mere wanderers in a land of other wanderers), and lastly the question of
> the extent of the country possessed, or over which they wandered, as the case
> may be. No evidence upon the issues plaintiff desires to prove would enable
> plaintiff to escape the controlling effect of public law and public administra-
> tion, which the Court judicially knows, which cannot be controverted by
> evidence and which requires dismissal of the case.[2]

All the evidence gathered up to that time by Hanna, Light, and Mahone was
reduced to an opinion not five pages long. Ling's reasoning — once he struck
out on his own and departed from the railroad's argument — made little sense.
What did he mean when he stated that the government had "conceded" the
points enumerated above? It did no such thing. Stranger still was Ling's point
that the only evidence the government could offer would — alongside a discussion of Hualapai social organization — answer the question of the Hualapais'
territorial possessions. Well . . . that was exactly the point! The evidence
Hanna presented to the court was designed to show the tribe's aboriginal
territory, but to Ling such evidence was irrelevant. It made no difference to
him that the tribe *might* have occupied or wandered over a particular territory.
What mattered was that U.S. policy, beginning with the grant to the Atlantic
and Pacific in 1866, had consistently chipped away at any rights to the territory that the tribe might have had. The decision was free of citations; it relied
on no authority other than judicial knowledge.

Hanna and company wasted no time. Within days of losing their case in the
District Court they began to bat about the possibility of an appeal. Hanna and
Collier spent March, April, and May working to convince the Justice Depart-
ment that an appeal was necessary; the questions were too important to be let
go, they reasoned. By late May Justice had tentatively agreed to push forward.
Arguing that the Hualapais' aboriginal title to land inside and outside the
reservation had never been extinguished, Assistant Attorney General Norman
Littell thought the Hualapais' claim deserved a trial. "Litigation of this nature

should not be summarily dismissed," Littell wrote. "A cause of this importance merits a full and complete hearing, with the submission of all evidentiary, factual and historical data available." But a month later, in a stunning reversal — mirroring the apostasy of Seth Richardson years earlier — Littell changed his mind. Citing the Hualapais' lack of property rights under Mexican law and the lack of protection the Treaty of Guadalupe Hidalgo offered, Littell was now convinced an appeal would fail.[3]

But for the Interior Department the case had become too important to let go. When Justice abandoned the case Assistant Secretary of the Interior Oscar Chapman tried to impart the magnitude of the case to the attorney general, saying, "This case is of truly overwhelming importance not only to the Walapai Tribe but to the Indian Service as well. The Tribe is fully aware of its moral right, and, I believe rightly, thinks it has a legal right as well. In addition, the case is a celebrated one and is being watched by Indians all over the country and Indian welfare groups everywhere."[4]

John Collier was convinced that "there is an adverse and uncooperative attitude at a certain level at the Department of Justice." But then, a week after his dismissal, Littell circled back to the position he had staked out a month earlier — albeit with far less conviction. He reluctantly agreed to an appeal; although there was little hope of success, he thought the case deserved review by an appellate court. Literally cutting and pasting most of his argument for dismissal into his new opinion in favor of appeal, Littell acquiesced only in the face of Interior's interest in an appeal, not from any newfound conviction concerning the Hualapais' claim. After what Collier called "a good deal of fighting" between Justice and Interior a decision was finally reached in mid-July: they would appeal the case.[5] Hanna and his partner William Brophy spent the rest of the summer and early fall working on their brief; they had a draft ready by the beginning of October.

As lawyers at the Department of Justice began work on the case, a familiar pattern reemerged: they began to look for legal excuses as to why the Hualapais would lose their case. Set off by the doubts that Littell had voiced in the late spring, they began in the fall of 1939 to make a concerted effort to rid themselves of the case. For more than three years Richard Hanna had managed the case with little or no interference from Justice — he worked more for Collier and the BIA than he did for the attorney general. After Ling's dismissal in the spring, however, Justice began to reevaluate its commitment to the tribe. Except for Hanna's role — less a symbol of the department's alacrity than a sign of Collier's influence — Justice had never taken more than a grudging interest in the case.

Two issues bothered the Justice Department's attorneys in particular. They were skeptical that a court would find that the Hualapais or any other tribe living in formerly Mexican territory had the right of occupancy accorded tribes elsewhere in the United States. And, echoing Ling, they worried that legislation such as the 1925 act designed to split the reservation in two could be construed as an extinguishment of Indian title—if, of course, the Hualapais had title in the first place.[6] Norman MacDonald, another in the long line of Justice attorneys devoted to weakening the tribe's claim—a list that included Iverson, Gung'l, and Richardson—voiced these concerns in October, and by December he made up his mind: the Hualapai could not claim title to the lands inside or outside their reservation. As a result, he urged that the government's appeal abandon *any* effort to prove that the Hualapai had title based on occupancy.

MacDonald claimed, first, that the tribe lost title when Congress granted the land to the railroad, and second, that the reports of explorers and surveyors attesting to Hualapai occupancy of the land were meaningless. Taking his cue from the railroad's brief on the motion to dismiss, MacDonald agreed with the railroad that such reports were moot because they "were without any authority." (Unless, of course, they were used, as the railroad used them, as evidence of the Hualapais' savage state.) Hanna had attempted to use the reports as proof of Hualapai occupancy; MacDonald threw out any claims based on this evidence. MacDonald argued that because the purposes of, say, the Sitgreaves expedition had not been to determine Indian title—whether they observed Hualapais living in their claimed territory or not—any references to Hualapais were outside their expertise. The BIA's chief counsel, MacDonald claimed, assured him that John Collier would have no objections to the extreme change in strategy, and, assuming that Hanna also saw things their way, Justice was now prepared to drop all claims to occupancy from the appeal.[7] Neither Collier nor Hanna ever considered changing the appeal in such a way; proving occupancy was at the heart of their claim.

Hanna, in Albuquerque, was not given a chance to protest. He was unaware of the machinations going on in Washington. Norman Littell, despite Hanna's wishes to remain involved, now held the reins. Without significant input from Hanna, Littell filed an anemic brief with the Circuit Court of Appeals on 11 December 1939. And then, because Hanna's services were no longer necessary, Littell fired him.[8]

The Justice Department had all but given up on the case, thought Hanna. Unwilling to take a careful look at the mountain of evidence he had amassed, Justice was resigned to losing. And now Hanna would have to cancel a trip to the reservation to depose further witnesses, testimony he thought would greatly help the Hualapais' case. Hanna knew he was right—the tribe had a strong case. He was nonetheless glad to be free of the "burden of the thing." Yet he could not help hanging on just a little longer. If Justice gave up, he reminded the attorney general in early January, the reservation would be cut in half. This was unthinkable, first, because the reservation was the Hualapais' home, and, second, because the railroad had never had title to the land in the first place. When the District Court had taken it on judicial notice—saying that no evidence to the contrary could be offered—that the tribe's title had been extinguished or never had existed, it had ignored all of Hanna's work. He hoped that Justice would not allow the Ninth Circuit to make the same mistake. And, of course, John Collier was angry. Belying the assurances that MacDonald had offered regarding Collier's complacency about the new appeal, Collier told Hanna that Justice's attitude did not surprise him. Collier thought it was part of a pattern in the Lands Division and vowed to "talk with Mr. Margold and see whether he thinks there is any way to get this matter rectified and to bring the Department of Justice around to serious prosecution of the Walapai case."[9]

But Justice was not simply uninterested in the Hualapai claim. It was so unprepared to manage the case that Littell had to ask Hanna—*after* the government's appeal had been filed and Hanna fired—what type of evidence he could provide in the event it won in the Ninth Circuit and was forced to proceed to trial. Hanna was stunned. How, he wondered, could he possibly answer such a question in a letter when "to include in a letter the nature and character of the evidence, is to write a book"? For him, Littell's failure to consider the evidence when writing the government's brief and his ignorance of the content and amount of evidence collected for the case summed up Justice's lack of commitment.[10] Littell's 24-page opinion on appeal, free of historical evidence, was no match for the railroad's 175-page tome.

Collier and Margold hoped to retain Hanna as the only hope for the Hualapais. Whereas Collier could barely contain his outrage, calling Justice's brief "boiled-down . . . denatured . . . debilitated," Margold counseled diplomacy. Believing that Littell seemed to have been "using his inordinate vigor and energies in directions which so far have done a lot more harm [than good] to the interest" of the Interior Department, Margold nonetheless wanted to believe that it was not based on hostility, but rather on Littell's "immature and poor judgement." Whatever the reason, Margold urged Collier to back down —with so many claims cases pending, and with Justice lawyers charged with defending Indians in the mounting treaty rights struggles in the Pacific Northwest, for example, he and Collier could scarcely afford to make more enemies in the department. Collier backed off, but he was worried by the railroad's unlimited resources. And, he sighed, with the "Department of Justice in an apologetic attitude, the Indians aren't going to have a chance." Hanna, not willing to back down, took his complaints directly to Littell and forcefully pointed out that the government's brief had conceded title to the railroad when Littell jettisoned the historical evidence that would prove occupancy — the crux of the case.[11]

Margold, Hanna, and Collier weren't the only ones who grasped the import of Littell's move. Apprising Carl Hayden of developments in the case, Joyce Cox, the railroad's lead attorney, wrote the senator toward the end of the year that the government had "jettisoned 99 per cent of what we spent so many days and so many reams of paper arguing about."[12] They were both delighted. Littell and MacDonald had forsaken everything that Fred Mahone and the Hualapai, not to mention their lawyers, had worked for.

Weakened argument in hand, the government presented its case to the Ninth Circuit Court of Appeals in March 1940. Collier and Margold had managed to convince Justice to allow Hanna to argue the case before the Ninth Circuit; Justice acceded to this request as long as MacDonald stood by his side. The two argued the case in Los Angeles in late March.[13] And then they waited. The court's opinion, issued several months later, was simply a more detailed version of Ling's. Upholding the lower court's decision, it echoed some of the more ethnocentric views of Judge Ling while also embracing MacDonald's and Littell's view of the Hualapais' appeal: that the Hualapais were nomadic savages with no property rights, and any land that might have been theirs had long been lost to the ATSF. To a greater extent than the District Court before it, the Ninth Circuit saw U.S. policy as a real estate license. With little or no restrictions, the United States had authority to dispense with Indian land; Indian title was mere permission to use the land until some other use was found for it. Although a railroad's title might be "burdened" by Indian occupancy — and in this case it wasn't — the railroad could still do what it wanted with its land. Indian title effectively meant nothing. The Ninth Circuit worked hard to find no room for any rights for the Hualapais to the land they claimed. In a common but flawed mode of argument the court stated that the absence of any explicit recognition by the United States that Indians in the Mexican cession had property rights was enough to prove that they did not. Of course, one could argue that the treaties made with other tribes such as the Navajos, the Utes, and the Paiutes implicitly recognized Indian property rights — otherwise, why negotiate treaties with tribes who had nothing to give?[14]

If the feeble argument made by the Ninth Circuit regarding rights to occupy formerly Mexican land was not enough, then surely the fact that the Hualapai could not prove occupancy would quash their claim. And in this regard the court had no need to spin out a weak argument. The government had already done so. Littell and MacDonald's brief used the Finney and Richardson opinions to show that the Hualapai had no proof of occupancy. Rather than take a look at the evidence collected by Hanna, Littell and MacDonald relied on work that long since had been discredited by Margold and Collier. The government's brief, purportedly written to defend the Hualapais, went some distance toward supplying the Ninth Circuit with a variety of reasons to deny the Hualapai's claim. While stating that because the Hualapais were denied a trial it must be assumed that they were still in possession of their land — but admitting that they just might have lost some of it — the brief reminded the court that time and again the tribe had been found to be without property rights. Littell and MacDonald noted in their introduction all the various instances in the course of the Peach Springs case when the government had declared that the Hualapais did not have title, such as the 1925 consolidation agreement.[15]

The brief's recounting ended with the Finney and Richardson opinions and the 1931 agreement. No mention was made of Hanna's research or of the depositions of Hualapais and settlers testifying to Hualapai occupancy. The brief stuck to the law of occupancy, not the facts of the tribe's history. The brief's main purpose was to convince the Circuit Court that the Hualapais deserved a chance to try to prove their claim, a chance denied them by the District Court. But it was toothless: it cited no evidence of their occupancy and twice pointed out that the Finney and Richardson opinions had found no proof of their occupancy. It was as if time had stopped in 1931 and Richard Hanna had never existed. The court parroted Littell and MacDonald by following Finney and Richardson and then upheld Ling's decision to take it on judicial notice that no evidence could be offered to show Hualapai occupancy.[16] Tribal history was worthless.

The uncritical acceptance of the worthlessness of any evidence that was contrary to what Judge Ling and the Ninth Circuit's Judge Wilbur already knew about the Hualapais suggests the power of what have come to be called master narratives. So deeply embedded in the judges' minds was a generic narrative of the native past — one in which savagery and aimless wandering combined to deny the tribe any valid claim to property — that they reflexively accepted a crudely rendered universal story rather than look at a specific set of historical circumstances.[17] And when they did, the Hualapai stood to lose half of their land. Judges Ling and Wilbur did not deny that the Hualapai might have occupied the land; it simply did not mean anything.

The Ninth Circuit's opinion dealt a swift but not fatal blow to the Hualapais' case. Reactions were predictable: Carl Hayden told Joyce Cox that he was "delighted that the Court saw it [the railroad's] way." Given the weakness of the government's case — at least as it was presented to the court — John Collier was not surprised by the opinion; he had expected it. Hanna, obviously, disagreed with the Ninth Circuit, holding firm to his belief that not only did all Indians residing on formerly Mexican land have Indian title but that the Hualapai could prove it. What bothered Hanna most was that the "evidence of the Indians themselves might be considered the best evidence upon the subject but they are denied their day in court." He fumed that the "scope of the matters directed to the judicial notice of the trial court go far beyond matters of common knowledge, and by no stretch of the imagination can they be denominated historical and therefore beyond dispute." Hanna and Brophy insisted that Interior push Justice to appeal to the Supreme Court. The assistant secretary of the interior also advocated an appeal on the same grounds: the evidence had not been heard, nor was there any reason to suppose that Indians living on land ceded by Mexico under the Treaty of Guadalupe Hidalgo had no rights.[18]

The court's opinion brought into relief the status of Indian history: easily ignored, ruled irrelevant, overrun by the law, it could tell the court nothing it did not already know. Throughout the 1920s the Hualapais had stuck to their story: we have always been here. In the 1930s, finally, the Hualapai version of the past, not seen by previous attorneys, slowly became visible. Other tribes joined the Hualapais, and the number of claims steadily increased throughout the decade. But as new readings of the Indian past emerged and Indians grew more and more active, resistance hardened. At the beginning of the 1930s, Indian history was still a mystery. George Stormont, the attorney in charge of Indians claims at Justice, admitted that few knew anything about the Indian past. Indian claims worried him, though. He was especially concerned about several bills designed to allow for a special Indian Claims Commission making their way through Congress in 1932. If passed, these "most unusual, revolutionary" bills "would establish dangerous precedents." Claims work was taking so much time, preparing tribal histories was costing so much money — more than one million dollars — and the financial consequences of successful claims were becoming so daunting — estimated rather precisely at $2,392,836,097.29 — that Justice was despairing of ever finding a solution. By the end of the decade, history began to scare the Department of Justice.[19]

And because the Hualapai case was particularly worrisome Littell and Mac-Donald had made it a sure loser; they attempted nothing less than completely ceding all control of the land to the railroad by virtue of the passage of the title to the railroad pursuant to the terms of the grant and by ignoring all evidence of Hualapai occupancy. (By forgoing a discussion of the evidence in their brief, of course, Littell gave the Ninth Circuit no opportunity to review it.) Littell and MacDonald wanted to lose. Because they worked for the Justice Department they were charged with defending the United States against suits by Indians. Between 1941 and 1945 Littell was either lead attorney in or was otherwise closely involved in responding to thirteen suits against the government. Mac-Donald, for his part, was involved in only one — *Northwestern Band of Shoshones v. United States,* which he saw through the Court of Claims and the Supreme Court. Justice Department lawyers throughout the 1930s — as before — both defended and fought Indians. Take another example: attorney Henry Blair advised Hanna about the Hualapai case while also defending the United States against Indian claims. The obvious conflict of interest did not suggest to Littell and MacDonald that they might recuse themselves from the Hualapai case. What's more, Collier claimed to have evidence that just before Hanna was fired the railroad made known that his "elimination" from the case was of paramount importance.[20] Eventually, Justice would no longer be able to reconcile its dual roles. The department's handling of the case, characterized by Littell's hostility and the obvious conflict of interest, was part of a larger antipathy to the pursuit of Indian rights. Afraid to lose these cases, the department's lawyers were also loath to grant Indians any increased legal autonomy.

The battle between the Interior Department and the Justice Department over Indians' legal rights went beyond land claims. Early in 1939 Justice and Interior agreed that something had to be done about federal Indian law; it was a mess. In 1934, the law was characterized by the legal scholar W. G. Rice as follows: "Besides the scores of Indian treaties still in force, there is special federal legislation for half a hundred different tribes and groups of tribes. Especially the land tenure legislation is bewildering. . . . [T]he federal statutes are so confused that they paralyze administrative action." Sense had to be made of the tangle of statutes, court decisions, treaties, attorneys' general opinions, solicitors' opinions, and land cessions. The monumental task was assigned to Felix Cohen.[21] Loaned to Justice to write a handbook on federal Indian law, Cohen intended it to be a guide to protecting Indian rights, but not everyone shared his view. And once the writing of what would become the *Handbook of Federal Indian Law* commenced, Cohen clashed with Justice Department attorney Robert Fabian and the project's supervisor, Norman Littell.

Littell had initially been enthusiastic about the project; he hoped that a manual for litigation would be of "inestimable value as an aid to government counsel." But his enthusiasm was buoyed by the hope — shared by Fabian — that the book would be an aid to government attorneys in cases *against* Indians. Cohen saw the handbook as an aid to tribes. For example, whereas Cohen had titled a chapter "Property Rights of Individual Indians," Fabian proposed changing it to "Rights of the United States with Respect to Property Rights of Individual Indians." By the fall of 1939 their differing views stymied progress. The committee convened to oversee the project—made up mostly of Littell's allies in Justice—recommended that the handbook concern itself with current litigation problems and forgo the opportunity to make a sweeping survey of Indian law. What the department wanted was a book about how to win Indian cases in court now, not a treatise on the development and theoretical underpinnings of federal Indian law, which was what Cohen had in mind. The handbook was quickly becoming useless—Cohen joked that if written as envisioned by Justice it would be "about as valuable as a treatise on the law of torts as established in cases won by red-headed lawyers."[22]

The committee set its sights on the historical aspects of the handbook, thinking that all the talk about the past—discussion of treaties, for example—was irrelevant. But as Theodore Haas, a colleague of Cohen's from Interior, argued, the "past and the present fuse indistinguishably" in almost all aspects of Indian law. Haas contended that after a close reading of eighteen hundred cases involving Indians the staff of the Indian law survey—the name for the group charged with compiling the data for the handbook—determined that in most cases historical matters took up much of courts' attention. Citing the Duwamish and the Sioux claims, for example, Haas stated that he did not see how it was possible to leave history out of the handbook. Fabian's and Littell's insistence on limiting the scope of the project was, according to Cohen, an example of "extreme bureaucratic provincialism." Secretary of the Interior Harold Ickes, who hoped the handbook would lead to the "elimination of injustices based upon ignorance of legal rights and responsibilities in our Indian Service," stepped in and tried mend the rift between Justice and Interior.[23] But rather than sanction the type of book Cohen wanted, Littell canceled the project at the end of October, claiming that the draft chapters were of such poor quality as to be useless.

Cohen was upset by the criticism—later found to be entirely unwarranted —but "very happy to be relieved of the necessity of working for the Department of Justice." His termination was a blessing. The project was handed off to Interior, and Cohen was back working for Margold. Even if it meant foregoing a salary, Cohen thought, that was a "light cost to pay for the privilege of working once more for superiors who know enough about my work to praise it intelligently instead of repeating, in parrot-like fashion, charges of disgruntled employees which show on their face that they emanate from prejudice, or ignorance, or both."[24] Cohen was miserable during his brief tenure at

Justice. His superiors were actually inferiors, and he found the working conditions so bad that "to put it mildly, [they are] inconsistent with ordinary standards of efficiency, economy and fair play in Government service." In fact, Cohen worried, the problems at Justice "may greatly discredit this Administration if they become generally known before the appropriate remedial steps are taken."[25]

After spending considerable time untangling himself from Justice — files and personnel needed to be transferred, and the charges leveled against the original drafts of the handbook had to answered — Cohen was finally allowed to set up shop at Interior in the summer of 1940. With Cohen again working for Margold, the original purpose of the handbook — a manual for attorneys working for the government, as well as Indians and their lawyers — would guide the government's work. Indeed, Margold committed himself to making all material collected for the handbook available to tribes and their attorneys after the manual was complete. And toward the end of the summer, once tempers had cooled, Attorney General Robert Jackson apologized for any misunderstanding between the two departments. Cohen, it turned out, had done a fine job on the handbook; Justice even looked forward to receiving a copy. Jackson put the problems down to the difference in their missions: Interior administered Indian affairs; Justice litigated Indian affairs. Knowing from the outset that they were often at odds with one another when it came to Indians, perhaps it had been a fool's errand all along. After all, Jackson was right: given the "natural differences of opinion" between the two, problems were inevitable.[26] Littell's two-front war — fighting Cohen on one front and Indians' claims on the other — was heating up. And now, with the *Handbook* completed, Cohen was about to move on to his next project: the Hualapai case.

The battle over the *Handbook of Federal Indian Law* was eclipsed by a more pressing concern: How could Justice represent the Hualapais and at the same time argue against other tribes' claims? Lawyers involved in the case finally realized in the fall of 1940 that they couldn't do both. Justice's two-pronged argument in other cases against Indians — that they did not possess property rights unless specifically granted by Congress and that, in particular, the "wild tribes" living in the Mexican cession never possessed any rights at all — put them in a difficult position when it came to the Hualapai, whom they were charged with representing. Justice began to take a close look at the consequences of a Hualapai victory in the Supreme Court. Raymond Nagle, a lawyer in the trial section, briefed the department on the implications and likelihood of a decision in favor of the Hualapais, realizing that if the Supreme Court reversed the Ninth Circuit, Justice's argument could collapse. And, what's more, "The importance of these contentions [denying Indian property claims] from a monetary standpoint cannot be stated even approximately without extensive research to determine the size and value of the areas which have not been affirmatively recognized as belonging to Indian tribes. But, generally, it can be stated that most of California, Nevada, Utah, Arizona, and parts of Wyoming, Colorado, and New Mexico are involved."[27] If the Hualapais won, the dam would break, and nothing could hold back a wave of cases from making their way to the Court of Claims and eventually to the Supreme Court. Several Court of Claims cases had affirmed Justice's view that, until recognized, Indian title sat "inchoate." Nagle took comfort in two cases from the early 1930s — *Duwamish v. United States* and *Coos Bay Indians v. United States* — which not only upheld Justice's contention, but were declined by the Supreme Court.

But Nagle knew better than to assume that the matter was settled. He got to work firming up the government's position, based on Justice's second contention: the United States has never recognized, nor did Spain and Mexico, any rights in the "savage tribes" — his words — who occupied the vast space ceded by Mexico after the Mexican-American war. Nagle was forced to admit, though, that the courts had used "loose language" when discussing the rights of Indians in the former Mexican territory. He cautioned that the cases which touch on the question should not "be given much weight either pro or con."[28] The question was unsettled, and Nagle's analysis forced him to concede that the Court could decide that the Hualapais had Indian title.

Norman Littell also weighed in, recommending that the Court take the case. And he also wondered how Justice could help the Hualapais and simultaneously defend the government. Littell based his recommendation on what he thought was the chief flaw of the Ninth Circuit's opinion: that the court had "disregarded the allegation in the complaint that the Walapai were and are now in possession" of the land they claimed as theirs. The Ninth Circuit's "disregard" should have come as no surprise to Littell — it was his fault. Oscillating between supporting and undermining the Hualapais' claim, he could not make up his mind. Although a strong argument could be made in support of the decision, the Supreme Court should have a chance to make a decision of its own. Janus-faced as ever, Littell cautioned the solicitor general that "a reversal of that decision might possibly have an adverse effect upon pending and potential Indian claims litigation handled by" the Lands Division.[29] In other words, the Hualapai deserve their day in court, but a decision in their favor would be very bad for the government.

The Justice Department decided that there was simply no way to adequately defend the Hualapais. After hashing it out with Interior and with Solicitor

General Warner Gardner, Charles Denny, chief of the appellate section, decided that in light of the obvious conflict "whoever handled the case on behalf of the Walapai should be completely free to argue that the tribal right of occupancy was not only effective against grantees of the Government [the railroad] but, until extinguished, was effective against the United States even in the absence of treaty recognition." Conceding that Indians might have compensable claims against the United States left Justice deeply concerned about what attorney Thomas Harris called the "staggering liability" the United States would face were the tribe to prevail. A Hualapai victory would allow other tribes to make claims against the government based on aboriginal title. Gardner boiled the conflict down to this: "As fiduciary, we cannot abandon an argument because it would cost the US large amounts, and as counsel for the Government we cannot urge it."[30]

By the fall of 1940, when more than one hundred tribes were suing the government in the Court of Claims and several victories totaling more than $10 million had been won in the Supreme Court, the Justice Department finally realized that it either had to fight or defend Indians. Doing both was no longer an option.[31] For four years, under the direction of Richard Hanna — whom John Collier had hired and Justice had fired — the Lands Division had been building a case that, if successful in the Supreme Court, would go a long ways toward crippling the government in cases against Indians. Justice already had enough work defending the government against claims based on breached treaties. It would be nearly impossible to fend off cases based on history.

The impact of a favorable decision was quickly becoming apparent to others also. In the late winter of 1941, Senator Carl Hayden, who by his own calculation had now been involved in the Hualapai case for twenty years, called the claim of the BIA on behalf of the tribe "entirely ridiculous." Confident that the Supreme Court would not grant certiorari and that if it did the Court would uphold the Ninth Circuit, a tinge of worry nonetheless colored Hayden's mood. For two decades he had been doing his best to separate the Hualapais from their land: he had sponsored the consolidation legislation designed to cut the reservation in half; he had encouraged Herbert Hagerman's efforts to settle the dispute in the railroad's favor; he had compiled the *Walapai Papers;* and he had regularly plied the railroad with evidence and advice. And now, if the Supreme Court did not see things his way, he would go further still and make certain Congress drafted legislation to keep the reservation out of Hualapai control. Responding to the perceived worries of the Arizona legislature that Indians and the federal government were taking over the state, Hayden committed himself to reserving for "white use . . . as much of the Walapai lands as possible." Rarely were his anti-Indian sentiments, which often leaked out of his missives, so explicit.[32]

Now that the implications of a decision in the Hualapais' favor were becoming clear, Justice lawyers must have felt chagrined. Francis Biddle, the attorney general, confessed to Hayden that he found the conflict of interest "embarrassing."[33] They had let the case get far beyond what Biddle had likely imagined when Richard Hanna was hired in 1936. Although few people — save perhaps Cohen, Hanna, Margold, Collier, and company — felt this way at the time, the irony now is almost comical (or tragic, depending on your point of view). Before Justice realized it, and after it was too late, the Hualapai case came to resemble other claims based on aboriginal possession. But because the Hualapai were fighting a third party (the ATSF) and not the government, Justice had agreed to take the case. For four years the department had funded the construction of a legal strategy that would be used against the U.S. government — and eventually governments in Canada, New Zealand, Australia, and South Africa, among other places — for the rest of the twentieth century.

That it took so long for Justice to figure all this out is a measure of the autonomy that Hanna had had for a time. But it is also a measure of how little power most attorneys seemed to accord Indian history. "The Government," Department of Justice attorney Thomas Harris wrote in 1940, "for years assumed that the Walapai claims were groundless." It had turned out to be impossible to ignore the fact of occupancy and the law of Indian title. Of course, not everyone agreed that the Hualapai had no past in the land they claimed. Writing in the popular western magazine *Arizona Highways* in 1941, Frances Sanita claimed confidently, "As far as is known, the Hualpai have always occupied the pine clad mountains for about a hundred miles along the southern side of the Grand Canyon. . . . Evidence of their undisputed occupancy, and ownership of this territory is contained in their family and tribal records, traditions and legends which are unwritten but have been faithfully transmitted from parent and leader to offspring and follower." Based on her observations of and interviews with Hualapais, Sanita's detailed article was a strong endorsement of the tribe's claims. By 1941 the Hualapais were able to marshal a version of their past and make it convincing to outsiders — but not to the courts, at least, not yet.[34]

Several years later, on the eve of the passage of the Indian Claims Commission Act in 1946, when the United States agreed to open itself up to hundreds of Indian suits, many based on aboriginal possession, President Harry Truman might have said it best when he expressed the hope that "we are not unloosening a Frankenstein."[35] The simple argument the Hualapai had been making since Fred Mahone returned to the reservation for good in 1921 — "we have always been here" — could no longer be ignored. The Justice Department solved its dilemma the only way it knew how: it let go of the Hualapai case late in the fall of 1940 and handed it over to the Interior Department, where it landed in the lap of Felix Cohen. Hanna and his partner William Brophy were promptly rehired. After being granted a sixty-day extension by the Supreme Court they made their way to Washington, and work on the appeal began.

12

The Supreme Court and the Power of History

Convincing the Court to grant certiorari would not be easy. The petition
—jointly authored by Cohen, Margold, Hanna, and Brophy—not only had to
persuade the Supreme Court to hear the case, but it also had to make up for
deficiencies in the work done by Littell and MacDonald. The petition critiqued
their brief in subtle but important ways. The thrust of the argument was the
same: the Hualapai have occupancy rights that all Indians in the formerly
Mexican territory also possess. But whereas Littell and MacDonald had
chosen to craft the opening of their brief to show that the government had
consistently found the Hualapais to be without title, the petition's authors
more accurately wrote that since 1919 the rights of the Hualapai had been
"investigated" by Interior and the Senate Committee on Indian Affairs. And
when writing about the Finney opinion, rather than suggest that Finney's was
the last word on Hualapai occupancy, the petition noted that the "meager
information then available was inadequate to establish" that the tribe had
Indian title.[1] On the basis of the government's previous brief one would not be
wrong in assuming that it had little faith in the Hualapais' claim; the petition
for certiorari, on the other hand, left it an open question for the Court to
decide.

Hanna, Cohen, Margold, and Brophy were restrained in their criticism of
Littell and MacDonald's work—they were colleagues of a sort, after all. They

showed no such reluctance when it came to the lower courts, calling their use of judicial notice "unprecedented and unjustifiable."[2] The District Court had decided that no evidence could be presented that could counter the railroad's contention that the Hualapais were merely a congeries of wandering savages without property rights. But it had not even looked at the government's evidence. The petition, on the other hand, exposed the courts' use of judicial notice for what it was: a misguided reading of history based on strongly held opinions about Indians. The lower courts had readily accepted the railroad's evidence — which was, according to the petition, an "inadequate and one-sided collection of reports presented by the defendant" — as being the only story one could tell about the Hualapais because that's what was within their intellectual grasp. On reading the defendant's presentation of its evidence, the lower courts recognized what they took to be *the* way of seeing the Indian past.

Several years after the Hualapai case had been decided, when the Northwestern Band of Shoshones lost their land claim in the Supreme Court, Felix Cohen distilled a common perception about Indian property rights into one sentence. He charged the Court, and by extension other judges, bureaucrats, and government attorneys, with thinking that "Indians are less than human and that their relation to their lands is not the human relation of ownership but rather something similar to the relation that animals bear to the areas in which they may be temporarily confined." He called this the "menagerie theory of Indian title." Though not yet named, it was this theory that persuaded the lower courts in the Hualapai case, Cohen wrote in his petition to the Supreme Court, to extend the "scope of judicial notice to difficult and controversial issues of anthropology with respect to the land tenure of an obscure Indian group and to equally difficult issues of history." During that case Cohen also began to learn about the "myth of the nomadic homeless Indian" — a myth that he claimed was "commonly accepted as a fact even by judges who are trained in the difficult art of reserving judgment in the absence of evidence." Whether they were so trained or not, there was plenty of evidence regarding Hualapai occupancy. But, the petition argued, the lower courts had accepted the railroad's version of Hualapai history and would not "consider evidence to the contrary."[3]

The lower courts' use of judicial notice troubled others besides Cohen and his colleagues. Supreme Court Justice Felix Frankfurter also seized on it. When working to decide whether to take case, what Frankfurter found particularly galling was the lower courts' acceptance on judicial notice of the Finney and Richardson opinions. For one thing, Frankfurter thought "allegations of possession ought not to be tried on a motion to dismiss by a reference to conclusions of government officers," who, he seemed to suggest, would not give Hualapai history a fair look. But it was even stranger that the lower courts, in a move that "seems hardly justifiable," took on judicial notice a question of fact that was "sought to be established by memoranda of some 150 pages in the record."[4] Frankfurter wondered: How could the lower courts simply say that 150 pages' worth of evidence would not tell them anything they did not already know?

Because of the power of the petition, combined with Frankfurter's obvious annoyance at the lower courts' willful disregard for Hualapai history, the Court took the case. Carl Hayden's anger and mystification were almost palpable. How could it be that the tribe's "entirely ridiculous" claims could place in jeopardy the property interests of white people? After all, according to Hayden, the Hualapais were "a dying race." And what's more, Hayden pointed out to Attorney General Francis Biddle, if the Hualapai won, a precedent would be established that would be "binding upon the Department of Justice, the Court of Claims, and the Congress and which will require the recognition of Indian claims based upon aboriginal possession." He urged Biddle to consider the outcome of such a decision. Congress would be called on "to pay out of the public treasury astronomical sums of money in settlement of Indian claims based upon possessory rights."[5] Hayden had cut to the heart of the matter: the Hualapais had only history on their side.

Cohen began to work on persuading the Supreme Court to reverse the lower courts. After the Court agreed to take the case, Richard Hanna played an ever smaller role. Though he was still collaborating with colleagues such as Brophy, the responsibility of writing the government's brief largely fell to Cohen.[6] When complete, the brief was a hefty 104 pages, a rock-solid defense of the Hualapais' claim. Cohen again struck hard at the lower courts' use of judicial notice. The courts' "findings" — the ironic quotation marks are Cohen's — were merely distillations of the railroad's "miscellaneous collection of reports of explorers and soldiers who, at various times, found the Walapai Indians in various places and occasionally reported that the Indians they found ate wild foods and dressed in skins." Given no chance to present evidence in favor of the Hualapais, the government had been barred from exposing some of the railroad's anti-Hualapai evidence as emanating from less-than-objective observers. For example, Cohen challenged the railroad's effort to prove "alleged Indian backwardness." By relying, for example, on the opinions of the Superintendent of Indian Affairs for Arizona, a man who in 1865 advocated Indian "extermination" and wrote, "I have no objection to seeing them burnt alive, men, women, and children," Cohen argued, the railroad had deliberately used "prejudiced sources." Cohen wondered how someone who advocated the destruction of Indians could be a reliable judge of "Indian backwardness," much less Hualapai occupancy rights. He claimed that he could find an equal if not greater number of missives from contemporaneous sources showing the opposite of what the railroad claimed and the lower courts believed. He argued that the "truth of any report or opinion on Walapai habits, movements and possessions is properly subject to proof."[7]

For the Supreme Court's benefit, Cohen attached fifty pages' worth of statutes, treaties, and archival evidence — what he called only a "token" of the available evidence — to show, first, that the railroad's evidence was selective and incomplete, second, that the material the lower courts refused to look at would refute the railroad's claim that the Hualapai "were disunited bands of non-agricultural, nomadic savages who occupied exclusively no definable territory and no place or places for any great length of time," and, finally, that the Hualapais had *not* surrendered title to the land to which the railroad laid claim. And all this was designed to get at what Cohen called "the primary issue in the case": to answer the question of whether the Hualapai "had an enforceable right of use and occupancy in those lands which . . . they had occupied continuously from time immemorial."[8]

In the Respondent's Brief the railroad made the lower courts' denial of Hualapai land rights the major feature of its argument. Pleased that the courts had found that the government had repeatedly denied the tribe any property rights, the railroad was adamant in its belief that the lower courts were entirely justified in ignoring evidence regarding Hualapai occupancy. But its argument was circular at best and teleological at worst. As the railroad argued, it was *because* the government believed that the Hualapais were merely nomadic savages that their rights had been denied in the first place. The lower courts had held that any evidence regarding occupation was "immaterial." The courts knew that the government had regarded them as one of the "savage tribes referred to in the Treaty of Guadalupe Hidalgo." By suppressing discussion of the Hualapais as anything but nomadic savages, the railroad had hoped to keep it that way. Of course, the railroad did not take it on faith that the courts would agree with its description. Knowing that if it could show the Hualapais to be merely a collection of nomadic savages the law was on its side, and not content to let past policy speak for itself, the Santa Fe's lengthy brief for the lower courts marshaled reams of evidence to prove that the Hualapais were mere wanderers — and just in case, they provided the Supreme Court with a summary of their evidence regarding occupancy.[9]

Things had been going well for the railroad; it had met with little resistance from the government and the courts. But now the government turned on the railroad, and it was stunned. Until that time, the Santa Fe claimed, the government had been acting in "an exactly opposite manner." In five previous appearances before the Supreme Court the question now before the Court had never been "presented or even hinted at." The railroad was confused. Well-settled matters of policy were being upended. According to its brief, "The counsel for the Walapai find themselves, with respect to the questions of Indian right, opposed, in a field indubitably one of political and not judicial cognizance, to everything that has been done by the United States in its sovereign and proprietary capacity, for more than ninety years." (That the railroad only now felt betrayed by the government is testimony to the radical departure that Cohen and his colleagues had taken from Littell's approach.) After all, what the railroad called the savage tribes had no land rights but those explicitly given to them by the sovereign.[10]

To the Santa Fe's surprise, the government was creating what the railroad called a "new sort of title." Because the government now argued that Indians had a property right that was good against the United States until extinguished by the sovereign, what scared the railroad was its perception that the government was prepared to jettison the idea that Indians had no more than a "mere right of possession." How could this be possible, the railroad wondered, when history had until then gone its way? Nearly one hundred years of policy and practice "have manifested and realized one clear purpose, to develop all the lands of Arizona with specified exceptions known as reservations, for and by white men." In the face of such history, a history that marched toward the goal of an Indian-free Arizona, the Hualapais' claim was absurd; their case had "no more weight than a shadow." The government's wish that a case be tried on the facts of occupancy would be a waste of time, the railroad reasoned. The facts were irrelevant. Trying a case such as the Hualapais', arguing that the fact of occupancy creates a property right heretofore unrecognized by the sovereign, was a brand of "reasoning [that] stands in marked repugnance to the actual course of history."[11]

Standing in opposition to history was, of course, the point. Cohen and his colleagues, and Mahone and the Hualapais before them, knew what they were doing. The railroad was right: U.S. policy had written the Hualapais out of their land. The government's apostasy rightfully came as a shock to the railroad. To argue, as Cohen did, that the Hualapai had a property right based on their long-term occupancy and not recognized or sanctioned by the sovereign was novel indeed. Even a sympathetic colleague such as Theodore Haas, one of Cohen's collaborators on the *Handbook of Federal Indian Law*, argued that Indians only had the rights that were granted to them.[12] Cohen's move was radical. The Department of Justice, and the railroad had a hard time with the notion that occupancy — centuries or more of living in the same place, cultivating crops, raising children, waging war — could have the stamp of legitimacy. Cohen argued that it did.

Cohen, Margold, and the attorneys for the railroad spent two days in late November 1941 — of which no records exist — arguing their respective cases before the Court. Owing to the complexity of the issues — so many facts, such a long case history, and such vast implications — the government and the railroad had each asked for an extra hour to make their case. The Court granted each side an extra fifteen minutes. Cohen and Margold had little more than an hour to sum up what had taken two decades to prepare. Three weeks later, on 8 December 1941, the Court issued its opinion. Writing for a unanimous Court, in an opinion that appeared to have caused little discord among the justices, William O. Douglas demolished the lower courts' opinions.[13] As Margold had done in 1934 when he completely reversed earlier attorneys' opinions concerning the Hualapais' claim, so Douglas did now: he found the lower courts' decisions to be without merit and reversed them.

It was not a very long opinion — only fifteen pages — but it said a great deal. In that short space, Douglas digested the essentials of this complicated case. Associate Justice Hugo Black told him it was "a remarkable feat to get the grasp you did." The opinion both affirmed many of the key principles laid down by the Marshall Court in the early nineteenth century and broke new ground. The Court declared that no positive affirmation of title from the sovereign was necessary because Indians had aboriginal title to their land based on occupancy from time immemorial. And thus, although the Hualapai lost title to land outside the reservation when they accepted its boundaries in 1883, their aboriginal title to land within the reservation had never been extinguished. The Court said that Indian "occupancy necessary to establish aboriginal possession is a question of fact to be determined as any other question of fact."[14] Previously, lawyers had argued, and courts had agreed, that because the Hualapais had no treaty or other similar recognition of their land rights they had none, *and* that no facts could be presented to prove otherwise. By making occupancy the basis of title, and by making proof of occupancy dependent on history, the Supreme Court threw out this line of reasoning.

The Court also found that the creation of the Colorado River Reservation, to which Finney and Richardson attached such importance, was, "so far as the Walapais were concerned, nothing more than an abortive attempt to solve a perplexing problem." In addition, it found that the forced removal that Finney and Richardson considered sufficient to extinguish title was nothing more than "a high-handed endeavor to wrest from these Indians lands which Congress never declared forfeited."[15] Finally, the Court settled the important question of the rights that native people had to land claimed by the United States in the Treaty of Guadalupe Hidalgo: Indian lands within the former Mexican territory have the same protections as lands elsewhere in the United States.

It took the Supreme Court only a few weeks to reach a decision about matters that had consumed Fred Mahone's life for more than twenty years. He must have been ecstatic. After losing twice in lower courts, the Hualapais had convinced the Supreme Court that they had been telling the truth: the land was theirs. No one had taken it away. Likewise, the decision must have made Carl Hayden angry. After all, the Court relied heavily on his pet publication, the *Walapai Papers,* to reach many of its conclusions regarding Hualapai occupancy. Hayden's effort to marshal history in the railroad's favor, not to mention Arizona's, had failed. The verdict was important to others as well. Writing to Alfred Kroeber shortly afterward, Cohen not only told him that he was "particularly gratified to find anthropologists making a very real contribution to the vindication of Indian rights" but also called it "one of the most important cases ever to reach the Supreme Court in the history of our Federal Indian law."[16]

United States v. Santa Fe Pacific Railroad Co. was the twentieth century's first major decision concerning Indian land rights. The various lawyers, bureaucrats, and other officials who weighed in against the Hualapais believed that applying nineteenth-century legal principles to twentieth-century Indians was not possible. Thus, as the case made its way through the administrative process and then the courts, it appeared at many times as if the basic principles laid down by the Marshall Court might be reinterpreted in the light of changed circumstances. The cases decided by the Marshall Court were forgotten. But the modern Court chose to protect Indian property rights by realizing that the law insulates Indians from the passage of time; rights guaranteed in the past could not be eroded by the powerful current of history. And perhaps most significant, the Court said that even though Congress still possessed ultimate power over Indian property it had to demonstrate a clear and plain intent to take away inherent, sovereign rights.[17] By validating the historical work that Mahone, the Hualapais, and other tribes and their attorneys had pioneered in the 1920s and 1930s, and by stating that aboriginal title was a "question of fact to be determined as any question of fact," the decision launched a new reading of the Indian past.

13

In the Wake of Hualpai

In April 1942, Felix Cohen and Fred Mahone finally met. In his mid-fifties now, Mahone began a new spring for the first time in more than twenty years not consumed by the effort to protect his people's property. Appointed by the Hualapai tribal council to aid in documenting Hualapai land use and to help individual Indians file land claims, Mahone showed Cohen the land he had helped save. Mahone and Cohen, along with Abe Barber from the General Land Office, spent part of April and May together. They toured "the claimed area," Cohen recalled, "in an old jalopy for about 1200 miles." They visited the entirety of the Hualapais' aboriginal lands — parts of three states all linked by the Colorado River — exploring numerous sites on the Hualapai reservation and interviewing Hualapais, Mojaves, Havasupais, Hopis, Paiutes, and others. For Cohen the trip was the "most interesting phase of the litigation." Impressed by "the way in which old Indians of different tribes who did not know each other and had not heard each other's testimony agreed on the specific rivers and mountains that marked their ancient inter-tribal boundaries," he believed now more than ever that the land was the Hualapais'.[1]

Charged with determining exactly what land the Hualapai occupied within the boundaries of their reservation and what land individual Hualapais might have occupied outside the reservation, Cohen came to answer some key questions — questions that historians, anthropologists, courts, and others would eventually ask of indigenous people across the United States and around the globe. Did the Hualapai occupy their land exclusively, as was now mandated by the Supreme Court? Had they occupied their land since time immemorial? How could they prove it? Although the Court made it clear that there had never been any clear and plain intent to extinguish Hualapai title, it had not ruled as to what land was Hualapai land when the reservation was created in 1883 — that was Cohen's job. In short, the same question that had been driving the case all along remained the same: Did the Hualapais have a valid claim to the land they said was theirs?

By the time Cohen and Barber arrived the Hualapais had learned to talk about their past and their property. In a series of several dozen reticent exchanges among Cohen, Barber, and individual Hualapais — as well as Mojaves, Paiutes, Yavapais, and Havasupais who attested to the boundaries of the Hualapais' aboriginal territory — a picture of Hualapai occupancy and history emerged. But the exchanges were not especially revealing, and little that was not already known resulted. Generally speaking, all agreed that each tribe's territory was recognized by the others and marked by specific features such as the Colorado River.[2]

The hearings showed that the Hualapai and their neighbors had learned to speak clearly about their *exclusive* aboriginal boundaries. In doing so, the hearings exposed one of the several implications of the Supreme Court's opinion in the Hualapai case. The exchange economy in which the Hualapai participated with all their neighbors was deemphasized in order to shore up claims to their land. Other Indians might have visited the Hualapais, but none stayed long enough to lay claim to their land or weaken the Hualapais' claim. The Mojave and Paiute witnesses, for example, described a world inhabited by discrete tribes who, after the rare occasions in which they encountered one another, quickly retreated to their own respective territories. The constant trading and occasional intermarriage went unexplored. The clearest example of the need to talk in terms of exclusive occupancy came when discussing the Havasupais. The obvious — and previously attested to — affinity between the Havasupais and the Pine Springs Hualapais was explicitly denied by some witnesses. They insisted that the two groups had no overlapping claims, had never occupied the same territory, and were completely unrelated to one another. But creeping into the testimony of several witnesses — Indian Honga (Hualapai), Coyote Jim (Havasupai), Jim Crook (Havasupai), and Young Beecher (Hualapai) — was evidence of both intermarriage and overlapping claims, especially to land in the east. When questioned, even by a sympathetic Felix Cohen, who often supplied the answer he wanted in the form of a question, it was difficult to keep up the pretense that, at a minimum, Pine Springs was not contested ground. Ten years earlier, when Fred Mahone was in the thick of documenting Hualapai land use in the Pine Springs country, Samuel Brosius of the Indian Rights Association had warned him to make sure that Hualapai and Havasupai claims did not overlap. Now it appeared as if both tribes had taken that advice to heart: Despite cracks in their claims, the Hualapais and the Havasupais agreed, in advance of Cohen and Barber's arrival, to testify that each tribe maintained an exclusive territory. They had learned to tell Cohen and Barber what they wanted — or needed — to hear, how to talk about their land in a new way. It was now property.[3]

Fred Mahone played along, but the idea seemed absurd. And so soon after he returned to Washington, Felix Cohen received a long letter from Mahone. Laced with the gratitude, frustration, and incredulity that Mahone had felt for decades, the letter was both a mark of how far he had come and a sign of his persistent befuddlement regarding a system he did not understand. The idea that land could be claimed by one party to the total exclusion of another left him bewildered; the notion that the United States could simply take what was obviously the Hualapais' angered him to no end. And although he had perfected the Hualapais' ability to make a sound claim and early in his career as an activist had learned that he would have to talk about Hualapai territory as property, Mahone was still baffled by the fact that the Hualapai way of "property" needed any justification. Their country, Mahone told Cohen, "was marked and bounded by . . . ancient laws and rulings. These laws and rulings, only made in mouth words, [are] just as powerful as the present white mans Western laws and rulings." Mahone wondered: How had it come to be that these laws prevailed and Hualapais' words did not? He answered the question with a rare bit of sarcasm, observing: "It was as if the Hualapais should go across the Ocean and come to small groups of nations and say: I discover a new country; a new people. Now, I have my laws and rulings; I have the right to put up notices on certain water and land, saying: this is my right, and it is my own. Now, you go away. And keep this up until every water hole or spring or stream, and all the land is taken away from people situated like the Hualapais are."[4] For Mahone, when all was said and done, that's what it boiled down to: using their own laws, white people came and took the Hualapais' land and water. And now that Mahone came to that realization, his long journey from Chilocco student to World War I veteran to activist to plaintiff before the Supreme Court was over.

The story of the Hualapai case, in many respects, ended with the Court's decision. After several years of legal wrangling, during which the Justice Department again tried to abandon the case, the railroad and the Hualapai finally settled out of court. It never went to trial. No longer able to sustain the fiction that the Hualapai had no history and no claim, the railroad gave up. Settling the case in 1947, the tribe got what it wanted: recognition that the land within the reservation was theirs, as well as the return of six thousand acres of land around Clay Springs. When he heard the news Felix Cohen was pleased, saying, it "makes me feel that my years at Interior have not been wholly wasted." The final settlement meant that "the principles of law that were established in the Supreme Court decision [were] more than high-sounding generalities."[5]

But Cohen's sigh of satisfaction masked his otherwise grim outlook on Indian affairs. Less than a year later, on 2 January 1948, he quit. On hearing the news of Cohen's departure one Alaska newspaper was ecstatic, claiming that Cohen's "theories are responsible for a great deal of the mess Alaska now has in connection with Indian property rights."[6] The Indian New Deal, of which the Hualapai case was both a high point and a turning point, was over. Catching the same wave of optimism that other young lawyers had ridden all the way to the capital, Cohen had arrived at the beginning of the New Deal in 1933. Thirteen years later, alone after most of his colleagues had left, he followed them. He knew what was coming: tribal termination and a renewed commitment to assimilation. The government had decided—again—to get out of the Indian business. When it did, Cohen decided to get out of the government.

When Cohen turned in his letter of resignation, his friends threw a party for him. Gathering at the Chinese Lantern in downtown Washington, D.C., friends, family, and colleagues spent a night together reminiscing about Cohen's career—one in which he'd helped draft the Indian Reorganization Act and tribal constitutions, written the *Handbook of Federal Indian Law,* secured voting rights for Indians in New Mexico and Arizona (the last states to keep Indians from voting), taken two precedent-setting cases to the Supreme Court, and co-drafted the Indian Claims Commission Act. Cohen had come to Washington at twenty-eight, armed already with a Ph.D. and a J.D. He was ready to change the world. That night at the Chinese Lantern all anybody wanted to do was remember the Indian New Deal. "All who came to Washington in 1933," Cohen fondly recalled, "will remember that many of us thought then that we were not far from the Divine Throne. The fate of the world seemed to rest on the wisdom and the power that the President brought to bear on the great problems" of the day.[7]

But Cohen was forty-one now and bitter, soured by what he thought was the government's betrayal of Indians. And though he could not wait to leave, he worried that everything he had worked for would be reversed—Indians would again become subject to ill-conceived programs aimed at their assimilation, their lands would again slip easily into white hands, already fragile property rights would crumble and blow away, and most important, the limited sovereignty and self-government Indians possessed would be replaced by total state control. Halfway through the twentieth century, and just four years before his life would be a tragically cut short by cancer, Cohen wished that Americans would finally realize that "Indian self-government is not a new but an ancient fact. The Federal government cannot really give self-government to the Indians, it can only get out of the way."[8]

Felix Cohen was tired of hearing the government—and well-meaning whites like himself—tell Indians how to be Americans. By way of analogy, Cohen wrote later that spring, "If anybody should tell me, a Jew of Russian descent, that I ought to be beneficially assimilated into the Anglo-Saxon protestant main stream of American life, my first impulse would be to punch my would-be reformer in the nose."[9] As far as I know, Cohen never did strike anyone—at least, not with his fists. His pen had always been a much more powerful weapon.

Fred Mahone lived for another thirty years. He was about eighty-two when he died in 1972. After the passage of the Indian Claims Commission Act, as the Hualapai litigated their land claim and a court finally heard the facts concerning their occupancy, Mahone again was at the forefront, reprising his role as tribal historian. He and Cohen must have met again because Cohen became the Hualapais' counsel in the case's early years. The ICC reached its final decision in 1967: the Hualapais were due compensation for 4.4 million acres of aboriginal land left out of their reservation and illegally taken by settlers and by the U.S. government. Figured down to the dollar, the ICC said the government owed them $2,974,612, which it made arrangements to pay in 1970. Variously going to healthcare, investments, and education, the money was a boon to the tribe's economy—which was not then, and is not now, robust. Each adult member of the tribe also received $70. What had begun just after World War I was now complete. The Hualapai proved what they had been saying all along: This land is ours and we've always been here.[10]

The case has had a long and productive life, affecting land claims in the United States and far beyond. The impact of the *Hualpai* decision was felt first in Alaska. Nathan Margold and Felix Cohen had wanted to pursue Alaska natives' claims but waited until the Court decided *Hualpai* before pushing forward. Immediately after the decision, government officials and native people used its principles to begin the long process of litigating Alaskan native land claims. Two months after the *Hualpai* decision was handed down Cohen wrote an official solicitor's opinion—which, like "Powers of Indian Tribes" eight years earlier, was attributed to Margold—affirming Alaska natives' fishing rights. Explicitly based on *Hualpai,* Cohen's opinion reasoned that because these rights had never been expressly extinguished by the United States, and because occupancy could likely be proved, they still existed. In response to the claims of the Tlingit and Haida villages of Klawock, Kake, and Hydaburg, the *Alaska Fishing News* wrote, "It must now be apparent to everyone that Secretary Ickes is planning one of the biggest land grabs ever attempted by a bureau chief." Though unsuccessful, the Tlingits and the Haidas saw the *Hualpai* decision as a way to claim ownership of a vast portion of the Tongass National Forest based on aboriginal title.[11]

Also on the heels of the Hualapai decision, in February 1943 William Paul of the Alaska Native Brotherhood, armed with a precedent he could use to bring the Tee-Hit-Ton Tlingits' claims to court, filed a brief in Alaska State Court that relied on the Supreme Court's rule that a clear and plain intent to extinguish title must be present. Paul accused the attorneys for Pacific American Fisheries, the defendants in the case, of distorting his aims by claiming that he and the Indians were after the entire state. Indeed, Paul wrote, "these same terroristic arguments were used in the Walapai case by defendant's attorneys and by the Attorney General of the State of Arizona as amicus curiae. It is significant that the Supreme Court believed such arguments so insignificant that it did not even dignify them with a refutation—they were simply ignored." Paul said that the Tee-Hit-Tons were merely attempting to retain the use of their aboriginal fishing grounds—and they would be using the precedent set down in *Hualpai* to do so. As Paul wrote to Cohen, "Careful study of the 'Walapai Indian Case' . . . leads me to the following conclusion, namely, that our supreme court has laid down once more the rights of Indians in lands and waters wherein their rights were not previously extinguished by our government." Paul took great comfort in the Court's decision.[12] After the *Hualpai* decision and the Margold opinion were written, Alaskan native land claims would dominate state politics for decades.

But Cohen's instincts about the way in which the government was moving were correct, and the initial promise of the *Hualpai* opinion soon began to fade. Although the decision paved the way for Alaskan land claims, it did not guarantee victory. Even with the clear and plain intent test, Congress still had almost total power over Indian land, and the Supreme Court was still staffed by justices who were unwilling to accord Indians land rights based on immemorial occupancy. The land rights of Alaskan natives were by no means safe or secured. In 1955, two years after Cohen's death, in what is widely considered one of the twentieth century's most strongly anti-Indian decisions, the Supreme Court found that without prior recognition of title by the sovereign Alaska natives did not have compensable claims under the Fifth Amendment. In *Tee-Hit-Ton Indians v. United States,* an opinion that is shocking in its ethnocentrism, shoddy in its history, and unfaithful to precedent, Justice Stanley Reed provided no clear explanation of why the Fifth Amendment's takings clause did not apply to Indians. Seizing on language in the Hualapai case to the effect that Congress's power over Indian land is supreme but ignoring the decision's clear and plain intent test, as well the fact that the *Hualpai* Court affirmed that title does not have to be based on a congressional grant, Reed did his best to make sure that the United States was not financially liable for violating native property rights. And as if that were not enough, in 1956 the Department of Justice, still afraid that Indian land claims would bleed the Treasury dry, lobbied Congress in an attempt to ensure that history played no part in Indian claims. When it became clear that Indians were able to show, via historical reconstructions of their pasts, that they had long-term ties to land, Justice worked hard to make sure that the law—common law and legislation —would not recognize history. The Justice Department wanted to bar all claims based on aboriginal occupancy from being heard by the Indian Claims Commission.[13]

The passage of the Indian Claims Commission Act had been Cohen's final effort at bringing some measure of justice to American Indians. He did not live to see how it played itself out. Created by Congress in 1946, the Indian Claims Commission (ICC) was long in the making. The idea of some sort of tribunal, or special court, to settle Indian claims against the government had been batted about since before World War I. And as more and more tribes launched an ever-increasing number of claims against the government in the 1920s and 1930s, Congress convened hearing after hearing in a vain search for a solution. By the mid-1940s the claims process had become so cumbersome, so costly, and so inefficient that most of those involved despaired of ever disposing of Indian claims. Most politicians, and of course the Justice Department, were leery of exposing the government to an endless barrage of suits. But they were not going away, and the process needed to be streamlined.

Two factors motivated Congress to finally act. Many in Congress hoped that the final adjudication of claims against the government would be the beginning of the end of the government's responsibility toward Indians. They had already cost the government too much. The termination era, marked by the policy of severing all ties with tribes, was just around the corner; settlement of all claims would be an auspicious start. But Congress did not only have self-interest in mind. After all, the bill that finally passed in 1946 was largely the product of Felix Cohen's efforts. The ICC did not live up to Cohen's expectations, nor Congress's — among other problems, tribes rarely received adequate compensation, Indians were largely left out of the process, claims took too long to settle, and the act certainly did not end tribes' relations with the government. Despite its failures, the act's passage marked a victory over powerful anti-Indian forces within the Department of Justice, forces opposed to the very idea of any sort of tribunal to hear Indian claims. And, as the first state-sponsored effort to put native history on trial, the ICC has become a model for other efforts at reconciling past wrongs.[14]

Beginning with the ICC, and as a result of the *Hualpai* case, land claims litigation has affected the ways in which scholars think about native history. Ethnohistory was born. In the early years of land claims this meant that the fluidity of the native past had to be denied, modified, glossed over, or simply never found by scholars searching for stability. The complexity of the past conflicted with the simplifications required by the law of property. The "tribe" became reified as anthropologists, working for Indians as well as the government, went in search of stable, identifiable groups of people who "owned" this or that piece of property. Because boundary lines did not exist in the fashion required by western notions of property, conflicting claims to common territory, for example, have caused the courts and native people significant problems.[15]

When the ICC adopted the Supreme Court's rule in *Hulapai* regarding exclusive occupancy of a definable territory, tribes and the Justice Department were compelled to research the history of native land use. Right from the start, when the earliest cases coming out of the ICC started citing *Hualpai* as the origin of the requirement that tribes show exclusive occupancy, claims proved troubling.[16] When the commissioners hearing cases before the ICC and the anthropologists charged with building cases for and against Indian occupancy adopted that decision as their standard, a whole series of questions came cascading down. How would exclusive occupancy be proved? What if it could not be shown? Was the law of property asking Indians and their historical and anthropological assistants to demonstrate something that never existed? How would anthropologists and others make Indian history legible to the law? And how would having to show exclusive occupancy affect the writing of Indian history, to say nothing of the historical consciousness of Indian people?

In order to debate some of these issues, anthropologists and historians involved in claims work founded a new journal in 1954 called *Ethnohistory*. In 1955 the journal devoted an entire issue to Indian claims. All of this was so new, so strange, really, that at first most of those involved were flummoxed. Ralph Barney, the attorney at Justice who was in charge of Indian claims, spoke for everyone when he said that "the law [of Indian claims] is essentially new and in some respects revolutionary." Barney singled out *Hualpai* when he noted that the "most difficult factual problem with which the Commission is faced . . . is the question of what definable territory the Indians occupied exclusively." That is when "the anthropologist comes into the picture." And when the anthropologists were called in claims became complicated, indeed. Exclusive aboriginal occupancy, though hard to prove, was, according to Barney, the only thing the ICC cared about. Writing to his anthropologist colleague Erminie Voegelin in 1956, Barney asked Voegelin to keep the research that she and her colleagues were doing focused on this issue only. Although he realized that Voegelin and others might be interested in other features of the Indian past, he cautioned her: if the evidence collected answers the question, then it is "of value: if it does not tend to answer the question it is wholly valueless to the Commission regardless of how interesting it might be to an anthropologist, or a historian or any one else."[17]

What did this new type of research mean for anthropologists? Verne F. Ray worried about scholars' getting involved in claims work because it "pits anthropologist against anthropologist in the presentation of anthropological data in the form of expert testimony." Until the ICC appeared, anthropologists had only rarely been used in Indian law; now, they became a critical component. Ray realized, too, that the volume of claims work was bound to have an effect on anthropology; new methodologies were already changing the field. Indeed, claims research and all its implications were among "the most important professional issues of the day." Julian Steward, one of the twentieth century's most influential anthropologists and a specialist on hunter-gatherers, noted the difficulties associated with the fact that lawyers and anthropologists did not speak a common language. Whereas lawyers attached a fixed meaning to concepts such as "property," anthropologists did not, knowing that it shifted from culture to culture. If anthropologists had "failed to come to grips with this crucially important problem of 'property' in detail and concreteness," how could lawyers assign any fixed meaning to the term, much less prove exclusive occupancy? Steward was frustrated — after all, cultures varied so much across time and space that one never knew from case to case what one was supposed to prove. Questions about aboriginal land tenure, as well as political organization and economic organization — questions that had largely been absent from anthropology as scholars pursued research into native belief systems, for instance — now rose to prominence. Because one of the key issues in claims research was proving exclusive occupancy of a definable territory, previously ignored or understudied matters such as the history of land use and native concepts of property became important.[18]

Alfred Kroeber also noted the difficulties associated with terminology, especially with the terms "tribe" and "property." Kroeber wanted to make it clear that indigenous people had organized themselves in a multitude of ways and used their land according to the peculiarities of each group's history and relationship with land. Like Steward, he found it difficult to reconcile a discipline that recognized flux — anthropology — with one that required fixity and stasis — law. To Kroeber, the term "tribe" was simply a "White man's creation of convenience for talking about Indians . . . an administrative fiction of the Caucasian." Because native groups rarely resembled what mid-twentieth-century lawyers and judges thought of as tribes — cohesive units of linguistically and culturally homogenous peoples organized into a stable group with a recognized leader and territory — Kroeber rightly recognized the term as problematic. Claims litigation potentially asked Indian people to represent themselves as something they never were.[19]

Anthropologists such as Ray, Steward, and Kroeber realized soon after beginning claims work that their theoretical positions, as well as the imposition of categories, would have profound effects in the real world. Steward, for his part, worked for the Justice Department in cases against the Northern Paiutes, the Utes, and the Shoshones. His views concerning property, derived from his work with the Great Basin Shoshonean peoples before and during his employment by Justice, became the basis for the government's position that hunting and gathering people did not have a strong enough concept of land ownership to warrant calling their land-holding "property." According to Steward, whose position was adopted wholesale by Justice, the hunting and gathering people of the Great Basin had to spend so much time simply scratching a living from the desert that territoriality was beyond their ken; they followed their noses in search of food, never able to organize themselves into anything resembling a band, much less a tribe, with a definable territory. That Steward developed key features of his theoretical position on hunter-gatherers' property while working for Justice, and with the benefit of no further fieldwork, suggests the influence of the political-legal context in which he operated. (The ICC disagreed with Steward and Justice in all three cases, siding with the Indian plaintiffs each time.)[20]

Kroeber, on the other hand, worked for Indians, specifically the Mojaves and the conglomeration known as the "Indians of California." Although he shared Steward's skeptical view regarding the law's ability to recognize aboriginal land use as akin to property ownership, he recognized that the problem was the category itself, not Indians' inability to fit into it. Steward, on the other hand, appeared unable to disabuse himself of the notion that hunting and gathering people could not own property.[21]

Nor could Robert Manners, Justice's expert in the Hualapais' claim, do so. Like Steward and Kroeber, Manners preferred not to use such terms as "tribe" and "band." He agreed with Kroeber: As far as Indians were concerned, they did not exist. The terms and the concepts they signified were non-Indian inventions, Manners wrote in a 1957 *Ethnohistory* essay about the Hualapais. Life before the ICC, Manners suggested, was simple for anthropologists. The ways in which native people organized themselves did not much matter outside academia; it was "only a matter for analytic and theoretical consideration." But now anthropologists were being called out of their offices to help sort out "the multi-billion dollar determination and distribution of awards." Observing that fictional entities were now suing the government, Manners made it his aim to expose such chicanery. After all, "some of the 'tribes' which are now suing, *as tribes,* for compensation for 'tribal' lands taken from them, are, in effect, suing for something which never existed."[22] This was especially so in the Hualapai case: because they operated as semiautonomous bands before contact, they were never a tribe. It seems not to have mattered to Manners that from the beginning of contact with the United States, for purposes of war, internment, service as scouts, and the creation of the reservation the Hualapais were considered a tribe. His and Steward's deconstruction of the term stemmed from a concern for disciplinary integrity, not from the application of the term as it affected Indian people.

Because of the adversarial nature of the law, claims work pitted anthropologists against one another. Regardless of any professed loyalty to objectivity and impartiality, an anthropologist's work was going to be used by lawyers as they saw fit to win their cases. By simply agreeing to be part of the process, anthropologists were opening up their work to possible manipulation and distortion. Steward made this point clear to his colleagues in the Department of Justice: "The simple and unhappy fact seems to me that, since the Indians' lawyers are committed to proving certain things in order to win their cases, the anthropologists are almost forced to attempt to prove what the lawyers consider necessary whether this is scientifically defensible or not." The same, of course, could be said for government lawyers; neither side, after all, wanted to lose.[23]

It is impossible to know how much Justice's needs influenced Manners's research. His faith in "rigorous scientific research" allowed him — at least in print — to slough off any affronts to his scholarly credibility in the form of accusations that he and his colleagues had the government's interests in mind. After all, he reasoned, when pursuing the truth there was no room for taking sides. Anthropologists were simply ciphers, objectively looking at the evidence. That might be true, but Manners knew the government's goal: the department did not hire him to learn whatever he could about the Hualapai; he was hired to help prove that they had no claim and that they were never a tribe. One of his colleagues, Nancy Lurie, made the very good point that neither side would hire someone it knew to be previously disposed against its position. The debate between Lurie and Manners, hashed out in the pages of *Ethnohistory*, was becoming more than an academic question. It was becoming a labor problem at Justice and a problem of disciplinary boundaries with anthropology. As the number of claims based on occupancy increased so, too, did the need for anthropologists. But, as Ralph Barney lamented in 1955, fewer and fewer were willing to do claims work. Staking out a position, either for the government or for the Indians, was increasingly troublesome to many of them. Barney worried that as a result it was becoming harder and harder to hire competent expert witnesses. A year later, Barney, no less worried but a little more reflective, thought that "American Anthropology is in a transitional stage of transcendental importance." Though some were still skeptical of merging their discipline with history, many had come around. History and ethnology, in Barney's mind, had melded into one discipline, ethnohistory — and this was the best method "to discover the *true* factual situation in any given case."[24]

Claims work led to an explosion of work on Indian history that, for better or worse, was results-oriented. Ethnohistory was instrumental history invented by anthropologists and historians embedded in the adversarial process of claims work. Their research, commissioned and produced to win cases, was an outgrowth of the historical consciousness that had developed among such tribes as the Hualapai during the 1920s and 1930s. It came about when the Supreme Court made provable occupancy the standard for claiming aboriginal title. The Court's decision effectively mandated the creation of Indian history as a distinct discipline.

The effects of the case reach further still, forcing native land claims and the meaning and content of native property rights onto the international indigenous rights agenda. The decision changed the way indigenous history was perceived, the way it was written, and for what purpose. The story of the way native peoples, lawyers, and courts have rethought the indigenous past as a way to ensure a more secure and just future is a global one. Indeed, to see the history of the case as only an American story would be to ignore a simple fact: the law affecting indigenous people is international in both origin and contemporary practice. And that story took a decisive turn with the United States Supreme Court's decision in *United States v. Santa Fe Pacific RR Co.*[25] In *Calder v. Attorney General,* Canada's first aboriginal title case, Justice Hall of the Canadian Supreme Court said that the "Hualpai case must be considered to be the

leading modern judgment on the question of aboriginal rights." The basic
assumptions about the past and native property have been drastically altered.
In 1992, in *Mabo and Others v. The State of Queensland* the Australian High
Court decided that Australia was not terra nullius when the British arrived in
the late eighteenth century. In 1997 the Canadian Supreme Court, in *Delgamuukw v. British Columbia*, ruled that aboriginal title existed in Canada, as
well. Both cases would never have come to court were it not for *Hualpai*. Today,
newspapers in Australia and Canada regularly cover the subject — the *Delgamuukw* decision was front-page news in the *New York Times*.[26]

Courts have not dealt with the question of aboriginal title because they
wanted to. Native people have forced the issue. Throughout the twentieth
century, native activists in Australia, Canada, and New Zealand struggled to
hold on to land by seeking political and legal solutions. Like Fred Mahone and
the Hualapais, native activists organized themselves for the purpose of securing land rights.[27] A brief example from Australia serves to highlight the role
played by indigenous activists, as well as the barriers to success set up by
powerful states armed with very particular notions of native property rights.

In the early 1920s aboriginal activists lead by Fred Maynard founded the
Australian Aboriginal Progressive Association, Australia's first pan-aboriginal
organization. Its founding marked the beginning of a sustained, organized
push for aboriginal rights. But, as in the United States, Aborigines faced stiff
opposition from a state that was widely perceived by Aborigines to be at odds
with their interests. In 1938 the aboriginal activist William Cooper, of the
Australian Aborigines League, pulled no punches and compared the Australian government, which he believed was committed to wiping out Aborigines,
to the Nazis. In Western Australia especially, the government was, according
to Cooper, "out Hitlering Hitler." As a form of protest, Cooper and other
activists organized a Day of Mourning in 1938 to serve as a counterpoint to
the government's celebration of 150 years of Australian history. History, in
fact, became Cooper's ally. Like Fred Mahone, Cooper seized upon the fact of
long-term aboriginal occupancy as his best defense against assertions that
Aborigines had no land rights.[28]

But Australians were just as mystified as Americans when it came to the
aboriginal past. Land claims based on history, in a country considered legally
terra nullius at the time of discovery, fell on deaf ears. Aboriginal people,
considered by anthropologists to be living relics of a timeless past, standing on
the shore watching the stream of history pass them by, were absent from the
story of Australia. Their past met much the same fate as the Hualapais': it was
ignored. It was not until anthropologists such as W. E. H. Stanner began to
radically rethink the Australian past and break what he called the "great
Australian silence" in the late 1950s and 60s, that Aborigines had any hope of

making successful land claims based on history. Like the Hualapais, Australian Aborigines needed powerful allies.[29]

As in the Hualapai case, Aborigines joined with sympathetic Anglos — lawyers, historians, anthropologists, and activists — to force the courts to hear their claims. One of those activists was Barrie Pittock, a young man who introduced the work of Felix Cohen to the Australian land claims community as a member of the Federal Council for Aboriginal Advancement. After spending a year in the United States in the early 1960s, Pittock returned to Australia convinced that something could be done about aboriginal land rights. While in America, Pittock had met John Collier and D'Arcy McNickle. At the recommendation of Collier, Pittock turned to the work of Felix Cohen, where he found a clear delineation of native Americans' rights to land. But he saw more: in an interview in the mid-1990s, he recalled that Cohen's writing anchored indigenous land rights in international law. And thus, the key to land rights in Australia was to be found there. Pittock's time in the United States was so pivotal that while still abroad his letters home were compiled and circulated amongst activists as "A Letter on the History of Land Rights of American Indians and Its Relevance to Australian Aborigines."[30] Within a few years of his return, he and a committed group of aboriginal and Anglo activists pushed land rights to the top of their agenda.

Pittock's campaign for aboriginal land rights meshed with the concerns of the Yolngu, in Australia's Northern Territory. Worried that their land was being sacrificed by the state to a mining company but consistently rebuffed by the government and the courts throughout the 1960s, the Yolngu needed sympathetic advocates. When Yolngu protestors such as Daymbalipu Mununggur and their most vocal supporter, Arthur Ellemor of the Methodist Commission on Aboriginal Affairs, teamed up with legal scholars and activist lawyers in the mid-1960s and determined that native title might apply to Australia, the slow unraveling of the doctrine of terra nullius began.[31]

The case that eventually reached the Supreme Court of the Northern Territory — *Milirrpum and Others v. Nabalco Pty. Ltd and the Commonwealth of Australia* — was the first of its kind in Australia. Decided in 1971, *Milirrpum*, like *Hualpai*, decided thirty years earlier, asked that aboriginal people and their lawyers, in tandem with anthropologists and historians, be allowed to present history to the court in defense of native title. Because Australia had no native title jurisprudence of its own, Justice Blackburn turned to international law. In an opinion that ran to more than 150 pages, Blackburn took Yolngu claims seriously. Still, the Yolngus lost: aboriginal title had never been legally recognized in Australia, and thus it did not exist.[32] Ignoring but not unaware of *Hualpai*, Blackburn claimed he could find no authority in American law for the proposition that occupancy gave title; nor could he locate any authority for the clear and plain intent test — then recently adopted in Canada, where native title was almost as dimly understood as in Australia. Further, Blackburn claimed that in order to exist aboriginal title must be granted by the sovereign. Despite turning to Felix Cohen's landmark 1947 article "Original Indian Title" for assistance, Blackburn was unmoved. The judge, "with some diffidence," would only be guided so far down a new path.[33]

But it was only a matter of time. The Yolngus might have lost, but further aboriginal activism in the 1970s and 1980s, as well as steps taken by the state such as passage of the Aboriginal Land Rights (Northern Territory) Act of 1976, eventually led to the decision in *Mabo* and the recognition of aboriginal title in 1992 — a case that came about as the result of a committed aboriginal activist and his allies. This brief sketch — to which the Maoris of New Zealand and the First Nations of Canada could be added — serves simply to suggest that though the Hualapais' story possesses its own peculiarities, it is also part of a much larger phenomenon.

The impact of the Court's *Hualpai* decision has been felt most strongly in three areas: the Court's mandate that Congress demonstrate a clear and plain intent to extinguish title, the requirement that in order to exist aboriginal title must be based on exclusive occupancy in a definable territory, and that native title is not dependent on a grant from the sovereign. The implications for future claims cases of the Supreme Court's insistence on exclusive occupancy have been profound because the mandate regarding occupancy has been adopted, explicitly or implicitly, by courts in the United States and abroad, making the business of land claims complicated indeed. The clear and plain intent test, which a federal judge in Canada in 1979 said has its origins in the Hualapai case and which the Australian High Court in 1992 called "patently the right rule," has forced states to rethink the origins of indigenous property rights.[34] Previously, absent a specific grant, indigenous people had no property rights; now, states that have acknowledged the existence of aboriginal title have to prove that those rights have been explicitly extinguished. Malaysia, where aboriginal title litigation began in the late 1990s, has most recently adopted the rule. And similar land claims litigation is under way in South Africa, where a space has opened up in the post-apartheid political landscape for indigenous land rights. Such claims, heretofore solely based on dispossession stemming from statutory law, now have recourse to history. In October 2003, South Africa's Constitutional Court found that the three thousand–member Richtersveld Nama community's land rights had not been extinguished in 1847 when the British annexed the land on which they live. History made it clear that the Nama possessed customary title based on their own system of law, and that title still existed. As a result, the Richtersvelders might win back land granted to the Alexkor Mining Company, as well as compensation for nearly a century of diamond mining on what turns out to have been their land all along. Thus, the doctrine of aboriginal title is making its way into yet another jurisdiction.[35] The clear and plain intent test, combined with providing proof of aboriginal occupancy, have become the standards of international indigenous claims law in the post-*Hualpai* world.

But history can be a difficult business; it can also be powerful. Before the Hualpai case was decided, when the principles of immemorial occupancy and clear and plain intent were not embedded in the minds of most lawyers and government bureaucrats, the sovereign had total power over native property. History did not matter; it now does. Yet when history is not clear, when native people cannot prove their occupancy, history can become their enemy, too. Courts have decided that the "tide of history" or the "increasing weight of history" has variously washed away or crushed native claims. Ever more complex versions of the native past have been needed as the implications and consequences of land claims have become more serious. In the Hualpai case, even though few had accorded the tribe a meaningful history in a specific place, and it took many years to get the claim to court, by contemporary standards the evidentiary bar was not terribly high. Now, courts demand — and, at times, accept — ever-increasing amounts and kinds of evidence. For example, when the Gitksan and the Wet'suwet'en took their claim to the Supreme Court of British Columbia in the late 1980s and early 1990s, the trial lasted four years — the longest trial of any kind in Canadian history — and the *Reasons for Judgement* ran to more than four hundred pages. Many types of evidence, and many days' testimony, had to be considered in coming to the conclusion that the plaintiffs possessed aboriginal title. In Australia, art became evidence when a group of aboriginal painters unveiled for the Native Title Tribunal a twenty-six by thirty-two foot painting depicting land use history.[36]

Proving a land claim has only become more complicated. Indeed, in Australia, in the wake of the *Mabo* and *Wik* decisions, the Native Title Act of 1993, and its revisions, both the legislature and the courts have gone to great lengths to subject title claims to intense scrutiny. A critical difference between the United States and Canada, on one hand, and Australia, on the other, is that in Australia the lower federal courts have interpreted the law to mean that native title is based on customary aboriginal law and the maintenance of "tradition." In order for native title to remain intact, Aborigines must maintain their customary legal practices — whatever they may be — across time as they have *always* been practiced. If customary law cannot be found among contemporary aboriginal claimants, or if that law has atrophied to such an extent as to be inoperative (washed away by the "tides of history"), then native title does not exist. Thus, Australian courts have taken the proof of occupancy rule set down in the Hualapai case to mean something much more than mere historical occupancy. "This," according to Kent McNeil, a leading scholar of native title, "is manifestly unjust." That native people's customary law once had a concept of property rights akin to what is now recognized by the courts is, as a matter of evidence, difficult to prove. But courts in Australia have nonetheless required that it be proved. And now the evidentiary bar for proving a land claim is being raised to unattainable heights. Land claims litigation has become so prominent that the battles over native title have left the confines of the courtroom. Whereas the discipline of history had once silenced Aborigines, courts cannot now ignore them and their past; this makes many people very angry. Venomous and very public "history wars" have been waged in innumerable newspaper and magazine articles between those who favor new readings of the past and those who do not, between, somewhat simply put, those who see terra nullius as fact and those who see it as fiction. Set off in part by the *Mabo* decision, the ammunition used in the history wars comes from books with such titles as *The Fabrication of Australian History* and *The Invention of* Terra Nullius on one side and *Telling the Truth about Aboriginal History* on the other.[37]

That a debate about the aboriginal past, however shrill at times, can be had so publicly in Australia—a debate that is a result of a land claims case very much like *Hualpai*—is a mark of a decidedly changed political climate (not one necessarily changed in favor of aboriginal rights but one in which aborigines are at least not silenced). When the Hualapai case was making its way through the courts, it was all but ignored by the public; only the principal players paid it any attention. Now, in Canada, Australia, and New Zealand, indigenous issues, especially land claims, are matters of great public concern. In the United States, Indian issues still are all but ignored, the concern only of those directly involved. Just as in Fred Mahone's time, when he and the Hualapais had to work long and hard to keep their land claim alive, Indians today must fight to make their voices heard. Outside the United States, a revision of the indigenous past, constructed by native people and their allies and sanctioned in part by the courts, has meant that the settlement history of entire nations has had to be rethought. No such public rethinking of the Indian past has ever taken place in the United States—the Indian Claims Commission was no such thing. But what is happening in Australia and elsewhere is a mark of the power of history. That power was unleashed by the Hualapai case.

Fred Mahone's and the Hualapais' activism, so critical to the case, was soon forgotten. Shortly after the Court released the opinion, *Indians at Work,* the glossy magazine published by the BIA during the New Deal, carried an article about the Hualapais' victory. Pleased, of course, by the opinion, Collier's BIA was just as pleased by the help that sympathetic whites provided the Hualapai. It was a validation of the policies of the Indian New Deal. Non-Indian re-formers, of course, played a major role in getting the case to court. Indeed, because of the obstacles that had stood in the tribe's way prior to John Collier's administration, the case was a measure of the new climate that held sway for a brief but important time in the 1930s and early 1940s. But the Hualapai were completely left out of the story. Looked at from the BIA's perspective, one would get the impression that well-meaning bureaucrats swept in, assessed the situation, and saved the reservation while the helpless Hualapais stood by and watched and then waved goodbye in gratitude.[38] Of course, there is little truth to that version.

The story in *Indians at Work* mirrored the absence of Hualapais in the stories told by government attorneys in the 1920s and 1930s; it is also an accurate reflection of the relatively minor role the BIA let Indians play in making many of the major policy decisions of the era. Further, it is symbolic of the place Indians as actors have played in the historiography of the Indian New Deal, to say nothing of the larger narrative of twentieth-century Ameri-can history. Indians have been largely absent. After reading the story, one could be forgiven if one thought that no Hualapais played a part in the case. Likewise, the reader of nearly all twentieth-century American history could be forgiven for thinking that Indians had disappeared. As the Hualapai case made its way to court, consciously and unconsciously, lawyers and bureau-crats wrote the Hualapai out of their land. Because their past was hard to see, it was largely assumed that they were not there. Likewise, the article wrote the tribe out of the history of the case. By the time it reached the courtroom, non-Indians had taken over and the Hualapais' instrumental role was forgotten. In turn, historians have written Indians out of twentieth-century American his-tory for many of the same reasons—their voices are hard to find, their lives tough to narrate, their role as actors generally thought to be minimal at best. But without the Hualapais, and especially Fred Mahone, the case never would have come to the attention of non-Indian reformers, much less reached a court. Hualapai activism was the critical ingredient, without it the story told in this book would never have taken place.

Notes

The following abbreviations are used in the notes. The descriptions of correspondence are taken from the sources.

AG   Attorney General
CCF   Central Classified Files
CHP   Carl Hayden Papers, Hayden Library, Arizona State University
CIA   Commissioner of Indian Affairs
FSC   Felix Solomon Cohen Papers, WA MSS-S 1325, Beinecke Library, Yale University
GLO   General Land Office
HEBP   Herbert Eugene Bolton Papers, Bancroft Library, University of California, Berkeley
JCP   John Collier Papers, microfilm edition, Sterling Memorial Library, Yale University
NA   National Archives
PSFFC   Peach Springs File, Law Offices of Fennemore Craig, Phoenix, Arizona
PIRA   Papers of the Indian Rights Association, microfilm edition, Sterling Memorial Library, Yale University
RBSC   Records and Briefs of the U.S. Supreme Court, Records of *United States, as Guardian of the Hualpai Indians of Arizona, v. Santa Fe Pacific Railroad Co.*, 314 U.S. 339 (1941)
RG   Record Group

RHP Richard Hanna Papers, Zimmerman Library Annex, University of New Mexico

SANSR Superintendents' Annual Narrative and Statistical Reports from Field Jurisdictions of the Bureau of Indian Affairs, 1907–1938, microfilm publication 1011, reels 151–152

SJTP Sara Jones Tucker Papers, Museum of Northern Arizona, Flagstaff, Arizona

SOI   Secretary of the Interior

WP   *Walapai Papers: Historical Reports, Documents, and Extracts from Publications Relating to the Walapai Indians of Arizona,* Sen. Doc. 273, 74th Cong., 2nd Sess., 1936

Introduction

1. On nomads' place in the world see Hugh Brody, *The Other Side of Eden: Hunters, Farmers and the Shaping of the World* (Vancouver: Douglas and McIntyre, 2000); the case is 314 U.S. 339 (1941). The first Cohen quotation is from Felix Cohen, "Indian Claims," in *The Legal Conscience: Selected Papers of Felix Cohen,* ed. Lucy Kramer Cohen (New Haven: Yale University Press, 1960), 265, originally published in *American Indian* 2:3 (Spring 1945): 3–11. For the second, see Felix Cohen to Thomas Dodge, 25 November 1946, CCF, file # 5 106, box 3534, RG 48, NA.

2. There is a massive literature on the early justifications for taking Indian land. As a starting point see Anthony Pagden, "Conquest and Settlement," in *Lords of All the World* (New Haven: Yale University Press, 1995), 63–102; Robert Williams, *The American Indian in Western Legal Thought* (New York: Oxford University Press, 1990); James Brown Scott, *The Spanish Origin of International Law: Lectures on Francisco de Victoria (1480–1546) and Francisco Suarez (1548–1617)* (Washington, D.C.: School of Foreign Service, Georgetown University, 1928 [lectures delivered 1927]), 13–70, a classic treatment; and Felix S. Cohen, "Original Indian Title," in *The Legal Conscience: Selected Papers of Felix Cohen,* ed. Lucy Kramer Cohen (New Haven: Yale University Press, 1960), 273–304, originally published in *Minnesota Law Review* 32 (1947): 28–59.

3. The years between ca. 1887 and 1920 are well covered by historians. For a detailed introduction to all of these issues see Francis Paul Prucha, *The Great Father: The United States Government and the American Indians,* vol. 2 (Lincoln: University of Nebraska Press, 1984); on the image of the vanishing Indian as a symbol and a political tool, see Brian Dippie, *The Vanishing American: White Attitudes and U.S. Indian Policy* (Lawrence: University Press of Kansas, 1982), esp. pt. 5; on population see Russell Thornton, *American Indian Holocaust and Survival* (Norman: University of Oklahoma Press, 1987); on boarding schools see David Wallace Adams, *Education for Extinction: American Indians and the Boarding School Experience, 1875–1928* (Lawrence: University Press of Kansas, 1995); on allotment and the erosion of Indian land holdings see Janet McDonnell, *The Dispossession of the American Indian, 1887–1934* (Bloomington: University of Indiana Press, 1991); on political power see Stephen Cornell, *The Return of the Native: American Indian Political Resurgence* (New York: Oxford University Press, 1988), esp. 51–67, and Donald L. Parman, *Indians and the American West in the Twen-*

tieth Century (Bloomington: Indiana University Press, 1994), esp. 1–58; on the intellectual underpinnings of policy in the period see Frederick E. Hoxie, *A Final Promise: The Campaign to Assimilate the Indians, 1880–1920* (Lincoln: University of Nebraska Press, 1984; reprint, New York: Cambridge University Press, 1989).

4. *Lone Wolf v. Hitchcock,* 187 U.S. 553 (1903); Blue Clark, Lone Wolf v. Hitchcock: *Treaty Rights and Indian Law at the End of the Nineteenth Century* (Lincoln: University of Nebraska Press, 1994), 95. The legal commentary on *Lone Wolf* is voluminous. For a clear, concise description of the case and its place in Indian law see Charles Wilkinson, *American Indians, Time, and the Law: Native Societies in a Modern Constitutional Democracy* (New Haven: Yale University Press, 1987). Joseph William Singer has recently said that *Lone Wolf* is "among the worst decisions ever made by the Supreme Court and is arguably the most unjust decision of all time in the field of federal Indian law." Singer, "*Lone Wolf,* Or How to Take Property by Calling It a 'Mere Change in the Form of Investment,'" *Tulsa Law Review* 28 (2002): 37; George Kennan, "Have Reservation Indians Any Vested Rights?" *Outlook,* 29 March 1902, 759–65; U.S. Department of the Interior, Natural Resource Board, *Indian Land Tenure, Economic Status, and Population Trends,* pt. 10 of *The Report on Land Planning* (Washington, D.C.: Government Printing Office, 1935), 1, cited in McDonnell, *Dispossession of the American Indian,* 121.

5. At the beginning of every volume in the Garland series American Indian Ethnohistory, which contains the expert witness reports submitted to the ICC, the introduction by Ralph A. Barney, the Justice Department attorney in charge of Indian claims, explains the principles of the *Hualpai* decision and its adoption by the ICC. On the importance of the case to the ICC see also Ralph A. Barney, "Legal Problems Peculiar to Indian Claims Litigation," *Ethnohistory* 2.4 (1955): 320. See also Harvey D. Rosenthal, *Their Day in Court: A History of the Indian Claims Commission* (New York: Garland, 1990), 146–47. The case is *United States, as Guardian of the Hualpai Indians of Arizona, v. Santa Fe Pacific Railroad Co.,* 314 U.S. 339, 343 (1941). The Supreme Court Reporter misspelled the tribe's name.

6. McNickle, remarks at farewell dinner, folder 1470, box 92, FSC.

7. Felix Cohen to Edgar E. Witt, Commissioner of the Indian Claims Commission, 18 November 1950, folder 906, box 57, FSC.

8. The metaphor is from Thomas D. Hall's description of the process of incorporation in *Social Change in the Southwest, 1350–1880* (Lawrence: University of Kansas Press, 1989), 21.

Chapter 1. The Hualapais

1. Henry F. Dobyns, *Hualapai Indians I: Prehistoric Indian Occupation Within the Eastern Area of the Yuman Complex; A Study in Applied Archaeology,* Indian Claims Commission, American Indian Ethnohistory: Indians of the Southwest (New York: Garland, 1974), 203–8. Dobyns's is the most thorough archaeological study of the Pai peoples. See also Robert C. Euler, "Walapai Culture History" (Ph.D. diss., University of New Mexico, 1958). For subsequent Hualapai history see Dennis G. Casebier, *Camp Beale's Springs and the Hualapai Indians* (Norco, Calif.: Tales of the Mojave Road, 1980); on

Hualapai history generally see Henry F. Dobyns and Robert C. Euler, *The Walapai People* (Phoenix: Indian Tribal Series, 1976). The latest scientific assessment of Hualapai origins is reviewed in David E. Purcell, *The Historic Hualapai Occupation at Hackberry, Mohave County, Arizona: Archival, Ethnohistorical, and Archeological Investigations* (Flagstaff, Ariz. SWCA, 1996), 14–19. For the confusion about Pai origins see also Connie L. Stone, *People of the Desert, Canyons and Pines: Prehistory of the Patayan Country in West Central Arizona,* Cultural Resource Series, Monograph no. 5 (Phoenix: Arizona State Office of the Bureau of Land Management, 1987), 51–62; Donald E. Simonis, "Western Prescott and Cohonina Traditions," in *Archaeology in West-Central Arizona: Proceedings of the 1996 Arizona Archaeological Council, Prescott Conference* (Prescott, Ariz.: Sharlot Hall Museum Press, 2000), 185–203.

In addition to these two, for summaries of the work done on western Arizona, including debates about terminology, commentary on scantiness of research, and other issues, see Albert H. Schroeder, "Prehistory: Hakataya," in *Handbook of North American Indians,* vol. 9, *The Southwest,* William C. Sturtevant, gen. ed., Alfonso Ortiz, vol. ed. (Washington, D.C.: Smithsonian Institution Press, 1979), 100–108; Linda S. Cordell, *The Prehistory of the Southwest* (Orlando: Academic, 1984), 75–79; Donald Hughes, *In the House of Stone and Light: A Human History of the Grand Canyon,* Bulletin no. 114 (Grand Canyon: Grand Canyon Natural History Association, 1978); Douglas W. Schwartz, *On the Edge of Splendor: Exploring the Grand Canyon's Human Past* (Santa Fe: School of American Research, 1988). For work done contemporaneously with the case — the Atchison, Topeka, and Santa Fe Railroad actually sponsored Colton's research — see Harold Sellers Colton, *An Archeological Survey of Northwestern Arizona Including the Descriptions of Fifteen New Pottery Types* (Flagstaff: Museum of Northern Arizona, 1939); Harold Sellars Colton, "Prehistoric Culture Units and Their Relationships in Northern Arizona," *Museum of Northern Arizona Bulletin* 17 (October 1939): 1–76; Lyndon L. Hargrave, "Results of a Study of the Cohohina Branch of the Patayan Culture in 1938," *Museum of Northern Arizona Museum Notes* 11.6 (1938): 43–50. For eastward migration of Yuman peoples see Malcolm J. Rogers, "An Outline of Yuman Prehistory," *Southwestern Journal of Anthropology* 1.1 (1945): 167–98.

For oscillation see Steadman Upham, "Nomads of the Desert West: A Shifting Continuum in Prehistory," *Journal of World Prehistory* 8.2 (1994): 113–67. The abandonment is well documented; the causes are in dispute. Climate change now takes the lead in the debate. For that view and a review of the debate see Robert C. Euler, George J. Gumerman, Thor N. V. Karlstrom, Jeffrey S. Dean, and Richard H. Hevly, "The Colorado Plateaus: Cultural Dynamics and Paleoenvironment," *Science* 205.4411 (1979): 1089–1101. Dobyns argued that the Hualapais had arrived by A.D.1150 but shared their land with another group, the Cohoninas, until they occupied the land exclusively by 1300. Dobyns, *Hualapai Indians I: Prehistoric Indian Occupation,* 198–208. Douglas Schwartz, in "Havasupai Prehistory: Thirteen Centuries of Cultural Development" (Ph.D. diss., Yale University, 1955), argued that the Cohoninas became the Havasupais, but evidence for the presence of the Cohoninas fades away around A.D.1150, leading others to say that Schwartz was wrong. For a clear critique of Schwartz and a sound argument that backs up Dobyns and Euler's contention that the Hualapais and the Havasupais are both descended from the Cerbats and not the Cohoninas, see John F. Martin,

"The Prehistory and Ethnohistory of Havasupai-Hualapai Relations," *Ethnohistory* 32.2 (1985): 135–53; for further discussion of the gap see Robert C. Euler and Dee F. Green, "An Archeological Reconnaissance of Middle Havasu Canyon," Cultural Resources Report, No. 22, USDA, Forest Service, Southwestern Region, Albuquerque, N.M., August, 1978.

2. For a discussion of using science and oral history in tandem see Roger C. Echo-Hawk, "Ancient History in the New World: Integrating Oral Traditions and the Archaeological Record in Deep Time," *American Antiquity* 65.2 (2000): 267–90. See the numerous examples of such convergences in Colin Calloway, *One Vast Winter Count: The North American West Before Lewis and Clark* (Lincoln: University of Nebraska Press, 2003), esp. 56–57; Henry P. Ewing, *The Origin of the Pai Tribes*, ed. Henry F. Dobyns and Robert C. Euler, reprinted in *Kiva* 26.3 (1961): 8–23. Two years later George Wharton James collected the Hualapai origin story in *The Indians of the Painted Desert Region: Hopis, Navajos, Wallapais, and Havasupais* (Boston: Little, Brown, 1903), 188–98. Then, in 1929, Alfred Kroeber and a team of anthropologists collected data for the first and only ethnography of the tribe, A. L. Kroeber et al., *Walapai Ethnography*, Memoirs of the American Anthropological Association no. 42 (Menasha, Wis.: American Anthropological Association, 1935). See G. A. MacGregor, "Origin Myth," told by Kuni, in ibid., 16–26; Elenora Mapatis, translated and transcribed by Lucille J. Watahomigie, "Hualapai: Origin of the People," *Plateau* 53.2 (1981): 24–26. Fred Mahone told a brief version of the migration and Madwida stories in Interview with Fred Mahone, 25 June 1968, 541–42, 545, Prescott College Hualapai Oral Tradition Project, Prescott, Arizona.

For a version by the Yuma that differs slightly but agrees in many of the particulars, such as the migration of the Hualapais and Havasupais to the northeast away from Wikame (in this case spelled *Avikwaame*), see John Peabody Harrington, "A Yuma Account of Origins," *Journal of American Folklore* 21.82 (1908): 324–48, esp. 345–46; for a Mojave account see John Gregory Bourke, "Notes on the Cosmogony and Theogony of the Mojave Indians of the Rio Colorado, Arizona," *Journal of American Folklore* 2.6 (1889): 169–89, esp. 180, on Hualapai migration, and 172, where Bourke's informant tells him about "Spirit Mountain," where the world was made — this is the same mountain as in all the Hualapai origin stories. For an excellent discussion of the various origin stories of all the Yuman peoples see Jack D. Forbes, *Warriors of the Colorado: The Yumas of the Quechan Nation and Their Neighbors* (Norman: University of Oklahoma Press, 1965), 5–44. Almost forty years later, Forbes's extraordinary book still is likely the best book about the lower Colorado River Indian world. My rendering of the story is condensed from the various Hualapai versions cited above. Details vary, but the basic structure remains the same. For example, in the Ewing version, which Dobyns and Euler consider the most accurate and detailed, the Mojaves, the Paiutes, and the Navajos came with the Hualapais, the Havasupais, the Yavapais, and the Hopis to Madwida, rather than breaking off beforehand. The list tends to vary, but the Hualapais, the Havasupais, the Mojaves, the Hopis, and the Yavapais are always included. The Mapatis version, for instance, is the only one that includes the Quechans and the Chemehuevis. The prevailing consensus is that the Hualapais are a single ethnic group and that the Havasupais are now a separate tribe that was once part of the same larger group. This view is supported by all anthropologists and archaeologists writing about the Hualapais with the exception of Robert Manners. Manners was the government's expert witness in the Hualapai's Indian Claims Commission case. He argued, perhaps unsurprisingly, that the Hualapais were never a unified tribe occupying a definable territory. All subsequent work disagrees with this position, as did the ICC. Robert Manners, "Tribe and Tribal Boundaries: The Walapai," *Ethnohistory* 4.1 (1957): 1–26; Robert Manners, *An Ethnological Report on the Hualapai (Walapai) Indians of Arizona,* American Indian Ethnohistory: Indians of the Southwest (New York: Garland, 1974). Timothy Braatz believes that the precontact social organization among the Pai was less formal than Dobyns and Euler thought but does not go so far as to say they that were not an identifiable tribe. Timothy Braatz, "The Question of Regional Bands and Subtribes Among the Pre-Conquest Pai (Hualapai and Havasupai) Indians of Northwestern Arizona," *American Indian Quarterly* 22.1–2 (1998): 1–7 (Web pagination).

3. Dobyns limits this figure regarding one-quarter of trade goods to pottery remains. But this does not mean that the Hualapais were trading for pottery; earthen vessels were used to transport trade goods such as corn and melons. See his discussion in *Prehistoric Indian Occupation,* 101–11. For a general description of Hualapai boundaries see Henry F. Dobyns and Richard C. Euler, *Wauba Yuma's People: The Comparative Socio-Political Structure of the Pai Indians of Arizona* (Prescott, Ariz.: Prescott College Press, 1970), 7–8. For horses among the Havasupais in 1776 see Elliott Coues, ed., *On the Trail of a Spanish Pioneer: The Diary and Itinerary of Francisco Garcés in His Travels Through Sonora, Arizona, and California, 1775–1776* (New York: Francis P. Harper, 1900), 2:337–38. Garcés found the horses among the people who are now known as the Havasupais but then were likely only considered one of the thirteen bands of Pais. On Upland Yumans (Hualapais, Havasupais, or Yavapais) as slaves see David M. Brugge, *Navajo in the Catholic Church Records of New Mexico, 1694–1875* (Tsaile, Ariz.: Navajo Community College Press, 1985), 22–23. On trade goods among the Hualapais in 1776 see Coues, *On the Trail of a Spanish Pioneer,* 319–320.

Albert Shroeder claims that the first definite mention of the Havasupais in the Spanish documents occurred in 1665, when Governor Don Diego de Peñalosa of New Mexico mentioned his reduction of the Coninas (a Hopi term for the Havasupais) while being interrogated during the Inquisition. Albert H. Schroeder, "A Brief History of the Havasupai," *Plateau* 25.3 (1953): 46. Schroeder offers tantalizing but far from definitive evidence that Spaniards explored the area west of the Hopi mesas before Garcés made his journey north from Mexico. On early Spanish references see also Dobyns, *Hualapai Indians I: Prehistoric Indian Occupation,* 1:9–20. On the importance of shells see Henry P. Ewing, "The Pai Tribes," ed. Robert C. Euler and Henry Dobyns, reprinted in *Ethnohistory* 7.1 (1960): 65. Further evidence about trade and marriage comes from oral and archaeological evidence. For trade in general see M. A. Mook, "Trade and Transport," in A. L. Kroeber et al., *Walapai Ethnography,* Memoirs of the American Anthropological Association, no. 42 (Menasha, Wis.: American Anthropological Association, 1935) 164–67; for the shell trade between California and the Colorado River Yumans in Arizona see Malcolm J. Rogers, "Aboriginal Cultural Relations Between Southern California and the Southwest," *San Diego Museum Bulletin* 5.3 (1941): 1–6; on marriage with Mojaves see A. L. Kroeber, *A Mohave Historical Epic,* Anthropological Records vol. 11, no. 2 (Berkeley: University of California Press, 1963), 105–7; on Paiutes living with the Hualapais see "The Paiute Residence Among the Walapai," in Leslie Spier, *Havasupai Ethnography* (New York: Anthropological Papers of the American Museum of Natural History, 1928), vol. 29, pt. 3, 360–62; for marriage with Paiutes see "Statement of Smokey Little Jim," Exhibit N, 1 May 1942, "Final Hearing on Claims to Released Railroad Lands in Northwestern Arizona," in Abe Barber and Felix Cohen, "Examiners' Report on Tribal Claims to the Released Railroad Lands in Northwestern Arizona," *Hualapai Tribe of the Hualapai Reservation, Arizona v. The United States of America*, Indian Claims Commission Docket No. 90, box 1055, RG 279 (Records of the Indian Claims Commission), NA.; for marriage see also Informant B, interview with the author, 26 September 2002, Peach Springs, Arizona. For relations with the Yavapais see E. W. Gifford, *Northeastern and Western Yavapai*, University of California Publications in American Archaeology and Ethnology vol. 34, no. 4 (Berkeley: University of California, 1942); Leslie Spier, "The Walapai and Havasupai Raid the Yavapai," in *Havasupai Ethnography* (New York: Anthropological Papers of the American Museum of Natural History, 1928), vol. 29, pt. 3, 368–69.

4. On the collecting and selling of pine nuts, which, according to the *Mohave County Miner*, Hualapai women did every year, see the edition of 3 September 1910, 2; Lucille J. Watahomigie, Malinda Powskey, Jorigine Bender, *Ethnobotany of the Hualapai*, recounted in Hualapai by Elenor Mapatis (Peach Springs, Ariz.: Hualapai Bilingual Program, 1982), 30, 31, 13; Charline G. Smith, "*Selé*, A Major Vegetal Component of the Aboriginal Hualapai Diet," *Plateau* 45.2 (1973): 102–10.

5. For a discussion of the regional differences in Hualapai and Havasupai agriculture and gathering see Martin, "Prehistory and Ethnohistory of Havasupai-Hualapai Relations." See also John F. Martin, "On the Estimation of the Sizes of Local Groups in a Hunting and Gathering Environment," *American Anthropologist* 75.5 (1973): 1448–68.

6. See WP, 7–8. The Garcés material found in WP is faithfully reproduced from Coues, *On the Trail of a Spanish Pioneer*, 1:322–35. Most of the cited passage is taken up with Coues's copious footnotes and not Garcés's reporting about the Hualapais. For an annotated discussion of the Garcés trip see Dobyns, *Hualapai Indians I: Prehistoric Indian Occupation*, 1:24–33. Garcés learned of the Hualapais from the Mojaves.

7. Bill Williams was alleged to have spent the winter of 1834–35 with the Hualapais, but the account is unreliable. See Frederic E. Voelker, "William Sherley (Old Bill) Williams," in *Mountain Men and Fur Trappers of the Old West* (Lincoln: University of Nebraska Press, 1965), 207. For a concise summary of the expeditions see Robert C. Euler, "Havasupai Historical Data," in *Havasupai Indians* (New York: Garland, 1974), 286–91. On government exploration of the Colorado Plateau during the period generally see William H. Goetzmann, *Army Exploration in the American West, 1803–1863* (New Haven: Yale University Press, 1959). For Ives's remarks see WP 32 (grizzly soup), 30 (profitless locality).

8. On cornfields see Report of John Sherburne, 21 April 1868, WP, 70. For the Hualapai War and the general changes rapidly occurring in Hualapai country see documents collection in WP; see also Henry F. Dobyns and Robert C. Euler, "The Nine Lives of Cherum, the Pai Tokumhet," *American Indian Quarterly* 22.3 (1998): 1–15 (Web pagination); Dobyns and Euler, *The Walapai People* (Phoenix: Indian Tribal Series, 1976). On

the Mojaves see especially the oral history of Mojave warfare collected by Kroeber in 1903, A. L. Kroeber and C. B. Kroeber, *A Mohave War Reminiscence, 1854–1880,* University of California Publications in Anthropology, no. 10 (Berkeley: University of California Press, 1973). On the Paiutes' being drawn into regional war and Anglo contact see Martha C. Knack, *Boundaries Between: The Southern Paiutes, 1775–1995* (Lincoln: University of Nebraska Press, 2001), 95–130; on regional interaction in general and war with Anglos see Forbes, *Warriors of the Colorado,* 297–340.

9. On the use of Hualapais and Apaches as scouts against the Apaches see Thomas Dunlay, *Wolves for the Blue Soldiers: Indian Scouts and Auxiliaries with the United States Army, 1860–90* (Lincoln: University of Nebraska Press, 1982), 165–86; for the early use of Hualapais as allies against the Apaches see John G. Bourke, *On the Border with Crook* (1891; reprint, Lincoln: University of Nebraska Press, 1971), 167–71. The number of Hualapai men and women who received pensions does not reflect accurately the number of Hualapais that served as scouts. As of 4 January 1931, 27 Hualapais, living and deceased, had received $34,409.93 for services rendered. For this figure see Amounts Paid to Indian War Pensioners, folder 14, box 622, CHP. Between 1872 and 1875, 140 Hualapais served as scouts, but I do not have figures for service in the 1880s. For these numbers see Alphabetical List of Hualapai Indian Scouts, 1872–1875, box 34, Hualapai Indians, Records Supporting Claims for Service During the Indian Wars, Records of Indian Scouts, Department of Veterans Affairs, RG 15, NA. For "Sahara of the Colorado" see Thomas Byrne to Assistant Adjutant General, 17 December 1874, WP, 99. See also Jeffrey P. Shepherd, "Building an American Indian Community: The Hualapai Nation in the Twentieth Century" (Ph.D. diss., Arizona State University, 2002), esp. 69–84.

10. For "every stream" see Major J. W. Mason, Whipple Barracks, Arizona Territory, to Assistant Adjutant General, Headquarters, Department of Arizona, 16 June 1882, in WP, 140–42. On wanting to stem further losses see Dobyns and Euler, *Walapai People,* 61. O. B. Willcox, Colonel, Twelfth Infantry, Brevet Major General Commanding Department of Arizona to Headquarters, Department of Arizona, 19 September 1881, Letters Received, #17606, Special Case 1, "Hualapai and Havasupai," box 1, ser. 102, RG 75, NA.

11. On Spencer as a scout and Indian fighter see Dan L. Thrapp, *The Conquest of Apacheria* (Norman: University of Oklahoma Press, 1967), 44–45. The Indian agent William Light also thought Spencer was a scout and not an officially appointed agent but that, after fighting Indians, he decided to marry one. William Light to CIA, 7 February 1928, CCF 31229-23-313, pt. 2, box 26, RG 75, NA. The first mention of Spencer living among the Hualapais comes from George Wilson, 1st Lieutenant, 12th Infantry, to Asst. Adjutant General, 18 November 1879, WP, 127, who said that Spencer had lived with them for years. The quotation from Spencer is in Spencer to Department Commander, Fort Whipple, 20 September 1882, WP, 144. On Spencer's Ranch see Major J. W. Mason to Assistant Adjutant General, 16 June 1882, WP, 142. On Spencer's efforts to mark out a reservation territory for the Hualapais see S. N. Benjamin, Asst. Adjutant General, to Major A. K. Arnold, 6th Cavalry, Acting Asst. Adjutant General, 16 September 1881, WP, 137, and J. W. Mason, Whipple Barracks, Arizona Territory, to Assistant Adjutant General, Headquarters, Department of Arizona, 16 June 1882 WP, 141 all in WP.

In 1880 there were four Hualapais actually living at Spencer's Ranch; see Spencer's

Ranch, Mohave County, Arizona Territory, 4 June 1880, Manuscript Census, RG 29, reel 36, NA. For "taken by newcomers" see Statement of Jim Fielding, submitted by H. O. Davidson, 12 October 1928, box 2, entry 824, RG 48, NA. For Fielding's being a teenager see Truxton Cañon School Reservation, Mohave County, Arizona Territory, 6 June 1900, Manuscript Census, RG 29, reel 46, NA, which lists Fielding's age as thirty, making him a young teenager in the 1880s. For Mike Sue's and Nora Schrum's testimony see Affidavit of Mike Sue and Affidavit of Kwath a yan ya or Nora Schrum, taken by William A. Light, both 23 February 1928, and affidavit of Snyje, n.d., all in Records Concerning U.S. v. Santa Fe Pacific Railroad Company, box 2, entry 824, RG 48, NA. Deposition of Jim Smith, 17 August 1929, folder 3/5, box 30b, and Deposition of W. F. Grounds, 7 December 1927, folder 1/5, box 30b, both in Phoenix Area Office, Accession #NRHL-075-00-115, RG 75, Laguna Niguel, Pacific Region, NA. As will become clear, Grounds was not a friend to the Hualapais. He was to be a major witness against them in the court case. He claimed that Spencer had the reservation set aside for his own purposes — if he could rid the region of other whites, he would have the land to himself. No one else ever made that claim, however. Grounds's deposition is useful because even if he was wrong with regard to Spencer's motivations, his statements about Spencer's critical role in setting aside the reservation do square with the statements of others.

12. William Redwood Price to S. N. Benjamin, Asst. Adjutant General, Department of Arizona, 1 July 1881, WP, 134–35.

13. Hiram Price to Secretary of the Interior, 22 July 1881, in WP, 133.

14. Contract between Walapai Indians and Mohave and Prescott Toll Road Company, July 15, 1865, WP, 34. On Cherum see Henry F. Dobyns and Robert C. Euler, "The Nine Lives of Cherum, the Pai Tokumhet," *American Indian Quarterly* 22:3 (1998): 1–15 (Web pagination). On Wauba Yuma see Dobyns and Euler, *Wauba Yuma's People;* for the clearest delineation of Hualapai sociopolitical structure see ibid., esp. 10–51, and on hereditary leadership see specifically "hereditary index," 45. For a somewhat later look at social structure, using Kate Crozier as an informant, see Philip Drucker, *Culture Element Distributions: XVII Yuman Piman,* Anthropological Records 6.3 (Berkeley: University of California Press, 1941), 132. The question of Hualapai political structure has recently, and bitterly, been debated in a series of five articles in the *American Indian Quarterly.* For the most important points see Timothy Braatz, "The Question of Regional Bands and Subtribes Among the Pre-Conquest Pai (Hualapai and Havasupai) Indians of Northwestern Arizona," *American Indian Quarterly* 22:1–2 (1999): 1 (Web pagination). Braatz argues that although the Pai bands varied they did so along geographical lines, not social-political boundaries. See the response of Henry F. Dobyns and Robert C. Euler, "Band of Gardeners," *American Indian Quarterly* 23.3, 4 (1999): 1–10 (Web pagination).

15. On this point see, e.g., Henry F. Dobyns and Robert C. Euler, *The Ghost Dance of 1889 Among the Pai Indians of Northwestern Arizona* (Prescott, Ariz.: Prescott College Press, 1967), 19–24. Dobyns and Euler discuss the factionalism of the various bands in relation to Hualapai participation in the Ghost Dance.

16. Between 1882 and 1888 the Hualapais virtually abandoned Pine Springs. In 1882 J. W. Mason reported that ninety-five individuals were living at Pine Springs; in 1888 G. M. Brayton reported that fifty members of the Pine Springs band had left for Peach

Springs to work on the railroad. See Major J. W. Mason, Whipple Barracks, Arizona Territory, to Assistant Adjutant General, Headquarters, Department of Arizona, 16 June 1882, and G. M. Brayton to Assistant Adjutant General, Department of Arizona, 8 June 1888, both in WP, 142, 167. For a brief description of the Pine Springs country as the territory of a Hualapai band see Fred B. Kniffen, "Geography," in A. L. Kroeber et al., *Walapai Ethnography*, Memoirs of the American Anthropological Association no. 42 (Menasha, Wis.: American Anthropological Association, 1935), 41–42. For nationalities see Hackberry, Mohave County, Arizona Territory, 13 June 1880, Manuscript Census, RG 29, reel 36, NA. For the quotation see George Wilson to Asst. Adjutant General, 18 November 1879, WP, 127. For occupations of Hualapai men and women see the census taken by G. M. Brayton, 8 June 1888, WP, 165–68. For disease and death see "Report of E. B. Robertson, Ninth Infantry, on the Condition of the Hualapai, 1887," in WP, 153; for Hackberry in general see Purcell, *Historic Hualapai Occupation,* 59–61.

17. Dobyns and Euler, *Ghost Dance of 1889.*

18. Truxton Cañon School Reservation, Mohave County, Arizona Territory, 2 June 1900, Manuscript Census, RG 29, reel 46, NA.

Chapter 2. The Conflict

1. On the history of the Atchison, Topeka, and Santa Fe (ATSF) and its land grant see Thomas Doniphan Best, "The Role of the Atchison, Topeka, and Santa Fe Railway System in the Economic Development of Southwestern United States, 1859–1954" (Ph.D. diss., Northwestern University, 1959); Glenn Danford Bradley, *The Story of the Santa Fe* (Boston: Badger, 1920); Keith L. Bryant, *History of the Atchison, Topeka and Santa Fe Railway* (New York: Macmillan, 1974); James H. Ducker, *Men of the Steel Rails: Workers on the Atchison, Topeka & Santa Fe Railroad, 1869–1900* (Lincoln: University of Nebraska Press, 1983); William S. Greever, *Arid Domain: The Santa Fe Railroad and Its Western Land Grant* (Stanford: Stanford University Press, 1954); James Leslie Marshall, *Santa Fe: The Railroad That Built an Empire* (New York: Random House, 1945); David Myrick, *The Santa Fe Route: Railroads of Arizona,* vol. 4 (Visalia, Calif.: Signature, 1998); L. L. Waters, *Steel Trails to Santa Fe* (Lawrence: University of Kansas Press, 1950); Kurt Peters, "Watering the Flower: The Laguna Pueblo Indians and the Santa Fe Railroad" (Ph.D. diss., University of California at Berkeley, 1997); Sanford Mosk, *Land Tenure Problems in the Santa Fe Railroad Grant Area,* Publications of the Bureau of Business and Economic Research, University of California (Berkeley: University of California Press, 1944); Herbert Andrew Wisby Jr., "A History of the Santa Fe Railroad in Arizona to 1917" (master's thesis, University of Arizona, at Tucson, 1946); Russell Wahmann, "The Historical Geography of the Santa Fe Railroad in Northern Arizona" (master's thesis, Northern Arizona University at Flagstaff, 1971).

Almost without exception the literature on the railroad is devoid of discussion of Indians, the Peters dissertation being the obvious exception. Mosk and Greever discuss the Santa Fe's legal problems with the Hualapais and other tribes in some detail; Wisby mentions the creation of the Hualapai reservation and the attendant legal troubles over the course of two sentences (124). The date of the railroad's arrival in Peach Springs is hard to pin down, but the bulk of the evidence, especially that in the railroad's own records, makes it clear that the reservation was set aside *before* the railroad arrived. In his detailed history of the railroad's route through Arizona, Donald Myrick (*Santa Fe Route*, 49) says that the tracks reached Peach Springs later in January 1883. But he has no notes and thus I have no way to verify his sources. The *Railway Age*, a weekly trade journal for the industry, tracked railroad construction. It reported in its 25 January 1883 issue that "track is now completed west from Albuquerque to Peach Tree Spring, almost 450 miles west from the Atchison, Topeka, and Sata Fe railway and 110 miles east from Colorado crossing" (53). See also the issue of 22 February 1883: "The Atlantic and Pacific is rapidly pushing across the Arizona wilds. Trains are running to Peach Springs, 465 miles west of Albuquerque, and track has been laid a few days ago six miles farther, leaving 121 miles to be ironed to reach the Colorado river" (101). And in the same issue it reports, "General passenger agent C. R. Williams announces completion of this line to Peach Spring, Arizona, 465 miles west of Albuquerque" (110). But then we get conflicting information from the same source; see the issue of 21 December 1882: "Track on this road has now been laid for a distance of about 500 miles from Albuquerque, Mex. [*sic*], and within about 70 miles of the Colorado river to a junction with the Southern Pacific" (726). But 28 November 1882 issue reported: "This road has advanced its western operating terminus from Williams to Ash Fork, 400½ miles west of Albuquerque" (679). *Railroad Gazette* published the same report from C. R. Williams in its 22 February 1883 issue: "the train had reached Peach Springs" (131).

Further confusion comes from ATSF sources. The *Santa Fe Splinters*, a collection of documents compiled by ATSF employee Joseph Weidel in 1940 for the Interstate Commerce Commission's valuation division, contains information culled from the railroad's records. According to data found there, the railroad first entered the reservation at Nelson, milepost 446.8, on 22 January 1883 and made it to Peach Springs, milepost 453.11, on 30 January 1883, where construction continued until 9 February 1883, to milepost 457.2. See "Statement of Chronological Data on Construction of the Atlantic and Pacific Railroad, from Isleta, New Mexico, to the Colorado River showing Dates when Track Construction reached certain designated places," sheet 2/5, p. 261, of "Two Decades of the Atlantic and Pacific Railroad Company: The Western Division from the Congressional Act of July 27, 1866 until the Financial Plan and Agreement to Extend into California at End of 1881, No. 2," vol. 14, *Santa Fe Splinters*, Atchison, Topeka, and Santa Fe Railway Collection, Kansas State Historical Society, Topeka. See also the annotated chronology of construction compiled by Weidel in which he quotes a 24 January 1883 letter in which Lewis Kingman writes of the *impending* arrival of the track and an 8 February 1883 letter in which Kingman wrote that Peach Springs was now delivering water, p. 266, both in ibid.

2. The first definite sign of interest in the question of who owned the rights to the spring came in 1909. There may be earlier discussions of the issue, but I have not found them. In any case, after 1909 interest in what became known as the Peach Springs controversy never let up. See John Charles, Inspection Report, Subject: Report on Investigation of Water Rights, 18 October 1909, box 69, entry 953, Inspection Reports, 1908–40, Inspection Division, RG 75, NA.

3. For details of the Hualapais' new cattle operation see Charles E. Shell, "Development of the Stock Industry on the Walapai Indian Reservation, Ariz.," in *Forty-Eighth*

Annual Report of the Board of Indian Commissioners (Washington, D.C.: Government Printing Office, 1917), 365; the Shell quotation is found in Charles E. Shell, superintendent, to CIA, 6 June 1914, CCF 1907-39-68188-14-371 — Truxton Canyon, box 37, RG 75, NA.

4. C. F. Hauke, chief clerk, to Charles E. Shell, 14 July 1914, CCF 68188-14-371 — Truxton Canyon, box 37, RG 75, NA; for the earlier survey and the quotation see Henry P. Ewing to CIA, 15 October 1899, CCF 1897–1951, file 300-Land, folder 2/2, Pacific Region, Laguna Niguel, RG 75, NA; for Hauke's finding the report see C. F. Hauke, chief clerk, to Charles E. Shell, 14 July 1914, CCF 68188-14-371 — Truxton Canyon, box 37, RG 75, NA; Major J. W. Mason, Whipple Barracks, Arizona Territory, to Assistant Adjutant General, Headquarters, Department of Arizona, 16 June 1882, in WP, 140–42.

5. J. A. Christie, Superintendent, Atchison, Topeka, and Santa Fe Railway, to Charles Shell, 14 October 1914, CCF 68188-14-371 — Truxton Canyon, box 37, RG 75, NA.

6. Charles Shell to CIA, 22 October 1914, CCF 68188-14-371 — Truxton Canyon, box 37, RG 75, NA.

7. E. B. Merritt, Assistant CIA, to Commissioner of the General Land Office, 11 November 1914; Commissioner of the GLO to E. B. Merrit, 14 November 1914; E. B. Merritt, Asst. CIA, to Charles Shell, 4 December 1914, all in CCF 68188-14-371 — Truxton Canyon, box 37, RG 75, NA.

8. Charles Shell to W. F. Grounds, 14 December 1914; W. F. Grounds to Charles Shell, 18 December 1914; W. B. Ridenour to Charles Shell, 14 December 1914; Mrs. T. G. Walter to Charles Shell, 8 January 1915, all in CCF 68188-14-371 — Truxton Canyon, box 37, RG 75, NA.

9. Charles Shell to CIA, 7 January 1915, CCF 68188-14-371 — Truxton Canyon, box 37, RG 75, NA.

10. Ibid.

11. On the suggestion to close the road see Charles Shell to CIA, 23 October 1915. The CIA's response to Shell, on 15 December 1915, shows that his frustration with Shell's ambivalence is clear; the quotation is from Charles Shell to CIA, 1 January 1916. All are in CCF 68188-14-371 — Truxton Canyon, box 37, RG 75, NA.

Chapter 3. The Hualapai Awakening

1. Fred Mahone to Cato Sells, CIA, 29 July 1918, CCF 66662-18-823 — Truxton Canyon, box 49, RG 75, NA.

2. The profiles so deftly sketched by historians such as David Rich Lewis, Loretta Fowler, Frederick Hoxie, and Melissa Meyer, among others, of educated Indians who both frustrate and facilitate interactions between Anglos and Indians and gain positions of leadership are models for this chapter. Mahone, however, does not fit the cultural broker model, nor was he an intermediary or middleman. David Rich Lewis, "Reservation Leadership and the Progressive-Traditional Dichotomy: William Wash and the Northern Utes, 1865–1928," *Ethnohistory* 38:2 (1991): 124–48; Melissa Meyer, "Warehouses and Sharks: The Social and Economic Basis of Political Factionalism," in *The White Earth Tragedy: Ethnicity and Dispossession at a Minnesota Anishinabe Reservation, 1889–1920* (Lincoln: University of Nebraska Press, 1994). For an excellent profile

of a contemporaneous leader who, as a returned student, has interesting parallels to Mahone, see Frederick E. Hoxie and Timothy Bernardis, "Yellowtail: Crow," in *The New Warriors: Native American Leaders Since 1900,* ed. David R. Edmunds (Lincoln: University of Nebraska Press, 2001), 55–77. For a fuller treatment of Robert Yellowtail within the context of Crow history see Hoxie, *Parading Through History: The Making of the Crow Nation in America, 1805–1935* (Cambridge: Cambridge University Press, 1995); Loretta Fowler, "Political Middlemen and the Headman Tradition Among the Twentieth Century Gros Ventre of Fort Belknap Reservation," *Journal of the West* 23:3 (1984): 54–64; Walter L. Williams, "Twentieth Century Indian Leaders: Brokers and Providers," *Journal of the West* 23:3 (1984): 3–6. On the culture broker see Margaret Szasz, *Between Indian and White Worlds: The Cultural Broker* (Norman: University of Oklahoma Press, 1994); R. David Edmunds, ed., American Indian Leaders: Studies in Diversity (Lincoln: University of Nebraska Press, 1980).

3. Ben Beecher, interview with the author, 25 May 2001, Peach Springs, Ariz., trans. Ronald Mann Susanyatame; author interview with Mabelene Mahone and Ardith Bell, Fred Mahone's daughters, 5 June 2002, Phoenix. On Mahone's fear see Fred Mahone to Jonathan Steere, president of the Indian Rights Association, 13 March 1931, reel 47, PIRA. On the myriad problems that returned students faced see David Wallace Adams, *Education for Extinction: American Indians and the Boarding School Experience, 1875–1928* (Lawrence: University Press of Kansas Press, 1995), 292–306.

4. Mahone to Sells, 29 July 1918.

5. Henry P. Ewing, "Report of Industrial Teacher in Charge of Hualapais and Yava Supais," 21 July 1897, in WP, 181. Details about Fred Mahone's life come from a variety of sources: see e.g., Fred Mahone to ?, 28 January 1921, CCF 34163-21-175, pt. 1, General Service, box 447, RG 75, NA. According to Mahone, he was at Chilocco for three and a half years, but then he says his dates of enrollment were 9 December 1914 to 15 December 1917. The discrepancy is slight, but worth mentioning. I have also tracked Mahone's life via Hualapai census material, reels 580–81, Indian Census Rolls, 1885–1940, microfilm publication 595, RG 75, NA See also the obituary for Fred Ward Mahone in *Gum-U,* a Hualapai newsletter, March 1971, 1. See also a copy of Mahone's honorable discharge and enlistment record (which gives his age at time of enlistment as twenty-nine), PIRA, reel 46. These dates, of course, mean that Mahone would have been twenty-six when he went to Chilocco. This seems like an old age for boarding school, but I have found nothing to contradict this information. On speaking, reading, writing English by age ten, see Truxton Cañon School Reservation, Mohave County, Arizona Territory, 2 June 1900, Manuscript Census, RG 29, reel 46, NA. On TB see *Contagious and Infectious Diseases Among the Indians,* 62nd Cong., 3rd sess., Doc. 1038, 1914, 41.

6. Hazel W. Hertzberg, *The Search for an American Indian Identity: Modern Pan-Indian Movements* (Syracuse: Syracuse University Press, 1971), 36, 72–74. On the ideology of assimilation see Frederick E. Hoxie, *A Final Promise: The Campaign to Assimilate the Indians, 1880–1920* (1984; reprint, New York: Cambridge University Press, 1989), 239–44. On political activism, pan-Indianism, and the boarding school experience see Stephen Cornell, *The Return of the Native: American Indian Political Resurgence* (New York: Oxford University Press, 1988), esp. 110–18. On the SAI, Cornell and all other historians follow Hertzberg, who argues that pan-Indianism's decline should be blamed

on the general demise in the reform spirit that had characterized the Progressive Era but had vanished in the 1920s. As an external factor this might be true. See Hertzberg, *Search for an American Indian Identity,* 209.

7. This is not to say that the SAI's appeal was nonexistent; for one example of the SAI's influence in western Washington see Alexandra Harmon, *Indians in the Making: Ethnic Relations and Indian Identities Around Puget Sound* (Berkeley: University of California Press, 1998), 178–79. On the SAI and its leaders, including Charles Eastman and Arthur C. Parker, and the version of Indianness they fed to America — Indian and non-Indian — see Philip J. Deloria, *Playing Indian* (New Haven: Yale University Press, 1998), 122–25. On this aspect of Parker's life and its impact on the SAI see also Joy Porter, *To Be an Indian: The Life of Iroquois-Seneca Arthur Caswell Parker* (Norman: University of Oklahoma Press, 2001), 91–142. Parker's statement about playing Indian is quoted in Hertzberg, *Search for an American Indian Identity,* 57. For "American Race" see Arthur C. Parker, "The Red Man Is Not a Tanned Mongolian," *Indian School Journal,* March 1915, 269 (emphasis in original), For disarming non-Indians' views of Indians as savages see Philip Deloria, who puts it this way: "Arthur C. Parker, Charles Alexander Eastman, and many others wanted to become bridge figures, using primitive antimodern primitivism to defend native cultures against the negative stereotypes left over from colonial conquest" (*Playing Indian,* 122), vigorously asserting that Americanness is a version of what Matthew Jacobson has called "vindictive assimilationism." Matthew Frye Jacobson, *Barbarian Virtues: The United States Encounters Foreign Peoples at Home and Abroad, 1876–1917* (New York: Hill and Wang, 2000), 209.

8. Arthur Parker, editorial, *Quarterly Journal* 1:1 (1913), quoted in Hertzberg, *Search for an American Indian Identity,* 103; Chief Francisco Patencio, as told to Margaret Boynton, "Speech Making in Minneapolis," in *Stories and Legends of the Palm Springs Indians* (Los Angeles: Times-Mirror, 1943), 64–66.

9. *Indigenismo,* a non-Indian discourse, sought to celebrate Indians' good qualities while dragging them into the modern world. Indigenismo and antimodernism are, in many respects, strikingly similar. For a review of the literature, which suggests fruitful comparisons between the United States and the rest of the Americas, see Mark Carey, "The Legacy of Race in Latin America: Indigenismo in Peru and Mexico," seminar paper, University of California at Davis, 15 June 2001. For Australia see Patrick Wolfe, "On Being Woken Up: The Dreamtime in Anthropology and in Australian Settler Discourse," *Comparative Studies in Society and History* 33:2 (1991): 197– 224, and Patrick Wolfe, "Repressive Authenticity," in *Settler Colonialism and the Transformation of Anthropology: The Politics and Poetics of an Ethnographic Event* (London: Cassell, 1999). For an examination of indigenismo discourse and its relation to Mexican immigrants to the United States during a period of nationalistic fervor in Mexico see George J. Sánchez, *Becoming Mexican American: Ethnicity, Culture, and Identity in Chicano Los Angeles, 1900–1945* (New York: Oxford University Press, 1994), 119–21.

10. The first two quotations are from Arthur C. Parker, "The Legal Status of the Indian," *Red Man* 4.10 (1912): 461–63; the third is from Arthur C. Parker, "Problems of Race Assimilation in America, with Special Reference to the American Indian," *Quarterly Journal of the Society of American Indians* 4.2 (October–December 1916): 285–304, 301 (emphasis mine).

11. For the point about Eastman and for many of the general ideas about Indian cultural and intellectual figures see Frederick E. Hoxie, "Exploring a Cultural Borderland: Native American Journeys of Discovery in the Early Twentieth Century," *Journal of American History* 79.3 (1992): 969–95, 981. Virility and manhood during the period as such are beyond the scope of this book, but for a good introduction to the complexity and importance of the terms for an analysis of people such as Parker and his views of Indians see Gail Bederman, *Manliness and Civilization: A Cultural History of Gender and Race in the United States, 1880–1917* (Chicago: University of Chicago Press, 1995), esp. "Remaking Manhood Through Race and Civilization."

12. For Mahone's thoughts about the importance of a Chilocco education and his organization see Mahone to Sells, 29 July 1918. On the diversity of the school's student body see K. Tsianina Lomawaima, *They Called It Prairie Light: The Story of Chilocco Indian School* (Lincoln: University of Nebraska Press, 1994), 11. Lomawaima found that more than one hundred Chilocco students served in the war (21). Russel Barsh found that almost all eligible men from boarding schools went to war, and 90 percent of them were volunteers; Russel Lawrence Barsh, "American Indians in the Great War," *Ethnohistory* 8.3 (1991): 278. The high rate of volunteerism was noted at the time, too. An editorial in the *Dallas News* claimed that 85 percent of Indians in the armed forces were volunteers. *Dallas News*, "Their Country," 18 February 1918, quoted in the *Indian School Journal*, March 1918. On the ways in which Indians made it into the army, especially the citizenship requirement, see Thomas A. Britten, "The Draft and Enlistment of American Indians," in *American Indians in World War I: At Home and Abroad* (Albuquerque: University of New Mexico Press, 1997). On keeping up with the news see Fred Mahone to the monthly Chilocco newletter *Indian School Journal: An Illustrated Monthly Magazine About Native Americans*, 4 August 1918, *Indian School Journal*, September 1918, 28, including photograph. The quotations about service are from "In the Council Tepee: Following the Flag," *Indian School Journal*, September, 1917, 583. By November 1918, 131 former Chilocco students were in the armed forces. See "Chilocco Students Who Have Answered Their Country's Call," *Indian School Journal*, November, 1918, 124. Mahone enlisted on 9 February 1918. Card File Relating to Indians in World War I, 1916–20, entry 977B, box 11, RG 75, NA.

13. Britten, *American Indians in World War I* (see especially the quotations on 173 from veterans about the transformative effects of the wartime service). See also Barsh, "American Indians in the Great War," 296–97. For the effects of the war more generally see Donald Parman, *Indians and the American West in the Twentieth Century* (Bloomington: University of Indiana Press, 1994), 59–66; Michael L. Tate, "From Scout to Doughboy: The National Debate over Integrating American Indians into the Military, 1891–1918," *Western Historical Quarterly* 17.4 (1986): 417–38. Not all Indians embraced the war; indeed, some protested Indian enlistment with great vigor. See David L. Wood, "Gosiute-Shoshone Draft Resistance, 1917–18," *Utah Historical Quarterly* 49.2 (1981): 173–88; Eric M. Zissu, "Conscription, Sovereignty, and Land: American Indian Resistance During World War I," *Pacific Historical Review* 64.4 (1995): 537–566.

14. Thomas Britten discusses the image of the Indian warrior during the war at length in *American Indians in World War I*; see esp. "American Indians as 'Doughboys': The Influence of Stereotypes." The Sells quotation is found in Cato Sells, untitled article in *Salt*

Lake City News, 13 February 1918, quoted in Barsh, "American Indians in the Great War," 292.

15. For a thoughtful analysis of Parker's views of education see Hazel W. Hertzberg, "Nationality, Anthropology, and pan-Indianism in the Life of Arthur C. Parker (Seneca)," *Proceedings of the American Philosophical Society* 123.1 (1979): 59; Parker is quoted in Hertzberg, *Search for an American Indian Identity,* 62.

16. Details of Mahone's time at Valparaiso University are taken from Mel Doering, Valparaiso University archivist, pers. comm., 13 February 2002.

17. Inspectors E. B. Linnen and T. B. Roberts wrote to CIA Burke in July that "the majority of these southern Mission Indians are under the spell and control of this man Tibbet." For this statement and the quotation in the text see Linnen and Roberts to Burke, 12 July 1921, file #216628, straight numerical files, box 3586, RG 60 (Department of Justice), NA. For the support of the MIF and the general disruption its leader, Jonathan Tibbet, caused among the Mission Indians see George W. Armijo, "General Conditions," Inspection Report, 2 October 1921, p. 5, CCF 82891-1923-150—Mission, box 12, RG 75, NA. On the board see E. M. Sweet, Inspection Report, 19 January 1921, in Inspection Reports, 1908–40, Inspection Division, entry 953, box 42, RG 75, NA; see also their newspaper, *The California Indian Herald.* On California Indian claims, including the role of Collett and the Indian Board of Cooperation, see "Indian Tribes of California," Hearing Before a Subcommittee of the Committee on Indian Affairs, House, pt. 1, 23 March 1920.

18. For "Enemy of the government" see Sweet, Inspection Report, 19 January 1921, 9. On the early influence of Tibbett and the beginnings of the MIF see Sweet Report, 19 January 1921; see also E. M. Sweet Jr., Inspection Report, 9 May 1921, CCF 86894-1920-150—Mission, box 12. For an outline of the MIF's goals see Walter Robert Baggs, "An Unfortunate Kind of Leadership: Jonathan Tibbet and the Mission Indian Federation," master's thesis (University of California at Riverside, 1978), 35; Anna Rose Monguia, "The Mission Indian Federation: A Study in Indian Political Resistance," master's thesis (University of California at Los Angeles, 1975). Tibbett is quoted in "Testimony of Jonathan Tibbett, 26 May 1920," in "Indians of the United States: Investigation of the Field Service," Hearing by a Subcommittee of the Committee on Indian Affairs, H. 231, vol. 3, pts. 3–9. None of this is to say that the MIF had no use for activists such as Montezuma or that they did not share some if not many of the values and goals. Montezuma published essays in *The Indian: A Runner from Tribe to Tribe; The Magazine of the Mission Indian Federation.* On Montezuma see Hertzberg, *Search for an American Indian Identity,* and Peter C. Iverson, *Carlos Montezuma and the Changing World of American Indians* (Albuquerque: University of New Mexico Press, 1982); for his views of the reservation system see Carlos Montezuma, "The Indian Reservation System," *Quarterly Journal of the Society of American Indians* 1.3 (July–September 1913): 359–60, and Carlos Montezuma, "The Reservation Is Fatal to the Development of Good Citizenship," *Quarterly Journal of the Society of American Indians* 2:1 (January–March 1914): 64–68.

On the MIF and the climate of discontent in southern California see Tanis C. Thorne, "On the Fault Line: Political Violence at Campo Fiesta and National Reform in Indian Policy," *Journal of California and Great Basin Anthropology* 21.2 (1999): 182–212, and John Collier, "The Mission Indians: The Mission Indian Federation, and the Allegations of Mr. Purl Williams and Mr. Adam Castillo," n.d. [1933], CCF 33247-33-155 — Mission Agency, pt. 1, folder 2/3, box 16, RG 75, NA. This document gives a short history of the organization from the perspective of Collier and suggests the BIA's continued anxiety about the MIF. See also "The Story of the Mission Indian Federation, by Its President [Adam Castillo]," in "Fact-Finding Study of Social and Economic Conditions of Indians of San Diego County, California and Reports from Specialists in Allied Fields," folder 24 — Mission Indians of California, Study of Social Conditions, box 47, RG 46 (Records of the U.S. Congress), Records of the Senate Subcommittee on Indian Affairs, 1928–1953, Center for Legislative Archives, NA.

19. For information about the fall meeting of the Indian Board of Cooperation see E. M. Sweet Jr., Inspection Report, 9 May 1921, CCF 86894-1920-150 — Mission, box 12. For the meetings with Tibbett see Armijo, "General Conditions," Inspection Report, 2 October 1921, and Sweet, Inspection Report, 19 January 1921. For the spring meeting see "Indians Ask for Rights," *Los Angeles Times*, 24 April 1921, 1, 4, which reported that Indians came from the Grand Canyon country to the meeting. On Hualapai attendance see William A. Light to CIA, 17 June 1921, CCF 34163-21-175 — General Service, pt. 1, box 447, RG 75, NA. On Mojave interest in the MIF see W. E. Thackrey, Supt. at Fort Mojave School, 14 June 1921, CCF 34163-21-175 — General Service, pt. 1, box 447, RG 75, NA.

20. Tibbett first inquired about visiting the Mission Reservations in 1917; the superintendent at Pala gave him permission to do so. See Richard Maxfield Thomas, "The Mission Indians: A Study of Leadership and Culture Change," Ed.D. diss. (University of California at Los Angeles, 1964), 87. Ironically, and probably much to his later chagrin, their tour of Indian reservations in the region had been facilitated by Arizona representative Carl Hayden, who in a matter of years would fight the Hualapais and their land claim. But in 1920 he was eager to grant Tibbett's wish to have "freedom of the reservations." And in doing so he made it possible for the MIF message to spread throughout the region unabated. Jonathan Tibbett to Carl Hayden, 28 February 1920; Carl Hayden to Cato Sells, 5 March 1920, both in CCF 4840-20121 — Malki, box 1, RG 75, NA. For "absolutely necessary" see Charles Burke to SOI Albert Fall, 22 July 1921, straight numerical file #216628, box 3586, RG 60, NA. On the BIA's fear of the MIF see Burke to SOI Albert Fall, [illegible] July 1921, #216628, box 3586, RG 60, NA; Albert Fall to Attorney General, 21 July 1921, in ibid. For "very unfortunate uprising" see Raymond Benjamin, Asst. Dist. Atty. to AG, telegram, 2 August 1921, in ibid. The indictment was for violating section 2113 of the revised statutes, "Attempt to Alienate the Confidence of the Indians from the Government of the United States." The case eventually became Criminal Case 2979, *United States v. Jonathan Tibbet, Joe Pete, J. H. Jones and F. U. S. Hughes*, United States District Court for the Southern District of California (1921). For "strike down" see Joseph Burke, Asst. AG to John W. Crim, Asst. U.S. Atty., 22 March 1922, #216628, box 3586, RG 60, NA; for "unless stopped" see Raymond Benjamin to the AG, 19 August 1921, #216628, box 3586, RG 60, NA. On Pete see various documents in file #19803, box 2830, concerning his efforts to resist the BIA's survey of Indian eligibility for service, RG 60, NA. For a more sympathetic view of Pete's continued role as a leader see Vera L. Connolly, "The End of the Road," *Good Housekeeping*, May 1929, 169–70.

21. For "we are all depressed" and "ruled like slaves" see Statement of Fred Mahone, 28 June 1921, CCF 34163-21-175 — General Service, pt. 1, box 447, RG 75, NA. On Mahone as a "splendid fellow" see "Fred Mahone, Wallapai Officer, in Air Service," *Mojave County Miner,* 3 June 1921, 7. On Swaskegame's body lying in state and Mahone's role as a pallbearer for him, see "Wallapai Boy, Who Gave His Life for Uncle Sam, Laid to Rest Here," *Mohave County Miner,* 20 September 1921; on Swaskegame's death see "Sam Swaskegame, Local Indian, Killed in Action," *Mohave County Miner,* 30 November 1918, 1, 5. On naming the post see "Kingman Branch of American Legion Formed This Week," *Mohave County Miner,* 12 July 1918, 1. On the funeral events see "Wallapais to Have Big Pow-wow in Memory of Hero," *Mohave County Miner,* 6 May 1921; "Wallapais to Hold Big Pow-wow Monday," *Mohave County Miner,* 17 June 1921; "Big 'Cry' Comemorated [*sic*] Sam Swaskegame's Death," *Mohave County Miner,* 1 July 1921, 7; "Sam Swaskegame World War Hero Funeral Sunday," *Mohave County Miner,* 23 September 1921, 1. For an account of the funeral based on interviews with participants, witnesses, and newspaper stories see Dick Waters, "The Day Sam Swaskegame Came Home," *Mohave Magazine,* 20 May 1971, 17. It is unclear why Watson is not mentioned in this article. Dolores Honga's grandfather was present at the funeral, and he passed on his stories of the event to her. She remembers her grandfather and other elders talking about the funeral as a turning point when she was growing up in the 1940s. Author interview with Dolores Honga, 23 September 2002, Peach Springs, Ariz.

The funeral in Kingman was not an isolated incident. Returning soldiers — living or dead — were feted across the country, American Legion posts sprang up on Indian reservations, and funerals combining Indian and non-Indian rituals were not uncommon. A virtually identical funeral took place in 1921 when two thousand residents of the town of Thomas, Oklahoma, held a memorial service in honor of, and named an American Legion post after, Henry Goodbear. Goodbear was either Cheyenne or Arapaho. Donald Parman, *Indians and the American West in the Twentieth Century* (Bloomington: University of Indiana Press, 1994), 63. For the positive reception Indians received on returning home see Britten, *American Indians in World War I,* 159–60; on American Legion posts, see ibid., 166, and Barsh, "American Indians in the Great War," 295, 296 (for funerals).

22. Details about when and where the group was formed are unknown. "Supai" was quickly dropped from the group's title. For the date of formation see Statement of Fred Mahone, 28 June 1921, CCF 34163-21-175 — General Service, pt. 1, box 447, RG 75, NA. For "Human Rights and Home Rule," "With our counselor," and other details see Fred Mahone to Governor Campbell of Arizona and J. Maddock, state highway engineer, 21 July 1921, and on the organization of Mahone's group under the by-laws and constitution of the MIF see Fred Mahone to CIA, 29 August 1921, both in ibid.

23. Statement of Fred Mahone, 28 June 1921.

24. Burke to Fred Mahone, 28 September 1921, ibid.

25. On leadership see A. L. Kroeber et al., *Walapai Ethnography,* Memoirs of the American Anthropological Association no. 42 (Menasha, Wis.: American Anthropological Association, 1935), 154–56; the phrase "good talker" is from Blind Tom (156). The Pine Springs country to the east of Peach Springs is an example; see Ch. 1, n. 16, above concerning the population there. On Hualapais as laborers and the consequent moving to towns see Henry F. Dobyns and Robert C. Euler, "The Nine Lives of Cherum, the Pai Tokumhet," *American Indian Quarterly* 22.3 (1998): 363–86. The point about new

residential patterns based on availability of work is further fleshed out in Jeffrey P. Shepard, "Land, Labor, and Leadership: The Political Economy of Hualapai Community Building, 1910–1940," in *Native Pathways: American Indian Culture and Economic Development in the Twentieth Century,* ed. Brian Hosmer and Colleen O'Neill (Niwot: University of Colorado Press, 2004), 209–37, esp. 217.

26. Interview with Jacob Honga, 12 August 1968, pp. 739–40, Prescott College Hualapai Oral Tradition Project, Prescott, Arizona. Many thanks to Jeff Shepard for making this source available to me. For the letter and quotation concerning Mahone see May E. Young, "Jim Mahone, Hual[a]pai Scout," *Desert Magazine,* February 1957, 8, and "Jim Mahone, Big Walapai Brave, Deserves Pension," *Mohave County Miner,* 14 July 1922, 14, reporting that the letter was written by Crook himself. On Mahone in general see John R. Winslowe, "Maha'Navie—Hualapai Warrior: He Spent a Lifetime Fighting His Own People," *Westerner,* May–June 1970, 10–13, 50–51; for a contemporaneous sketch of Jim Mahone's life see A. P. Miller, "Mu-Ko-Hoi-Na-Vie, Jim Mahone, Sr., Indian Scout of the Hualapai Indian Tribe," June, 1937, MS in Dennis Casebier Collection, Mohave Desert Archives, Goffs Schoolhouse, Essex, Calif. (hereafter Casebier Collection). For Mahone's pensions see Declaration for Survivor's Pension—Indian Wars, 15 August 1922, CCF 58388-22-725—Truxton Canyon, box 42, RG 75, NA.

For Hualapais who received pensions see Ch. 1, n. 9, above. On the importance of scouting among the Hualapais see, e.g., Huya's pension record, the case file for which was obtained via a Privacy/Freedom of Information Act request. File #XC 2 581 427, deposition of Huya, 17 October 1927, claim #19935, in the author's possession. On his age and further biographical and geographical information see "Affidavit of Captain Huya," 9 August 1932, reel 49, PIRA.

27. On Fielding's bid for power, of which few details are known, see "Insurgency Among the Wallapais," *Mohave County Miner,* 11 June 1910, 2. All quotations by Fielding are in "Speech of Jim Fielding, Chief of the Hualapais, made Monday, October 14, 1922," Exhibit E, in John M. Atwater, "Investigation Report on Charges Against the Administration of Superintendent Light, Truxton Canyon Agency and School," made October 4–24, 1922, Inspection Reports 1909–40, Inspection Division, entry 953, box 70, RG 75, NA (hereafter Atwater Report). For more on Fielding and his place among the Hualapais see A. P. Miller, "The Passing of Chief Pachilawa," undated but written on the occasion of Fielding's death, 31 May 1936, Casebier Collection.

28. See Petition to the Hon. President of the United States, Warren G. Harding, 26 May 1921, signed by thirty-nine leaders from reservations in southern California, in Beaver Lake in Nevada, and by Yumas, Hualapais, and Havasupais in Arizona, in Atwater Report. On Steve Leve-Leve becoming the leader of the Hualapais see "New Wallapai Chief Heads Local Indians," *Mohave County Miner,* 14 August 1920, 1. On the elder Leve-Leve see Henry F. Dobyns and Robert C. Euler, *Wauba Yuma's People: The Comparative Socio-Political Structure of the Pai Indians of Arizona* (Prescott, Ariz.: Prescott College Press, 1970), 27–28.

29. On concerns about the plot see George J. Laten [?] to CIA, 21 April 1921, CCF 34163-21-175—General Service, pt. 1, box 447, RG 75, NA. The Mahone quotation comes from Fred Mahone to Alben B. Fall, Secretary of the Interior, 1 July 1921; he discusses his pending August discharge in another letter to Fall, 8 July 1921, both in ibid.

30. For the quotations from and characterizations of Magee and Crozier see William

Light to CIA, 17 June 1921, CCF 34163-21-175 — General Service, pt. 1, box 447, RG 75, NA; on the returned students see Light, Annual Report, 20 June 1921, SANSR.

31. For "The organization" see Statement of Fred Mahone, 28 June 1921; for "settle it" see Fred Mahone to Governor Campbell and State Highway Engineer Maddock, 21 July 1921, both in CCF 34163-21-175 — General Service, pt. 1, box 447, RG 75, NA.

32. For "white friends" and "to carry out" see Statement of Fred Mahone, 28 June 1921. Statement of Richard McGee, n.d. (this is the same person mentioned in the text above as Richard Magee; names were often spelled a variety of ways), CCF 34163-21-175, pt. 1, box 447, RG 75, NA. All Havatone quotations are from Statement of Roger Havatone, 28 June 1921, in ibid.

33. William Light to CIA, 25 August 1921, CCF 34163-21-175, pt. 1, box 447, RG 75, NA.

34. Ibid. Light threatened to take away the Hualapais' land and used almost the same language he had earlier that same year. In reference to a newspaper article about white interest in the reservation, Light had said: "This illustrates the sentiment of the people of the country. They want it all, and if the Indian does not show an inclination to use it, and to improve his industry, character, and usefulness, I should not defend him against the plans of the white man. The Indian should either use the reservation for his self support, or he should surrender it to men who will use it." Light, Annual Report, 18 January 1921, SANSR, reel 151.

35. Mahone's letters and statements made their way into the file on Tibbett at the request of Inspector E. B. Linnen. Linnen wrote to Commissioner of Indian Affairs Charles Burke requesting that Mahone's writings be forwarded to the Assistant U.S. Attorney in Los Angeles to be used as evidence in the case against Tibbett and his co-conspirators. E. B. Linnen to Charles Burke, 7 October 1921, CCF 34163-21-175 — General Service, pt. 1, box 447, RG 75, NA.

36. Steve Levey Levey [sic], 1st Chief, and Fred W. Mahone, Chief's Secretary, to CIA, 3 December 1921, J. M. Stewart to CIA, 2 January 1922, and Charles Burke to J. M. Stewart, 14 January 1922, all in CCF 34163-21-175 — General Service, pt. 2, box 447, RG 75, NA. The petition came from S. D. Stewart, a Kingman attorney representing the Hualapais in some fashion. Stewart remains in the shadows. It's possible that he had the Hualapais' best interests in mind, but there is also a chance that he wanted the reservation opened to mining, and with the Hualapais, not the government, in charge that would be easier.

37. On property and marriage see G. A Mook, "Property," in A. L. Kroeber et al., *Walapai Ethnography,* Memoirs of the American Anthropological Association, no. 42 (Menasha, Wis.: American Anthropological Association, 1935), 160–62. Details of the incident may be found in Light to CIA, 1 February 1922; on having Fielding fired see Charles Burke to S. D. Stewart, 14 February 1922, both in CCF 34163-21-175 — General Service, pt. 2, box 447, RG 75, NA.

38. For "self styled" see William Light to CIA, 29 June 1923, CCF 30310-23174.1 — Truxton Canyon, box 11, RG 75, NA; all other quotations in the paragraph are from William Light to CIA, 1 February 1922, CCF 34163-21-175 — General Service, pt. 2, box 447, RG 75, NA.

39. L. E. Murphy to CIA, 18 February 1922, CCF 34163-21-175 — General Service, pt. 2, box 447, RG 75, NA.

40. Ibid.

41. Statement of Indian Beecher (Young) of Pine Springs, Exhibit D, Atwater Report.

42. "Speech of Jim Fielding, Chief of the Hualapais, made Monday, October 16, 1922," Exhibit E, Atwater Report. On Fielding's getting the cattle operation under way see Beecher interview, 24 September 2002. Fred Mahone estimated that the Sanford Cattle Company grazed 6,500 head, Abe Cauffman 1,000, in the Pine Springs area. Fred Mahone, "Present and Previous Livestock," 23 April 1923, CCF 30310-230174.1 — Truxton Canyon, box 11, RG 75, NA. For other estimates of cattle numbers see Jeffrey Shepard, "Building an American Indian Community: The Hualapai Nation in the Twentieth Century," Ph.D. diss. (Arizona State University at Tempe, 2002).

43. For "foremost urgent need" see Fred Mahone to Senator Henry A. Ashurst and Congressmen Carl Hayden and Clyde Kelly, 6 April 1923, CCF 30310-230174.1 — Truxton Canyon, box 11, RG 75, NA. On the contract with Du Four see "Power of Attorney' contract," 6 April 1923, CCF 30310-230174.1 — Truxton Canyon, box 11, RG 75, NA. This file contains a variety of documents that Fred Mahone compiled on behalf of the Hualapais in order to buttress their claim to the land around Peach Springs. It is not clear how Du Four came to the attention of the Hualapais, nor is it evident that he actually did any work for them. It is possible that Du Four was of the class of lawyers that preyed on Indians, getting them to sign away valuable mineral rights, for example, in return for promises of sovereignty. This was the initial, and quite sensible, reason the BIA forbade Indians, except with BIA permission, to hire their own counsel. Later, of course, restrictions on the hiring of attorneys would become a bar to acquiring adequate legal aid. For "ill treatment" see Mahone to Ashurst, Hayden, and Kelly, 6 April 1932. It was Hayden who sent the petition and supporting documents to the CIA. Carl Hayden to CIA, 10 April 1923. Both are in CCF 30310-23-174.1 — Truxton Canyon, box 11, RG 75, NA.

44. For non-Indian uses of the reservation see "Previous and Present Livestock, sheets 1–3, supporting petition." Despite the title Mahone discusses such businesses as the Nelson Lime and Cement Company, which operated on the eastern border of the reservation, claiming that they mined on the reservation side of the line. For "Chester A. Arthur set aside" see "Petition," 6 April 1923, CCF 30310-23-174.1 — Truxton Canyon, box 11, RG 75, NA.

45. "Sheet #13, Supporting Petition," 6 April 1923, CCF 30310-23-174.1 — Truxton Canyon, box 11, RG 75, NA.

46. For "sent out a call" see Fred Mahone, "Explanatory history accompanying renewed petition by Hualapai Indians to United States Congress," 6 April 1923, and for the rest of the quotations see in Mahone to Ashurst, Hayden, and Kelly, 6 April 1923, sheet #3, Supporting Petition, both in CCF 30310-23174.1 — Truxton Canyon, box 11, RG 75, NA. On the Hualapai War see Dan Thrapp, *The Conquest of Apacheria* (Norman: University of Oklahoma Press, 1967), 39–52. On the use of Hualapais and Apaches as scouts against the Apaches see Thomas Dunlay, *Wolves for the Blue Soldiers: Indian Scouts and Auxiliaries with the United States Army, 1860–90* (Lincoln: University of Nebraska Press, 1982), 165–86; for the early use of Hualapais as allies against the Apaches see John G. Bourke, *On the Border with Crook* (1891; reprint, Lincoln: University of Nebraska Press, 1971), 167–71.

47. For "advancing with equal rights" see "Question 2, sheet 7, Petition," 6 April 1923,

and for "treaty of brotherhood" see "Answer 6, sheet 11, Petition," 6 April 1923, both in CCF 30310-230174.1 — Truxton Canyon, box 11, RG 75, NA.

Chapter 4. The Government Versus the Hualapais

1. Clay Fallman, Commissioner, GLO, to SOI, 19 April 1919, CCF 65843-18-307.2 — Havasupai, box 7, RG 75, NA.

2. Cato Sells to SOI, 13 May 1919; Alexander Vogelsang, First Asst. SOI, to Commissioner, GLO, 2 October 1919; Cato Sells to Alexander Vogelsang, 27 December 1919; Alexander Vogelsang to Cato Sells, 26 January 1920, all in CCF 65843-18-307.2 — Havasupai, box 7, RG 75, NA. Sells wanted to craft an argument in favor of the Hualapais based on occupancy; in order to do so he had the lands division examine the question in a couple of memos. For Sells's initial interest in examining the question see E. S. McMahon to Garber and Shipe, 17 July 1919, in ibid.; for Sells's supporters see CDM [possibly the chief of the land division, Marschalk], "Memorandum for Secretary Vogelsang, RE Hualapai Indian Reservation," n.d., in ibid.; J. M. Shipe, "Memorandum Relative to the Proposed Withdrawal of Railroad Land from the Walapai Reservation," n.d., in ibid.

3. The suggestion to split the reservation in two is in Vogelsang to Sells, 26 January 1920. The legal counsel to the SOI agreed that a split was the best solution, reasoning that getting congressional approval for an exchange or enlargement would be difficult. Charles Mahaffie, solicitor of the Department of the Interior, to Alexander Vogelsang, 26 January 1919, CCF 65843-18-307.2 — Havasupai, box 7, RG 75, NA. Alexander Vogelsang to CIA, 16 June 1920, in ibid. See also Cato Sells, CIA, to Britton and Gray, 12 December 1920, in ibid., on the exchange. This includes the memo "Justification for item to authorize the consolidation into two separate tracts or blocks the holdings of Southern Pacific Railroad Company within the Hualapai Indian Reservation in Arizona." See Britton and Gray to Sells, 27 December 1920, and Sells to Britton and Gray, 8 January 1921, both in ibid. The mistake of calling the Santa Fe the Southern Pacific was not noted in the subsequent letters cited by Sells or by Britton and Gray.

4. Britton and Gray, Santa Fe attorneys, to CIA, 20 August 1923, in CCF 65843-18-307.2 — Havasupai, box 7, RG 75, NA; W. A. Marschalk, Memorandum for Commissioner Burke, n.d., and Charles Burke to SOI, 9 September 1923, both in ibid. For Hayden's continuing support see Carl Hayden to Charles Burke, CIA, 26 April 1923, and on finally agreeing to split the reservation in half see Herbert Work, SOI, to Charles Burke, 28 September 1923, both in ibid. Work suggested that Burke take a look at the act of March 3, 1921 (41 Stat. 1239), which might provide him with a model for writing his own piece of consolidation legislation; the attorneys complained to the Indian Office that the Hualapais were cutting trees and grazing cattle on their sections without proper compensation to the railroad. Britton and Gray to CIA, in ibid. For "reduce by about one-half" see Hubert Work, SOI, to Homer P. Snyder, Chairman, Committee on Indian Affairs, House of Representatives, 6 December 1923, in ibid. A week later the Indian Office informed Britton and Gray, the ATSF's attorneys, of their move to introduce a bill. E. B. Merritt, Asst. CIA, to Britton and Gray, 13 December 1923, in ibid. In order to consolidate the checkerboard on the Navajo reservation, Work facilitated a very similar deal there in

1925. Realizing that this plan, too, would cut Navajo holdings in the Western-Leupp area in half, Work rationalized it the same way: expediency. See Lawrence C. Kelly, *The Navajo Indian and Federal Indian Policy, 1900–1935* (Tucson: University of Arizona Press, 1968), 118.

5. The spring fell inside Section 2, Township 25, Range 11 West. For the first mention of this definite location see Charles A. Burke, CIA, to SOI, 16 July 1924, CCF 31229-23-303 —Truxton Canyon, pt. 1, folder 2/2, box 26, RG 75, NA.

6. See E. C. Finney, 1st Asst. SOI, to Harlan Fiske Stone, AG, 22 July 1924, forwarding the Burke letter cited in n. 5 recommending that the Department of Justice initiate the suit, and Stone to Work, 25 July 1924, notifying him that the U.S. attorney in Phoenix had been asked to begin legal proceedings, both in CCF 31229-23-303 —Truxton Canyon, pt. 1, folder 2/2, box 26, RG 75, NA. For the question of the settlers' right to sell to the railroad and the matter of Hualapai use of the spring see Ira Wells, Asst. U.S. AG, to Frederic H Bernard, Asst. U.S. Attorney for Arizona, 25 July 1924, #227235, box 3944, entry 112, straight numerical files, central files, Department of Justice, RG 60, NA.

7. The instructions for the U.S. attorney are in Ira Wells to Hubert Work, 12 February 1925, #227235, box 3944, RG 60, NA; the consolidation law is in *U.S. Statutes at Large* 43 (1925), 954. For details of the exchange see Thomas G. Havell, Acting Comm., GLO, Circular no. 1029, "Regulations for Exchange of Lands in the Walapai Indian Reservation, Arizona," 8 September 1925, box 42, Subject Files, Walapai, Records of the Senate Subcommittee on Indian Affairs, 1928–1953, RG 46, Center for Legislative Archives, NA. On the railroad's decision to wait see Charles Burke to Carl Hayden, 7 July 1925, CCF 65843-18-307.2 —Havasupai, RG 75, NA. On Light's concerns about cattle see William Light to Carl Hayden, 24 March 1925, and "Facts Concerning the Wallapai Indian Reservation," both in box 42, RG 46; on Hill and his visit see George Hill to AG, 1 December 1925, file #227235, box 3944, RG 60, NA; George Hill to CIA, 1 December 1925, CCF 31229-23-313, pt. 1, box 26, RG 75, NA.

8. All quotations are from H. O. Davidson to CIA, 25 November 1925, Phoenix Area Office, Accession #NRHL-075-00-115, folder: memoranda, box 27b, RG 75, NA, Pacific Region, Laguna Niguel, Calif. This file is part of an accession made in fall 2000 by the National Archives. When I looked at it in May 2001 it had been minimally processed. The folder and box numbers are temporary. Anyone interested in looking at the material should consult the National Archives in Laguna Niguel for current cataloging information. Davidson was a Mojave Indian who, at various times, represented the Hualapais' and the Mojaves' interests to the Indian Office. On his membership in the MIF see items concerning Davidson in *The Indian: A Runner from Tribe to Tribe: The Magazine of the Mission Indian Federation*, May 1922, p. 5, and June 1922, p. 9.

9. Hill filed two reports on the same day that differed in wording but agreed in content. The quotation is from George Hill to Charles Burke, 1 December 1925, CCF 31229-23-303, folder 2/2, box 26, RG 75, NA; see also George Hill to AG, 1 December 1925, #227235, folder 1, box 3944, RG 60, NA.

10. John Edwards, Asst. SOI, to AG, 16 January 1926, #5 106, Peach Springs, entry 749, CCF 1907–36, box 1500, Department of the Interior, RG 48, NA.

11. For "If . . . as some things" see B. M. Parmenter, Asst. A.G., to Hubert Work, 11 February 1926, CCF 31229-23-303 —Truxton Canyon, folder 2/2, box 26, RG 75, NA;

for "merely wandered" and "having no doubt" see B. M. Parmenter to John B. Wright, U.S. Attorney for Arizona, 11 February 1926, #227235, folder 1, box 3944, RG 60, NA.

12. For "drove off the Indians" and information about the reservation see George R. Hill, Asst. U.S. attorney for Arizona, to B. M. Parmenter, 17 February 1926, CCF 31229-23-303 — Truxton Canyon, folder 2/2, box 26, RG 75, NA; for "fed up with conferences and delays" and the suit see Parmenter's memo to Wright, 9 July 1926, "Re: Proposed suit against the Atchison, Topeka, and Santa Fe Pacific Railway Company, involving Peach Springs on the Walapai Indian Reservation, Arizona," #227235, folder 2, box 3944, RG 60, NA. George Hill to Ethelbert Ward, 24 August 1926, Phoenix Area Office, Accession #NRHL-075-00-115, folder 227235, box 27b, RG 75, Laguna Niguel, NA.

13. For the railroad see E. E. McInnis, general solicitor of the ATSF, to Charles Burke, 15 October 1926, CCF 31229-23-313, pt. 1, folder 2/2, box 26, RG 75, NA. Hayden's continued support is documented in the telegram between the attorneys of 25 August 1927, PSFFC. When talking about Hayden in telegrams the lawyers used a code; the files retain the coded telegram and a translation. These files are still the property of the firm and are not public documents. Because of a confidentiality agreement, I cannot quote from any correspondence, memos, or other material in the firm's Peach Springs file, nor can I use names. Agreement on file with author and Fennemore Craig. For the exchange between Interior and Justice about putting the investigation on hold see [no first name] Campbell, "Memorandum relative to the Proposed Suit Against the Atchison, Topeka, and Santa Fe Railroad Company Involving Peach Springs on the Walapai Indian Reservation," 21 September 1926, CCF 31229-23-303 — Truxton Canyon, folder 1/2, box 26, RG 75; [no first name] Marshalk, "Memorandum Relative [to] Walapai Indian Reservation, Arizona," 12 November 1926, B. M. Parmenter to Hubert Work, 16 December 1926; John Edwards, Asst. SOI, to B. M. Parmenter, 2 January 1927, and B. M. Parmenter to Hubert Work, 8 January 1927, all in ibid. See also John Edwards to AG, 4 January 1927, CCF #5 106, Peach Springs, box 1500, RG 48, NA. All quotations are from a four-page letter written by Bob Schrum and signed also by Jim Fielding, Kate Crozier, John Huya, Honga, and Jim Smith to Inspector Herbert Fiske, 31 July 1927, CCF 45077-28-806 — Truxton Canyon, RG 75, NA. On Schrum as a leader of the Peach Springs band see Statement of George Walker (informant G) in A. L. Kroeber et al., *Walapai Ethnography*, Memoirs of the American Anthropological Association, no. 42 (Menasha, Wis.: American Anthropological Association, 1935), 155.

14. On the decision to sue see E. C. Finney, first Asst. SOI, 22 August 1927, "*In re* Atchison, Topeka, and Santa Fe Railway Company. Application Denied. Application for Recall of Departmental Recommendation," and John H. Edwards, Asst. SOI, to AG, 15 September 1927, both in CCF file #5 106, Peach Springs, box 1500, RG 48, NA.

15. The railroad's concerns and its information regarding the government's case are in letters between attorneys, 6 September 1927, 27 September 1927, and 8 October 1927, and Hill's promise to alert the railroad is in letter between attorneys, 22 September 1927, all in PSFFC.

16. *Winters v. United States*, 207 U.S. 564 (1908); *Cramer v. United States*, 261 U.S. 219 (1921). Ward worked on Indian water rights cases that arose from the *Winters* decision stating that Indians had a prior right to water flowing across their reservations

that was superior to the rights of non-Indian users. On Ward and his influence and expertise see John Shurts, *Indian Reserved Water Rights: The* Winters *Doctrine in Its Social and Legal Context, 1880s to 1930s* (Norman: University of Oklahoma Press, 2000), 205–6. For "The proposed suit" and Ward's opinions on the case see Ethelbert Ward to AG, 16 November 1927, CCF 31229-3-313, folder 1/2, box 36, RG 75, NA. Because of Interior's constant wavering Ward had looked into the Peach Springs matter in December 1926, before the suit had, again, been officially authorized in 1927. Considering that communications needed to get from one agency to the other and then be dispatched to field agents, it should not be surprising that Ward, for example, would have embarked on an assignment before learning of a change in course. I am relying on both of Ward's opinions and will cite the specific one when quoting.

17. Ethelbert Ward to John B. Wright, U.S. Atty. for Arizona, 18 November 1927; Ethelbert Ward, "Proposed Suit by U.S. against Santa Fe Pacific Railroad concerning land and water rights on the Hualpai [*sic*] Indian Reservation, Arizona," addressed to the AG, 4 December 1926, both in CCF 31229-23-313, folder 1/2, box 26, RG 75, NA.

18. Ward's response to Parmenter is in Ethelbert Ward to AG, 11 January 1928, #227235, box 3944, RG 60, NA. Tthe quotation is from his fourteen-page memo "Proposed Suit by U.S.," emphasis mine. For consent and international law see M. F. Lindley, *The Acquisition and Government of Backward Territory in International Law: Being a Treatise on the Law and Practice Relating to Colonial Expansion* (London: Longmans, Green, 1926), 342.

19. Grounds is cited in William A. Light to CIA, 26 April 1926, CCF 31229-23-313, folder 2/2, box 26, RG 75, NA. Affidavit of John A. Bozarth, April 1928, in "Proposed Suit Against the Atchison, Topeka, and Santa Fe Railroad Company, Involving Peach Springs in the Walapai Indian Reservation, Digest of Facts Taken from Affidavits and Deposition," CCF 31229-23-313, pt. 2, box 26, RG 75, NA. "Statement of Harvey Hubbs, of Kingman, Ariz., on the matter of use and ownership of the waters Peach Springs, on the Wallapai Reservation, Ariz." Interrogatory form, n.d., box 2, entry 824, RG 48, NA. Hubbs's statement was recorded by William Light, which means that it was likely taken down while Light worked on the other statements between 1926 and 1928. On Hubbs as a miner living in Cerbat see Cerbat, Mohave County, Arizona Territory, 7 June 1880, Manuscript Census, RG 29, reel 36, NA. For the railroad's witnesses see Abstract of Deposition of T. F. Garner, 21 June 1929, witness for the railroad, and James B. Rothwell, n.d., both in box 2, entry 824, RG 48, NA. Deposition of John T. Hewlett, 24 June 1929, folder 1/5, box 30b, Phoenix Area Office, Accession #NRHL-075-00-115, RG 75, NA, Laguna Niguel, NA. Information about Hewlett as a star witness is in letter between attorneys, 17 October 1927, PSFFC. O. W. Decker, dictated to his wife, to William A. Light, 10 June 1926, Phoenix Area Office, Accession #NRHL-075-00-115, folder 227235, box 27b, RG 75, NA, Laguna Niguel, NA.

The evidence suggests that before the government claimed title to Indian land, the settlers recognized the Hualapais as owners and entered into some form of agreement with them concerning use. This is similar to other pre-governmental land use arrangements in settler societies. Ann Parsonson's research into Maori-white land use agreements that predate the extinguishment by the Crown of native title shows a similar pattern. Whites acknowledged that they leased land at the sufferance of the Maoris. Of course, as in the United States, in New Zealand these leases were invalidated, in this case by the Crown. By following the doctrine laid out in *Johnson v. M'Intosh,* the Crown declared that native title did not provide for a right to alienate land to anyone but the sovereign. See Ann Parsonson, "The Fate of Maori Land Rights in Early Colonial New Zealand: The Limits of the Treaty of Waitangi and the Doctrine of Aboriginal Title," in *Law, History, Colonialism: The Reach of Empire,* ed. Diane Kirkby and Catherine Coleborne (Manchester, U.K.: Manchester University Press, 2001): 173–89; see also the detailed report by Light regarding interviews and correspondence with Grounds, Decker, and Crozier in William Light to CIA, 26 April 1926, CCF 31229-23-313, folder 2/2, box 26, RG 75, NA.

20. From my reading about him in the archives it is clear that Davidson is the man described, anonymously, as the chairman of the Mohave and Hualapai Welfare Committee in Institute for Government Research, *The Problem of Indian Administration: Report of a Survey Made at the Request of the Honorable Hubert Work, Secretary of the Interior, and Submitted to him, February 21, 1928* (Baltimore: Johns Hopkins University Press, 1928), 698, otherwise known as "the Meriam Report." This description of him as an agitator comes from that reading. On Davidson as a shyster see F. T. Mann to CIA, 11 September 1928, CCF 44178-28-320 — Truxton Canyon, box 29, RG 75, NA. Details about Davidson also come from author interviews with Dolores Honga and Vera Watoname, 25 September 2002, Peach Springs, Ariz. On persuading Frazier see Lynn Frazier to Hubert Work, SOI, 23 January 1928, and to John G. Sargent, AG, 30 April 1928, box 42, RG 46, NA.

21. H. O. Davidson to Lynn Frazier, n.d. [after 30 January 1928], box 42, RG 46, NA.

22. For the Hualapais' working on their own history see ibid. Henry Dobyns traced specific Hualapai occupancy to ca. 1790. See "Genealogy Chart — Peach Springs Band (Yi Kwat Pa'a), The Captain George Lineage," Claimant's Exhibit 119G, *Hualapai Tribe of the Hualapai Reservation, Arizona v. The United States of America,* Indian Claims Commission Docket No. 90, box 1055, RG 279 (Records of the Indian Claims Commission), NA. On the Peach Springs band see the affidavits of Jim Smith, Mike Sue, W. F. Grounds — a non-Indian who testified that when he arrived in country in 1873 the Hualapais were in full possession of the springs — John Smith, Jane Huya, and Kwath a yan ya (Nora Schrum), recorded on 19 and 22 December 1927, CCF 31229-23-313, folder 3/3, box 26, RG 75, NA. Grounds, however, was not a very reliable witness. In a deposition taken 7 September 1927, he said virtually the opposite. "I don't remember that I was ever there when there were any Indians around. . . . No settlement to amount to anything there, you might say, outside of renegades who would go there and gather feed and one thing and another." In "Proposed Suit against the Atchison, Topeka, and Santa Fe Railroad Company, Involving Peach Springs in the Walapai Indian Reservation, Digest of Facts taken from Affidavits and Deposition," CCF 31229-23-313, pt. 2, box 26, RG 75, NA. On supplying the Hualapais with attorneys see "Made and done by H. O. Davidson, Acting Secretary of Mohave and Walapai Tribes, on behalf of Chief Aniyarre Askit (Joseph Goodman), Pete Lambert, and Sherman Ross of the Mohave Tribe Committee and Chief Bob Schrum, Philip Quasalla, and Captain Jim Fielding of the Walapai Tribe Committee to Hubert S. Works [*sic*]," 17 January 1928, CCF 31229-23-313, pt. 2, box 26, RG 75, NA.

23. William A. Light to B. E. Marks, Asst. U.S. atty. for Arizona, 8 May 1928, box 2, Records Concerning U.S. v. Santa Fe Pacific Railroad Company, 1919–43, entry 824, Records of the Office of the Solicitor, RG 48, NA (hereafter entry 824, RG 48, NA). Citations are to box number only. These records are not filed in any order, nor are there folder numbers. They occupy three boxes.

24. Ibid.

25. See affidavit of William H. Nelson, 24 April 1928, affidavit of Warren E. Day [?], April 1928, and affidavit of Snyje, n.d., all in box 2, entry 824, RG 48, NA. For Cureton's remarks see James Cureton, deposition on behalf of the Santa Fe Pacific Railroad, 13 January 1928, folder 2/5, box 30b, Phoenix Area Office, Accession #NRHL-075-00-115, RG 75, Laguna Niguel, NA. Of course, depositions have to be read carefully. Often, questions were phrased so as to elicit a specific type of answer, such as the following, asked of Frank Shelton by Thomas G. Nairn, attorney for the railroad: "Do you really ever recall seeing more than a few roving Indians camped around Peach Springs?" Answer: "No." Deposition of Frank Shelton, 17 June 1930, 13, box 2, entry 824, RG 48, NA. In another example, the following was asked of Jim Fielding by Lemuel Matthews, a lawyer for the government: "Wallapai Indians, have they always lived around this country? — around Peach Springs and this country?" Answer: "Yes." Deposition of Jim Fielding, 17 August 1929, 4, in ibid. When lawyers supplied the answer in advance they got it. Also, as with the Grounds deposition and affidavit (see text below), oral statements — from Indians or whites — can be unreliable. Cureton was asked, "What influence did Cherum have over the Walapais?" He answered, "Absolutely none, I think." "Was he — " "He was their leader simply because he was a more intelligent man, lots of force about him, and whatever he said would go." Cherum, then, was simultaneously with and without influence. Cureton's deposition is riddled with such contradictions. Deposition of John Cureton, 28 October 1937, 13, in ibid.

26. On the IRA's interest see Herbert Welsh to CIA and Gentlemen, 30 August 1927, folder 1/2, and Samuel Brosius to the President, 12 October 1928, folder 2/3, both in CCF 31229-23-313, pt. 2, box 26, RG 75, NA. For Interior's reply see Roy O. West, SOI, to Samuel Brosius, 22 October 1928, #5 106, Peach Springs, box 1500, RG 48, NA. For the Brosius quotation see Samuel Brosius to Herbert Fiske, Indian Inspector, 22 October 1928, CCF 31229-23-313, pt. 2, folder 2/3, box 26, RG 75, NA. John H. Edwards, Asst. SOI, to AG, 21 January 1928, file 5 106, box 1500, RG 48, NA. Ethelbert Ward to AG, 2 February 1928, folder 227235, box 27a. For the exchange between Ward and Parmenter see Parmenter to Ward, 9 February 1928, Ward to Parmenter, 24 February 1928, Parmenter to Ward, 6 March 1928, and Ward to Parmenter, 10 March 1928, all in Phoenix Area Office, Accession #NRHL-075-00-115, RG 75, NA, Laguna Niguel, CA. Parmenter's letter of 6 March echoes one he had received from the assistant SOI, advising him that Interior felt that enough evidence had been gathered to press on. See John H. Edwards, Asst. SOI, to B. M. Parmenter, 2 March 1928, file 5 106, box 1500, RG 48, NA.

27. For "wild, shiftless" see G. A. Iverson, Special Asst. AG, "Memorandum Opinion: Proposed suit *United States v. Atchison, Topeka, and Santa Fe Railway Company,* involving the right to use the waters of Peach Springs in the Walapai Indian Reservation, Arizona," 11 May 1928, folder 5/5, box 30c, Phoenix Area Office, Accession #NRHL-075-00-115, RG 75, Laguna Niguel, NA. On Iverson's misrepresenting testimony see G. A. Iverson, "Memo for

Mr. Parmenter re Controversy between the United States and the Atchison, Topeka, and Santa Fe Railway Company relative to the right to appropriate and use the waters of Peach Springs in the Walapai (Hualpi) Indian Reservation, Arizona," 24 September 1928, CCF 31229-3-212, pt. 2, box 26, RG 75, NA; O. W. Decker, dictated to his wife, to William A. Light, 10 June 1926, Phoenix Area Office, Accession #NRHL-075-00-115, folder 227235, box 27b, RG 75, NA, Laguna Niguel, CA; William Light to O. W. Decker, 19 June 1926, CCF 45077-28-806 — Truxton Canyon, box 46, RG 75, NA. See also Deposition of Mrs. O. W. Decker, Halfway, Oregon, 3 March 1928, box 2, entry 824, RG 48, NA. Her support of the Hualapais' claim is also mentioned in Mrs. O. W. Decker to attorneys, 28 December 1927, PSFFC. Ida Crozier is quoted in "Sworn statement in interrogatory form of Mrs. Ida Crozier," 18 February 1928, p. 4, box 2, entry 824, RG 48, NA; see also Deposition of Lydia C. Crozier, 29 June 1929, folder 2/5, box 30b, Phoenix Area Office, Accession #NRHL-075-00-115, RG 75, Laguna Niguel, NA. When the occupation of the eastern section of the reservation was questioned four years later, she reiterated this claim. See the statement of Ida Crozier, 5 July 1932, in Mathew K. Sniffen, "Notes on the Walapai Controversy," 30 July 1932, box 42, RG 46, NA. For Mike Sue's and Nora Schrum's testimony see Affidavit of Mike Sue and Affidavit of Kwath a yan ya or Nora Schrum, taken by William A. Light, both 23 February 1928, box 2, entry 824, RG 48, NA. On nothing convincing Iverson, and on his trip, see Letter between attorneys, 13 July 1928, PSFFC.

28. The statements about the railroad and Cureton are in letter between attorneys, 17 October 1927, PSFFC. For Grounds's unreliability see n. 22 in this chapter.

29. Iverson, "Memo for Mr. Parmenter," 24 September 1928.

30. On the pressure from Interior see John Sargent, AG, to Roy O. West, SOI, 29 September 1928, CCF 31229-23-313, pt. 2, box 26, RG 75, NA. For "come under much criticism" see Joseph Edwards, Asst. SOI, to John Sargent, 11 October 1928, file #5 106, Peach Springs, box 1500, RG 48, NA.

31. For "how much we own" see Statement of Jim Fielding, submitted by H. O. Davidson, 12 October 1928, box, entry 824, RG 48, NA. For "for white people" and "Executive Order" see Petition of Jim Fielding and Bob Schrum, prepared by H. O. Davidson, 4 September 1928, CCF 44178-28-320 — Truxton Canyon, box 29, RG 75, NA. On the success of the cattle operation and Fielding and other Hualapais' interest in making it even more their own see Chester Faris, Supervisor of Indian Industries, to CIA, 5 August 1929, box 42, RG 46, NA. On going to the governor and Ward's being a good water attorney see Captain Jim Fielding, Chief Philip Quasala, and Chief Bob Schrum to Gov. George Hunt, Arizona, 21 September 1927, box 3a, Governor's Papers — George Hunt, RG 1, Arizona Department of Library, Archives, and Public Records, History and Archives Division.

32. For "I am now of the opinion" see Ethelbert Ward to Seth Richardson, 20 May 1929, file #227235, box 3944, RG 60, NA. See also Seth Richardson to Ethelbert Ward, 14 May 1929, letter and "Digest of Correspondence — Old Army Officers, etc.," Phoenix Area Office, Accession #NRHL-075-00-115, folder 227235, box 27a, RG 75, Laguna Niguel, NA; Seth Richardson to John Gung'l, U.S. Atty., Arizona, 30 May 1929, file 227235, folder 4, box 3944, RG 60, NA.

33. For "these Indians lived" and "evidence of the Indians" see Seth Richardson to John

Gung'l, 9 September 1929 (emphasis added); for "among the ancient Indians" see Seth Richardson, Asst. AG, to John Gung'l, 27 March 1930; for "de facto reservation" see Seth W. Richardson, Asst. AG, to John Gung'l, 27 March 1930; on going ahead with the suit, see Richardson to Gung'l, 2 October 1929, all in file #227235, folder 4, box 3944, RG 60, NA. "United States Sues Santa Fe Railway in Peach Springs Case," *Arizona Republican,* 1 November 1929.

Chapter 5. Taking Hualapai Land

1. On hiring Hagerman see Joseph M. Dixon, First Asst. SOI, to AG, 18 December 1925, #5 106, Peach Springs, box 1500, RG 48, NA. The meeting in Chicago is mentioned in a letter between attorneys, 2 February 1930, and the close relationship between Hagerman and the Santa Fe, as well as worries about evidence and Hagerman's impending visit, are in letters between attorneys of 2 February 1930, 6 February 1930, and 21 February 1930, all in PSFFC.

2. On the controversy about executive order reservations as opposed to treaty reservations see Francis Paul Prucha, *The Great Father: The United States Government and the American Indians,* unabridged edition (Lincoln: University of Nebraska Press, 1984), 887–88; Lawrence Kelly, "Defending the Title to Indian Reservations, 1922–27," in *The Assault on Assimilation: John Collier and the Origins of Indian Policy Reform* (Albuquerque: University of New Mexico Press, 1983); Janet McDonnell, *The Dispossession of the American Indian, 1887–1934* (Bloomington: Indiana University Press, 1991), 51–55. On the council and Hagerman's relations with the Navajo in general see Lawrence Kelly, *The Navajo Indians and Federal Indian Policy, 1900–1935* (Tucson: University of Arizona Press, 1968), 61–75, 191–94; see also Kathleen P. Chamberlain, *Under Sacred Ground: A History of Navajo Oil, 1922–1986* (Albuquerque: University of New Mexico Press, 2000). For Fall's position see Albert B. Fall, "An Appeal from the General Land Office," 9 June 1922, in "Development of Oil and Gas Mining Leases on Indian Reservations," Hearings Before a Subcommittee of the Senate Committee on Indian Affairs, 69th Cong., 1st sess., on S. 1772, February 27, March 5, 9, and 10, 1926, 25–29 (hereafter Oil and Gas Hearings). Hagerman's financial ties are tough to pin down, but the organization he ran, the New Mexico Taxpayers Association, counted as its major donor the ATSF. See Hearings Before a Subcommittee of the Committee on Indian Affairs, U.S. Senate, 71st Cong., 3rd sess., pursuant to S. Res. 79, 308, 263, A Resolution Directing the Committee on Indian Affairs of the United States Senate to Make a General Survey of the Conditions of the Indians of the United States, pt. 11, hearings held 30–31 January and 3, 5 February 1931. Hagerman's brief testimony was on 31 January, p. 4548.

3. The railroad's hope that a compromise would be forged at the meeting is found in a letter between attorneys, 5 March 1930, PSFFC; on the exchange see E. E. McInnis to Hagerman, 6 March 1930, CCF 31229-23-313, folder 2/3, pt. 2, box 26, RG 75, NA. The meeting is also mentioned in the letter between attorneys, 11 March 1930, PSFFC. For "inevitable delays" see Hagerman to C. J. Rhoads, CIA, 10 March 1930, CCF 31229-23-313, folder 2/3, part 2, box 26, RG 75, NA. Details regarding the Santa Fe's trip to the reservation, their discussion of a compromise, and passing that information on

to Hagerman and the railroad in Chicago are in letter between attorneys, 11 March 1930, PSFFC.

4. For the visit by Gung'l visit and his sense of what the Hualapais wanted see John Gung'l to AG, 25 April 1930, CCF 31229-23-13, pt. 2, box 26, RG 75, NA, and letter between attorneys, 22 April 1930, PSFFC.

5. Gung'l to AG, 25 April 1930.

6. Details of the discussion of a compromise between Gung'l and the Santa Fe are in a letter between attorneys, 22 April 1930, PSFFC.

7. The details in this paragraph are from ibid. and a letter between attorneys, 3 May 1930, PSFFC.

8. For "vigorous prosecution" see Richardson to Gung'l, 2 May 1930; he implores Gung'l to hurry in a second letter written later the same day, both in #227235, folder 4, box 3944, RG 60, NA. The lack of familiarity is described in Gung'l to railroad attorneys, 9 May 1930, and a letter between attorneys, 22 May 1930, PSFFC.

9. On the agreement see Memorandum made at Truxton Canyon Agency, 21 May 1930, CCF 31229-23-12, pt 2, folder 1/3, box 26, RG 75, NA. No Hualapais were present at this meeting. Only Hagerman, district supervisor Chester Faris, agent D. H. Wattson, and railroad representatives Collinson and McInnis were there. Also included in the proposed deal were some future rights to land for the railroad, and access to adequate timber for the Hualapai. The figure of 200,000 acres would eventually be re- fined to 170,000 acres; for Hagerman's concerns see Hagerman to C. J. Rhoads, CIA, 21 May 1930, in ibid.

10. Notes of a Meeting held in the Truxton Canyon Indian School auditorium, Valen- tine, Arizona, May 22, 1930, 9 A.M., CCF 31229-23-312, pt. 2, folder 1/3, box 26, RG 75, NA.

11. Ibid.

12. This account comes from Fred Mahone's version of the May meeting. Statement Referring to Hagerman, Faris, Two Railroad Officials, & Supt. Watson [sic] of Truxton Canyon Agency, Valentine, Arizona, 12 August 1930, reel 47, PIRA.

13. The Mahone quotations are in Fred Mahone to Brosius, 16 August 1930, reel 46, PIRA. The quotations from and information about the meeting are in Statement Refer- ring to Hagerman, 12 August 1930, reel 47, PIRA.

14. Both quotations are in Statement Referring to Hagerman (emphasis in original).

15. John Gung'l to AG, telegram, 11 June 1930, file #227235, folder 4, box 3944, RG 60, NA.

16. The appearance by Gung'l at the Arizona attorneys' office is mentioned in letter between attorneys, 19 July 1930, and the contact with the Chicago office regarding prevailing on Rhoads is in a telegram between attorneys, 19 July 1930, both in PSFFC.

17. The railroad's concerns about giving away water and its priority are discussed in letters between attorneys, 26 June 1930, 1 July 1930; details about the domestic water supply and assurances from Gung'l that no Hualapais would use the water are in a letter between attorneys, 1 July 1930; attempts to appease the BIA are found in a letter between attorneys, 19 July 1930, all in PSFFC.

18. Details about Gung'l's fear of reprisal and his belief that the government would win are in a letter between attorneys, 19 July 1930, PSFFC.

19. This series of events is described in letters between an attorney and the railroad, 24 July 1930, and 4 August 1930, both in PSFFC; Hagerman to Indian Office, telegram, 24 July 1930, CCF 31229-23-313, pt. 2, folder 1/3, box 26, RG 75; then two telegrams from SOI to AG, 25 July 1930, file 5106, box 1500, RG 48; then AG to Gung'l, 25 July 1930, file #227235, folder 4, box 3944, RG 60, NA; and finally, letter between attorneys, 2 August 1930, PSFFC.

20. On waiting see C. J. Rhoads to Herbert Hagerman, 15 August 1930, CCF 31229-23-313, pt. 2, folder 1/3, box 27, RG 75, NA. On meeting with Hayden see Herbert Hagerman to Indian Office, telegram, 19 September 1930; on meeting and agreeing see Hagerman's twenty-one-page memo on the exchange, 13 October 1930, 13–14, all in ibid. On the meeting see also "Hayden Confers with Collinson and Hagerman," *Mohave County Miner*, 26 September 1930; Carl Hayden to Major General Charles H. Bridges, Adjutant General of the Army, 24 September 1930, folder 40, box 620, ser. 1, Indian Affairs, CHP.

21. The Mahone quotation is from Statement Referring to Hagerman. On the meeting with the U.S. attorney see "Notes of a privately held meeting," 28 November 1930, Ray T. Winfred, interpreter, per Fred W. Mahone, including sworn, notarized statements of Kate Crozier (Haka, 2001/4 [the number Crozier bore as a scout]), Jim Mahone, Little Jim (Jim Smith, Myorthy, Yateveja), and Prescott Jim (Gee-Gody), 28 November 1930, box 42, RG 46, NA.

22. On Mahone as a "well known Wallapai" see "Wallapais to Petition for More Lands," *Mohave County Miner*, 22 August 1930, 4. As of April 1930 Mahone owned property worth $1,000, considerably more than any other Hualapai. He was working as a stockman on the open range; see Fourteenth Census of the United States, Population Schedule, Hualapai Indian Reservation, sheet 3B, microfilm publication T-626, reel 55, RG 29, NA. Samuel Brosius to Matthew K. Sniffen, 15 August 1930, reel 46, PIRA. On Mahone's trip to Kingman see "Wallapais to Petition for More Lands," 4. PETITION: To the Honorable Carl Hayden and Henry F. Ashurst, United States Senate for the State of Arizona, and to Lewis W. Douglas, Member of the United States House of Representatives from the State of Arizona," n.d., CCF 31229-23-313/2, box 26, RG 75, NA.

23. "PETITION: To the Honorable Carl Hayden and Henry F. Ashurst, United States Senators for the State of Arizona, and Lewis W. Douglas, member of the U.S. House of Representatives from the State of Arizona," 5 August 1930, CCF 31229-23-312, pt. 2, folder 1/3, box 26, RG 75, NA. On the petition see also "Indians Seeking Rail Lands for Grazing Cattle," *Arizona Republic*, 22 August 1930, which claimed that Fred Mahone delivered the petition in person to Washington, D.C. I can find no evidence of Mahone making a trip to Washington.

24. The two men were confused about the details. They thought that General Nelson Miles called the meeting, but Miles did not assume command in Arizona until 1886. The Hualapais served in 1872–73, 1877, and 1881–82. They scouted for several different commanders, and the welter of names must have been hard to keep straight. Fred Mahone thought it was General Willcox, in 1881, not Miles, and, in a later statement, both Jim Mahone and Crozier said it was Willcox. On Hualapai service in the 1870s see Dennis G. Casebier, *Camp Beale's Springs and the Hualapai Indians* (Norco, Calif.: Tales of the Mojave Road, 1980), 63–75. At the Senate subcommittee hearings held on the reservation

in 1931 — discussed in Chapter 7 — the subject of Jim Mahone's service came up. Senator Lynn Frazier asked about the dates of his service. Fred Mahone, acting as interpreter, said, "He do not understand years, what year it was, because he was not educated to put down figures like the white people and the years; so he do not understand what year it was but it was away back in the early days." Fred Mahone thought that Jim Mahone was referring to Miles. WP, 248–49. For the statements that they served under Willcox see Affidavits of Jim Mahone and Kate Crozier, 12 December 1930, CCF 31229-23-313, pt. 3, folder 3/3, box 27, RG 75, NA; for Crozier's service see "Deposition of Kate Crozier or Kid or Hu-ka-qua-ta No. 19937," n.d. [claim heard in September 1927], Records Supporting Claims for Service During the Indian Wars, Records of Indian Scouts, Hualapai Indians, box 34, RG 15 (Department of Veterans Affairs), NA.

25. "The Walapai Lands," *Native American*, 6 December 1930, 242; Samuel Brosius to CIA, 15 August 1930, CCF 31229-23-313, pt. 2, folder 1/3, box 26, RG 75, NA; Eighteen Hualapai men to Samuel Brosius, 23 August 1930, reel 46, PIRA.

Chapter 6. Writing Indians out of Their Land

1. Mary E. Dewey, *12th Annual Report of the Massachusetts Indian Association* (Boston: Massachusetts Indian Association, 1894), 11. On the association's purchase of land among the Hualapais see Mary E. Dewey, "The Condition of the Hualapai," *Indian's Friend*, January 1898, 7.

2. All quotations are from Robert Lowie, "Oral Tradition and History," *Journal of American Folklore* 30.114 (1917): 165, 164, except "I cannot attach," which is from Robert Lowie, "Oral Tradition and History," *American Anthropologist* 17, 3 (1915): 598. This brief essay was written in response to Dixon and Swanton's article "Primitive American History," discussed below. For Lowie's support of the existence of individual property rights see Marvin Harris, *The Rise of Anthropological Theory: A History of Theories of Culture* (New York: Crowell, 1968), 357–62. I am not the first to use Lowie's approach as an example of a particularly outmoded way of seeing the Indian past. See Peter Nabokov, *A Forest of Time: American Indian Ways of Seeing History* (New York: Cambridge University Press, 2002), esp. 114–18 on the Shoshones; David Hurst Thomas, *Skull Wars: Kennewick Man, Archaeology, and the Battle for Native American Identity* (New York: Basic, 2000), 99–101. That Indians had sophisticated ways of thinking about and using the past in the nineteenth century is the subject of Maureen Konkle's *Writing Indian Nations: Native Intellectuals and the Politics of Historiography, 1827–1865* (Chapel Hill: University of North Carolina Press, 2004).

3. William A. Light, Annual Report, 18 January 1921; D. H. Wattson, Annual Report, 30 June 1930, both in reel 151, SANSR. For a survey of the state of the field see Alfred Kidder, "Speculations on New World Prehistory," in *Essays in Anthropology, Presented to A. L. Kroeber in Celebration of His Sixtieth Birthday, June 11, 1936*, ed. Robert Lowie (Berkeley: University of California Press, 1926), 143–52. For the practice of archaeology and the little that was known at the time about the southwestern United States see Douglas W. Schwartz, "Kidder and the Synthesis of Southwestern Archeology," in *An Introduction to the Study of Southwestern Archaeology*, by Alfred Vincent Kidder (1924; reprint, New Haven: Yale University Press, 2000). Kidder's book is an excellent measure

of the inchoate nature of the field. See also Robert L. Schuyler, "The History of American Archeology: An Examination of Procedure," *American Antiquity* 36.4 (1971): 383–409.

On dendrochronology and on the advances in the field in the late 1920s and 1930s that radically altered the chronology of, in particular, the pre-contact period in the Southwest, see Stephen Edward Nash, *Time, Trees, and Prehistory: Tree-Ring Dating and the Development of North American Archaeology, 1914–1950* (Salt Lake City: University of Utah Press, 1999); see p. 2 for specific reference to the newfound importance of chronology in the 1920s. For a survey of all of these issue see Don D. Fowler, *A Laboratory for Anthropology: Science and Romanticism in the American Southwest, 1846–1930* (Albuquerque: University of New Mexico Press, 2000). For the railroad-sponsored work see Harold Sellers Colton, *An Archeological Survey of Northwestern Arizona Including the Descriptions of Fifteen New Pottery Types* (Flagstaff: Museum of Northern Arizona, 1939); Harold Sellers Colton, "Prehistoric Culture Units and Their Relationships in Northern Arizona," *Museum of Northern Arizona Bulletin* 17 (October 1939): 1–76; Lyndon L. Hargrave, "Results of a Study of the Cohohina Branch of the Patayan Culture in 1938," *Museum of Northern Arizona Museum Notes* 11.6 (1938): 43–50.

For a survey of archaeological work on Hualapai country see Robert C. Euler, "Archaeological Problems in Western and Northwestern Arizona, 1962," *Plateau* 35.3 (1963): 78–85. For the quotation see Leslie Spier, "Problems Arising from the Cultural Position of the Havasupai," *American Anthropologist* 31.2 (1929): 219. See also Spier's monograph on the Havasupais, in which he writes, "The description of even the material culture in the only spot in the United States [the Southwest] where it remains in anything like its pristine condition has hardly been begun." Leslie Spier, *Havasupai Ethnography* (New York: Anthropological Papers of the American Museum of Natural History, 1928), vol. 29, pt. 3, 84. William Duncan Strong, "An Analysis of Southwestern Society," *American Anthropologist* 29.1 (1927): 5; the precursor of this article was Strong's 1926 dissertation at the University of California. For the lack of historical knowledge of the native population of the Southwest and a call for further research see Alfred Kroeber, *Native Culture of the Southwest,* 23.9 (Berkeley: University of California Publications in Archeology and Ethnology, 1928); see especially Kroeber's comments on Indians as objects as opposed to subjects, 398. See also H. S. Gladwyn, "An Outline of Southwestern Prehistoric," *Arizona Historical Review* 3.1 (1930): 71–87.

4. John R. Swanton and Roland B. Dixon, "Primitive American History," *American Anthropologist* 16.3 (1914): 376–412. On historians writing during the late nineteenth and early twentieth centuries and the absence of Indians in their work see Richard L. Haan, "Another Example of Stereotypes on the Early American Frontier: The Imperialist Historians and the American Indian," *Ethnohistory* 20.2 (1973): 143–52 (for the quotation from Herbert Levi Osgood see 147); Edward Lazarus, *Black Hills, White Justice: The Sioux Nation versus the United States, 1775 to the Present* (New York: HarperCollins, 1991); Alexandra Harmon, *Indians in the Making: Ethnic Relations and Indian Identities Around Puget Sound* (Berkeley: University of California Press, 1998), 182–89; Laurence M. Hauptman, *The Iroquois and the New Deal* (Syracuse: Syracuse University Press, 1981), 11–18.

5. On the Crows, see Frederick E. Hoxie, *Parading Through History: The Making of the Crow Nation in America, 1805–1935* (New York: Cambridge University Press,

1995), 312–14; "Crow Indian Claims," Hearing Before a Subcommittee of the Committee on Indian Affairs, House, 69th Cong., 1st sess., 13 April 1926, 14. On the Shoshones see Steven J. Crum, *The Road on Which We Came: A History of the Western Shoshone* (Salt Lake City: University of Utah Press, 1994), 77; Spokane et al., "Statement of Charlie Thompson," in "Claims of the Lower Spokane and Lower Pend D'Oreille or Lower Kalispell Indians," Hearing Before the Subcommittee of the Committee on Indian Affairs, House, 70th Cong., 1st sess., 14 January 1928, 22; "Claims of the Colville and Okanogan Indians," Hearing Before a Subcommittee of the Committee on Indian Affairs, House, 69th Cong., 1st sess., 6 April 1926. On the Colvilles and Okanogans see also "Authorizing Certain Indian Tribes in the State of Washington to Present Their Claims to the Court of Claims," Hearing Before the Committee on Indian Affairs, Senate, 16 April 1926.

As for California, nearly three hundred pages' worth of testimony and documentary evidence were aired in "Indian Tribes of California," Hearings Before a Subcommittee of the Committee on Indian Affairs, House, 66th Cong., 2nd sess., pt. 1, 23 March 1930, and 67th Cong., 2nd sess., pt. 2, 28 and 29 April 1922. See especially the testimony of C. Hart Merriam, in which he details the violent history of early contact (206–8), testimony of Alfred C. Gillis (222), and Statement of Indian Auxiliary Delegates, Board of Indian Cooperation (249). See also Donald G. Shanahan, "Compensation for the Loss of the Aboriginal Lands of the California Indians," *Southern California Quarterly* 57.3 (1975): 297–320. On the federation and the claims of Indians in Washington see "Indian Tribes of Washington," Hearings Before the Committee on Indian Affairs, House, 68th Cong., 1st sess., H.R. 2694, 2 February 1924 (see especially testimony of Wilfred Steve of the Northwestern Federation of American Indians, 19–27). For Satiacum's statement see Affadavit of Charles Satiacum, 6 July 1916, in "Indian Tribes of Washington," Hearings Before a Subcommittee of the Committee on Indian Affairs, House, 67th Cong., 2nd Sess., H.R. 2423 and 2424, pts. 1 and 2, May 24 and June 5, 1922. On the origins of the federation see Harmon, *Indians in the Making*, 178–85; "Wichita and Affiliated Bands, on H.R. 6044," Hearing Before the Committee on Indian Affairs, House, 67th Cong, 2nd Sess., 9 March 1922, 37–39. For the Omahas see Melvin R. Gilmore, "Indian Tribal Boundary-Lines and Monuments," *Indian Notes* 5 (1928): 59–63.

6. Harvey D. Rosenthal, *Their Day in Court: A History of the Indian Claims Commission* (New York: Garland, 1990), 17; E. B. Smith, *Indian Tribal Claims Decided in the Court of Claims of the United States, Briefed and Compiled to June 30, 1947*, 2 vols. (Washington, D.C.: University Publications of America, 1976; originally compiled by E. B. Smith, Chief, Indian Tribal Claims Section, United States General Accounting Office, 1947). For their historical complexity see "Annual Report of the Attorney General of the United States" (Washington, D.C.: Government Printing Office, 1922), 56–57; to get a fuller sense of the scope of the claims, and opinions on them from Indians, their advocates, and bureaucrats, see the 328-page report "Survey of Conditions of the Indians in the United States," Hearings Before a Subcommittee of the Committee on Indian Affairs, Senate, pt. 25, 72nd Cong., 1st sess., January, March, November, and December, 1930 and May and June, 1931. For the cost of the claims exceeding that of World War I, see testimony of Homer Snyder in "Indian Tribes of Washington," 2 February 1924, 24; for the amount claimed see "Annual Report of the Attorney General of the United States" (Washington, D.C.: Government Printing Office, 1930), 67. The exact figure was

$1,450,571,129.72. For most important litigation see the attorney general's report for 1931, p. 72; by 1934 the number of cases had reached 104, see the attorney general's report for that year.

7. For an excellent analysis of the origins of the reverence for farming as opposed to wandering, and some of the legal consequences thereof, see James Tully, "Rediscovering America: The *Two Treatises* and Aboriginal Rights," in *An Approach to Political Philosophy: Locke in Contexts* (Cambridge; Cambridge University Press, 1993). Stuart Banner has argued that Locke's influence on day-to-day land policy was not significant and that colonists nonetheless made purchases from Indians on the basis of their belief that Indians were property owners. Banner does not discuss Locke's influence on the thinking of courts; in addition, though Locke may not have had profound influence in the eighteenth century, his ideas nonetheless became canonical in the nineteenth and early twentieth centuries. Stuart Banner, *How the Indians Lost Their Land: Law and Power on the Frontier* (Cambridge: Harvard University Press, 2005), 46–48. On the history of evolutionism and anthropology see Marvin Harris, *The Rise of Anthropological Theory: A History of Theories of Culture* (New York: Crowell, 1968), 25–38 and chap. 6, "Evolutionism: Methods." For a thoughtful analysis of Morgan from an anthropologist of the generation that was directly under his sway, see Robert H. Lowie, *The History of Ethnological Theory* (New York: Holt, Rinehart, Winston, 1937), 54–67.

For the general consensus among anthropologists by the 1920s that individually property ownership did not exist see Harris, *Rise of Anthropological Theory,* 357. For an overview of anthropological thinking about property, especially as it relates to dispossession, see Paul Nadasdy, " 'Property' and Aboriginal Land Claims in the Canadian Subarctic: Some Theoretical Considerations," *American Anthropologist* 104.1 (2003): 247–61. For the place of hunters and gatherers in the world see generally Hugh Brody, *The Other Side of Eden: Hunters, Farmers and the Shaping of the World* (New York: North Point, 2001). And on the rise of farming and its displacement of hunters and gatherers see Jared Diamond, *Guns, Germs, and Steel: The Fates of Human Societies* (New York: Norton, 1997).

8. George Bird Grinnell, "Tenure of Land Among the Indians," *American Anthropologist* 9.1 (1907): 1; Frank G. Speck, "The Indians and Game Preservation," *Red Man,* 1913, 21–25, quoted in Harvey A. Feit, "The Construction of Algonquian Hunting Territories: Private Property as Moral Lesson, Policy Advocacy, and Ethnographic Error," in *Colonial Situations: Essays on the Contextualization of Ethnographic Knowledge,* ed. George Stocking (Madison: University of Wisconsin Press, 1991), 123; Frank G. Speck, "The Family Hunting Band as the Basis of Algonkian Social Organization," *American Anthropologist* 17.2 (1915): 289–305; Frank G. Speck, "The Basis of Indian Ownership of Land and Game," *Southern Workman* 42.1 (January 1914): 38; Frank G. Speck, "Land Ownership Among Hunting Peoples in Primitive America and the World's Marginal Areas," in *Proceedings of the Twenty-Second Annual Congress of Americanists* (Rome: Congress of Americanists, 1928), 323–32. For Speck's influence, the controversy surrounding his theories, and his reification of property see Nadasdy, " 'Property' and Aboriginal Land Claims"; on Speck's early advocacy of Indian property rights and the possibility that he let his politics shape his research, see Feit, "Construction of Algonquian Hunting Territories"; for a contemporaneous view of property, though not exclu-

sively focused on land, which argues that native people did indeed *own* things and that the Morganian evolutionary model should be jettisoned, see Robert H. Lowie, "Incorporeal Property in Primitive Society," *Yale Law Journal* 37.5 (1928): 551–63.

9. The most thorough scholarly estimate circulating in the early twentieth century was James Mooney's. In 1910 Mooney estimated that approximately 1.1 million Indians inhabited North America (846,000 in the United States, 220,000 in Canada, 72,000 in Alaska, and 10,000 in Greenland) when Europeans proffered their first estimates. But, as Mooney admitted, his figure might be low because Europeans only began to wonder about the native population after extensive contact had occurred and after the population had dramatically declined. Mooney's colleagues at the Smithsonian's Bureau of American Ethnology considered his number high, preferring 500,000. See James Mooney, "Population," in *Handbook of American Indians North of Mexico,* ed. Frederick W. Hodge, Bureau of American Ethnology Bulletin no. 30 (Washington, D.C.: Government Printing Office, 1910), 2:286–87. For a detailed discussion of the work of Mooney and others see Russell Thornton, "American Indian Population in 1492," in *American Indian Holocaust and Survival: A Population History Since 1492* (Norman: University Oklahoma Press, 1987), esp. 25–29; for the U.S. Census figure see 17. For a thorough and slightly more recent review of the literature and the debate see John Daniels, "The Indian Population of North America in 1492," *William and Mary Quarterly* 49.2 (1992): 298–320. On Mooney, Powell, the BAE, and population see also Brian Dippie, *The Vanishing American: White Attitudes and U.S. Indian Policy* (1982; reprint, Lawrence: University Press of Kansas, 1991), 236–41 (citations are to reprint ed.). Dippie makes the point that, either way, high or low, Indians could not win. If the pre-contact population was high, then their demographic decline was evidence that they were the weak race; if it was low, that was evidence that few had ever existed and thus their claims to the continent were weak (xv–xvii). I am not concerned with the actual numbers; rather, I am interested in the political and legal uses of the various estimates.

10. Flora Warren Seymour, "Our Indian Problem: I: The Delusion of the Sentimentalists," *Forum,* March 1924, 274. For an earlier and more detailed exploration of the use of population figures to justify conquest see Francis Jennings, "Widowed Land," in *The Invasion of America: Indians, Colonialism, and the Cant of Conquest* (New York: Norton, 1975), 15–31.

11. Seymour, "Our Indian Problem" 274.

12. See Cyrus Thomas, introduction to *Indian Land Cessions in the United States,* by Charles C. Royce, reprinted in *Eighteenth Annual Report of the Bureau of American Ethnology, 1896–97,* by J. W. Powell, pt. 2 (Washington, D.C.: Government Printing Office, 1899), 537 (figures), 538 (all quotations but the last). For "it is an inevitable" see Cyrus Thomas and W. J. McGee, *The Indians of North America in Historic Times* (Philadelphia: Printed for subscribers only by G. Barrie, 1903), ix. For other examples of legal commentary on Indians that generally take a social evolutionary perspective see Cuthbert Pound, "Nationals Without a Nation: The New York State Tribal Indians," *Columbia Law Review* 22.2 (1922): 97–102; Horace H. Hagan, "Tribal Law of the American Indian," *Case and Comment* 23.9 (February 1917): 735–38.

13. Frank T. Mann, "Wild People," *Native American,* 27 September 1930, 170, 169. This article was reprinted from *Southern Workman,* 8 August, 1930, 360–64. The *Native*

American, the newspaper of the Phoenix Indian School, called itself "A fortnightly journal devoted to Indian education"; Dewey, *12th Annual Report,* 11.

14. Mary Roberts Coolidge, *The Rain-Makers: The Indians of Arizona and New Mexico* (1929; reprint, Santa Fe: William Gannon, 1975), 10, 302 (citations are to reprint ed.).

15. G. E. E. Lindquist, *The Red Man in America: An Intimate Study of the Social, Economic, and Religious Life of the American Indian* (New York: Doran, 1923), 308–10. The survey claims that the Havasupai were formerly a Pueblo tribe (they were not), that the nearest train was found at Valentine although it was at Peach Springs, on the reservation, and that the school at Valentine was founded in 1894, not 1901. On Lindquist and his place in Indian affairs see David W. Daily, *Battle for the BIA: G. E. E. Lindquist and the Missionary Crusade Against John Collier* (Tucson: University of Arizona Press, 2004).

16. George Wharton James, *The Indians of the Painted Desert Region: Hopis, Navajos, Wallapais, and Havasupais* (Boston: Little, Brown, 1903), 172–98. James continued to write about the Southwest. In two later books about the Grand Canyon he says little or nothing about the Hualapais. In *The Grand Canyon of Arizona: How to See It* (Boston: Little, Brown, 1910) James included only a couple of sentences (210–11) about the Hualapais while devoting a chapter to the Havasupais. And in *In and Around the Grand Canyon: The Grand Canyon of Colorado River in Arizona* (Boston: Little, Brown, 1910), the chapter on Peach Springs does not mention the Hualapais, but a chapter is devoted to the Havasupais. For a much fuller discussion that surveys the literature on the Southwest, see Christian W. McMillen, "Rewriting History and Proving Property Rights: Hualapai Indian Activism and the Law of Land Claims in the Twentieth Century" (Ph.D. diss., Yale University, 2004), esp. 36–41.

17. Sherry L. Smith, *Reimagining Indians: Native Americans Through Anglo Eyes, 1880–1934* (New York: Oxford University Press, 2000); Carter Jones, " 'Hope for the Race of Man': Indians, Intellectuals, and the Regeneration of Modern America, 1917–1934" (Ph.D. diss., Brown University, 1991); Margaret Jacobs, *Engendered Encounters: Feminism and Pueblo Cultures, 1879–1934* (Lincoln: University of Nebraska Press, 1999); Philip J. Deloria, *Playing Indian* (New Haven: Yale University Press, 1998), esp. 95–127; Patrick Wolfe, *Settler Colonialism and the Transformation of Anthropology: The Politics and Poetics of an Ethnographic Event* (London: Cassell, 1999), 163–214.

18. For Collier's awakening see John Collier, *From Every Zenith: A Memoir and Some Essays on Life and Thought* (Denver: Sage, 1963), esp. 125–26; John Collier, "The Red Atlantis," *Survey,* October 1922, 15–20, 63, 66. Mary Austin, whom I discuss below, spent time among some of the Southern California tribes, see *Land of Little Rain* (Boston: Houghton Mifflin, 1903).

19. For "nastiest human beings" see Charles Fletcher Lummis, *Letters from the Southwest: September 20, 1884–March 14, 1885,* ed. James W. Byrkit (Tucson: University of Arizona Press, 1989), 261; for "thrashed into submission" see Charles Fletcher Lummis, *A Tramp Across the Continent* (1892; reprint, New York: Charles Scribner's Sons, 1909), 249; for "worthless" and "don't make blankets" see Smith, *Reimagining Indians,* 124; for "miscarriage" see Lummis, *Letters,* 261.

20. Sherry Smith may be right when she says about Austin and the others in her study of

changing attitudes toward Indians that "for all their intellectual shortcomings, these people helped create new conceptions of Indians which, in turn, made a place for Native Americans—culturally and politically—in the twentieth century." Smith, *Reimagining Indians*, 216. The quotation is from Mary Austin, "Our Indian Problem II: The Folly of the Officials," *Forum* 71.3 (March 1924): 285.

21. Mary Austin, "Why Americanize the Indian?" *Forum* 82.3 (September 1929): 170, 172.

22. For a more critical view of Austin and her associates see Jacobs, *Engendered Encounters*. Although Jacobs recognizes that the antimoderns placed Pueblo Indians outside history, that they believed in social evolution, and that they, to a crippling degree, constructed Indians as primitive for their own ends, she still is committed to the idea that the antimoderns worked for the defense of Indian religious and land rights. For another critical view of the antimoderns see Shari M. Huhndorf, *Going Native: Indians in the American Cultural Imagination* (Ithaca: Cornell University Press, 2001), esp. 1–18. Mary Ellen Kelm has shown that, just as it was with the law, so it was with medicine: the discourse of antimodernism hardly helped Indians confronted by doctors who thought their primitive ways were the cause of their pathologies. See Kelm, "Diagnosing the Discursive Indian: Medicine, Gender, and the 'Dying Race,'" *Ethnohistory* 52.2 (2005): 371–406, esp. 381. Austin surely did write in support of, for example, the Pueblos' right to carry on their various dances. But she did so in her celebration of antimodernism and her belief that Indians were national treasures to be used beneficially by spiritually enervated whites. See Austin, "Our Indian Problem II." Mabel Dodge Luhan and Austin *did* help stir up interest in the Bursum bill, interest that appears to have been instrumental in preventing its passage. See Lawrence Kelly, *The Assault on Assimilation: John Collier and the Origins of Indian Policy Reform* (Albuquerque: University of New Mexico Press, 1983), ch. 7; and Smith, *Reimagining Indians*, 176.

Chapter 7. The Hualapais and History

1. Ray Tokespeta Winifred, "The Wallapai Indians and Their Prehistoric Homeland," 30 September 1930, box 42, RG 46, NA.

2. For "at least in part" see Herbert H. Fiske, 25 August 1927, Inspection Report, entry 953, Inspection Division, Inspection Reports 1908–1940, p. 14, box 70, RG 75, NA. Statement of Indian Honga, 22 May 1931, WP. Mahone's paraphrasing of Dr. Tommy and the quotation are from Statement of Fred W. Mahone, 30 September 1930, reel 46, PIRA. For information about Dr. Tommy see Informant A, interview with the author, 23 September 2002 (this gentleman asked that I not use his name); Dolores Honga, interview with the author, pt. 2, 25 September 2002, both in Peach Springs, Ariz. She remembers hearing her grandparents talk about Dr. Tommy's work in the Clay Springs country, too. On living at Diamond Creek see Informant B, interview with the author, Peach Springs, Ariz., 26 September 2002.

3. Charles Shell, 31 August 1911, Annual Report, Truxton Canyon Agency, Superintendents' Annual Narrative and Statistical Reports from Field Jurisdictions of the Bureau of Indian Affairs, 1907–1938, reel 151, microfilm publication 1011, RG 75, NA. On Pine Springs see Herbert Hagerman to Charles Rhoads, 30 August 1930, and on being gone by

1940 or 1950 see Hagerman to Rhoads, 24 June 1930, both in CCF 31229-23-313, pt. 2, box 26, RG 75, NA. Gung'l made this same assertion in his 25 April memo. For "dying race" see Hayden to AG, 21 March 1941, folder 17, box 649, CHP. Information about Gung'l is in letter between attorneys, 22 April 1930, PSFFC (a confidentiality agreement prevents identifying the correspondents). D. H. Wattson to CIA, 30 August 1930, CCF 31229-23-313, pt. 3, folder 3/3, box 27, RG 75, NA; D. H. Wattson, Annual Report, 30 June 1930, "Superintendents' Annual Narrative and Statistical Reports from Field Jurisdictions of the Bureau of Indian Affairs, 1907–1938," microfilm publication 1011, reel 151, RG 75, NA.

4. For a brief description of the Pine Springs country as the territory of a Hualapai band see Fred B. Kniffen, "Geography," in A. L. Kroeber et al., *Walapai Ethnography*, Memoirs of the American Anthropological Association, no. 42 (Menasha, Wis.: American Anthropological Association, 1935), 41–42; Henry Dobyns estimated that the area used by Pine Springs band was approximately 669,670 acres, making it the second largest Hualapai use area. Henry Dobyns, "Area of Territory Used Exclusively by Hualapais, Post 1827 to the Hualapai War and Pacification," Claimant's Exhibit 121, *Hualapai Tribe of the Hualapai Reservation, Arizona v. The United States of America,* Indian Claims Commission Docket No. 90, box 1055, RG 279 (Records of the Indian Claims Commission), NA.

5. Statement of Dr. Tommy, or Wa'thee'ima, 30 September 1930, reel 46, PIRA. Mahone described this statement thus: "Historical Views of Early Walapais Garden Ground and Ruins. By Dr. Tommy, old man still active[.] This is an ancient story told after told to the people of the Walapai Indian." For further evidence that Dr. Tommy's family lived in the Pine Springs county see the oral acccount "Yavapai Raid of 1855," collected in Leslie Spier, *Havasupai Ethnography* (New York: Anthropological Papers of the American Museum of Natural History, 1928), vol. 29, pt. 3, 358. Spier's informant, Sinyella, told him about Dr. Tommy's father's camp in the Pine Springs country. Spier identifies Dr. Tommy as a shaman (243). Additional information about Dr. Tommy comes from formal and informal conversations with Hualapai elders. Informant A, interview with the author, 23 September 2002. On Dr. Tommy as a doctor for the Havasupai see the many references to him in Mark Hanna, *Man of the Canyon: An Old Indian Remembers His Life as Told to Richard G. Emerick* (Orono, Me.: Northern Lights Books, 1992); see, e.g., p. 49, where Hanna discusses Dr. Tommy's caring for his sick uncle in Mohawk Canyon.

6. Statement of Mrs. Philip Sullivan (Headama), 30 September 1930, reel 46, PIRA; Statement of Frank Beecher, dictated to and translated by Fred Mahone, 23 October 1930, 30 September 1930, box 42, RG 46, NA. I learned that everyone else in the area knew about Beecher's "secret" well during a visit to the spot on 22 September 2002 with Ronald Mann Susanyatame.

7. When the dates are vague it is because I am basing them only on internal clues in the statement, such as the name of the superintendent. Statement of [Indian] Honga and Jacob Honga, dictated to and translated by Fred Mahone, 29 October 1930, box 42, RG 46, NA. The Hongas and Frank Beecher included photographs of their gardens with their statements. For more on Hualapais' attempts to settle on the eastern portion of the reservation see Matthew K. Sniffen to C. J. Rhoads, 7 August 1931, box 42, RG 46, NA. I also learned a lot about this spot from Indian Honga's grandson Ronald Mann Sus-

anyatame on a visit there, 22 September 2002. For "they'd shoot us" see Interview with Jane Honga, 11 July 1968, p. 673, Prescott College Hualapai Oral Tradition Project, Prescott, Ariz. Many thanks to Jeff Shepard for making this source available to me. Jane Honga also remembered Samuel Brosius as one of the white men who worked on the ATSF case (673).

8. Statement of Kate Crozier, n.d. but with others from late September 1929, reel 46, PIRA; see also Statement of Charles McGee, 29 September 1929, reel 46, PIRA. On building the house see also Hanna, *Man of the Canyon*, 71–72.

9. William Light to CIA, 29 June 1923, CCF 30310-23-174.1 — Truxton, box 11, RG 75, NA.

10. Mahone's list is dated 29 September 1930 and is found in S. M. Brosius, Indian Rights Association to CIA, 10 October 1930, CCF 31229-23-313, pt. 3, folder 3/3, box 27, RG 75, NA. PETITION: To the Honorable Carl Hayden and Henry F. Ashurst, United States Senators for the State of Arizona, and to Lewis W. Douglas, Member of the United States House of Representatives from the State of Arizona, n.d., CCF 31229-23-313, pt. 2, folder 1/2, box 26. On the superiority of the eastern half to the western half see also affidavit of John Neal, 12 October 1930, reel 47, PIRA; M. J. Musser to The Right Honorable President Hoover, 10 November 1930, CCF 60287-30-313, Truxton Canyon, box 29, RG 75, NA. This is the same Mary J. Musser as the one listed among the petition's signatories.

11. On the early history of the IRA see William Hagan, *The Indian Rights Association: The Herbert Welsh Years, 1888–1904* (Tucson: University of Arizona Press, 1985); for the quotation and their official views of the case see Indian Rights Association, *45th Annual Report of the Board of Directors, 1927* (Philadelphia: Indian Rights Association, 1928), 18–20. On Brosius, the IRA, and the *Lone Wolf* case see Blue Clark, Lone Wolf v. Hitchcock: *Treaty Rights and Indian Law at the End of the Nineteenth Century* (Lincoln: University of Nebraska Press, 1994), esp. 65, 74–77. On federal power over Indian affairs and the impact of *Lone Wolf* see Nell Jessup Newton, "Federal Power Over Indians: Its Sources, Scope, and Limitations," *University of Pennsylvania Law Review* 132 (January 1984): 195–288. Brosius and the IRA first took an interest in the Hualapai case in July 1927. But their initial interest did not amount to much. See Brosius to Herbert Welsh, 7 July 1927, reel 44, PIRA.

12. Fred W. Mahone to William A. Light, 25 November 1930, CCF 31229-23-313, pt. 3, folder 3/3, box 27, RG 75, NA. On getting Light interested see Brosius to Light, 26 September 1930, reel 46, PIRA.

13. Fred W. Mahone to William A. Light, 25 November 1930. I say that "perhaps" Brosius influenced Mahone and the Hualapais because below the statement referring to the treaty Mahone says in parentheses, "The above said Treaty of Guadaloupe Hidalgo in 1848 of Mexico, was extracted by our Representative, Mr. S. M. Brosius." What he exactly means is hard to say, but I think it's at least clear that it could mean that it was Brosius who first brought the treaty to the attention of Mahone. Brosius had just broached this topic with the president of the IRA. Samuel Brosius to J. M. Steere, 4 November 1930, reel 47, PIRA.

14. Like many of the developments in this case, one has to follow this thread through several record groups, and the path is not always clear. It remains uncertain exactly when

this deal was agreed to, but it was more than likely sometime in the first couple of weeks of December. First telegram between the railroad and attorneys, 15 December 1930, PSFFC; Joseph M. Dixon, First Asst. SOI, to AG, 31229-23-313, pt. 3, 18 December 1930, folder 3/3, box 27, RG 75; letter between attorneys, 23 December 1930, PSFFC. For transmission of the stipulation (agreement) see Dixon to AG, 3 January 1931, file #5 106, Peach Springs, box 1500, RG 48; and for the stipulation itself see "In the District Court of the United States for the District of Arizona, The United States of America, Plaintiff v. Atchison, Topeka, and Santa Fe Railway Company, a corporation, Defendant, No. L-388 Prescott," 3 January 1931, file #227235, RG 60, NA.

15. Samuel Brosius to Matthew K. Sniffen, 19 January 1931, reel 47, PIRA.

16. Letter between attorneys, 14 January 1931, PSFFC.

17. For the quotations see Mahone to Rhoads and Mahone to President Hoover, both 28 January 1931, CCF 31229-23-313, pt. 3, folder 3/3, box 27, RG 75, NA. On knowing about Gung'l and sending his material see Mahone to Frazier, 28 January 1931, reel 47, PIRA; Mahone to Rhoads, CIA, 28 January 1931, CCF 31229-23-313, pt. 3, folder 3/3, box 27, RG 75, NA.

18. Charles Rhoads to Fred Mahone, 3 March 1931, CCF file #5 106, Peach Springs, box 1500, RG 48, NA. Rhoads's "very kind letter" is in Mahone to Jonathan M. Steere, 13 March 1931, reel 47, PIRA.

19. For Fielding's and Davidson's opposition to Mahone see Matthew Sniffen to Samuel Brosius, 27 August 1930, reel 46, PIRA.

20. Mahone to Steere, 13 March 1931, reel 47, PIRA.

21. Brosius to Mahone, 25 March 1931, reel 47, PIRA.

22. For the Interior Department's support of the consent decree see Joseph M. Dixon, Asst. SOI, to AG, 7 May 1931, file #5 106, Peach Springs, box 1500, RG 48, NA.

23. Mahone to J. M. Pepperday, publisher, and H. P. Pickerill, editor, *Albuquerque Journal*, 18 May 1931, box 42, RG 46, NA. In anticipation of the hearings, Mahone urged the *Albuquerque Journal* to publicize the hearings and publish the Hualapais' statement of opposition to the Hagerman agreement. The paper agreed to publish Mahone's views in a letter to the editor. See J. M. Pepperday to R. H. Hanna, 20 May 1931, ibid.

24. A newspaper article in the Mohave County Historical Society's Hualapai file (n.d. but likely from the spring of 1931, as indicated by its reference to upcoming hearings at Valentine) lists the Swaskegame Post of the American Legion, the Oasis Temple of the Pythian Sisters, the Kingman Thursday Afternoon Club, the Charles Poston chapter of the National Society of the Daughters of the American Revolution, and the Kingman Business and Professional Women's Club as supporters of the Hualapais' claim. The article also calls Fred Mahone the official spokesman of the tribe.

25. Kathleen P. Chamberlain, *Under Sacred Ground: A History of Navajo Oil, 1922–1982* (Albuquerque: University of New Mexico Press, 2000), 63–64; Robert Gessner, *Massacre: A Survey of Today's American Indian* (New York: Jonathan Cape and Harrison Smith, 1931). Gessner was secretary of the American Civil Liberties Union's Committee on Indian Civil Rights; Nathan Margold was the chair. The Indian Rights Association thought Gessner went too far in his criticism of Rhoads and Scattergood and that, "because of his extreme bias and recklessness in accepting without question any allega-

tion that might fit in with his preconceived ideas, he disqualifies himself as a reliable source of information." *Indian Truth*, March 1931, 3–4. On Wheeler as a heckler"of the witnesses," and on the hearings in the Southwest in general, see also Erna Fergusson, "Senators Investigate Indians," *American Mercury*, 1931, 464–68; for an earlier assessment of the hearings see John Collier, "Senators and Indians," *Survey*, 1 January 1929, 425–28, 457; "Indian Affairs Committee at Valentine Now," *Mohave County Miner*, 22 May 1931; "U.S. Senators Investigate Indian Post: Subcommittee Hears Testimony of Rails and Redskins," *Mohave County Miner*, 29 May 1931. Transcripts of the hearings are printed in WP.

26. Mahone's version of events is found in Mahone to S. M. Brosius, 18 August 1931, reel 47, PIRA; see also WP, 242, 244–45.

27. WP, 247–50; the quotation is on 250.

28. Ibid., 251.

29. For "clash" see Mahone to Brosius, 18 August 1931, reel 47, PIRA. For Wheeler and the second set of Mahone quotations see WP, 252–54.

30. Mahone to Indian Rights Association (Attn: S. M. Brosius), 13 June 1931, reel 47, PIRA.

31. Mahone to Frazier, 15 August 1931, CCF 31229-23-313, pt. 3, folder 2/3, box 27, RG 75, NA. There is another copy of this letter, identically worded but dated 31 August, on reel 47, PIRA.

32. Wattson to CIA, 7 August 1931, CCF 31229-23-313, pt. 3, folder 2/3, box 27, RG 75, NA, expressing the Hualapais' concerns about the case. On the influence of the Hualapais on Sniffen and for the quotation see S. M Brosius to Mahone, 31 August 1931, reel 47, PIRA. Brosius tells Mahone: "It is to your credit that he has been enabled to see more clearly the need of the tribe, and that all the lands should be kept for them." Sniffen to Rhoads, 7 August 1931, CCF 312239-23-313, pt. 3, folder 3/3, box 27, RG 75, NA.

33. Gung'l to AG, 7 July 1931, file #227235, folder 4, box 3944, RG 60, NA; Mahone to Frazier, 7 July 1931, reel 47, PIRA. The affidavits, unfortunately, were not filed with the letter.

34. Hayden to Hagerman, 31 July 1931, correspondence with Hayden, Carl, Senator, box 4, Herbert Hagerman Papers, Laguna Niguel, NA.

35. The subcommittee's views are expressed in Joseph M. Dixon, Asst. SOI to AG, 30 July 1931, # 5 106, Peach Springs, box 1500, RG 48, NA; Frazier to Ray Lyman Wilbur, SOI and William D. Mitchell, AG, 12 August 1931, folder 2/3, box, 27, CCF 31229-23-313, pt. 3, RG 75, NA.

36. The Indian Office asked that the solicitor render a formal opinion in advance of the attorney general's. See J. Henry Scattergood to SOI, 24 August 1931, CCF 31229-23-313, pt. 3, folder 2/3, box 27, RG 75, NA. E. C. Finney, "Atlantic and Pacific Railroad Grant — Walapai Indian Lands," 16 September 1931, *Decisions of the Department of the Interior*, vol. 53, 1 January 1930–30 June 1932 (Washington, D.C.: Government Printing Office, 1932), 481–91 (hereafter Finney Opinion). Finney had personal knowledge of and had participated in the case since at least 1924. He in fact had at one time recommended that the suit proceed. On his involvement in his capacity as First Assistant SOI since 1924 see E. C. Finney, 1st Asst. SOI to Harlan Fiske Stone, AG, 22 July 1924, forwarding CIA Burke's letter recommending that the Department of Justice initiate a suit, file #227235, box 3944,

RG 60; for his recommendation of a continuation of litigation proceedings after the railroad attempted to have the suit stopped see E. C. Finney, 22 August 1927, "*In re* Atchison, Topeka, and Santa Fe Railway Company. Application Denied. Application for Recall of Departmental Recommendation," CCF file #5 106, Peach Springs, box 1500, RG 48, NA.

37. Finney Opinion, 486.

38. Ibid., 490.

39. Brosius to Mahone, 30 September 1931, reel 48, PIRA.

40. Because there was no case actually pending in court, Assistant Attorney General Seth Richardson hesitated to submit the matter to the attorney general for a formal opinion. Instead, he gave his own informal views of the case in early November, 1931. All quotations are from Richardson to Joseph M. Dixon, First Asst. SOI, 12 November 1912, CCF 31229-23-313 — Truxton, pt. 3, folder 2/3, box 27, RG 75. The SOI had asked for the AG's formal opinion in September, after the Finney Opinion appeared. SOI to AG, 30 September 1931, #5 106, Peach Springs, box 1500, RG 48, NA.

41. A. C. Monahan, "Memorandum to the Commissioner of Indian Affairs, Relative to the Railroad Claims to Lands on the Walapai (Hualapai) Reservation, Arizona," Walapai, Records of the Board of Indian Commissioners, entry 1387, box 22, RG 75, NA.

Chapter 8. Land and Law

1. Frederick Edwin Smith, Earl of Birkenhead, "The Southern Rhodesia Land Case," *Famous Trials of History* (London: Hutchinson, 1926), 208. After surveying the law on native title, Kent McNeil could say with some confidence that approaches to native property rights were largely ad hoc. Kent McNeil, *Common Law Aboriginal Title* (Oxford: Clarendon, 1989), 2. For a view from New Zealand based on archival research that suggests the same thing see Mark Hickford, "Making 'Territorial Rights of the Natives': Britain and New Zealand, 1830–1847" (D.Phil. thesis, University of Oxford 1999).

2. The vicissitudes of Indian law and the ways in which precedent is used to serve many masters is a routine subject for scholarship concerning federal Indian law, which is now voluminous. I have relied on Jill Norgren, "Protection of What Rights They Have: Original Principles of Indian Law," *North Dakota Law Review* 64.73 (1988): 73–120; Charles Wilkinson, *American Indians, Time, and the Law: Native Societies in a Modern Constitutional Democracy* (New Haven: Yale University Press, 1987); David Wilkins, *American Indian Sovereignty and the U.S. Supreme Court: The Masking of Justice* (Austin: University of Texas Press, 1997); Philip P. Frickey, "Adjudication and Its Discontents: Coherence and Conciliation in Federal Indian Law," *Harvard Law Review* 110 (1997): 1754–84. Between 1880 and 1900 the Court heard 112 cases involving Indians; between 1900 and 1940 it heard 266. See Blake A. Watson, "The Thrust and Parry of Federal Indian Law," *University of Dayton Law Review* 23 (1998): 437–514, appendix. On lawyers' ignorance of Indians see Karl J. Knoepfler, "Legal Status of the American Indian and His Property," *Iowa Law Bulletin* 7:3 (1922): 232. On the lack of expertise in Indian law see Lewis Meriam and the Institute for Government Research, *The Problem of Indian Administration: A Report of a Survey Made at the Request of the Honorable Hubert Work, Secretary of the Interior, and Submitted to Him, February 21, 1928* (Bal-

timore: Johns Hopkins University Press, 1928), 808 (hereafter Meriam Report). For the quotation see Tho[ma]s J. Tydings, "Rights of Indians on Public Lands," *Case and Comment* 23.9 (February, 1917): 743. For the changes in colonial land policies and practices see Stuart Banner, *How the Indians Lost Their Land: Law and Power on the Frontier* (Cambridge: Harvard University Press, 2005).

3. The same was true for most nineteenth-century property cases: the Court may or may not have ruled in favor of Indians, but the fact of occupancy was not in question. For example, the Court decided in *United States v. Cook*, 86 U.S. 591 (1873), that the Menominee did, indeed, possess Indian title — their presence on their land was not questioned — but they didn't have the right to sell the timber on the land for a profit.

4. *Fletcher v. Peck*, 10 U.S. 87 (1810). On earlier uses of Indian title in cases that have had little if any impact on Indian law see Tim Alan Garrison, *The Legal Ideology of Removal: The Southern Judiciary and the Sovereignty of Native American Nations* (Athens: University of Georgia Press, 2002), 258, n. 26. For a general overview of the Marshall Court's Indian decisions within the larger context of American law, see G. Edward White, *The Marshall Court and Cultural Change, 1815–1835* (New York: MacMillan, 1986), 703–40. Despite White's title he does include *Fletcher.* On the importance of *Fletcher,* the potential impact of Johnson's dissent, and the vagueness of Marshall's opinion, see Nell Jessup Newton, "At the Whim of the Sovereign: Aboriginal Title Reconsidered," *Hastings Law Journal* 31.3 (1980): 1220–21; James Youngblood Henderson, "Unraveling the Riddle of Aboriginal Title," *American Indian Law Review* 5.1 (1977): 83–87; Robert Williams, *The American Indian in Western Legal Thought: The Discourses of Conquest* (New York: Oxford University Press, 1990), 3089; Garrison, *Legal Ideology of Removal,* 73–87. On the case in general, but with no discussion of Indian title, see C. Peter Magrath, *Yazoo: Law and Politics in the New Republic; The Case of Fletcher v. Peck* (Providence: Brown University Press, 1966).

5. *Johnson v. M'Intosh*, 21 U.S. 543 (1923). For much more on *Johnson* and on Marshall's reasoning see Eric Kades, "History and Interpretation of the Great Case of *Johnson v. M'Intosh,*" *Law and History Review* 19.1 (2001). http://www.historycooperative.org/journals/lhr/19.1okades, paras. 111– 21. For a discussion of one colony, Massachusetts, see Neal Salisbury, *Manitou and Providence: Indians, Europeans and the Making of New England, 1500–1643* (New York: Oxford University Press, 1982), 190–202. Salisbury contends, in fact, that when the magistrates of Massachusetts Bay famously threw out Williams it was not for his religious views but because Williams questioned the king's right to patent land that belonged to Indians (199). For an argument that as a general matter nearly all purchases of Indian land needed to be officially sanctioned, and for how this idea was manifested in *Johnson,* see Banner, *How the Indians Lost Their Land,* 10–48, 183–84. For the decision and how it manipulated the history of colonial land policy to suggest that Indians never had anything but occupancy rights see Lindsay G. Robertson, *Conquest by Law: How the Discovery of America Dispossessed Indigenous People of Their Lands* (New York: Oxford University Press, 2005), 95–116; for the wider historical context surrounding *Johnson* see Jill Norgren's excellent *The Cherokee Cases: The Confrontation of Law and Politics* (New York: McGraw-Hill, 1996). For a full understanding of *Johnson* and the evolution of Indian title and occupancy rights, the Robertson, Norgren, and Banner books are essential reading.

6. On the importance of occupancy see Gordon I. Bennett, "Aboriginal Title in the Common Law: A Stony Path Through Feudal Doctrine," *Buffalo Law Review* 27.4 (1978): 621–22. See generally Daniel G. Kelly Jr., "Indian Title: The Rights of American Natives in the Land They Have Occupied Since Time Immemorial," *Columbia Law Review* 75.3 (1975): 655–86.

7. Felix S. Cohen, "Original Indian Title," in *The Legal Conscience: The Collected Papers of Felix Cohen,* ed. Lucy Kramer Cohen (New Haven: Yale University Press, 1960), 292 (first published in *Minnesota Law Review,* 1947).

8. For "Brilliant compromise" see Newton, "At the Whim of the Sovereign," 1223; for "judicial mythology" see Howard W. Berman, "The Concept of Aboriginal Rights in the Early Legal History of the United States," *Buffalo Law Review* 27.4 (1978): 643. For a position that is somewhere between the two—recognizing that Marshall largely made up his rationale on the spot but also preserved a modicum of Indian land rights—see David Wilkins, *American Indian Sovereignty and the U.S. Supreme Court: The Masking of Justice* (Austin: University of Texas Press, 1997), 27–35; for Marshall's confession see *Johnson v. M'Intosh,* 21 U.S. 543, (1923) 591–92; for an analysis of this passage see Milner S. Ball, "Constitution, Court, Indian Tribes," *American Bar Foundation Research Journal* 1987.1: 28–29; on the power of colonialism see especially Philip P. Frickey, "Marshalling Past and Present: Colonialism, Constitutionalism, and Interpretation in Federal Indian Law," *Harvard Law Review* 107 (1993): 389. As Robert Williams put it: "Perhaps most important, *Johnson's* acceptance of the Doctrine of Discovery into United States Law preserved the legacy of 1,000 years of European racism and colonialism directed against non-Western peoples." *American Indian in Western Legal Thought,* 317.

9. *Worcester v. Georgia,* 6 Pet. 515 (1832); *Mitchel v. United States,* 31 U.S. 711 (1835). The other famous case of the Marshall era, *Cherokee Nation v. Georgia,* 30 U.S. 1 (1831), was not part of the line of cases affecting aboriginal title. My interpretation follows Frickey, Newton, Berman, Norgren, and Ball; for a recent, clearly written elaboration of the principle that discovery only gives the discoverer the first right to purchase, or, in the authors' words, "preemptive discovery," see David E. Wilkins and K. Tsianina Lomawaima, " 'The Law of Nations': The Doctrine of Discovery," in *Uneven Ground: American Indian Sovereignty and Federal Law* (Norman: University of Oklahoma Press, 2001), 19–63. For "ongoing process of colonialism" see Frickey, "Marshalling Past and Present," 396 (the quotation is on 401). On states and Indian sovereignty see Sydney Haring, "*Corn Tassel*: State and Federal Conflict Over Tribal Sovereignty," in *Crow Dog's Case: American Indian Sovereignty, Tribal Law, and United States Law in the Nineteenth Century* (New York: Cambridge University Press, 1994). For state courts and Indian rights see also Brad Asher, *Beyond the Reservation: Indians, Settlers, and the Law in Washington Territory, 1853–1889* (Norman: University of Oklahoma Press, 1999).

10. *Mitchel v. United States,* 746. For the most detailed treatment of *Mitchel* see David E. Wilkins, "*Johnson v. M'Intosh* Revisited: Through the Eyes of *Mitchel v. United States,*" *American Indian Law Review* 19.1 (1994): 159–81; see also Cohen, "Original Indian Title," 295–96.

11. "Opinion of William Burge, 1836," in Edward Sweetman, *The Unsigned New Zealand Treaty* (Melbourne: Arrow Printery, 1939), 117–20. In 1841 the Superior Court of New South Wales, though not explicitly citing U.S. case law, did discuss the state of

American law regarding Indians. See *R. v. Bonjon*, Supreme Court of New South Wales, Willis, J., 16 September 1841, Melbourne, available, along with many other early Australian cases, on the extraordinary Web site run by Bruce Kercher at Macquarie University. http://law.mq.edu.au/scnsw/index.htm.

12. On *Johnson*'s applicability see esp. Hickford, "Making 'Territorial Rights of the Natives.'" Henry Chapman, "The English, the French, and the New Zealanders," *New Zealand Journal*, 4 April 1840. "Gipps Defends the New Zealand Bill," 9 July 1840, in Sweetman, *Unsigned New Zealand Treaty*, 110 (the original is in the Public Record Office, London). For the roles that Gipps and Wentworth played in debates about land policy see Hickford, "Making 'Territorial Rights of the Natives'"; David V. Williams, "*The Queen v. Symonds* Reconsidered," *Victoria University of Wellington Law Review* 19.4 (1989): 392; Peter Adams, *Fatal Necessity: British Intervention in New Zealand, 1830–1847* (Auckland: Auckland University Press, 1977).

13. *R. v. Symonds*, [1847] N.Z.P.C.C. 387. See generally Paul G. McHugh, *The Maori Magna Carta: New Zealand Law and the Treaty of Waitangi* (Auckland: Oxford University Press, 1991); see 108–20 for *Symonds*, aboriginal title in the nineteenth century generally, and the influence of *Johnson*. On the relation between *Johnson* and *Symonds* see also McHugh, *Aboriginal Societies and the Common Law: A History of Sovereignty, Status, and Self-Determination* (New York: Oxford University Press, 2004), 42. Mark Hickford, "'Settling Some Very Important Principles of Colonial Law': Three 'Forgotten' Cases of the 1840s," *Victoria University of Wellington Law Review* 34 (2003): 1–30. Williams, "*The Queen v. Symonds* Reconsidered," 385–402.

14. For the foregoing discussion I have relied on Ann Parsonson, "The Fate of Maori Land Rights in Early Colonial New Zealand: The Limits of the Treaty of Waitangi and the Doctrine of Aboriginal Title," in *Law, History, Colonialism: The Reach of Empire*, ed. Diane Kirkby and Catharine Coleborne (Manchester, U.K.: Manchester University Press, 2001), 173–89; M. P. K. Sorrenson, "The Settlement of New Zealand from 1835," in *Indigenous Peoples' Rights in Australia, Canada, and New Zealand*, ed. Paul Haveman (Auckland: Oxford University Press, 1999), 162–79; Claudia Orange, *The Treaty of Waitangi* (Wellington: Allen & Unwin, 1987); McNeil, *Common Law Aboriginal Title*, 188–191; Geoffrey S. Lester, "The Territorial Rights of the Inuit of the Canadian Northwest Territories: A Legal Argument" (D.Jur. diss., York University, York, Ont., 1981), 3:723–846; F. M. (Jock) Brookfield, *Waitangi and Indigenous Rights: Revolution, Law and Legitimation* (Auckland: Auckland University Press, 1999); Shaunnaugh Dorsett and Lee Godden, *A Guide to Overseas Precedents of Relevance to Native Title* (Canberra: Native Title Research Institute, Australian Institute of Aboriginal and Torres Strait Islander Studies, 1998), 92–96. For a concise legislative history see McHugh, *Aboriginal Societies and the Common Law*, 185–89. The favorable case is *Nireaha Tamaki v Baker*, [1901] N.Z.P.C.C. 371. For the neglect of *Symonds* see McHugh, *Maori Magna Carta*, 122; Williams, "*The Queen v Symonds* Reconsidered."

15. *Cooper v. Stuart*, [1889] 14 App. Cas. 286. That the land was empty was a favorite conceit of not only historians — amateur and professional — but also of judges. See Tom Griffiths, "Past Silences," in *Hunters and Collectors: The Antiquarian Imagination in Australia* (Melbourne: Cambridge University Press, 1996); Bain Attwood, "The Past as Future: Aborigines, Australia and the (Dis)course of History," in *In the Age of Mabo: History, Aborigines and Australia,* ed. Bain Attwood (Crows Nest, N.S.W.: Allen &

Unwin, 1996), vii–xxxviii. Gerry Simpson described *Cooper* thus: "[T]he people that did inhabit the land were redefined as physically present but legally irrelevant and their history was obliterated." Simpson, "*Mabo,* International Law, *Terra Nullius* and the Stories of Settlement: An Unresolved Jurisprudence," *Melbourne University Law Review* 19.1 (1993): 200. Simpson shows how in successive decisions after *Cooper* the doctrine of terra nullius was redefined by the Australian Supreme Court to fit current political trends but always went against Aborigines. He calls this "enlarged *terra nullius*"; on the historical evolution and application of terra nullius see Alan Frost, "New South Wales as *Terra Nullius:* The British Denial of Aboriginal Land Rights," *Historical Studies* 19.77 (1981): 513–23. For a discussion of the legal theorists of the late nineteenth century and their influence on the Australian law of terra nullius see Henry Reynolds, *Aboriginal Sovereignty: Three Nations, One Australia?* (Crows Nest, N.S.W.: Allen & Unwin, 1996), 1–15, 39–59, and Antony Anghie, "Finding the Peripheries: Sovereignty and Colonialism in Nineteenth Century International Law," *Harvard International Law Journal* 40 (Winter, 1999): 50–51. For a sense of how naturalized terra nullius had become by World War II see Ernest Scott, "Taking Possession of Australia — The Doctrine of 'Terra Nullius' (No Man's Land)," *Royal Australian Historical Society: Journal and Proceedings* 26.1 (1940): 1–19. Scott does not discuss Aborigines. Rather, he accepts the doctrine of terra nullius and discusses the contests between European powers for control of Australia as terra nullius.

16. For Cook and his instructions to seek consent see Stuart Banner, "Why *Terra Nullius?* Anthropology and Property Law in Early Australia," *Law and History Review* 23.1 (2005) para. 5, http://www.historycooperative.org/journals/lhr/23.1/banner.html; see also Henry Reynolds, *The Law of the Land* (Victoria, Australia: Penguin, 1987), 125–48. For terra nullius and its hazy origins, as well as a discussion of early recognition of Aboriginal land rights, see Bruce Kercher, "Native Title in the Shadows: The Origins of the Myth of *Terra Nullius* in Early New South Wales Courts," in *Colonialism and the Modern World: Selected Studies,* ed. Gregory Blue, Martin Bunton, and Ralph Crozier (Armonk, N.Y.: Sharpe, 2002), 100–119. The first quotation by Stephen is in Banner, "Why *Terra Nullius?*" para. 38; the second is in Hickford, "Making 'Territorial Rights of the Natives,' " 240. On debates about aboriginal legal rights see Banner, "Why *Terra Nullius?*" paras. 49–59. For a focused discussion of the courts see Bruce Kercher, "The Recognition of Aboriginal Status in the Supreme Court of New South Wales Under Forbes, C.J., 1824–1836," in *Land and Freedom: Law, Property Rights, and the British Diaspora,* ed. A. R. Buck, John McLaren, and Nancy Wright (London: Ashgate, 2001), 83–102. Henry Reynolds's work on the humanitarian impulse to protect Aborigines' legal rights, most clearly manifested by the Aborigines Protection Society, which he suggested was representative of a consensus on aboriginal rights, has come under fire recently. Historians now see that policy, rhetoric, and action were not settled, nor was there a consensus. For this view see Daman Ward, "A Means and Measure of Civilisation: Colonial Authorities and Indigenous Law in Australia," *History Compass* 1 (2003): 1–24; Bain Attwood, "*The Law of Land* or the Law of the Land? History, Law and Narrative in a Settler Society," *History Compass* 2 (2004): 1–30, both available at www.history-compass.com. The *South Australian Register* is cited in Banner, "Why *Terra Nullius?*" para. 72.

17. For an excellent discussion of Indian title in British Columbia in the late nineteenth

century, including the knowledge that provincial officials had of *Symonds,* see Hamar Foster, "Letting Go the Bone: The Idea of Indian Title in British Columbia, 1849–1927," in *Essays in the History of Canadian Law,* vol. 6, *British Columbia and the Yukon,* ed. Hamar Foster and John McLaren (Toronto: Published for the Osgoode Society for Legal History by University of Toronto Press, 1995), 28–86. On the early recognition of native peoples' property interests see Paul Tennant, *Aboriginal Peoples and Politics: The Indian Land Question in British Columbia, 1849–1989* (Vancouver: University of British Columbia Press, 1990), 17–25; McNeil, *Common Law Aboriginal Title,* 273. For a history of the *St. Catherine's* case, 14 App. Cas. 46 (1888), and the recognition of the existence of Indian title by Minister of Interior David Mills in 1876 see S. Barry Cottam, "Indian Title as a 'Celestial Institution': David Mills and the *St. Catherine's* Case," in *Aboriginal Resource Use in Canada: Historical and Legal Aspects,* ed. Kerry M. Abel and Jean Friesen (Winnipeg: University of Manitoba Press, 1991), 247–65 (the quotation is on 259). This was the same Mills who as Minister of the Interior had defended Indian title. Cottam tracks his change of mind. See Kent McNeil, "Social Darwinism and Judicial Conceptions of Indian Title in Canada in the 1880s," *Journal of the West* 38.1 (1999): 68–76.

18. *Delgamuukw v. British Columbia,* 3 SCR 1010 (1997). J. A. J. McKenna, "Indian Title in British Columbia," *Canadian Magazine,* 1920, 471–74; the quotation is on 474. Since the *Delgamuukw* decision was handed down, the literature about aboriginal title in Canada has grown quite voluminous. For the history of this topic I have relied on McNeil, *Common Law Aboriginal Title;* Kent McNeil, "Aboriginal Rights in Canada: From Title to Land to Territorial Sovereignty," in *Emerging Justice? Essays on Indigenous Rights in Canada and Australia* (Saskatoon: Native Law Centre, University of Saskatchewan, 2001); Kent McNeil, "The Meaning of Aboriginal Title," in *Aboriginal and Treaty Rights in Canada: Essays on Law, Equality, and Respect for Difference,* ed. Michael Asch (Vancouver: University of British Columbia Press, 1997), 135–54; Brian Slattery, "The Nature of Aboriginal Title," in *Beyond the Nass Valley: National Implications of the Supreme Court's* Delgamuukw *Decision,* ed. Owen Lippert (Vancouver: Fraser Institute, 2000), 11–33; Dara Culhane, *The Pleasure of the Crown: Anthropology, Law, and First Nations* (Burnaby, B.C.: Talonbooks, 1998).

19. On native activism see Tennant, "Douglas Treaties." For "until such time" see R. M. Galois, "The Indian Rights Association, Native Protest Activity, and the 'Land Question' in British Columbia, 1903–1916," *Native Studies Review* 8.2 (1992): 1–34. *Statement of the Allied Tribes of British Columbia for the Government of British Columbia* (Vancouver: Cowan and Brookhouse, 1919). For a brief history of Canadian law and policy, including a discussion of the treaty process, see Hamar Foster, "Canadian Indians, Time, and the Law," *Western Legal History* 7.1 (1994): 69–112. Statement of Duncan Campbell Scott, 18 March 1927, in "To Inquire into the Claims of the Allied Tribes of British Columbia, as Set Forth in Their Petition Submitted to Parliament in June 1926," Proceedings, Reports and the Evidence, House of Commons, Special Committees of the Senate and House of Commons, sess. 1926–27, p. 6.

20. *Re. Southern Rhodesia,* [1919] A.C. 211; *Amodu Tijani v. Secretary, Southern Nigeria,* 2 A.C. 399. John H. Harris, *The Greatest Land Case in British History: The Struggle for Native Rights in Rhodesia Before the Judicial Committee of His Majesty's*

Privy Council (London: Anti-Slavery and Aborigines' Protection Society, n.d.). For the context of the case and the struggle for native land rights see Robin Palmer, *Land and Racial Domination in Rhodesia* (Berkeley: University of California Press, 1977), esp. 133–35 (on the case); Brian Wilson, "The Anti-Slavery and Aborigines Protection Society and the South African Natives' Land Act of 1913," *Journal of African History* 20.1 (1979): 83–102; Rachel Whitehead, "The Aborigines' Protection Society and White Settlers in Rhodesia, 1889–1930," Collected Papers on the Societies of Southern Africa in the Nineteenth and Twentieth Centuries, October 1971–June 1972, vol. 3 (London: University of London, Institute of Commonwealth Studies); Charles Swaisland, "The Aborigines Protection Society, 1837–1909," *Slavery and Abolition* 21.2 (2000): 265–80. Re. *Southern Rhodesia*, 233, 234.

21. *Amodu Tijani*, 403, 404. With regard to the case see O. Adewoye, "The Tijani Land Case (1915–1921): A Study in British Colonial Justice," *Odu: A Journal of West African Studies* 13 (1976): 21–39; for the legal significance of the case see A. E. W. Park, "The Cessions of Territory and Private Land Rights: A Reconsideration of the Tijani Case," *Nigerian Law Journal* 1.1 (1964): 38–49.

22. *Cramer v. United States*, 261 U.S. 219 (1921), at 229.

23. Ibid., 230.

24. Though never a robust branch of legal scholarship, jurisdiction in Indian country occupied a number of commentators in the nineteenth century. Only a few articles that could be considered scholarly were published, most of them dealing with jurisdiction, criminal law, and ways to bring Indians more fully under the law of the United States, among other things. For a survey of legal treatises and handbooks dealing with federal courts—the courts that hear Indian cases—and their generally brief or nonexistent treatment of Indians see Judith Resnik, "Dependent Sovereigns: Indian Tribes, States, and the Federal Courts," *University of Chicago Law Review* 56 (1989): 683, n. 44. Some representative publications from the nineteenth century are James Bradley Thayer, "A People Without Law," *Atlantic Monthly*, October 1891, 540–51; William Justin Harsha, "Law for the Indians," *North American Review*, March 1882, no. 134, 271–92; George F. Canfield, "The Legal Position of the American Indian," *American Law Review* 15 (January 1881): 21–37; Austin Abbot, "Indians and the Law," *Harvard Law Review* 2.4 (1888): 167–79. For Indian law in the nineteenth century in general see Sydney Haring, *Crow Dog's Case: American Indian Sovereignty, Tribal Law, and United States Law in the Nineteenth Century* (New York: Cambridge University Press, 1994); Isaac Franklin Russell, "The Indian Before the Law," *Yale Law Journal* 18.5 (1909): 328–37 (the quotation is on 331–32). Writing in the same year, Samuel T. Bledsoe, future president of the ATSF, published his massive treatise *Indian Land Laws: Being a Treatise of the Law of Acquiring Title to, and Alienation of, Allotted Indian Lands. Also a Compilation of Treaties, Agreements and Statutes Applicable Thereto* (Kansas City, Mo.: Pipes-Reed, 1909). Despite the title, the book concerned itself only with land of the so-called Five Civilized Tribes of Oklahoma, whose land title was, in significant ways, different from that of Indians elsewhere. Bledsoe dispenses with the general matter of Indian title in three paragraphs on pages 2–3.

25. Russell, "Indian Before the Law," 330, 337.

26. Grant Foreman, "The U.S. Court and the Indian: Where the Red Man Gets a

Square Deal," *Overland Monthly,* June 1913, 573; Clinton R. Flynn, "The Legal Status of the Indians in the United States," *Central Law Journal* 62:1 (May 25, 1906): 399–404.

27. For the quotation see Flora Warren Seymour, "Our Indian Land Policy," *Journal of Land and Public Utility Economics* 2 (June–October 1926): 97. To be fair to Seymour, she was a vocal critic of the allotment policy and couched her article in those terms; for her feelings about allotment see Flora Warren Seymour, *The Story of the Red Man* (New York: Longmans, Green, 1929), 365–81; for her thoughts about the Court and Indian policy see Flora Warren Seymour, "Land Titles in the Pueblo Indian Country," *American Bar Association Journal* 10.1 (1924): 37. See also Flora Warren Seymour, "Burlesquing the American Indian," *Woman Lawyers' Journal* 13.2 (1924): 3–6.

28. For "fitting the aborigines" see Alpheus Henry Snow, *The Question of Aborigines in the Law and Practice of Nations Including a Collection of Authorities and Documents Written at the Request of the Department of State* (Washington, D.C.: Government Printing Office, 1919), 6. For "economic competition" see Alpheus Henry Snow, *The Question of Aborigines in the Law and Practice of Nations Including a Collection of Authorities and Documents Written at the Request of the Department of State* (New York: G. P. Putnam's Sons, Knickerbocker Press, 1921), 134.

29. M. F. Lindley, *The Acquisition and Government of Backward Territory in International Law: Being a Treatise on the Law and Practice Relating to Colonial Expansion* (London: Longmans, Green, 1926).

30. For an excellent breakdown of the long history of thinking about indigenous people and the law see Paul Havemann, "Chronology One: Euro-American Law of Nations and Indigenous Rights," in *Indigenous Peoples' Rights in Australia, Canada, and New Zealand,* ed. Paul Havemann (Auckland: Oxford University Press, 1999), 13–17; see also Robert A. Williams Jr., *The American Indian in Western Legal Thought: The Discourses of Conquest* (New York: Oxford University Press, 1990). For the quotation see Lindley, *Acquisition and Government,* 11. For an excellent introduction to Victoria see James Brown Scott, *The Spanish Origin of International Law: Lectures on Francisco de Victoria (1480–1546) and Francisco Suarez (1548–1617)* (Washington, D.C.: School of Foreign Service, Georgetown University, 1928), 13–70 (the lectures were delivered in 1927). For Lindley's view of Vattel, see *Acquisition and Government,* 17; 304–42; on Vattel see Anthony Pagden, *Lords of All the World: Ideologies of Empire in Spain, Britain, and France, c. 1500–1800* (New Haven: Yale University Press, 1995), 78–79; for a clear exposition of the influence of Vattel and others on Australia's first major land rights case in the twentieth century, *Milirrpum v. Nabalco Pty. Ltd.,* 17 FLR 141 (1971), see Nancy M. Williams, *The Yolngu and Their Land: A System of Land Tenure and the Fight for Its Recognition* (Stanford: Stanford University Press, 1986), 109–38.

31. John Westlake, "Territorial Sovereignty, Especially with Relation to Uncivilised Regions," in *Imperialism,* ed. Philip D. Curtin (London: Macmillan, 1971), 52. For the positivists' rising influence see Lindley, *Acquisition and Government,* 21, and for their being contested see vi. For a succinct survey of the rise of legal positivism and *Westlake et al.* see S. James Anaya, *Indigenous Peoples in International Law* (New York: Oxford University Press, 1996), 19–23. For a much fuller discussion of the ways in which the colonial dispossession of indigenous peoples was rationalized via legal positivism see Antony Anghie, "Finding the Peripheries: Sovereignty and Colonialism in Nineteenth

Century International Law," *Harvard International Law Journal* 40 (Winter 1999): 1–80. According to Anghie, "The naturalist international law that had applied in the sixteenth and seventeenth centuries asserted that a universal international law deriving from human reason applied to all peoples, European or non-European. By contrast, positivist international law distinguished between civilized states and non-civilized states and asserted further that international law applied only to the sovereign states that composed the civilized 'Family of Nations'" (5). For Lindley's views of subsistence and compensation see *Acquisition and Government*, 352–53.

32. Chauncey Shafter Goodrich, "The Legal Status of the California Indian, part 2," *California Law Review* 14.2 (1926): 158. On the paucity of writing about Indians and the law see Rory SnowArrow Faussett and Judith V. Royster, "Courts and Indians: Sixty-Five Years of Legal Analysis; Bibliography of Periodical Articles Relating to Native American Law, 1922–1986," *Legal Reference Services Quarterly* 7.2–4 (1987): 111–15.

33. Jenning C. Wise, *Red Man in the New World Drama: A Politico-Legal Study, with a Pageantry of American Indian History* (Washington, D.C.: Roberts, 1931); Jennings C. Wise, "The Indians Held Their Lands Under the Communal System, the Rights of the Tribal Members Being Those of Commoners," *California Indian Herald,* July 1924, 12. The other articles are "The Indian Title and Estate Under the Laws of the United States," May 1924, 13–14; "The Indian Title and Estate Under the Laws of the United States," June 1924, 7, 13–14. These essays, marred by convoluted prose and likely read by few, could not have had much impact on the practice of Indian law. But he kept at it, managing to get a lengthy essay printed in the *Congressional Record* at the end of 1925 that was later abridged and published in the *American Bar Association Journal*. Jennings C. Wise, "Indian Law and Needed Reforms," *American Bar Association Journal* 12.1 (January 1926): 37–40. Jennings C. Wise, "A Plea for the Indian Citizens of the United States," 15 December 1925, *Congressional Record*, 69th Cong., 1st sess., 818–27, originally published as a pamphlet in 1925.

34. Both quotations are from Wise, "Plea for the Indian Citizens," 823.

Chapter 9. Saving Hualapai Land

1. Mahone to Brosius, 3 October 1931; the quotations are found in Wattson to CIA, 15 October 1931, both in CCF 56172-31-155 — Truxton Canyon, box 9, RG 75, NA. On Wattson's belief that no Hualapais lived in the east see Wattson to Hagerman, 9 October 1931, CCF 31229-23-313, pt. 3, folder 2/3, box 27, RG 75, NA.

2. Statement of Kate Crozier, 27 July 1931, reel 47, PIRA. For suspicions concerning Wattson see Ray T. Winfred, Oscar ?, Auggie Smith (his thumb mark), and Bob Schrum, 1st Chief (his thumb mark) to CIA, 16 October 1931, box 42, RG 46, NA; D. H. Wattson, 30 June 1930, Annual Report, reel 151, SANSR; Hagerman memo, "Walapai Exchanges," 13 October 1930, CCF 31229-23-313, pt. 3, folder 3/3, box 27, RG 75, NA.

3. On warning Mahone see Brosius to Mahone, 21 October 1931; for "legal officials" see Brosius to Mahone, 10 October 1931; on there still being hope see Brosius to Mahone, 22 October 1931; for "great stumbling block" see Brosius to Mahone, 9 September 1931, reel 47; Mahone to Brosius, 7 November 1931, sending him the petition; Brosius to

Frazier, 17 November 1931, sending the petition to the subcommittee, all but 9 September 1931 on reel 48, PIRA.

4. Frazier to Rhoads, 11 February 1932, CCF 31229-23-313, pt. 3, folder 2/3, box 27, RG 75, NA. For the quotations and the subcommittee's request to stop consolidation and to continue investigating the Hualapais' claim see Frazier to Wilbur, 17 June 1932, box 42, RG 46, NA. Wilbur complied and wrote to the railroad, saying, "We are delaying action in the matter due mainly to a formal request to the Department by the Chairman of the Senate Committee on Indian Affairs, that the proposed consolidation be deferred until the Committee considers the matter of prior rights, if any, that the Walapais may have to the lands." Ray Lyman Wilbur, SOI to Collinson, ATSF land commissioner, 20 June 1932, CCF 31229-23-313, pt. 3, folder 1/3, box 27, RG 75, NA. For the official cessation of the consolidation see S. Res. 273, 72nd Cong., 1st sess.: "Resolved, That the Secretary of the Interior is hereby requested to delay the final consummation of the proposed exchange of lands within the Walapai Indian Reservation with the Atchison, Topeka and Santa Fe Railway Company, pursuant to the act entitled 'An Act to provide for exchanges of Government and privately owned lands in the Walapai Indian Reservation, Arizona,' approved February 20, 1925, pending further investigation of the proposal by the Senate Committee on Indian Affairs and the final disposition by the Seventy-second Congress of such additional legislation as the committee may recommend in connection therewith," 11 July 1932, box 42, RG 46, NA. Frazier introduced the resolution in Congress on 13 July. See *Congressional Record*, 72nd Cong., 1st sess., 15175.

The trip to the Southwest did more, of course, than promote consideration of the Hualapai case. Anthony Godfrey, author of the most extensive treatment of the survey, argues that the trip was critical in the formation of subsequent Indian policy. The committee's two-month trip led to critiques on several fronts, among them the inefficiencies of the BIA — the committee especially disliked the agency farmers and found that the Klamath agency had one BIA employee for every Indian; the mismanagement of the tribal trust fund, which seemed to benefit non-Indian BIA employees more than it did Indians; the inadequacy of the Pueblo Lands Board, especially its chair, Herbert Hagerman. This all lead the committee, according to Godfrey, to come closer to the position later advocated by Collier: Indians should handle their own affairs. Anthony Godfrey, "Congressional-Indian Politics: Senate Survey of Conditions Among the Indians of the United States" (Ph.D. diss., University of Utah, 1985), 218–50.

5. Assessments of Collier's performance keep pouring in, and the bibliography to date is quite large. Most recently Collier's policies have come under tremendous scrutiny and have been found wanting. Some books that are critical of Collier are Graham D. Taylor, *The New Deal and American Indian Tribalism: The Administration of the Indian Reorganization Act, 1934–45* (Lincoln: University of Nebraska Press, 1980); Thomas Biliosi, *Organizing the Lakota: The Political Economy of the New Deal on the Pine Ridge and Rosebud Reservations* (Tucson: University of Arizona Press, 1992); Vine Deloria Jr. and Clifford M. Lytle, *The Nations Within: The Past and Future of American Indian Sovereignty* (Austin: University of Texas Press, 1984); Vine Deloria Jr. and and Clifford M. Lytle, *American Indians, American Justice* (Austin: University of Texas Press, 1983); Russell Lawrence Barsh and James Youngblood Henderson, *The Road: Indian Tribes and Political Liberty* (Berkeley: University of California Press, 1980); Frank Pommersheim, *Braid of Feathers: American Indian Law and Contemporary Tribal Life* (Berkeley: Uni-

versity of California Press, 1995); Laurence M. Hauptman, "Africa View: John Collier, the British Colonial Service and American Indian Policy, 1933–1945," *Historian* 48.3 (1986): 359–74; Laurence M. Hauptman, *The Iroquois and the Indian New Deal* (Syracuse: Syracuse University Press, 1981). Stephen Cornell's *The Return of the Native: American Indian Political Resurgence* (New York: Oxford University Press, 1988) is measured in its criticism of the Indian New Deal. In the chapter concerning the Navajo in *The Roots of Dependency: Subsistence, Environment, and Social Change Among the Choctaws, Pawnees, and Navajos* (Lincoln: University of Nebraska Press, 1983), Richard White takes a critical look at Collier's policies regarding sheep reduction. Elmer Rusco's detailed reevaluation of Collier and the Indian New Deal is a measured appraisal, focusing on the positive side of the ledger. Elmer Rusco, *A Fateful Time: The Legislative History of the Indian Reorganization Act* (Reno: University of Nevada Press, 2000). For his accident and continued interest in the case from the hospital see Collier to A. A. Grorud, 8 July 1932, and "Friday," American Indian Defense Association file, both in folder 2, box 1, RG 46.

6. Collier, "Shall the Hagerman Agreement Divesting the Walapai Tribe of Arizona Be Confirmed?" 30 May 1932, pp. 7, 10, pt. 1, #273, reel 9, JCP (emphasis in original).

7. Hagerman to Rhoads, 8 June 1932, CCF 31229-23-313, pt. 3, folder 2/3, box 27, RG 75, NA.

8. See Rhoads to Hagerman, 3 June 1932, in ibid., transmitting the Collier memo.

9. For the first two quotations see John Collier, "The Interior Department's and Indian Bureau's Defenses of Its Proposed (and Partially Completed) Destruction of Walapai Property Rights in Behalf of the Santa Fe Railway," 11 June 1932, reel 9, doc. 273, frame 358, JCP; for "hypnotic sway" see unsigned, undated memo, reel 9, doc. 273, frame 371, JCP. The tone and content of the memo are clearly Collier's.

10. For "Within this framework" see Collier, "Interior Department's and Indian Bureau's Defenses." For the Santa Fe's sway over Richardson and Finney, as well as the Indian Service and Interior, see John Collier, "Shall the Forced Departure of Herbert J. Hagerman from Government Employ be Memorialized Through the Consummation of a Betrayal of the Walapai Indian Tribe of Arizona[?]" n.d., reel 9, doc. 273, frame 374, JCP; see also John Collier, "The Question of the Walapai Ancestral Boundaries," 25 June 1932, reel 9, doc. 273, frame 362, JCP. He further charged that both Finney and Richardson had a long record of anti-Indian decisions. Finney was in fact working on two fronts: not only was he writing the Hualapais out of their land, but just then he was crafting a similar opinion that would forestall the claims of the Blackfeet to hunting rights within Glacier National Park based on some of the same faulty reasoning and crafted from some of the same legal and historical fictions. Several historians have interrogated the Blackfeet claim and the legal machinations used to deprive them of their land. For Finney and the Blackfeet's fight for rights to hunt in the park see Louis S. Warren, *The Hunter's Game: Poachers and Conservationists in Twentieth-Century America* (New Haven: Yale University Press, 1997), 150; Mark David Spence, "Crown of the Continent, Backbone of the World: The American Wilderness Ideal and the Blackfeet Exclusion from Glacier National Park," *Environmental History* (Summer 1996): 38; and Robert H. Keller and Michael F. Turek, *American Indians and National Parks* (Tucson: University of Arizona Press, 1998), 59.

11. On Mahone's knowledge of the consolidation see A. A. Grorud to Mahone, 16

June 1932; J. Hubert Smith, Hualapai attorney, to Collier, 9 June 1932, both in Walapai file, box 42, RG 46, NA. For Mahone's optimism and appreciation of white support see his letter to the people of Mohave County, reprinted in "Gratitude of Indians Told by Wallapais," *Mohave County Miner,* 18 March 1932, 1, 8, and Mahone to Collier, 18 June 1932, box 42, RG 46, NA; for Brosius's contribution see Brosius to Frazier, 27 February 1932, in ibid. Collier, "Forced Departure of Herbert J. Hagerman. Eighteen Hualapais held a meeting approving the hiring of counsel. Fred Mahone eighteen others (with thumbmarks) to Brosius, 13 April 1932, 27 February 1932, box 42, RG 46, NA.

12. "Minutes of a Meeting of Hon. Chas. J. Rhoads, Commissioner of Indian Affairs, with Walapai Indians at Peach Springs, Arizona, July 12, 1932," p. 3, CCF 31229-23-313, pt. 3, folder 1/3, box 27, RG 75, NA.

13. Testimony of Honga, Huya, and Annie Beecher, as well as Richard Mcgee's statement concerning ruins as proof of Hualapai occupancy, in "Minutes of a Meeting of Hon. Chas. J. Rhoads, Commissioner of Indian Affairs, with Walapai Indians at Peach Springs, Arizona, July 12, 1932," p. 3, CCF 31229-23-313, pt. 3, folder 1/3, box 27, RG 75, NA.

14. Testimony of Kate Crozier, ibid., p. 2.

15. Affidavit of Ida C. Crozier, 28 September 1932, Walapai file, box 42, RG 46, NA. See also Ida C. Crozier to [?], 5 July 1932, reel 49, PIRA. Deposition of Jim Smith, 17 August 1929, 7, Deposition of Mike Sue, 17 August 1929, 6, and Deposition of John Smith, 15 August 1929, 8–10, 21, 23, all in *United States of America v. The Atchison, Topeka, and Santa Fe Railway Company,* Equity No. 139, Phoenix Area Office, Accession #NRHL-075-00-115, folder 3/5, box 30b, RG 75, Laguna Niguel, NA. For the eastern bands of the Hualapais hiding out in the canyons that flow toward the Colorado River see Henry F. Dobyns and Robert C. Euler, "A Brief History of the Northeastern Pai," *Plateau* 32.3 (1960): 54–55.

16. Remarks of Charles Rhoads, in "Minutes of a Meeting," 7. Brosius thought Rhoads was heavily influenced by Hagerman; see Brosius to Sniffen, 29 July 1932. On Rhoads's ridicule see Brosius to Sniffen, 14 September 1932, both on reel 49, PIRA. Brosius and Rhoads had known each for some time. Recall that Rhoads was the former president of the IRA and that Brosius had worked for the organization since the late nineteenth century. Brosius's assessment of Rhoads must be taken seriously.

17. On the IRA's increased interest in the case see an untitled resolution calling for the consent decree to be set aside and for a suit to be filed on behalf of the Hualapais, 9 June 1932, reel 47, PIRA. Brosius to Sniffen, 13 June 1932; for "so many angles" see Brosius to Sniffen, 17 June 1932; for "revolve around" see Brosius to Sniffen, 18 June 1932; for "it is the land" see Brosius to Sniffen, 17 June 1932; on Brosius being encouraged see Brosius to Sniffen, 18 June 1932; for "should make no admission" see Brosius to Sniffen, 24 June 1932, all on reel 49, PIRA.

18. Brosius to Mahone, 23 June 1932; Brosius to Sniffen, 19 July 1932, both on reel 49, PIRA.

19. Mahone to Brosius, 28 June 1932, reel 49, PIRA. On Hualapais' traveling to trade on the Fourth of July see author interview with Jeanie Jackson, 26 September 2002, Peach Springs, Arizona.

20. Mahone to Brosius, 28 June 1932, reel 49, PIRA. On the Hualapais' fighting with their enemies see the nine war tales depicting clashes between the Hualapais and the

Yavapais that are collected in E. W. Gifford, *Northeastern and Western Yavapai* 34.4 (Berkeley: University of California Publications in American Archaeology and Ethnology, 1942); see also "The Walapai and the Havasupai Raid the Yavapai," in Leslie Spier, *Havasupai Ethnography* (New York: Anthropological Papers of the American Museum of Natural History, 1928), vol. 29, pt. 3, 386–69.

21. Matthew K. Sniffen, "Notes on the Walapai Controversy," n.d. (written concerning his visit of July 21–27, 1932, to the reservation), box 42, RG 46, NA. See also Sniffen to Brosius, 25 July 1932, reel 49, PIRA. And see "The Walapai Controversy," *Indian Truth,* September, 1932, 2–4. Sniffen had also spent July 12 on the reservation and had a day-long meeting with the Hualapais at which they related the news of the discouraging meeting with Rhoads. Sniffen to Brosius, 13 July 1932, reel 49, PIRA.

22. Mahone to Jonathan M. Steere, President of the IRA, 26 August 1932, reel 49, PIRA.

23. "Agreement for Employment of Attorneys," 16 November 1932, reel 49, PIRA.

24. Ray A. Brown, "The United States of America's New Departure in Dealing with Its Native Indian Population," *Journal of Comparative Legislation* 18 (1936): 129. All the Indian Congresses have now been compiled and published as *The Indian Reorganization Act: Congresses and Bills,* ed. Vine Deloria Jr. (Norman: University of Oklahoma Press, 2002). On Mahone's visit to Phoenix see Mahone to Edgar Howard, Committee on Indian Affairs, 20 March 1934, CCF 14654-34-313 — Truxton, box 29, RG 75; and on the conference itself see "Phoenix Congress," 15–16 March 1934, entry 1011, CCF 4894-34-066, part 1-B, box 2, RG 75, NA, Records of the Indian Organization Division, Records Concerning the Wheeler-Howard Act, 1933–1937 (hereafter Wheeler-Howard Records). A delegate from Truxton Canyon, presumably Mahone, attended the meeting, but the minutes appear to be incomplete, for at the end of the meeting delegates from each of the reservations made speeches, and the last one, by a delegate from the Colorado River reservation, is left incomplete. Thomas Biolsi, *Organizing the Lakota: The Political Economy of the New Deal on the Pine Ridge and Rosebud Reservations* (Tucson: University of Arizona Press, 1992), 75–76. For the radical opposition to the IRA see Laurence M. Hauptman, "The American Indian Federation and the Indian New Deal: A Reinterpretation," *Pacific Historical Review* 52.2 (1983): 378–402.

25. Indiana [*sic*] Commissioner to A. C. Monahan, 3 March 1934, telegram, CCF 4894-34-066/part 11-C, folder 2/2, box 10, Wheeler-Howard Records.

26. For Mahone's having read Collier's essays about Hagerman and the Hualapais' fight for the their land see Mahone to Collier, 18 June 1932, reel 49 PIRA; as recently as January 1933 the American Indian Defense Association advocated the return of the entire reservation. "The Walapai Indians' 400,000 Acres," *American Indian Life,* bulletin no. 21, January 1933, 32. Hobgood to CIA, 20 July 1933, CCF 31229-23-313, pt. 3, folder 1/3, box 27, RG 75, NA; Kate Crozier to AG, 2 February 1933, #2272735, folder 4, box 3944, RG 60, NA.

27. Mahone to Collier, 4 May 1933, CCF 31229-23-313, pt. 3, folder 1/3, box 27, RG 75, NA; Mahone to AG, 8 May 1933, #227235, folder 4, box 3944, RG 60.

28. Collier pointed out that (1) "the Atchison, Topeka, and Santa Fe Railroad has no just and legal claim for any land within the present Walapai Reservation"; (2) "all patents issued to the Atchison, Topeka, and Santa Fe Railroad to lands west of the reservation

and in the old Walapai territory (and perhaps in the Mojave territory) should be cancelled as illegally issued"; (3) "the United States is entitled to recover from the railroad the money received by it for such lands patented to it and sold by it"; and (4) "the railroad is entitled to lieu lands, and entitled also to reimbursement of $30,000 paid by it in 1920–22 for the land survey of the Walapai Reservation." Collier's demands, including his request for a solicitor's opinion, are found in "Memorandum to the Secretary: Walapai Reservation (Arizona) Land Matter," 2 August 1933, CCF 31229-23-313, pt. 3, folder 1/3, box 27, RG 75, NA. See also Harold Ickes, "Memorandum to the Solicitor," 3 August 1933, file 5 106, Peach Springs, box 1500, RG 48, NA. For "plans for the development" see Collier to Hobgood, 9 August 1933, CCF 31229-23-313, pt. 3, folder 1/3, box 27, RG 75, NA.

29. Mahone wrote two very similar letters to Collier, both dated sometime in January 1934, Casebier Collection, Mohave Desert Archives, Goffs Schoolhouse, Essex, Calif. (hereafter Casebier Collection).

30. The details of the Mahone-Miller relationship come from a number of documents in the Casebier Collection. Their correspondence might have started earlier than 1930, but that is the date of the first letter. See Fred Mahone to A. P. Miller, 28 November 1930. On preserving the Hualapai past see Miller to Mahone, 15 February 1934, Casebier Collection.

31. Mahone told Miller in a letter that he would be using "all of [his] photos before a legal Representatives who hold the Walapai land and water question"; Mahone to Miller, 28 November 1930. For the commentary on the hearings and concern about being fired see Miller to Mahone, 17 March 1932, both in Casebier Collection.

32. For the addition of Long Mesa see Barbara J. Morehouse, *A Place Called Grand Canyon: Contested Geographies* (Tucson: University of Arizona Press, 1996), 56. Michael F. Anderson's *Living at the Edge: Explorers, Exploiters and Settlers of the Grand Canyon Region* (Grand Canyon, Ariz.: Grand Canyon Association, 1998) is an excellent history of the rise of tourism and development in general at the canyon; for the history of the Santa Fe at the Grand Canyon see Al Richmond, *Cowboys, Miners, Presidents and Kings: The Story of the Grand Canyon Railway* (Flagstaff, Ariz.: Grand Canyon Railway, 1989). Although distinctly not a history of tourism at the Grand Canyon see also Stephen J. Pyne, *How the Canyon Became Grand: A Short History* (New York: Viking Penguin, 1998), esp. 117–39.

33. For the quotation see Santa Fe Railroad and Harveycars, *Indian Detours Through New Mexico and Arizona* (Chicago: Rand McNally, 1930), 47. The Atchison, Topeka, and Santa Fe and the Fred Harvey Company pioneered tourism in the Southwest, offering trips through timeless wilderness. The relation between the two, and their role in inventing the "Indian Southwest," though interesting, has been written about by many authors and is not part of the focus of this book, except in a tangential way. See Leah Dilworth, *Imagining Indians in the Southwest: Persistent Visions of a Primitive Past* (Washington, D.C.: Smithsonian Institution Press, 1996); Kathleen Howard, Diana F. Pardue, and the Heard Museum, *Inventing the Southwest: The Fred Harvey Company and Native American Art* (Flagstaff, Ariz.: Northland, 1996); T. C. McLuhan and William E. Kopplin, *Dream Tracks: The Railroad and the American Indian, 1890–1930* (New York: Abrams,

1985); Diane Thomas, *The Southwestern Indian Detours: The Story of the Fred Harvey/ Santa Fe Railway Experiment in Detourism* (Phoenix: Hunter, 1978); Marta Weigle, "Exposition and Mediation: Mary Colter, Erna Fergusson, and the Santa Fe/Harvey Popularization of the Native Southwest, 1902–1940," *Frontiers* 12.3 (1991): 117–50; Marta Weigle, "From Desert to Disney World: The Santa Fe Railway and the Fred Harvey Company Display the Indian Southwest," *Journal of Anthropological Research* 45 (1989): 115–37; Marta Weigle, Barbara A. Babcock, and the Heard Museum, *The Great Southwest of the Fred Harvey Company and the Santa Fe Railway* (Phoenix: Heard Museum, 1996). For a history of the relation between Fred Harvey and the ATSF see Keith L. Bryant, *The History of the Atchison, Topeka, and Santa Fe Railway* (New York: MacMillan, 1974), 106–22.

34. Santa Fe Railway, *Indian Detours* (1930), 1 (for archaeology), 19 (for the remaining quotations), 31–32 (for the map); Santa Fe Railway, "Conquest: The Story of the Santa Fe and the Men Who Built It," n.d., Santa Fe Pamphlets, the Bancroft Library, University of California, Berkeley.

35. For the suggestion of a billboard see Miller to Mahone, 12 November 1930; on Diamond Creek see Mahone to Miller, 18 January 1932; for the quotations see Mahone to Miller, 28 November 1930, all in Casebier Collection. In March 1883, only two months after the Atlantic and Pacific arrived in Peach Springs, Julius and Cecilia Farlee had opened a stage line down Peach Springs canyon, leading tourists to their modest hotel. After about a decade, the hotel closed. Anderson, *Living at the Edge,* 38–39; George Wharton James, *In and Around the Grand Canyon: The Grand Canyon of the Colorado River in Arizona* (Boston: Little, Brown, 1900), 207.

36. For a brief history of the Hualapais' relations with Grand Canyon National Park and Colorado River management see Robert H. Keller and Michael F. Turek, *American Indians and National Parks* (Tucson: University of Arizona Press, 1998), 141–48.

37. "A Proposition to Assist the People of the Walapai Indian Tribe to Become Self Supporting * * * * Our Unerring Aim," n.d., Casebier Collection.

38. For the quotation see Mahone to Miller, 18 January 1932, and for the Madwida plans see Mahone to Miller, 29 March 1932, both in the Casebier Collection.

39. On the dissent see Mahone to Miller, January 1934, and Miller to Mahone, 16 January 1934, both in the Casebier Collection.

40. Mahone to Miller, 28 November 1930, Casebier Collection.

41. Beginning in 1933, the BIA started running Indian Emergency Conservation Work and Civilian Conservation Corps — Indian Division work crews on the reservation as a way to employ out-of-work Hualapais, teach them skills, and do a variety of conservation projects. See Jeffrey Shepard, "Building an American Indian Community: The Hualapai Nation in the Twentieth Century" (Ph.D. diss., Arizona State University, 2002), 176–86; Hualapai Livestock and Protective Association to CIA, 30 March 1934, and Mahone to CIA, 8 May 1934, both in CCF 23135-34-310 — Truxton Canyon, box 25, RG 75, NA.

42. Mahone to CIA, 8 May 1934, CCF 23135-34-310 — Truxton Canyon, box 25, RG 75, NA. Collier temporarily put the matter to rest when he wrote Mahone that the railroad would not sell the land around Clay Springs. Only if the Hualapais and the BIA

agreed to the consolidation agreement would the railroad hand over the deed to Clay Springs. And the BIA was not going to do that, so Mahone was not to worry. Collier to Mahone, 3 July 1934, CCF 23135-34-310 — Truxton Canyon, box 25, RG 75, NA.

43. Fielding to Collier, 19 May 1934, and Wattson to Collier, 12 June 1934, both in CCF 26880-34-155 — Truxton Canyon, box 9, RG 75, NA.

44. Hobgood to Collier, 9 August 1934, CCF 39903-34-260 — Truxton Canyon, box 22, RG 75, NA.

45. Superintendent Guy Hobgood reported to Collier that there was little dissent about accepting the IRA; most Hualapais were in favor of the legislation, and discussions of it appeared to be causing few rifts among tribe members. See Hobgood to Collier, 12 May 1934, Records of the Wheeler-Howard Act, part 3-C, folder 1/1, box 5, RG 75, NA; Resolution of the Walapai Livestock and Protective Association (signed by Ray Parker, president; Swim Fielding, vice president; Carl Amis, secretary/treasurer), 10 February 1934, Records of the Wheeler-Howard Act, 4894-34-066,part 1-A, folder 7/8, box 1, RG 75. In an interview Jacob Honga remembered that the elders agreed to form a tribal council, presumably under the IRA (because he was discussing the Indian New Deal), only after it was clear that the council would help fight the land case. Interview with Jacob Honga, 12 August 1968, p. 746, Prescott College Hualapai Oral Tradition Project, Prescott, Arizona. For the Hualapais' unwillingness to vote for the IRA and Mahone's influence see Hobgood to Collier, 7 July 1934, Records of the Wheeler-Howard Act, pt. 12-A, folder 4/4, box 11; for the Hualapais' reluctance and desire for Collier to come personally to the reservation see Hobgood to Collier, 25 June 1934, CCF 32244-34-013 — Truxton, box 1, both in RG 75, NA. The Secretary of the Interior approved the Hualapais' constitution on 17 December 1939; see the state-by-state chart showing dates of approval for tribal charters and constitutions, 16 October 1939, in Records of the Wheeler-Howard Act, pt. 12-C, box 12, RG 75, NA. For a fuller discussion of the IRA and the Hualapais, including the details of their eventual acceptance of the bill, see Shepard, "Building an American Indian Community," 188–92.

46. "Wallapais to Celebrate Return of Indian Lands." The newspaper clipping in the Mohave County Historical Society has no name or date, but from the font it appears to be from the *Mohave County Miner,* and from the content it seems to have been published a week or so before the events of the weekend of 19 May 1934. Details of this event also come from a participant. Informant A, interview with author, Peach Springs, 23 September 2002.

Chapter 10. Building a Case

1. Felix Frankfurter to Senator Bronson Cutting, 11 January 1933, Nathan R. Margold Personnel File (hereafter Margold File), Federal Personnel Records Center, St. Louis, Mo., on file with the author. On Margold's fitness for the job see also "The Little Cabinet," *Survey,* May, 1933, 208. On lawyers during the New Deal generally see Jerold S. Auerbach, *Unequal Justice: Lawyers and Social Change in America* (New York: Oxford University Press, 1976), 158–231. Auerbach discusses Margold and the NAACP, for example, at 213–14; for Margold's work for the NAACP, including a summary of the so-called Margold Report (which argued that attacking the constitutionality of segregation

was misguided and that showing how segregation as practiced was illegal—because separate but equal facilities were inherently *not* equal—was the better strategy), see Mark V. Tushnet, *The NAACP's Legal Strategy Against Segregated Education* (Chapel Hill: University of North Carolina Press, 1988), 15–17. Tushnet again stresses Margold's importance in the history of civil rights for African Americans in *Making Civil Rights Law: Thurgood Marshall and the Supreme Court, 1936–1961* (New York: Oxford University Press, 1994), 12. See also Richard Kluger, *Simple Justice: The History of* Brown v. Board of Education *and Black America's Struggle for Equality* (New York: Vintage, 1975), 133–38.

2. Nathan R. Margold, "A BILL to create an Indian claims commission to provide for the powers, duties, and functions thereof, and for other purposes," in *Indian Claims Against the Government: Survey of Conditions of the Indians in the United States,* pt. 25, 72nd Cong., 1st sess. (Washington, D.C.: Government Printing Office, 1932). For a clear delineation of the series of bills and proposals designed to take care of Indian claims, that finally resulted in passage of the Indian Claims Commission Act in 1946, see Harvey D. Rosenthal, "The Evolution of the Indian Claims Commission," in *Their Day in Court: A History of the Indian Claims Commission* (New York: Garland, 1990), 47–109. For details of Margold's career see "Nathan R. Margold: Record," in Margold File; see also Elmer R. Rusco, *A Fateful Time: The Background and Legislative History of the Indian Reorganization Act* (Reno: University of Nevada Press, 2000), 164–65; Kluger, *Simple Justice,* 138. Margold also kept his hand in African-American affairs. Working for the NAACP, he took *Nixon v. Condon*—a white primary suit from Texas—to the Supreme Court in 1932. *Nixon* v. *Condon,* 286 U.S. 73 (1931).

3. Nathan R. Margold, "The Plight of the Pueblos," *Nation,* 4 January 1931, 121. Hanna and Margold worked together on an appeal for a writ of certiorari in the case of *Pueblo de San Juan v. United States,* 47 F.2d 446 (1931), cert. was denied, 284 U.S. 626 (1931).

4. Nathan R. Margold, Solicitor of the Department of the Interior, "Memorandum to the Secretary," 9 October 1924, pp. 148–52, file #5 106, Peach Springs, box 1500, RG 48, NA. For a contemporaneous examination of the problem of accommodating business or corporate interests instead of those of Indians, especially with regard to land rights, see Ray A. Brown, "The Indian Problem and the Law," *Yale Law Journal* 39.3 (1930): 307–31.

5. Margold, "Memorandum to the Secretary," 68 (for the quotaton); see also 41–42, 44–65. Before the passage of the Indian Claims Commission Act in 1946, expert testimony from anthropologists or historians had been heard only three times in the Court of Claims. Nancy Oestreich Lurie, "The Indian Claims Commission Act," *Annals of the American Academy of Political and Social Science* 311 (May 1957): 60. On the relative novelty of using expert testimony in claims cases see Donald C. Gormley, "The Role of the Expert Witness," *Ethnohistory* 2.4 (1955): 326–46; see generally Lawrence Rosen, "The Anthropologist as Expert Witness," *American Anthropologist* 79.3 (1977): 555–78. For some legal scholars, not needing formal recognition by Congress is the most important feature of the Hualapais' eventual victory in the Supreme Court. See Charles Wilkinson and John M. Volkman, "Judicial Review of Indian Treaty Abrogation: 'As Long as Water Flows, or Grass Grows Upon the Earth'—How Long Is That?" *California Law Review* 63 (1975): 617.

6. On knowing nothing about Indians see Dalia Tsuk, "The New Deal Origins of American Legal Pluralism," *Florida State University Law Review* 29 (2001): 213; on Cohen see Felix S. Cohen Personnel File, Federal Personnel Records Center, St. Louis, Mo., on file with the author; Jill E. Martin, " 'A Year and Spring of My Existence': Felix S. Cohen and the Handbook of Federal Indian Law," *Western Legal History* 8 (1995): 35–60; Jill E. Martin, "The Miner's Canary: Felix S. Cohen's Philosophy of Indian Rights," *American Indian Law Review* 23 (Summer 1999): 165–79; Martin P. Golding, "Realism and Functionalism in the Legal Thought of Felix S. Cohen," *Cornell Law Review* 66.5 (1981): 1032–57; Joel R. Cornwell, "From Hedonism to Human Rights: Felix Cohen's Alternative to Nihilism," *Temple Law Review* 68 (Spring 1995): 197–221; Stephen M. Feldman, "Felix S. Cohen and His Jurisprudence: Reflections on Federal Indian Law," *Buffalo Law Review* 35.2 (1986): 479–525; Stephen Haycox, "Felix S. Cohen and the Legacy of the Indian New Deal," *Yale University Library Gazette* 68.3–4 (1994): 135–56. Dalia Tsuk has recently argued in two articles that Cohen's legal philosophy was deeply influenced by pluralism, which led him, after his work with Indians, to try to create a more pluralistic, tolerant society. Dalia Tsuk, "Pluralisms: The Indian New Deal as a Model," *Margins* 1 (2001): 393; and especially Dalia Tsuk, "The New Deal Origins of American Legal Pluralism." See also Edward A. Purcell Jr., *The Crisis of Democratic Theory: Scientific Naturalism and the Problem of Value* (Lexington: University Press of Kentucky, 1973).

7. For "revolutionary" see Vine Deloria Jr. and Clifford M. Lytle, *The Nations Within: The Past and Future of American Indian Sovereignty* (Austin: University of Texas Press, 1984), 159; for a discussion of the opinion see 158–61. Ralph Johnson contends, probably with little argument from anyone, that before Cohen's work no such field existed. Ralph Johnson, " 'In Simple Justice to a Downtrodden People': Justice Douglas and the American Indian Cases," in *"He Shall Not Pass This Way Again": The Legacy of Justice William O. Douglas,* ed. Stephen L. Wasby (Pittsburgh: University of Pittsburgh Press, 1990), 191. On Cohen's writing the opinion see Fred Kirgis to Cohen, n.d., folder 11, box 8, FSC, in which Kirgis congratulates Cohen on a job well done. For the quotation about Cohen see David H. Getches, Charles F. Wilkinson, and Robert A. Williams, *Cases and Materials on Federal Indian Law,* 4th ed. (St. Paul: West, 1998), 201–2. For "the most basic principle" see "Powers of Indian Tribes," 10 October 1934, in *Decisions of the Department of the Interior,* vol. 55, October 1, 1934–September 9, 1936 (Washington, D.C.: Government Printing Office, 1938), 19 (emphasis in original); for "regulate the use" see ibid., 66.

8. Russell Barsh and James Youngblood Henderson have written that "[a]ll subsequent developments in doctrine must be measured from this foundation." Barsh and Henderson, *The Road: Indian Tribes and Political Liberty* (Berkeley: University of California Press, 1980), 111. Charles Wilkinson agrees, stating that Cohen's work regarding sovereignty "lays the conceptual outlines" for the field of federal Indian law. Charles Wilkinson, *American Indians, Time, and the Law: Native Societies in a Modern Constitutional Democracy* (New Haven: Yale University Press, 1987), 62. For the beginning of modern sovereignty and the distinction between inherent and delegated powers see Deloria and Lytle, *Nations Within,* 160.

9. Legal realism has inspired a vast literature among legal scholars, virtually none of it

recognizing the movement's effects on Indian law. Discussions of legal realism include Morton Horwitz, *The Transformation of American Law, 1870–1960: The Crisis of Legal Orthodoxy* (New York: Oxford University Press, 1992), 169–212; Laura Kalman, *Legal Realism at Yale, 1927–1960* (Chapel Hill: University of North Carolina Press, 1986). Joseph Singer provides the best one-sentence summation available: "By arguing against the practice of deducing rules from abstractions, the realists hoped to focus attention on the facts of specific cases and to understand the development of law in terms of situation types." Joseph Singer, "Legal Realism Now," *California Law Review* 76 (1988): 500. For the Cohen quotation see Felix Cohen, "Petition to the Congress and the President of the United States, Requesting Disapproval of H.R. 1113, the so-called Indian Emancipation Bill," 1948, Correspondence Files, folder 5, box 36, Records of the Association on American Indian Affairs, Seeley Mudd Library, Princeton University (hereafter AAIA).

10. Brown, "Indian Problem and the Law," 327. For "we must recognize" and "vital question" see the thirty-page memo that Cohen wrote concerning Indian affairs in folder 139, box 10, FSC. On voting rights in particular see Memorandum from Nathan Margold to SOI, 13 August 1937, folder 74, box 6, FSC, in which Margold recommends a test case in at least three of the states that prohibited Indians from voting: Arizona, Colorado, Idaho, New Mexico, North Carolina, Utah, and Washington. When the Supreme Court of New Mexico claimed that it had sovereignty over Indian affairs when the U.S. Constitution was silent, Cohen called the court's view "clearly erroneous." Cohen to Collier, 29 February 1940, folder 65, box 5, FSC. The establishment of tribal councils and tribal governments during the New Deal has been much criticized. For the standard critique see Graham Taylor, *The New Deal and American Indian Tribalism* (Tucson: University of Arizona Press, 1980), 63–118; for a detailed discussion of the Indian New Deal generally and of tribal government specifically that largely shares my view of Cohen, see Thomas Biolsi, *Organizing the Lakota: The Political Economy of the New Deal on the Pine Ridge and Rosebud Reservations* (Tucson: University of Arizona Press, 1992); for a study that sees the Indian New Deal governments as having, on balance a positive effect, see Paul C. Rosier, *The Rebirth of the Blackfeet Nation, 1912–1954* (Lincoln: University of Nebraska Press, 2001). For "as I have already" see Cohen to Roubideaux, 3 May 1940, folder 65, box 5, FSC; for the government's not doing enough see Cohen's notes of 20 October 1938, and 5 November 1938, on a draft of a statement on the history of Indian policy by John Collier, folder 138, box 10, in ibid.

11. Felix S. Cohen, "Anthropology and Indian Administration," in *The Legal Conscience: The Collected Papers of Felix Cohen*, ed. Lucy Kramer Cohen (New Haven: Yale University Press, 1960), 218 (for the first quotation), 213–14 (for the second) (originally published in the *Southwestern Social Science Quarterly* 18.2 (1937): 1–10). See also Lawrence C. Kelly, "Anthropology and Anthropologists in the Indian New Deal," *Journal of the History of the Behavioral Sciences* 16 (1980): 6–24; William H. Kelly, "Applied Anthropology in the Southwest," *American Anthropologist* 56.4 (1954): 709–14.

12. See Wilcomb E. Washburn and Bruce E. Trigger, "Native Peoples in Euro-American Historiography," in *The Cambridge History of the Native Peoples of the Americas,* vol. 1, *North America,* pt. 2, ed. Bruce G. Trigger and Wilcomb E. Washburn (New York: Cambridge University Press, 1996), 61–124, esp. 97–100; Kerwin Lee Klein, *Frontiers of*

Historical Imagination: Narrating the European Conquest of Native America, 1890–1990 (Berkeley: University of California Press, 1997), 144–48. Klein writes that "Indian history after [Frederick Jackson] Turner's dissertation scarcely existed. . . . For most historians they were an anachronism dispensed with in an introductory paragraph or chapter" (144). For another measure of the paucity of historical work being done by professional historians see William N. Fenton, "The Training of Historical Anthropologists in America," *American Anthropologist* 54.3 (1952): 328–39. For the lack of influence of anthropological work on historians see Richard L. Haan, "Another Example of Stereotypes on the Early American Frontier: The Imperialist Historians and the American Indian," *Ethnohistory* 20.2 (1973): 143–52, esp. his discussion of Charles M. Andrews's work in the 1930s on 148–49. For the twentieth-century exceptions see Ellen H. Fitzpatrick, "Native Americans and the Moral Compass of History," in *History's Memory: Writing America's Past, 1890–1990* (Cambridge: Harvard University Press, 2002), 98–140. Fitzpatrick's efforts to uncover the historians who wrote about Indians is to be commended, yet despite her good work I argue that Indians were largely left out of historiographical consciousness; Klein's work makes this evident. Fitzpatrick's analysis is limited to work that was strictly historical and does not take into account anthropologists who did historical work, such as John Swanton. For the Kroeber quotation see Alfred L. Kroeber, "The Work of John R. Swanton," in *Essays in Historical Anthropology of North America,* Published in Honor of John R. Swanton, Smithsonian Miscellaneous Publications (Washington, D.C: Smithsonian Institution, 1940), 6.

13. For my account of structural functionalism I have relied on Marvin Harris, "British Social Anthropology," in *The Rise of Anthropological Theory: A History of Theories of Culture* (New York: Crowell, 1968). For a contemporary critique of this school see Robert Lowie, *The History of Ethnological Theory* (New York: Holt, Rinehart, Winston 1937), 228–48. For the ways in which a structuralist view of the aboriginal world became hegemonic and was woven into contemporary debates about aboriginal title in Australia, thus locking Aborigines into *a* way of being and of using land, see Patrick Wolfe's discussion of Radcliffe-Brown in *Settler Colonialism and the Transformation of Anthropology: The Politics and Poetics of an Ethnographic Event* (London: Cassell, 1999), 190–204. For a critique offered by one of their British contemporaries see E. E. Evans-Pritchard, *Anthropology and History: A Lecture* (Manchester, U.K.: University of Manchester Press, 1961); see also Nicholas Thomas, *Out of Time: History and Evolution in Anthropological Discourse* (Cambridge: Cambridge University Press, 1989). Although Boas's legacy is that of a historicist, Kroeber did not see him that way, thinking that his methodology was very narrowly historical and really more functional. See Alfred L. Kroeber, "Science and History in Anthropology," *American Anthropologist* 37.4 (1935): 539–69, esp. 541. For a contemporary view of the functionalist-historicist debate see the exchange between Leslie White and Alfred Kroeber: Leslie A. White, "History, Evolutionism, and Functionalism: Three Types of Interpretation of Culture," *Southwestern Journal of Anthropology* 1 (1945): 221–248; Alfred L. Kroeber, "History and Evolution," *Southwestern Journal of Anthropology* 2 (1946): 1–15. Redfield is quoted in George Stocking, "Ideas and Institutions in American Anthropology: Thoughts Toward a History of the Interwar Years," in *The Ethnographer's Magic and Other Essays in the History of Anthropology* (Madison: University of Wisconsin Press, 1992), 140. On structure as it was

found see John W. Burton, "Shadows of Twilight: A Note on the History of the Ethnographic Present," *Papers of the American Philosophical Society* 132 (1988): 420–33. Burton's is a superb intellectual history of the notion that primitive peoples have no history but simply lived in one never-changing moment — the ethnographic present.

14. Kroeber, "Science and History in Anthropology," 548, 550–51.

15. On the importance of narrative and the creation of historical consciousness see Michael Harkin, "History, Narrative, and Temporality: Examples from the Northwest Coast," *Ethnohistory* 35.2 (1988): 99–130, esp. 101.

16. On Hanna's work sorting out Pueblo land titles see Hanna to A. A. Jones, telegram, 6 December 1920; Hanna to Cato Sells, CIA, 6 December 1920, Richard H. Hanna Personnel File, Federal Personnel Records Center, St. Louis, Mo. (hereafter Hanna Personnel File), all on file with the author. For Hanna's AIDA work see Lawrence C. Kelly, *The Assault on Assimilation: John Collier and the Origins of Indian Policy Reform* (Albuquerque: University of New Mexico Press, 1983), 195, 340; John Collier, *From Every Zenith: A Memoir, and Some Essays on Life and Thought* (Denver: Sage, 1963), 159. On Collier's approaching Hanna, see Collier to Hanna, 7 September 1935, frame 972, #148, reel 13, JCP.

17. After hearing from the Board of Supervisors of Coconino County, Arizona, which advocated consolidation because it feared losing tax revenues if more Indian land was created, Hayden reiterated to Collier his interest in the matter. See "Resolution of the Board of Supervisors of Coconino County," in Board of Supervisors to Hayden and Ashurst, 6 May 1935, CCF 31229-23-313, pt. 3, folder 1/3, box 27, RG 75, NA; Hayden to Collier, 22 May 1935, in ibid. Collier responded to Hayden by saying that there was evidence that the Hualapais had been long-term occupants of the land and thus he could not say what would come of the consolidation; see Collier to Hayden, 15 June 1935, in ibid.

18. For the complexity of the case and the Justice Department's opinion of the hiring of Hanna see Harry W. Blair, Asst. AG, "Memorandum for Mr. McMahon," 1 November 1935, Hanna Personnel File; for the quotations and the recommendation of Hanna see Ickes to AG, 29 October 1935, file #5 106, Peach Springs, box 1500, RG 48, NA. Ickes's letter to the AG parrots the recommendation made by Assistant Solicitor Frederick Bernays Wiener, "Memorandum for the Under Secretary: Re: Walapai (Hualpai) Indians," 11 October 1935, CCF 31229-23-313, pt. 3, folder 1/3, box 27, RG 75, NA; for background on Hanna and for Collier's promotion of his fitness for the job see Collier to Wiener, 12 October 1935, and for Collier's informal offer and Hanna's acceptance, contingent on being formally offered the position, see Collier to Hanna, 12 October 1935, and Hanna to Collier, 15 October 1935, both in ibid. For endorsements from Dennis Chavez and Carl Hatch see Hanna Personnel File; for the formal offer see Harry Blair, Asst. AG to Hanna (telegram), 20 December 1935, and for Hanna's acceptance see Hanna to Blair (telegram), 20 December 1935, both in #227235, folder 5, RG 60, NA. On coming to Washington see Hanna to Collier, 21 December 1935, CCF 31229-23-313, pt. 4, folder 2/2, box 27, RG 75, NA. For "Gabriel's trumpet" see Hanna to Collier, 31 March 1941, Collier correspondence, box 14, RHP. The sixty or so boxes that make up Hanna's papers are unprocessed and have no finding aid. Unfortunately, they contain little that is related to the case.

19. On being in touch with Light see Hanna to Stewart, 15 June 1936, in CCF 31229-23-313, pt. 4, folder 2/2, box 27, RG 75, NA. For "lack of complete records" see Hanna to Blair, 15 April 1936, and for "long lapse" see Hanna to J. M. Stewart, Director of Lands for the BIA, 24 March 1936, in ibid.; on previous interest in claiming nonreservation land see, e.g., J. M. Stewart to Hobgood, 4 January 1936, in which Stewart mentions that Justice had in mind an alternative strategy, namely, claiming land outside the reservation, for the exact nature of the confusion over Peach Springs see William Zimmerman, Asst. CIA to Fred Johnson, General Land Office, 10 April 1936, in ibid. The 1931 consent decree located the spring at sections 2 and 3, T25N, R11W, Gila & Salt River Meridian, but "it is now proposed that this decree be set aside on the ground that the springs are actually located in section 34, T26N, R11W, and section 14, T25W, R11W"; Hanna to Stewart, 25 March 1936, in ibid.

20. Sworn statement of Tomanata, 21 January 1936, CCF 4466-36-175.2 — Truxton Canyon, box 12, RG 75, NA. For Fielding's statement see Robert Marshall to CIA, 11 October 1935, CCF 56499-35-301 — Truxton Canyon, box 24, RG 75, NA.

21. Ibid. Statement of Jim Smith, 25 January 1936, and Statement of Indian Huya, n.d. but filed with others from January and February, Entry 824, 1936, Records Concerning U.S. v. Santa Fe Pacific Railroad Company, 1919–1943, box 2, RG 48, NA.

22. On early settlers see, e.g., Deposition of John Bozarth, 26 October 1937, pp. 37–39, folder 2, box 38, RG 21 (Records of the District Court of the United States for the District of Arizona), Laguna Niguel, Pacific Region, NA. On the Hualapais' urging Hanna to visit see Hanna to Blair, 29 April 1936, and on Hanna's visit see Hanna to Stewart, 28 May 1936, both in #227235, folder 6, box 3945, RG 60, NA. The Grounds and Matuthania statements are found in Ruth D. Kolling to Walter Woehlke, Chief of Operations, Project for Technical Cooperation with the Bureau of Indian Affairs, 8 April 1936, Project Records, 1936–1939 — Hualapai, Records of the Soil Conservation Service, RG 114, NA. Indian Sampson's statement is found in an unlabeled statement taken by Katherine Grounds, 27 April 1936, translated by Fred Mahone, Entry 824, Records Concerning U.S. v. Santa Fe Pacific Railroad Company, 1919–1943, box 2, RG 48, NA. On Hanna's growing interest see Hanna to Stewart, 15 June 1936, CCF 31229-23-313, pt. 4, folder 2/2, box 27, RG 75, NA. Hanna wrote to Stewart again that same day and reiterated his interest in looking into the possibility that the survey was faulty.

23. Hanna to Blair, 15 June 1936, #227235, folder 6, box 3945, RG 60, NA; on the search for army files see Oscar Chapman, First Asst. SOI to Sec. of War, 22 June 1936, file #5 106, Peach Springs, box 1500, RG 48, NA; on being discouraged see Hanna to Blair, 20 July 1936, and on the lack of a survey in the army's records see Secretary of War to SOI, 22 July 1936, both in CCF 31229-23-313, pt. 4, folder 2/2, box 27, RG 75, NA.

24. Joseph F. Schaffhausen, "Report on the Investigation of the Alleged Western Boundary of the Hualapai Indian Reservation," 28 September 1936, Entry 824, Records Concerning U.S. v. Santa Fe Pacific Railroad Company, 1919–1943, box 2, RG 48, NA. The troubled relations between Willis and the Hualapais have a lengthy history that dates back to at least 1917, when Willis may have absconded with some Hualapai horses and cattle. The details are beyond the scope of this project. See esp. L. F. Michael, special supervisor, to Mather Willis, 14 February 1918, alleging that Willis approved of non-Indian leases that the Hualapais specifically did not want, that Willis did not account for

all cattle in the spring roundup of 1917 and on being accused of this by the Hualapais used profane and abusive language against them, and that Willis used government saddle horses to do work on his own ranch, in L. F. Michael, Inspection Report, 19 February 1918, Inspection Division, Inspection Reports, 1908–40, entry 953, box 70, RG 75, NA. The report affidavits against Willis by Metuck and Jim Fielding, among others.

25. Hanna received the report in October from Hobgood and read it in December; see Hobgood to Hanna, 21 October 1936, Hanna to Collier, 1 December 1936, and, for the quotation, Hanna to Frank Chamber, Asst. AG, 4 March 1937, all in CCF 31229-23-313, pt. 4, folders 1/2 and 2/2, box 27, RG 75, NA; "Memorandum[:] Hualapai Controversy," 28 August 1936, PSFFC.

26. Hanna to Collier, 16 October 1936, CCF 31229-23-313, part 4, folder 2/2, box 27, RG 75, NA (first quotation); for "trunks and boxes" see Oscar Chapman, Asst. SOI to Secretary of War, 4 May 1936, file 5106 Peach Springs, box 1500, RG 48, NA; for the quotation about occupancy in Hanna to Frank Chambers, Asst. AG, 4 March 1937, CCF 31229-23-313, pt. 4, folder 1/2, box 27, RG 75, NA; on having enough to prove occupancy see Hanna to Collier, 12 March 1937, CCF 31229-23-312, pt. 5, folder 3/3, box 28, RG 75, NA; Hanna to Harlow Akers, 28 May 1928, file #227235, folder 6, box 3945, RG 60, NA.

27. Richard Hanna, 7 May 1937, "Memorandum for Carl McFarland, Assistant Attorney General, Re: Proposed Case of United States of America, as Guardian of the Indians of the Tribe of Haulpai [sic] in the State of Arizona, vs. The Santa Fe Pacific Railroad Company," CCF 31229-23-313, pt. 5, folder 3/3, box 28, RG 75, NA.

28. For the dissent see H. S. Julian, 12 May 1937, "Memorandum for Mr. Collett, Re: Walapai Tribe Matter," CCF 31229-23-313, pt. 5, folder 3/3, box 28, RG 75, NA; for Collier's ambivalence about which route to take see Collier to Collett, 13 May 1937, 31229-23-313, pt. 4, folder 1/2, box 27, RG 75, NA.

29. Hanna to J. M Stewart, director of lands, BIA, 26 May 1937, CCF 31229-23-313, pt. 4, folder 1/2, box 27, RG 75, NA. On the continuing efforts of Hanna's assistant to prove occupancy inside and outside the reservation see Harlow H. Akers to Hanna, 28 May 1937, file 227235, folder 7, box 3945, RG 60, NA; 2 June, 1937; 4 June 1937; 17 June 1937; and W. C. LeFebvre, "Memorandum" on the sources of Cataract Creek and Santa Maria River, 17 June 1927, all in folder containing data and correspondence, box 27b, Phoenix Area Office, Accession #NRHL-075-00-115, RG 75, NA, Pacific Region, Laguna Niguel, CA.

30. On employing Tucker see Fay Cooper-Cole to Tucker, 30 October 1936, and on her keeping secret her affiliation with the railroad and her subsequent embarrassment, see Tucker to Charles Woods, attorney for the Santa Fe, 2 February 1937, both in box 1, MS-183-0, SJTP. Tucker's research, though thorough in most respects, was mistaken in one regard. She claims to have interviewed Hualapai medicine man Dr. Tommy in February 1938; see "Dr. Tommie, 2/15/38," box 1, SJTP. But Dr. Tommy, according to his gravestone, died in 1931; see photograph of the gravestone in the author's possession. On turning the railroad down see Leslie Spier to Carl Hayden, 27 March 1937, folder 40, box 620, Indian Affairs, ser. 1, CHP; for the Spier quotation, which was in reference to the railroad's request, see Spier to Hanna, 27 September 1938, folder "misc. correspondence," box 29c, Phoenix Area Office, Accession #NRHL-075-00-115, RG 75, NL, NA.

Bolton to Cox, 13 April 1937, box 150, outgoing correspondence, BANC MSS C-B 840, pt. 2; Herbert Eugene Bolton, "Garces's Route from the Colorado River to Kingman," n.d., in "Garces Notes and Drafts," carton 19, BANC MSS C-B 840, pt. 3, both in HEBP. On Bolton's influence and legacy see David Weber, "Turner, the Boltonians, and the Spanish Borderlands," in *Myth and the History of the Hispanic Southwest* (Albuquerque: University of New Mexico Press, 1988); Hargrave, "Preliminary Report on the Joint Expedition of the A.T.S.F. Ry. and the Museum of Northern Arizona," Summer 1938, SJTP.

31. On Hayden's welcoming the railroad to examine his files as he compiled *The Walapai Papers* see Paul Roca, Hayden's assistant, to E. J. Engel, 15 July 1936, folder 40; for "I had it prepared" see Hayden to Mrs. J. M. Keith, Secretary, Arizona Cattle Growers Association, 12 November 1943, folder 7, both in box 620, Indian Affairs, ser. 1., CHP; Cohen quotation in Abe Barber and Felix Cohen, "Examiners' Report on Tribal Claims to the Released Railroad Lands in Northwestern Arizona," *Hualapai Tribe of the Hualapai Reservation, Arizona v. The United States of America,* Indian Claims Commission Docket No. 90, box 1055, RG 279 (Records of the Indian Claims Commission), 12. For passing on documents to the Santa Fe see Hayden to Cox, 25 January 1938; for keeping in touch with Tucker see Tucker to Roca, 20 April 1937; for helping with her research see Hayden to Tucker, 16 November 1937, all in folder 40, box 620, Indian Affairs, ser. 1, CHP. For offering "all of the assistance of my office" see Hayden to E. L. Jameson, 20 February 1941, folder 17, box 649, Interior, ser. 1, CHP.

32. On Hanna's frustration with the Justice Department and his threat to resign see Allan Harper to Oliver LaFarge, 29 June 1937, folder 16, box 359, AAIA. On the railroad's problems with the complaint and its desire for further clarification of details see Hanna to Joyce Cox, Law Department, ATSF, 24 September 1937; Hanna to Collier, 25 September 1937; Cox to Hanna, 15 October 1937, including the railroad's "Motion for Further Particulars"; Charles West, Under SOI to AG, 22 October 1937, all in CCF 31229-23-313, pt. 4, folder 1/2, box 27, RG 75, NA. On the railroad's refusal to relinquish title see Carl McFarland, Asst. AG to Collier, 28 October 1937, in ibid. On the SOI's unwillingness to acquiesce to the railroad see Oscar Chapman, Asst. SOI, to AG, 26 November 1937, file 5 106, Peach Spring, box 1500, RG 48, NA. The Justice Department, too, rejected the railroad's offers of a compromise; see McFarland to Hanna, 1 December 1937, file 227235, folder 7, RG 60, NA. On filing the motion to dismiss see Hanna to AG, 31 January 1938, Cox to Hanna, 29 March 1938, and Hanna to J. M. Stewart, 1 April 1938, all in 31229-23-313, pt. 4, folder 1/2, box 27, RG 75, NA.

33. "Excerpts from Brief of Defendant Santa Fe Pacific Railroad in Support of Its Motion to Dismiss the Complaint," in RBSC, 134–35.

34. "Memorandum of Points and Authorities in Support of Defendant's Motion to Dismiss Plaintiff's Complaint," RBSC, 30, 38–39, 39.

35. Ibid., 67, 68, 73, 84.

36. Hayden to Joyce Cox, 9 May 1938, folder 40, box 620, Indian Affairs, ser. 1, CHP.

37. Quoted in "Conway Charges U.S. Land 'Steal' Attempt," *Arizona Republic,* 18 August 1938.

38. For "assuming" see Hanna to Collier, 6 May 1938, CCF 31229-23-313, pt. 4, folder 1/2, box 27, RG 75, NA.

39. Hanna to AG, 19 April 1938, file 227235, folder 7, box 3945, RG 60, NA.

40. On the motion see Hanna to Collier, 1 August 1938, CCF 31229-23-313, pt. 4, folder 1/2, box 27, RG 75, NA; on Hanna's confidence in his ability to have the motion rejected see Hanna to Collett, Asst. AG, file 227235, folder 8, box 3945, RG 60, NA.

41. On the five days spent arguing see Hanna to Collett, 23 August 1938, file 227235, folder 8, box 3945, RG 60, NA; see also Hanna to Collier, 23 August 1938, CCF 31229-23-313, pt. 5, folder 3/3, box 28, RG 75, NA. Hayden communicated with his staff via government-rate telegram, asking them to secure copies from government files of Senate Committee land hearings to be sent by airmail to the railroad's attorney during the hearing. Hayden to Dix W. Price, 10 August 1938, folder 40, box 620, Indian Affairs, ser. 1, CHP.

Chapter 11. The Case in Court

1. Carl Hayden to Joyce Cox, 1 March 1939 (telegram), and Hayden to Cox, 3 March 1939, both in folder 40, box 620, Indian Affairs, ser. 1, CHP. For Collier's initial reaction see Collier to Hanna, 6 March 1939, CCF 31229-23-313, pt. 5, folder 3/3, box 28, RG 75, NA. For "like tenpins," see Testimony of John Collier, 25 March 1939, in "California Indians Jurisdictional Act," *Hearings Before the Committee on Indian Affairs,* House, 76th Cong., 1st sess., 17.

2. Judge David Ling, "Supplemental Order and Opinion," 6 March 1939, CCF 31229-23-313, pt. 5, folder 3/3, box 28, RG 75, NA.

3. For the Justice Department's agreement to take the case and the Littell quotation see Norman Littell, "Memorandum for the Solicitor," 31 May 1939, #5 106, Peach Springs, folder 10, box 3945, RG 60, NA; for his about-face see Littell, "Memorandum for the Solicitor General: Recommending Dismissal of Appeal Taken to the Circuit Court of Appeals for the Ninth Circuit," #227235, 23 June 1939, folder 10, box 3945, RG 60, NA.

4. For the importance of the case see Oscar Chapman, Asst. SOI, to AG, 28 June 1939, file 5 106, box 3534, RG 48, NA; for the quotation see Chapman to AG, 11 July 1939, in ibid.

5. For "adverse and uncooperative" see Collier to Hanna, 28 June 1939, ser. 2, subser. 148, reel 13, JCP. Littell, "Memorandum for the Solicitor General: Recommending That the Appeal Taken to the Circuit Court of Appeals for the Ninth Circuit Be Prosecuted," #227235, 30 June 1939, folder 12, box 3946, RG 60, NA. For "good deal of fighting" see Collier to Hanna, 6 July 1939, reel 13, JCP. On the solicitor general's deciding to appeal see C. W. Leaphart, chief of appellate section, "Memo for Collett," #227235, 12 July 1939, folder 12, box 3946, RG 60, NA.

6. Norman MacDonald, "Memorandum for C. R. Denny, Acting Chief, Appellate Section, RE: United States v. Santa Fe Pacific Railway Company," 5 October 1939, #227235, folder 12, box 3946, RG 60, NA.

7. MacDonald, "Memorandum for the Files, RE: The United States v. Santa Fe Pacific Railroad Company," 5 December 1939, #227235, folder 12, box 3946, RG 60, NA. MacDonald also urged that the government abandon two other points on appeal, saying that they were important to the case but had little bearing on the larger issues of Indian

title. He argued that the government should not try to prove that the railroad forfeited its right to the land when it failed to live up to the original terms of its grant—specifically, by not complying with its construction schedule. Likewise, he wanted the government to abandon its attempt to prove that the Hualapais had title based on adverse possession.

8. On Hanna's wanting to stay involved and implying, when he told Littell how long it took the mail to go from Albuquerque to San Francisco, where the Ninth Circuit is, that he was prepared to send his own version of the brief, see Hanna to Littell, 7 December 1939; for Littell's bypassing Hanna and mailing the brief directly from Washington see Littell to Hanna (telegram), 11 December 1939, both in folder 12, box 3946, RG 60, NA; Hanna to Collier, 30 December 1939, reel 13, JCP; Edward Kemp, Asst. to the AG, to Hanna, 13 and 15 December 1939, Richard H. Hanna Personnel File, Federal Personnel Records Center, St. Louis, Mo.

9. On the Justice Department and canceling his trip see Hanna to Edward Kemp, Asst. to the AG, 2 January 1940, Hanna Personnel File. For the "burden of the thing" see Hanna to Collier, 30 December 1939; Hanna to AG, 2 January 1940; Collier to Hanna, 8 January 1940, all on reel 13, JCP.

10. Hanna to Collier, 12 January 1940; see also William Brophy to Collier, 13 January 1940, in which he criticizes the Justice Department's lack of familiarity with the facts in the case, expresses dismay that the District Court took so much on judicial notice, and makes clear that the only person who knows Hualapai history well enough to argue for occupancy is Hanna, both in CCF 31229-23313, pt. 4, folder 1/3, box 28, RG 75, NA.

11. On retaining Hanna see Collier, "Memorandum to the Secretary of the Interior," 19 January 1940, reel 13, JCP. For the Collier quotations see Collier to Ickes, 6 February 1940, #5 106, Peach Springs, box 3534, RG 48, NA. For the Margold quotations see Margold to Collier, 20 January 1940, reel 13, JCP. Hanna to Littell, 2 February 1940, folder 13, box 3846, RG 60, NA.

12. Cox to Hayden, 21 December 1939, folder 17, box 649, CHP.

13. On authorizing Hanna to travel to Los Angeles and participate in oral argument see Hanna to Littell, 13 March 1940, #227235, folder 13, box 3946, RG 60, NA; see also Littell to Hanna (telegram), 18 March 1940; on MacDonald helping see Littell to Hanna, 14 March 1940; Hanna to Littell (telegram), 15 March 1940, all in ibid. See also Richard H. Hanna, "Hanna Memorandum on Presentment of Walapai Case to the Circuit Court of Appeals, March 29, 1940, at Los Angeles," folder titled "appeal," box 27a, Phoenix Area Office, Accession #NRHL-075-00-115, RG 75, NL, NA. On rehiring Hanna to aid Justice in its appeal to the Ninth Circuit—although there is little or no evidence that Hanna actually influenced the DOJ—see Robert Jackson to Hanna, 31 January 1940, and for termination once oral argument was completed see Jackson to Hanna, 8 April 1940, both in Hanna Personnel File.

14. Like Littell and MacDonald before him, Judge Wilbur, the judge for the Ninth Circuit Court, placed great stock in *Buttz v. Northern Pacific Railroad*,. 119 U.S. 55 (1886). The opinion in this case said that the Northern Pacific possessed the fee title to its grant merely because of the grant, and the government's brief argued that *Buttz* controlled the Hualapai case. The court and the DOJ attorneys failed, however, to recognize the difference between the present case and *Buttz*. The Atlantic and Pacific's grant made clear that title could only be extinguished with the consent of the Indians. But because the court agreed that the title passed to the railroad subject to the Hualapais' original Indian

title, Wilbur asked, did the Hualapais have the right of occupancy? Of course, they could only have the right of occupancy if they had in fact occupied the land. The court conceded that tribes had Indian title to all land actually occupied by them at the time they came under the sovereignty of the United States, and, further, that said title was good against all but the government — with one exception. Respecting Indian title had been the "common practice [of the government] in dealing with tribes occupying lands other than lands within the area ceded by Mexico." Why? Because, in effect, the court said so. "[S]ince the whole of the Indians' title depends entirely upon the policy of the federal government, it is obvious that what may have seemed the best policy in dealing with Indians in territories acquired prior to the treaty of Guadalupe Hidalgo might not have seemed the best policy in dealing with Indians occupying the area ceded by Mexico." But what was that alternate policy? The court cited two cases — *Bates v. Clark.*, 95 U.S. 204 (1877), and *Spaulding v. Chandler*, 160 U.S. 394 (1896) — that both upheld the principle that Indians hold title until it is extinguished by the government. Yet neither decision says anything about land ceded by Mexico, and no other authorities are cited. (In a long list of cases the government cited *Spaulding*, too — and also read it wrong. It hoped to use it to show that Indian land was protected by the Treaty of Guadalupe Hidalgo.) *United States, as Guardians of the Indians of the Tribe of Hualapai in the State of Arizona, Appellant v. Santa Fe Pacific Railroad Company, a Corporation, Appellee*, no. 9271, 114 F.2d 420, 422 (1940). For the government's reliance on *Spaulding* see "Brief for the United States," in *Records and Briefs of the Supreme Court* for 114 F.2d 420, pp. 10–11. Neither the government nor the Santa Fe cited *Bates*.

15. "Brief for the United States," 2–6.

16. Ibid.; *Santa Fe Pacific*, 114 F.2d 420, 425–26.

17. On the ways in which certain narratives can become so conventional as to become banal see Jerome Bruner, "The Narrative Construction of Reality," *Critical Inquiry* 18.1 (1981): 1–21, esp. 9; see also Kerwin Lee Klein, "In Search of Narrative Mastery: Postmodernism and the People Without History," *History and Theory* 34.5 (1995): 275–98. The literature on narrative is large. But anyone interested in reading some of the most perceptive work on the power of narratives and the ways in which they are constructed and disseminated should consult Hayden White's *The Content of the Form: Narrative Discourse and Historical Representation* (Baltimore: John Hopkins University Press, 1987) and *Tropics of Discourse: Essays in Cultural Criticism* (Baltimore: Johns Hopkins University Press, 1978).

18. Hayden to Joyce Cox, 6 September 1940, folder 17, box 649, CHP. For Collier's lack of surprise see Collier to Hanna, 10 September 1940, box 14, RHP. For "evidence of the Indians" and "scope" see "Hanna Memorandum on Appeal," n.d., Phoenix Area Office, Accession #NRHL-075-00-115, folder: appeal, box 27c, RG 75, NA, Pacific Region, Laguna Niguel,, Calif.; for Hanna's and Brophy's wish to appeal see Hanna to J. M. Stewart, Director of Lands, BIA, 13 September 1940, and William Brophy to Collier, 16 and 17 September 1940, CCF 31229-23-313, pt. 6b, box 29, RG 75, NA; A. J. Wirtz, Acting Secretary of the Interior, 10 October 1940, file 5 106, box 3534, RG 48, NA.

19. On not knowing Indian history see George T. Stormont to Asst. AG Blair, memo on Indian claims, 3 March 1934, box 11, FSC; for "most unusual" see George T. Stormont, "Memorandum for Attorney General Rugg, Re: S. 4397, S. 4578, H.R. 10927, and H.R. 11925, 72nd Congress, 1st Session," subject file 90-2-20-0, Federal Records Center Car-

ton 119, RG 60, NA. For a history of Indian claims within the Justice Department and the associated costs see Raymond Nagle, "Indians; Claims Against the United States; Nature, Problem, Handling," 25 December 1937, and for the estimated cost to U.S. Treasury of Indian claims, see George T. Stormont, "Memorandum for Mr. Nagle, Re: Indian Tribal Suits in the Court of Claims," both in subject file 90-2-20-0, Federal Records Center carton 119, RG 60, NA. Harvey D. Rosenthal, *Their Day in Court: A History of the Indian Claims Commission* (New York: Garland, 1990), 150–51; Ward Churchill, "Charades Anyone? The Indian Claims Commission in Context," *American Indian Culture and Research Journal* 24.1 (2000): 43–68, esp. 55.

20. Collier to SOI Ickes, 2 February 1940, reel 13, JCP.

21. W. G. Rice, "The Position of the American Indian in the Law of the United States," *Journal of Comparative Legislation and International Law* 16.1 (1934): 90. Much of what follows is based on a superb article by Jill Martin detailing the writing of and battle for the *Handbook of Federal Indian Law.* Jill E. Martin, "'A Year and Spring of My Existence': Felix S. Cohen and the *Handbook of Federal Indian Law,*" *Western Legal History* 8.1 (1995): 35–60. I have done extensive research in the Cohen papers and the files of the Department of the Interior. Cohen's papers contain copies of all the relevant archival material concerning the creation of the *Handbook.* And Martin's article is the only guide necessary for someone interested in its history. Unless otherwise noted I have used Martin's article rather than cite archival material.

22. Littell to AG, 14 April 1939, folder 154, box 11, FSC. On changing the chapter title see Martin, "'A Year and Spring,'" 43–44; the Cohen quotation is at 45.

23. Theodore Haas, "Memorandum for Mr. Cohen, Chief, Indian Law Survey," 20 September 1939, folder 179, box 13, FSC. For the Cohen quotation see Martin, "'A Year and Spring,'" 44. Ickes to AG, 4 December 1939, file 1–142 (general, pt. 3), CCF 1937–53, box 2677, RG 48, NA.

24. For "light cost to pay" see Cohen to Margold, 21 December 1939, folder 181, box 13, FSC.

25. Felix Cohen, "Memo to the Solicitor," n.d., folder 247, box 14, FSC.

26. On moving back to Interior see Martin, "'A Year and Spring,'" 48–55. Margold to Ernest L. Wilkinson, 2[?] May 1940 (Wilkinson was the attorney for several tribes that were suing the government over land claims), and Jackson to Ickes, 2 August 1940, both in box 2677, file 1–142 (general, pt. 3), CCF 1937–53, RG 48, NA.

27. Raymond T. Nagle, "Memorandum for Robt. E. Mulroney, Chief, Trial Section," 14 October 1940, #227235, box 3946, RG 60, NA.

28. Ibid.

29. Norman M. Littell, Asst. AG, "Memorandum for the Solicitor General, Recommending That a Petition for Certiorari Be Filed," 15 October 1940, #227235, box 3946, RG 60, NA.

30. Charles R. Denny, "Memorandum for Norman M. Littell, Assistant Attorney General, RE: Further Developments in the Walapai Indian Case," 23 October 1940, #227235, box 3946, RG 60, NA; see also Collier to Margold, 7 November 1940, CCF 31229-23-313, pt. 6, folder 1, box 28, RG 75, NA; Warner Gardner, handwritten note on Thomas Harris, "Memorandum for the Solicitor General," 25 October 1940, #227235, box 3946, RG 60, NA. For further debate about taking the case to the Supreme Court see

"Memorandum of a Conference held 12/20/40 (Friday) with Hon. Felix Cohen and Hon. Norman McDonald," miscellaneous memo folder, box 27c, Phoenix Area Office, Accession #NRHL-075-00-115, RG 75, NA, Laguna Niguel, Calif.

31. The cases, all heard on appeal from the Court of Claims, are *United States v. Klamath and Moadoc Tribes of Indian et al.*, 304 U.S. 119 (1938) ($5,313,347.32); *United States v. Creek Nation*, 295 U.S. 103 (1935) ($296,011.42); *Shoshone Tribe v. United States*, 299 U.S. 476 (1937) ($4,408,444.23). The case involving the Blackfeet et al. never made it to the Supreme Court, but the judgment, minus offsets, was large nonetheless. *United States v. Blackfeet, Blood, Peigan, Gros Ventre and Nez Perce*, 81 Ct. Cl. 969 (1935) (award: $6,130,874.88; offsets: $5,508,409.31; net: $622,465.57); *Indians of the Fort Berthold Reservation v. United States*, 71 Ct. Cl. 308 (1930) ($2,169,169.58). See also statistical tables in "Creation of Indian Claims Commission," Hearings Before the Committee on Indian Affairs, House of Representatives, 79th Cong. 1st sess., on H.R. 1198 and H.R. 1341, "Bills to Create an Indian Claims Commission, to Provide for the Powers, Duties and Functions Thereof, and for Other Purposes," March 2, 3, and 28, June 11 and 14, 1945, 163–75; E. B. Smith, *Indian Tribal Claims Decided in the Court of Claims of the United States, Briefed and Compiled to June 30, 1947*, 2 vols. (Washington, D.C.: University Publications of America, Inc., 1976; originally compiled by E. B. Smith, Chief, Indian Tribal Claims Section, United States General Accounting Office, 1947).

32. Hayden to E. L. Jameson, Chairman of Public Lands, 20 February 1941. Hayden was responding to Jameson's letter of 14 February; both are in folder 17, box 649, Interior, ser. 1, CHP.

33. Biddle to Hayden, 5 May 1941, in ibid.; see also the discussion of the DOJ's complicated and conflicting role in defending Indians against third parties while defending the government against Indian claims in *Annual Report of the Attorney General of the United States* (Washington, D.C.: Government Printing Office, 1940), 127–29.

34. Thomas Harris, "Memorandum for the Solicitor General, United States v. Santa Fe Pacific Railroad," 25 October 1940, #227235, box 3946, RG 60, NA; Frances B. Sanita, "The Hualpai," *Arizona Highways*, September 1941, 30–33.

35. Memo from Pres. Harry S. Truman to Director of the Budget, 25 February 1946, file 78-01-9, 114 — Classified Subject Files, RG 60. (There is no box number; this file was screened and made available to me at the National Archives and placed in a temporary box.)

Chapter 12. The Supreme Court and the Power of History

1. "Petition for Writ of Certiorari to the United States Circuit Court of Appeals for the Ninth Circuit," in *United States of America, as Guardian of the Indians of the Tribe of Hualpai in the State of Arizona vs. Santa Fe Pacific Railroad Company*, RBSC, 4–5.

2. Ibid. For Cohen's thoughts about judicial notice regarding Mexican and Spanish law concerning wandering peoples see "Memorandum of a Conference Held 12/20/40 (Friday) with Hon. Felix Cohen and Hon. Norman MacDonald," folder: miscellaneous memo 2/2, box 27c, Phoenix Area Office, Accession #NRHL-075-00-115, RG 75, PR, Laguna Niguel, NA.

3. For the first quotation see Felix S. Cohen, "Original Indian Title," in *The Legal*

Conscience: The Collected Papers of Felix Cohen, ed. Lucy Kramer Cohen (New Haven: Yale University Press, 1960), 303–4. "Petition for Writ of Certiorari," RBSC, 18. For the myth of the nomadic Indian see Felix Cohen, "Indian Claims," in *The Legal Conscience: Selected Papers of Felix S. Cohen*, ed. Lucy Kramer Cohen (New Haven: Yale University Press, 1960), 267 (originally published in *The American Indian* 2.3 (Spring 1945): 3–11); here he was talking about the decision in *Northwestern Band of Shoshone Indians v. United States* (1945). For the final quotation see "Brief for the United States," RBSC, 95.

4. Felix Frankfurter, "Memorandum to the Conference, Re: No. 717," 7 March 1941, pt. 1, Supreme Court File, box 67, William O. Douglas Papers, Library of Congress.

5. Hayden to AG, 21 March 1941, folder 17, box 649, Interior, ser. 1, CHP.

6. The brief is credited to Hanna, Margold, Brophy, and Cohen. But archival evidence overwhelmingly suggests that Cohen did the bulk of the work. The evidence also suggests that Margold simply served in an advisory capacity, allowing Cohen free reign. For example, Hanna told Collier that he and Brophy would be available to work on the case only through January 1941 (Hanna to Collier, CCF 312229-23-313/6b, box 27, RG 75, NA). Both he and Brophy were back in New Mexico by the spring of 1941, and Hanna was away for two months on vacation. Moreover, by late June 1941 Cohen wrote to Hanna asking whether Hanna and Brophy — still in practice together — had time to read the draft that Cohen had just finished (Cohen to Hanna, 10 July 1941, file #5 106, Peach Springs, CCF 1937, box 3454, RG 48). Other letters written over the summer make it clear that Cohen did most of the work with input from Brophy. In early September Cohen wrote to Brophy and thanked him for some helpful suggestions, apologizing in advance for likely not being able to send Brophy another copy before he submitted it to the Court because he was constantly revising it (Cohen to Brophy, in ibid.). See also Margold to Brophy, in ibid., in which he thanks Brophy for all his help over the years and expresses the hope the final version of the brief, as written by Cohen and Margold, will please him. Some of the best evidence for Cohen's primary role in writing the brief is found in the collection of papers related to the case, in which one will find Cohen's handwritten notes, memos, and so on (Phoenix Area Office, Accession no. NRHL-075-00-115, RG 75, NA, Pacific Region, Laguna Niguel, Calif.). And colleagues such as Ted Haas acknowledged that it was Cohen who took the Hualapai case to the Court and won (Haas, remarks at an Indian Claims Commission memorial service for Cohen, 4 December 1953, folder 1466, box 91, FSC). Of course, Cohen did not write the brief entirely on his own, but establishing Cohen's primary authorship is important because of his role as the acknowledged founder of modern federal Indian law. Few have written about Cohen's casework.

7. "Brief for the United States," RBSC, 96, 97, 101.

8. Ibid., 103, 15.

9. For "savage tribes" see "Respondent's Brief," 4, and for all the evidence see "Respondent's Brief: Appendix: Respondent's Presentation of Treaty and Laws Principally at Issue and Other Matters of Public Record, Part VI," 106–12, both in RBSC.

10. "Respondent's Brief," RSBC, 17, 21, 8, 8–9.

11. Ibid., 11–12, 76.

12. Cohen to Haas, 2 October 1941, folder 381, box 23, FSC. Haas had written a memo regarding occupancy rights of native Alaskans in which he argued, based on *Duwamish v. United States*, 79 Ct. Cl. 530 (1934), that Indians had no property rights other than those granted by the sovereign. I have Cohen's response but not the original memo.

13. Nathan Margold and Joyce Cox to Charles Cropley, clerk, Supreme Court of the United States, 7 November 1941, Appellate Case Files, folder 1, box 2538, Records of the Supreme Court, RG 267, NA. Cropley penciled in the following across the left side of the letter: "grant 15 minutes extra for each side." On the opinion galley in Douglas's papers each of the Justices wrote a brief note approving the opinion. None of them mentioned any significant difficulties in siding with Douglas. "Opinion galley," 1 December 1941, pt. 1, Supreme Court File, folder 2, box 67, William O. Douglas Papers, Library of Congress.

14. Hugo Black, handwritten note on galley of opinion, 1 December 1941, pt. 1, Supreme Court File, folder 2, box 67, William O. Douglas Papers, Library of Congress; *United States, As Guardian of the Hualpai Indians of Arizona, v. Santa Fe Pacific Railroad Co.,* 314 U.S. 339, 343 (1941). The Court misspelled the tribe's name.

15. Ibid., 355.

16. Felix Cohen to Alfred L. Kroeber, 25 February 1942, Entry 824, Records Concerning U.S. v. Santa Fe Pacific Railroad Company, 1919–1943, box 1, RG 48, NA.

17. This is perhaps the opinion's most powerful point; I discuss it in detail in chapter 13. On this point as it applies to Indian law generally see Charles F. Wilkinson, "Insulation Against Time," in *American Indians, Time, and the Law: Native Societies in a Modern Constitutional Democracy* (New Haven: Yale University Press, 1987). On Hualapais' being the twentieth-century affirmation of the Marshall court's Indian title decisions see Gene Bergman, "Defying Precedent: Can Abenaki Aboriginal Title Be Extinguished by the 'Weight of History'?" *American Indian Law Review* 18.2 (1993): 452–453. For a strong critique of the Hualapai decision that takes issue with the application by future courts of a famous line of *dicta* in Douglas's opinion — "whether it is done by treaty, by the sword, the purchase, by the exercise of complete dominion adverse to the right of occupancy, or otherwise, its justness is not open to inquiry in the courts" — see Joseph William Singer, "Well Settled? The Increasing Weight of History in the American Indian Land Claims," *Georgia Law Review* 28 (1994): 481–532. Although Singer's criticism of the decision — which he examined in light of the Vermont Supreme Court's 1991 finding that Abenaki title had been extinguished by the "increasing weight of history," based to an extent on that court's misapplication of some of features of *Hualpai* — is apt in some respects, he does not demonstrate that the Supreme Court was guilty of what he claims: namely, a naked taking of the tribe's title. In fact, Douglas's opinion went a long way toward making it clear that its title had not been extinguished by any kind of clear and unambiguous intent of Congress. Whether the power of Congress is absolute is not the point; it is, however, significant that although Douglas said that Congress's power is supreme it was not exercised in this case, and thus the Hualapais retained aboriginal title. For another view of the *Hualpai* decision, also examined in light of the Abenaki title case and also critical of the misapplication of *Hualpai* but more sympathetic to Douglas's opinion, see John P. Lowndes, "When History Outweighs Law: Extinguishment of Abenaki Aboriginal Title," *Buffalo Law Review* 42 (1994): 77–118.

Chapter 13. In the Wake of Hualpai

1. On Fred Mahone's appointment as aide and interpreter along with Carl Amis, see Minutes of Tribal Council meeting, 4 April 1942, CCF 22376-1937-054, box 3, RG 75, NA. The Cohen quotations are found in Cohen to Edgar Witt, chair of the ICC, 18

November 1950, folder 906, box 57, FSC. Hoping to make an administrative ruling on Hualapai occupancy in advance of a formal Court decision—which, considering the length of time it took the Hualapai case to get to court, could mean many more years of waiting—the Interior Departmentand the BIA dispatched Felix Cohen and Abe Barber, a lawyer from the General Land Office, to Hualapai country. On wanting an administrative ruling first see Joel Daniel Wolfsohn, Asst. Comm. GLO and John Collier, CIA, "Memorandum for the Secretary," 27 January 1942, file #5 106, Peach Springs, box 3534, RG 48, NA. The report filed by Cohen on his investigation was co-authored by Abe Barber. Barber went with Cohen to Hualapai country, but Cohen appears to have directed the hearings. Perhaps Barber helped Cohen write the report but did not otherwise participate. His name never appears in any references to the trip, and after his return to Washington, as the years went by, his name never reappeared. In addition, Hualapais remember Cohen as the one who saved their land, not Barber. My conclusion is that Cohen, based on his prior experience with tribe—writing the brief for the Supreme Court, for example—compiled and wrote the report, presided at the hearings, and was generally responsible for sorting out the Hualapais' claims.

2. Abe Barber and Felix Cohen, "Examiners' Report on Tribal Claims to the Released Railroad Lands in Northwestern Arizona," *Hualapai Tribe of the Hualapai Reservation, Arizona v. The United States of America,* Indian Claims Commission Docket No. 90, box 1055, RG 279 (Records of the Indian Claims Commission), NA.

3. Young Beecher, Exhibit L, Jim Crook, Exhibit CC, Coyote Jim, Exhibit EE, Indian Honga, Exhibit K, all in ibid. Brosius to Mahone, 23 June 1932, and Brosius to Matthew Sniffen, 19 July 1932, both on reel 49, PIRA. The evidence that there were overlapping claims comes from the 1953 testimony that Fred Mahone gave at the hearings regarding the Hualapais' case before the ICC. Mahone said that when the Hualapais and the Havasupais met in 1942 with Barber and Cohen the two tribes agreed that they had no overlapping claims to the land around Pine Springs. Testimony of Fred W. Mahone, 23 July 1953, box 1054, *Hualapai Tribe of the Hualapai Reservation.* Six weeks before Cohen and Barber arrived Collier had written to the Hualapais and urged them to have their stories straight regarding occupation. He did not ask them to make anything up but simply told them to be prepared for the coming hearings. Collier to Ralph M. Gelvin, Supt. Truxton Canyon Agency, 24 February 1942, file #5 106, Peach Springs, box 3534, RG 48, NA. For an excellent discussion of the ways in which property as a concept has impacted indigenous land rights, as well as a concise introduction to the history of property in anthropological discourse, see Paul Nadasdy, "'Property' and Aboriginal Land Claims in the Canadian Subarctic: Some Theoretical Considerations," *American Anthropologist* 104.1 (2002): 247–61; see also Paul Nadasdy, *Hunters and Bureaucrats: Power, Knowledge, and Aboriginal-State Relations in Southwest Yukon* (Vancouver: University of British Columbia Press, 2003), esp. 222–62.

4. Fred W. Mahone to Felix Cohen, 21 May 1942, box 1, Entry 824, Records Concerning U.S. v. Santa Fe Pacific Railroad Company, 1919–1943, Records of the Office of the Solicitor, Records of the Department of the Interior, RG 48, NA.

5. For details of the settlement see David L. Bazelon, "Memorandum for the Attorney General," 26 December 1946 (approved by Bazelon on 6 January 1947), and Judgment, Stipulation and Agreement, both in file #227235, enclosures, FRC carton 13, RG 60, NA. The Hualapais met with an official from the Justice Department in December 1946 and

approved the settlement in council; Martin G. White, Solicitor to Bazelon, 10 December 1946, in ibid. Cohen to William Brophy, 14 March 1947, folder 1350, box 86, FSC.

6. The newspaper clipping was sent with no date or name to Cohen by William Paul. Paul to Cohen, 31 December 1947, folder 1408, box 88, FSC.

7. Felix S. Cohen, remarks at farewell dinner, 17 January 1948, folder 1470, box 92, FSC.

8. Cohen's comments about government's getting out of the way are in Felix Cohen, remarks made at conference on Indian self-government sponsored by the Association on American Indian Affairs, 8 April 1949, folder 2, box 376, Records of the Association on American Indian Affairs Papers, Seeley Mudd Library, Princeton University (hereafter AAIA). For Cohen's thoughts about Indian policy in the termination era see "The Erosion of Indian Rights, 1950–1953: A Case Study in Bureaucracy," *Yale Law Journal* 62.3 (1953): 348–90.

9. Felix Cohen to Alexander Lesser, 18 May 1948, Correspondence Files, Folder 5, box 36, AAIA.

10. For the ICC's decision see 11 Ind. Cl. Comm. 447 (1962), 17 Ind. Cl. Comm. 465 (1966), and 18 Ind. Cl. Comm. 382 (1967), all titled *The Hualapai Tribe of the Hualapai Indian Reservation, Arizona v. The United States of America*, Docket Nos. 90 and 122. For the award see "Providing for the Disposition of Judgment Funds on Deposit to the Credit of the Hualapai Tribe of the Hualapai Reservation, Ariz., in Indian Claims Commission Dockets Nos. 90 and 122, and for Other Purposes," 27 August 1970, S. Rep. no. 91–1147, 91st Cong., 2nd sess. See also Jeffrey Shepard, "Building an American Indian Community: The Hualapai Nation in the Twentieth Century" (Ph.D. diss., Arizona State University, 2002), 265–68.

11. On waiting until the Court decided *Hualapai* to begin litigating Alaska natives' claims see Nathan Margold, "Memo for the Secretary [of the Interior]," 10 February 1942, folder 382, box 42, FSC; for the official opinion see Nathan R. Margold, "Aboriginal Fishing Rights in Alaska," 13 February 1942, in *Decisions of the Department of the Interior, March 1939–June 1942,* ed. Marie J. Turinsky (Washington, D.C.: Government Printing Office, 1945), 57:461–78. For Cohen's authorship of the opinion see Felix Cohen to Sec. of Interior, "Memorandum of Law on the Possessory Rights of Tlingit and Haida Indians[,] February 1942" (draft), 13 February 1942, folder 474, box 30, FSC. The wording of Cohen's draft, and the notes make it clear that Cohen was the author of the opinion. On the effects of this opinion and of the Supreme Court's opinion in *Hualpai* on southeastern Alaskan land rights, and for the quotation about Ickes, see Theodore Catton, "Dispossessing the Natives," in *Land Reborn: A History of Administration and Visitor Use in Glacier Bay National Park and Preserve* (1995). http://www.nps.gov/glba/adhi/adhi6.htm (accessed 17 May 2006). For the importance of the Hualapai case for Alaskan natives' land rights and the for the history of land claims in Alaskan politics and native activism, see Donald Craig Mitchell, *Sold American: The Story of Alaska Natives and Their Land, 1867–1959: The Army to Statehood* (Fairbanks: University of Alaska Press, 2003), esp. 319–20; for the importance of the decision to the Tlingit, the Haida, and the Tongass National Forest see Stephen W. Haycox, "Economic Development and Indian Land Rights in Modern Alaska: The 1947 Tongass Timber Act," *Western Historical Quarterly* 21.1 (1990): 20–46, 26–27.

12. William Paul, In the District Court for the District of Alaska, Territory of Alaska,

Division Number One, at Juneau, *William L. Paul v. Pacific American Fisheries,* Brief of Plaintiff on Defendant's Demurrers to Amended Complaint, 27 February 1942, file #90-2-11-2138, box 13802, RG 60, NA; Paul to Cohen, 3 June 1942, folder 450, box 28, FSC. On the Hualapais as inspiration for Alaskan natives' claims generally and *Tee-Hit-Ton* specifically, see Stephen Haycox, "*Tee-Hit-Ton* and Alaska Native Rights," in *Law for the Elephant, Law for the Beaver: Essays in the Legal History of of the North American West,* ed. John McLaren, Hamar Foster, and Chet Orloff (Regina, Sask.: Canadian Plains Research Center, University of Regina; Pasadena, Calif.: Ninth Judicial Circuit Historical Society, 1992): 127.

13. Nell Jessup Newton, "At the Whim of the Sovereign: Aboriginal Title Reconsidered," *Hastings Law Journal* 31.3 (1980), 1244–45; see also David E. Wilkins, *American Indian Sovereignty and the United States Supreme Court: The Masking of Justice* (Austin: University of Texas Press, 1997), 166–85; Joseph William Singer, "Well Settled? The Increasing Weight of History in American Indian Land Claims," *Georgia Law Review* 28 (1994): 519–527. For further elaboration regarding the narrowness of *Tee-Hot-Ton* see John P. Lowndes, "When History Outweighs Law: Extinguishment of Abenaki Aboriginal Title," *Buffalo Law Review* 42 (1994): 97. Just weeks after the Supreme Court decided *Tee-Hit-Ton Indians v. United States,* 348 U.S. 272 (1955), the Court of Claims ruled in favor of the Otoe and the Missouria Tribes, whose case was on appeal from the ICC. The Court of Claims found that under the provisions of the Indian Claims Commission Act of 1946 the Otoe and the Missouria had compensable claims based on aboriginal, not recognized, title. While not explicitly overturning *Tee-Hit-Ton,* the Supreme Court refused to hear an appeal and let stand the Court of Claims' opinion. See *Otoe and Missouria Tribe of Indians v. United States,* 131 Ct. Cls. 593 (1955). Regarding this case see Berlin Basil Chapman, *The Otoes and Missourias: A Study of Indian Removal and the Legal Aftermath* (Oklahoma City: Times Journal Publishing, 1965), 223–89. For the Justice Department and claims see House Committee on Interior and Insular Affairs, House Unpublished Hearings, *To Terminate the Existence of the Indian Claims Commission,* 84th Cong., 1st sess., May 2, 26–27, July 27, 1955; Senate Committee on Interior and Insular Affairs,, *Terminating the Existence of the Indian Claims Commission,* 84th Cong., 2nd sess., S. Rep. 1727; House Committee on Interior and Insular Affairs, *Terminating the Existence of the Indian Claims Commission,* 84th Cong., 2nd sess., H. Rep. 2719. See also Memorandum to All Clients, from Strasser, Speigelberg, Fried & Frank, "Original Indian Title Amendment to Indian Claims Commission Act," 12 April 1956 and 7 July 1956, frames 901–3, reel 45, JCP. The first memo warned the law firm's clients of the threat the amendment posed; the second relieved them of their concern—H.R. 5566 had failed. They wrote: "The defeat of that amendment is a significant victory, and shows the good that can come when Indians, their friends, and their attorneys make a united appeal to Congress."

14. All sources relating to the ICC note Cohen's role, but for the most thorough discussion see Dalia Tsuk, "The New Deal Origins of American Legal Pluralism," *Florida State University Law Review* 29 (2001): 189–268, esp. 250–63. The best book-length study of the workings of the ICC, whose authors cite all the periodical literature, is Mike Lieder and Jake Page, *Wild Justice: The People of Geronimo vs. the United States* (New York: Random House, 1997). For the most detailed legislative history of the ICC see

Harvey Rosenthal, *Their Day in Court: A History of the Indian Claims Commission* (New York: Garland, 1990). The most thorough review of Indian claims policy in general is Russel Lawrence Barsh, "Indian Land Claims Policy in the United States," *North Dakota Law Review* 58 (1982): 7–82; see also Ward Churchill, "Charades Anyone? The Indian Claims Commission in Context," *American Indian Culture and Research Journal* 24.1 (2000): 42–68. For the DOJ's persistent efforts to stop the ICCA from passing see Frank Chambers, "Memo for [Land] Section Files," 2 April 1946, file 78-01-9. This file was screened and made available to me on 14 August 2002. For an overview of state-sponsored reconciliation efforts, not all involving indigenous people, see Elazar Barkan, *The Guilt of Nations: Restitution and Negotiating Historical Injustices* (New York: Norton, 2000). For a comparison between the ICC and the Waitangi Tribunal in New Zealand (discussed below), see David Wishart, "Belated Justice? The Indian Claims Commission and the Waitangi Tribunal," *American Indian Culture and Research Journal* 25.1 (2001): 81–111. On the influence of ICC-generated anthropological research, as well as a discussion of the ICC's adoption of outdated research, see Arthur J. Ray, "Aboriginal Title and Treaty Rights Research: A Comparative Look at Australia, Canada, New Zealand, and the United States," *New Zealand Journal of History* 37.1 (2003): 5–21.

15. Ralph Barney of the DOJ explained the principles behind the Hualapai case in the introductions to the various volumes of the Garland Publishers series *American Indian Ethnohistory*. See also Ralph Barney, "Legal Problems Peculiar to Indian Claims Litigation," *Ethnohistory* 2.4 (1955): 320. See also Rosenthal, *Their Day in Court*, 146–47. There is a large literature on the origins of the ethnohistory and the historiography of Native America. Most authors note that ethnohistory as a distinct discipline began with the ICC; I am making no claim to originality in that regard. I do think that the date needs to be pushed back in order to acknowledge *Hualapai*'s singular influence on the ICC. Some of the most helpful works are Wilcomb E. Washburn and Bruce E. Trigger, "Native Peoples in Euro-American Historiography," in *The Cambridge History of the Native Peoples of the Americas*, vol. 1, *North America*, pt. 2, ed. Bruce G. Trigger and Wilcomb E. Washburn (New York: Cambridge University Press, 1996), 61–124; James Axtell, "Ethnohistory: An Historian's Viewpoint," in *The European and the Indian: Essays in the Ethnohistory of Colonial Native America* (New York: Oxford University Press, 1981), 3–15; Shepard Krech III, "The State of Ethnohistory," *Annual Review of Anthropology* 20 (1991): 345–75; Francis Jennings, "A Growing Partnership: Historians, Anthropologists and American Indian History," *Ethnohistory* 29.1 (1982): 21–34; Melissa L. Meyer and Kerwin Lee Klein, "Native American Studies and the End of Ethnohistory," in *Studying Native America: Problems and Prospects,* ed. Russell Thornton (Madison: University of Wisconsin Press, 1999), 183–216; Kerwin Lee Klein, *Frontiers of Historical Imagination: Narrating the European Conquest of Native America, 1890–1990* (Berkeley: University of California Press, 1997), esp. 129–85. Klein's book is essential reading for understanding the intellectual history of the writing of Indian history. On property see Nadasdy, " 'Property' and Aboriginal Land Claims." One can only imagine the chaos that would have been caused by a book such as James Brooks's *Captives and Cousins: Slavery, Kinship, and Community in the Southwest Borderlands* (Chapel Hill: University of North Carolina Press, 2002) if his thesis concerning the ever-shifting, never stable identity of Indians in the past had been published during the ICC years. A statement like the follow-

ing, entered as part of expert witness testimony, would have been totally mystifying to the Claims Commissioners — and, I might add, terribly unhelpful to both sides in land claims disputes. "A focus on the tensions and resolutions within a universally adoptive indigenous culture raises the possibility that native North America before the advent of political 'tribes' might have been more than a patchwork landscape of families and bands. Rather, the adoptive impulse wove a vast web of interethnic tensions and alliances that constituted a social formation equal in territorial scale and social complexity to that of Europe" (366). For a concise summary of the Navajo-Hopi land dispute as a construction of the American courts and government and not a historical dispute between the Navajo and Hopi, see Eric Cheyfitz, "The Navajo-Hopi Land Dispute: A Brief History," *Interventions* 2.2 (2000); see also David Brugge, *The Navajo-Hopi Land Dispute: An American Tragedy* (Albuquerque: University of New Mexico Press, 1994); Emily Benedek, *The Wind Won't Know Me: A History of the Navajo-Hopi Land Dispute* (New York: Random House, 1992). For one example of the ICC's effects on Indians see Pamela S. Wallace, "Indian Claims Commission: Political Complexity and Contrasting Concepts of Identity," *Ethnohistory* 49.4 (2002): 743–67, which deals with the conflicting claims of the Yuchi and the Creeks. For more examples of the problems associated with conflicting claims outside the United States see Adam Kuper, "The Return of the Native," *Current Anthropology* 44.3 (2003): 389–404.

16. The first case to cite *Hualpai* was *Pawnee Tribe of Indians v. United States,* 1 Ind. Cl. Comm. 230 (19xx). *Pawnee* then became the basis for other cases using the ruling laid down in *Hualpai. Mohave Tribe of Indians of Arizona, California, and Nevada v. United States,* 7 Ind. Cl. Comm. 219, 260 (1959), called *Hualpai* a "landmark case," in part because it made it impossible for the United States, in defending itself, to make the claim that hunting and gathering peoples living in the territory ceded to the United States by the Treaty of Guadalupe Hidalgo had no land rights. It might be useful to distinguish between anthropological or evidentiary use of *Hualpai* and its use by the judges.

17. Barney, "Legal Problems Peculiar to Indian Claims Litigation," 317, 320, 321; Barney to Voegelin, 29 August 1956, DOJ file #90-2-20-0, box 1, Justice Department Correspondence, Great Lakes–Ohio Valley Ethnohistorical Research Project records, 1953–1969, C105, Indiana University Archives, Bloomington, Indiana (hereafter GLOVERP).

18. Verne F. Ray, "Introduction to Anthropology and the Indian Claims Litigation: Papers Presented at a Symposium Held at Detroit in December, 1954," *Ethnohistory* 2.4 (1955): 287–91; for quotations see 287, 288. Before the passage of the Indian Claims Commission Act in 1946, expert testimony from anthropologists or historians had been heard only three times in the Court of Claims. Nancy Oestreich Lurie, "The Indian Claims Commission Act," *Annals of the American Academy of Political and Social Science* 311 (May 1957): 60; on the relative novelty of using expert testimony in claims cases see also Donald C. Gormley, "The Role of the Expert Witness," *Ethnohistory* 2.4 (1955): 326–46; and see generally Lawrence Rosen, "The Anthropologist as Expert Witness," *American Anthropologist* 79.3 (1977): 555–78; Julian H. Steward, "Theory and Application in a Social Science," *Ethnohistory* 2.4 (1955): 293. For new questions concerning land tenure, and Kroeber's thoughts in particular, see Ray, "Aboriginal Title and Treaty Research," 6.

19. Alfred L. Kroeber, "Nature of the Land-Holding Group," *Ethnohistory* 2.4 (1955): 314.

20. Steward's theoretical work and its influence on his work for the DOJ are described in Sheree Ronaasen, Richard O. Clemmer, and Mary Elizabeth Rudden, "Rethinking Cultural Ecology, Multilinear Evolution, and Expert Witnesses: Julian Steward and the Indian Claims Proceedings," in *Julian Steward and the Great Basin: The Making of an Anthropologist,* ed. Richard O. Clemmer, L. Daniel Myers, and Mary Elizabeth Rudden (Salt Lake City: University of Utah Press, 1999), 170–202.

21. For an excellent discussion of Kroeber's and Steward's work on land claims, as well as larger issues associated with research and claims, see Arthur J. Ray, "Aboriginal Title and Treaty Rights Research" and "Native History on Trial: Confessions of an Expert Witness," *Canadian Historical Review* 84.2 (2003): 255–73.

22. Robert A. Manners, "Tribe and Tribal Boundaries: The Walapai," *Ethnohistory* 4.1 (1957): 5.

23. Julian Steward, quoted in Barney to Voegelin, 9 June 1955, box 1, GLOVERP.

24. Robert A. Manners, "The Land Claims Cases: Anthropologists in Conflict," *Ethnohistory* 3.1 (1956): 78; Nancy O. Lurie, "A Reply to the Land Claims Cases: Anthropologists in Conflict," *Ethnohistory* 3.3 (1956): 260; for Barney's coments on the supply of experts see Barney to Ermine [*sic*] and Jay, 25 May 1955, and on the changes in anthropology see Barney to Voegelin, 4 April 1956, both in box 1, GLOVERP.

25. Current commentators might be right in suggesting that non-U.S. courts' reliance on U.S. precedent is faulty, but it was nonetheless important historically. For the notion that the Australian Supreme Court's reliance on the *Hualpai* case's doctrine of extinguishment of aboriginal title does not apply to Australia despite the high court's frequent citations to it in *Mabo,* see Kent McNeil, "Extinguishment of Native Title: The High Court and American Law," in *Emerging Justice? Essays on Indigenous Rights in Canada and Australia* (Saskatoon, Sask.: Native Law Centre, University of Saskatchewan, 2001), 409–15. For the inapplicability in general of American law to common-law jurisdictions, based on the notion that conquest was the prevailing method of acquiring land in the original thirteen colonies and thus irrelevant to places where "peaceful settlement" occurred, see Geoffrey S. Lester, "The Territorial Rights of the Inuit of the Canadian Northwest Territories: A Legal Argument" (D.Jur. diss., : York University, York, Ont., 1981), vol. 1. See also Kent McNeil's reservations about the applicability of American law outside the United States in *Common Law Aboriginal Title* (Oxford: Clarendon, 1989), 244–67. For the continued sharing of precedents, see Julie Cassidy, "Aboriginal Title: 'An Overgrown and Poorly Excavated Archeological Site'?" *International Legal Perspectives* 10 (1998): 39–110; Shaunnaugh Dorsett and Lee Godden, *A Guide to Overseas Precedents of Relevance to Native Title* (Canberra: Native Title Research Institute, Australian Institute of Aboriginal and Torres Strait Islander Studies, 1998); Ronald Sackville, "The Emerging Australian Law of Native Title: Some North American Comparisons," *Australian Law Journal* 74.12 (2000): 820–43. In *Hamlet of Baker Lake et al. v. Minister of Indian Affairs and Northern Development et al.,* 107 D.L.R. (3d) 513 (1979), a Canadian federal court said: "The value of early American decisions to a determination of the common law of Canada as it pertains to aboriginal rights is so well established in Canadian Courts, at all levels, as not now to require rationalization." The court specifically cited the Hualpai case. For a good discussion that explicitly recognizes the global trade in claims law as it applies to New Zealand see Ken S. Coates, "International Perspectives

on Relations with Indigenous Peoples," in *Kōkiri Ngātahi: Living Relationships: The Treaty of Waitangi in the New Millennium,* ed. Ken S. Coates and P. G. McHugh (Wellington, N.Z.: Victoria University Press, 1998).

26. *Calder v. Attorney General of British Columbia,* [1973] SCR 313, 391; *Mabo and Others v. The State of Queensland,* 107 ALK 1 (1992); *Delgamuukw v. British Columbia,* 3 SCR 1010 (1997). On *Hualpai* as the "leading modern judgment" in the common law before the explosion of aboriginal title litigation in Australia and Canada, see Gordon I. Bennett, "Aboriginal Title in the Common Law: A Stony Path Through Feudal Doctrine," *Buffalo Law Review* 27.4 (1978): 621; for a fuller discussion of post-*Hualpai* American claims, including the eastern land claims cases of the 1970s, among others, see Christian W. McMillen, "Rewriting History and Proving Property Rights: Hualapai Indian Activism and the Law of Land Claims in the Twentieth Century" (Ph.D. diss., Yale University, 2004), chap. 9. A great deal has been written about both *Mabo* and *Delgamuukw,* much of it legal commentary; for a comprehensive history of *Delgamuukw* that includes a thorough history of aboriginal title in Canada, see Dara Culhane, *The Pleasure of the Crown: Anthropology, Law and First Nations* (Burnaby, B.C.: Talonbooks, 1998). For a history of the *Mabo* case see Nonie Sharp, *No Ordinary Judgement: Mabo, The Murray Islanders' Case* (Canberra: Aboriginal Studies Press, 1996); Peter H. Russell, *Recognizing Aboriginal Title: The* Mabo *Case and Indigenous Resistance to English-Settler Colonialism* (Toronto: University of Toronto Press, 2005); Andrew Delbanco, "Canadian Indians Win a Ruling Vindicating Oral History," *New York Times,* 9 February 1998, A1.

27. For Australia see Bain Attwood, *Rights for Aborigines* (Crows Nest, N.S.W.: Allen & Unwin, 2003); Bain Attwood and Andrew Markus, *The Struggle for Aboriginal Rights: A Documentary History* (Crows Nest, N.S.W.: Allen & Unwin, 1999); Heather Goodall, *Invasion to Embassy: Land in Aboriginal Politics in New South Wales, 1770–1972* (Crows Nest, N.S.W.: Allen & Unwin, 1996); McMillen, "Rewriting History and Proving Property Rights," chap. 9. For New Zealand see Claudia Orange, *The Treaty of Waitangi* (Wellington, N.Z.: Allen & Unwin, 1987). For Canada see Paul Tennant, *Aboriginal Peoples and Politics: The Indian Land Question in British Columbia, 1849–1989* (Vancouver: University of British Columbia Press, 1990), 96–113; Daniel Raunet, *Without Surrender, Without Consent: A History of the Nishga Land Claims* (Vancouver: Douglas & McIntyre, 1984), and the sources cited in chapter 8 of this book, especially the work of Hamar Foster.

28. For the comparison to the Nazis and the Day of Mourning see Attwood, *Rights for Aborigines,* 23, 69–74. For "out Hitlering Hitler" see William Copper to the Chief Secretary or Minister for Native Affairs, Western Australia, 17 July 1938, quoted in Attwood and Markus, *Struggle for Aboriginal Rights: A Documentary History* (Crows Nest, N.S.W.: Allen & Unwin, 1999), 155–56. See also Goodall, *Invasion to Embassy.*

29. In the wake of *Mabo* a tremendous amount of work has been done on the role of history in Australian life and politics, especially as it relates to aboriginal land rights. For Australian historical writing and the absence of Aborigines see Richard Broome, "Historians, Aborigines, and Australia: Writing the National Past," and for the best discussion of the discourse of history in Australia and its effects on Aboriginal politics see Bain Attwood, "Introduction," both in Bain Attwood, ed., *In the Age of* Mabo: *History,*

Aborigines and Australia (Crows Nest, N.S.W.: Allen & Unwin, 1996), vi–xxxviii. For ideas about history in Australia and how they have impacted Aborigines and consciousness about the past see also Tom Griffiths, *Hunters and Collectors: The Antiquarian Imagination in Australia* (Melbourne: Cambridge University Press, 1996); for anthropological writing about Aborigines and how it led to a denial and eventual recognition of land rights see L. R. Hiatt, *Arguments About Aborigines: Australia and the Evolution of Social Anthropology* (Cambridge: Cambridge University Press, 1996), 13–35.

30. On Pittock see Attwood, *Rights for Aborigines*, 286–88; Interview with Barrie Pittock, 16 November 1996, Federal Council for the Advancement of Aborigines and Torres Strait Islanders, Oral History Project, MS 4009, Australian Institute of Aboriginal and Torres Strait Island Studies, Canberra. For the influence of Cohen on Pittock's views see A. Barrie Pittock, "Aboriginal Land Rights," in *Racism: The Australian Experience,* ed. F. S. Stevens (New York: Taplinger. 1972), 188–208, esp. 190. Bain Attwood has found that beginning in the 1930s reform-minded Australians involved in aboriginal affairs were heavily influenced by John Collier and the policies of the Indian New Deal generally. There is evidence that Collier, in turn, was influenced by British colonial policy in Africa. See Laurence M. Hauptman, "Africa View: John Collier, the British Colonial Service, and American Indian Policy, 1933–1945," *Historian* 48.3 (1986): 359–74.

31. For the best description of the politics and machinations of getting the case to court see Attwood, *Rights for Aborigines*, 283–306. For an anthropological account that describes Yolngu life, the court proceedings, and European notions of Native title in great depth see Nancy M. Williams, *The Yolngu and Their Land: A System of Land Tenure and the Fight for Its Recognition* (Stanford: Stanford University Press, 1986).

32. *Millirpum and Others v. Nabalco Pty. Ltd and the Commonwealth of Australia,* 17 FLR 141 (1971), at 244. For a good contemporaneous legal discussion of the case that illustrates its novelty at the time see John Hookey, "The Gove Rights Land Case: A Judicial Dispensation for the Taking of Aboriginal Lands in Australia," *Federal Law Review* 5.1 (1972): 85–114; John Hookey, "*Milirrpum* and the Maoris: The Significance of the Maori Lands Cases Outside New Zealand," *Otago Law Review* 3 (1973): 63–75. For a contemporaneous contrary view suggesting that *Johnson v. M'Intosh* was not an authority for common-law native title and thus that *Milirrpum* was decided correctly, see L. J. Priestly, "Communal Native Title and the Common Law: Further Thoughts on the Gove Rights Land Case," *Federal Law Review* 6 (1974): 150–73.

33. *Milirrpum,* 17 FLR, at 216–17, 292. That Blackburn was familiar with *Hualpai* is evident from the fact that he read "Original Indian Title"; Cohen cited *Hualpai* in the first sentence. On the novelty of *Calder* and the lack of knowledge regarding native title in general see K. Lysyk, "The Indian Title Question in Canada: An Appraisal in Light of *Calder,*" *Canadian Bar Review* 51 (September 1973): 450–80.

34. *Hamlet of Baker Lake et al. v. Minister of Indian Affairs and Northern Development et al.,* 107 D.L.R. (3d) 513 (1979), in which the court said: "It is apparent that the phrase 'clear and plain intention' has its origin in the *Santa Fe* decision" (344). As a measure of how embedded the clear and plain intent test is, one need only look to *R. v. Gladstone,* 2 S.C.R. 723 (1996), in which the court ruled that the Heiltsuk's aboriginal title had not been extinguished. In a concurring opinion, Justice L'Heureux-Dube wrote, "In the case at bar, the respondent argues that the [extinguishment] test is met when the

aboriginal right and the activities contemplated by the legislation cannot co-exist. Such an approach, based on the view adopted by the United States Supreme Court in United States v. Santa Fe Pacific Railroad Co., 314 U.S. 339 (1941), is irreconcilable with the 'clear and plain intention' test favoured in Canada" (809). The judge is wrong in two regards: *Santa Fe* does not say anything about the incompatibility of legislation and aboriginal rights, and the clear and plain intent test, though favored in Canada, has its origin in the United States. For Australia see *Mabo and Others v. State of Queensland,* 107 ALR 1 (1992), at 47. On the Hualapai case's influence on *Mabo* and the clear and plain intent test for extinguishment of native title see Richard Bartlett, *Native Title in Australia* (Sydney: Butterworths, 2000), 221, 229. In the 2003 update of *The Law of Land,* Henry Reynolds takes into account the history of Australian land claims in light of *Mabo* and *Wik.* Recognizing that extinguishment and the clear and plaint intent test are two of the most important features of the contemporary debate about aboriginal title, Reynolds cites the *Hualpai* decision as the case in which these "principles" are made most clear. Henry Reynolds, *The Law of the Land* (Victoria, Aus.: Penguin, 2003), 234.

35. The Malaysian High Court drew the rule regarding clear and plain intent from *Calder* and *Mabo,* which, of course, drew the rule from the Hualapai case. See especially *Nor Anak Nyawai and Others v Borneo Pulp Plantation and Others,* 6 MLJ 241 (12 May 2001). In *Sagong Bin Tasi and Others v Kerajaan Negeri Selangor and Others,* 2 MLJ 591 (12 April 2002) at 613, Justice Mohd Noor Ahmad embraced precedent from Australia, Canada, and the United States. See also Remy Bulan, "Native Title as a Proprietary Right Under the Constitution in Peninsula Malaysia: A Step in the Right Direction?" *Asia Pacific Law Review* 9.1 (2001): 83–101; Douglas Sanders, "Indigenous Land Rights in Malaysia: *Nor Nyawai v. Borneo Pulp and Plantation Sn Bhd,*" *Indigenous Law Bulletin* 5.14 (2002): 21–22.

Until recently, land claims in South Africa's national parks had received the most attention. See Bertus de Villiers, *Land Claims and National Parks — The Makuleke Experience* (Pretoria: Human Sciences Research Council, 1999). For land rights generally see Surplus People Project, *Land Claims in Namaqualand* (Cape Town: Surplus People Project, 1995). On the Native Lands Act and its impact on land rights see Elizabeth Mertz, "The Uses of History: Language, Ideology, and Law in the United States and South Africa," *Law and Society Review* 22.4 (1988): 661–85. For the place of South African indigenous people in early twentieth-century native rights schemes see Brian Willan, "The Anti-Slavery and Aborigines' Protection Society and the South African Natives' Land Act of 1913," *Journal of African History* 20.1 (1979): 83–102. On land claims and aboriginal title in South Africa see Steven Robins, "NGOs, 'Bushmen,' and Double Vision: The ≠khomani San Land Claim and the Cultural Politics of 'Community' and 'Development' in the Kalahari," *Journal of Southern African Studies* 27.4 (2001): 833–53; Steven Robins, "Land Struggles and the Politics and Ethics of Representing 'Bushman' History and Identity," *Kronos: Journal of Cape History* 26 (August 2000): 56–75; Renée Sylvain, "'Land, Water, and Truth': San Identity and Global Indigenism," *American Anthropologist* 104.4 (2002): 1074–85; William Ellis, "Bushman Identity, Land Claims and the Three Agendas," in *Africa's Indigenous Peoples: 'First Peoples' or 'Marginalized Minorities,'* ed. Alan Barnard and Justin Kenrick (Edinburgh: Centre for African Studies, University of Edinburgh, 2001): 255–72; John Sharp and Emile Boonzaier, "Ethnic Identity as Performance: Lessons from Namaqualand," *Journal of Southern African Studies* 20.3 (1994): 405–15; T. W. Bennett and C. H. Powell, "Aboriginal Title in South Africa Revisited," *South African Journal of Human Rights* 15.4 (1999), http://www.firstpeopl es.org/land _ rights/southern-africa/summary/aborig7E2.htm (accessed 17 May 2006); T. W. Bennett, "Redistribution of Land and the Doctrine of Aboriginal Title in South Africa," *South African Journal of Human Rights* 9 (1993): 443–76; Özlem Ülgen, "Developing the Doctrine of Aboriginal Title in South Africa: Source and Content," *Journal of African Law* 46.2 (2002): 131–54.

For reasons why aboriginal title is *not* the appropriate tack to take in South Africa see Karin Lehmann, "Aboriginal Title, Indigenous Rights and the Right to Culture," *South African Journal of Human Rights* 20.1 (2004): 86–118. In 2000 the South African Land Claims Court heard *Richtersveld Community v Alexkor Ltd and Another*, 2000 (1) SA 337 (LCC), denying the plaintiffs' claim that it lost land under the racially discriminatory practices of apartheid. The Richtersveld community appealed to the Supreme Court of Appeal, which, in March 2003, upheld the Land Claims Court's ruling but said that the Richtersveld community never lost communal title to its land. This case has opened to the door to further claims based on aboriginal title in South Africa. *Richtersveld Community and Others v Alexkor Ltd and Another*, 2003 (6) BCLR 583 (SCA). In October 2003 the Constitutional Court upheld the Court of Appeal's decision, saying, "The Court examined the nature of First Respondent's title, and concluded that the real character of the title that the Richtersveld Community possessed in the subject land was a right of communal ownership under indigenous law." *Alexkor Ltd and Another v Richtersveld Community and Others*, 2003 (12) BCLR 1301 (CC). Regarding this case see also Sharon LaFraniere, "The Diamond Mine May Not Be Forever, but It's a Start," *New York Times*, A3, 2 November 2003.

36. Geraldine Brooks, "The Painted Desert," *New Yorker*, 28 July 2003, 65. There is an ever-growing literature on the place of history as a discipline and the role it plays in land claims. For an excellent discussion of the uses of history in *Delgamuukw*, albeit before it was decided in the plaintiffs' favor in the Supreme Court, see Joel R. Fortune, "Construing *Delgamuukw*: Legal Arguments, Historical Argumentation, and the Philosophy of History," *University of Toronto Faculty of Law Review* 51.1 (1993): 80–117. For the same with regard to covering Australia, see Bain Attwood, "*The Law of the Land* or the Law of the Land? History, Law, and Narrative in a Settler Society," *History Compass* 2 (2004): 1–30. For the fragility of historical claims in Australia see David Ritter, "The Judgment of the World: The *Yorta Yorta* Case and the 'Tide of History,'" *Australian Historical Studies* 35.123 (2004): 106–21. For the problem of history and New Zealand claims see, among others, Alan Ward, "History and Historians Before the Waitangi Tribunal: Some Reflections on the Ngai Tahu Claim," *New Zealand Journal of History* 24.1 (1990): 150–67, including commentaries; Ewan Morris, "History Never Repeats? The Waitangi Tribunal and New Zealand History," *History Compass* 1 (2003): 1–13; Paul G. McHugh, "Law, History and the Treaty of Waitangi," *New Zealand Journal of History* 31.1 (1997): 38–57; J. G. A. Pocock, "Law, Sovereignty and History in a Divided Culture: The Case of New Zealand and the Treaty of Waitangi," *McGill Law Journal* 43 (1998): 481–506.

For a guide to the legal developments in the post-*Mabo* era see Bartlett, *Native Title in*

Australia; Janice Gray, "The Lost Promise of *Mabo:* An Update on the Legal Struggle for Land Rights in Australia with Particular Reference to the *Ward* and *Yorta Yorta* Decisions," *Canadian Journal of Native Studies* 23.2 (2003): 305–48. Contemporary courts in the United States have also crafted convoluted narratives about the past. For example, in 1991 the Vermont Supreme Court turned to history to explain why the Abenakis no longer have viable claims to their ancestral territory. The court reasoned that "the increasing weight of history" — or the accumulated decades of dispossession — had crushed the Abenakis' property rights. Citing no specific legislation and thus no clear and plain intent, the court simply said that time had washed away the tribe's title. See John P. Lowndes, "When History Outweighs Law: Extinguishment of Abenaki Aboriginal Title," *Buffalo Law Review* 42 (1994): 77–118; Joseph W. Singer, "Well Settled? The Increasing Weight of History in American Indian Land Claims," *Georgia Law Review* 28 (1994): 481–532; Aviam Soifer, "Objects in Mirror Are Closer Than They Appear," *Georgia Law Review* 28 (1994): 533–53.

37. Keith Windschuttle, *The Fabrication of Australian History* (Sydney: Macleay, 2002); Michael Connor, *The Invention of* Terra Nullius (Sydney: Macleay, 2005); Bain Attwood, *Telling the Truth about Aboriginal History* (Crows Nest, N.S.W.: Allen and Unwin, 2005). For a lucid explanation of the complicated state of affairs regarding the law see Lisa Strelein, "Conceptualising Native Title," *Sydney Law Review* 23 (March 2001): 95–124. For the McNeil quotation see Kent McNeil, "The Relevance of Traditional Laws and Customs to the Existence and Content of Native Title at Common Law," in *Emergeng Justice? Essays on Indigenous Rights in Canada and Australia* (Saskatoon, Sask.: Native Law Centre, University of Saskatchewan, 2001), 263. See *State of Western Australia v. Ward,* [2002] H.C.A. 28; *Risk v. Northern Territory of Australia,* [2006] F.C.A. 404; *Jango v. Northern Territory of Australia,* [2006] F.C.A. 318. This is how the judge puts it in the opinion summary in *Risk:* "12. The evidence shows that a combination of circumstances has, in various ways, interrupted or disturbed the presence of the Larrakia people in the Darwin area during several decades of the 20th century in a way that has affected their continued observance of, and enjoyment of, the traditional laws and customs of the Larrakia people that existed at sovereignty. The settlement of Darwin from 1869, the influx of other aboriginal groups into the claim area, the attempted assimilation of aboriginal people into the European community, and the consequences of the implementation of those attempts and other government policies (however one might judge their correctness), led to the reduction of the Larrakia population, the dispersal of many Larrakia people from the claim area, and a significant breakdown in Larrakia people's observance and acknowledgement of traditional laws and customs. 13. I have found that the effect of those circumstances is that the current Larrakia society, with its laws and customs, has not carried forward the traditional laws and customs of the Larrakia people so as to support the conclusion that those traditional laws and customs have had a continued existence and vitality since sovereignty. Some of the evidence reveals a correspondence between current and traditional laws and customs. But the oral evidence also reveals significant inconsistencies between members of the present applicants about what their laws and customs are, and the extent to which they are practiced. It reveals in many instances the adoption of knowledge of traditional laws and customs from those learned during the hearing of the Kenbi land claim concerning the Cox

Peninsula and then later from other research, as well as by direct inquiry of elderly Larrakia and non-Larrakia people. The oral evidence discloses a level of generality of knowledge which is not consistent with the acquisition of knowledge in accordance with the traditional laws and customs of the Larrakia people. Ultimately, I have concluded that during much of the 20th century, the evidence does not show the passing on of knowledge of the traditional laws and customs from generation to generation in accordance with those laws and customs. . . . 16. In those circumtances, I must dismiss the application."

38. *Indians at Work*, January 1942, 5–7.

Index

Abenaki Indians, 257*n*17, 268*n*36
Aboriginal title: in Australia, 86–88, 92, 94–95, 178–82, 263*n*25, 266*n*34, 268–69*n*37; in Canada, 86–88, 92, 95–97, 177–78, 180–82, 263*n*25; definition of, 86–87; in New Zealand, 86–88, 92–94, 178, 180, 182, 263*n*25; in Nigeria, 86, 92, 97–98; in Southern Rhodesia, 86, 92, 97, 98; Hualapai case expanded to recover lost aboriginal land, 134, 136, 138, 166–68; in South Africa, 180–81, 266*n*35. *See also* Australia; Canada; Hualapai case; Indian/native title; New Zealand
ACLU, 126, 225*n*25
Africa. *See* Nigeria; South Africa; Southern Rhodesia
Agriculture and gardening, 5, 63, 73–74
Ahmad, Mohd Noor, 266*n*35

AIDA. *See* American Indian Defense Association (AIDA)
Akers, Harlow, 134
Alaska, 169, 170–72, 256*n*12
Algonquins, 63–64
American Civil Liberties Union, 126, 225*n*25
American Indian Defense Association (AIDA), 106–8, 113, 133
American Wallapai and Supai Indian Association, 25–26, 29–35
Amodu Tijani v. Secretary, Southern Nigeria, 97–98
Anghie, Anthony, 234–35*n*31
Anthropology, 60, 61, 63–64, 127, 130–32, 173–77, 243*n*5, 246*n*12, 262*n*18
Apaches, 7, 27, 34, 68, 109, 112
Archaeology, 60–61
Army, U.S.: war between Indians and, 6–7; forced removal of Hualapais

British Columbia, 95–97, 181

Brooks, James, 261–62*n*15

Brophy, William, 133, 146, 151, 158, 159–60, 252*n*10, 256*n*6

Brosius, Samuel M.: and Indian politics in Washington, 46, 108; and Hagerman plan, 58; and *Lone Wolf v. Hitchcock*, 75; and Rhoads, 76–77, 110, 238*n*16; and Treaty of Guadalupe Hidalgo, 76, 224*n*13; and caution in corresponding with Mahone, 78; on Bureau of Indian Affairs (BIA)'s opinion on Hualapai case, 84; on Interior Department, 105; investigation of Hualapai case by, 110–12; on Havasupai claims, 111, 168; early interest in Hualapai case by, 224*n*11

Brown, Ray, 113, 129–30

Bureau of Indian Affairs (BIA): assimilation campaigns of, xiv; forced removal of Hualapais from homeland (1869–1883), 7, 41–42, 83–84; and water rights for Hualapai Indian Reservation, 14; and Mission Indian Federation (MIF), 22–24, 32; and American Wallapai and Supai Indian Association, 26; and Route 66, 29; and Light, 30–32; and railroad rights on Hualapai Indian Reservation, 37, 40–41, 50; distrust of, by Hualapais, 43–44; and Hagerman plan, 50, 51, 53–54, 57, 76, 77, 82; and Pine Springs country, 71–72; and Brosius, 77, 78; and Monahan's opinion of Hualapai case, 84–85, 107–8; Collier as commissioner of Indian affairs, 113–16, 119–21, 125, 239–40*n*28, 241–42*n*42; and tourism, 118; and anthropology, 130–31; and Indian New Deal, 182–83, 241*n*41; inefficiencies of, 236*n*4

Bureau of Reclamation, 118–19

Burge, William, 92

Burke, Charles, 24, 26, 30, 32, 48, 59, 206*n*4

Burton, John W., 247*n*13

Buttz v. Northern Pacific Railroad, 252*n*14

Byrnes, Thomas, 7

Calder v. Attorney General, 177–78

California, 22–24, 54, 62

Canada, xv, xviii, 86–88, 92, 95–97, 157, 177–78, 180–82, 263*n*25

Cattle: Anglo cattle ranching generally, 10; Light's management of cattle sales, 30–33, 38; leases for white ranchers on Hualapai Indian Reservation, 40, 43, 48, 122, 205*n*42; Hualapai cattle, 56, 80, 104, 105, 115, 118; water for, 56; Mahone's ownership of, 57; and Willis, 248–49*n*24

Cauffman, Abe, 48

Chapman, Henry, 92

Chapman, Oscar, 146

Charles, John, 13

Cherokee Nation v. Georgia, 229*n*9

Cherokees, 90, 229*n*9

Cherum, 8, 9, 27, 40, 211*n*25

Clark, Butch, 109, 113

Clay Springs, 51–53, 56, 75, 109, 115, 120, 136, 169, 241–42*n*42

Clear and plain intent test, 180

Cohen, Felix: on complexity of Hualapai case, xiii, xvi, 137–38; and Supreme Court appeal of Hualapai case, xvi, 128, 158, 159–65, 256*n*6; and Indian law, 125, 128–31, 152–54, 180; death of, 128; and Indian Reorganization Act (IRA), 128, 169; as Interior Department assistant solicitor, 128; and "Powers of Indian Tribes," 128–29, 171; as legal real-